LIA

Enjoy the journey

The MIRACLE of AFRICA

MIKE NEIL

TABLE OF CONTENTS

ACKNOWLEDGEMENTS

Special thanks goes to my loving and supportive wife Susan who followed me through the six years of writing this story. To my friend Chuck Lathrop, African hunter from Ellensburg, Washington, who encouraged me to read the African classic adventure novels. The stories he told about hunting with his wife Betty were the inspiration for this book. To Kenyan, Velma Abhiambo Odinga, who gave her perspective and helped with the Swahili dialogue. To Pierre Joubert, a professional hunter from Tanzania, who helped with the technical aspects of African hunting. To my editor, William Greenleaf, who believed in the story. Finally, to Mark and Becci Crowe, who took Sue and me on the trip of a lifetime to Botswana and Zambia on Safari in 2005.

DEDICATION
TO SUSANNE NEIL SCARINGI

The Lord took our daughter home on Wednesday morning September 27th, 2006 at the age of 27 when a van turned in front of her bicycle in Seattle. At one year old she contracted Viral Meningitis and we nearly lost her. Our third child, Ryan Neil, born January 1, 1981, came three months premature and lived only six weeks in intensive care. Having lost a little one and a big one neither is easy. You have the same hopes for them, but their footprint is much different. We loved our daughter as we love our oldest son James and his wife Heather, and we enjoy the times we have with them and our Grandkids, Grace and Hudson. We are so proud of the man James has become.

Susanne loved sports and became quite the accomplished figure skater in junior high; she played volleyball, and ran track in high school. In college she was a Heptathlete and was involved in YoungLife. After college she became an outdoor woman and climbed Mt. Rainier twice. She met and married Tony Scaringi, who worked for YoungLife. Tony has remarried and he and his wife Michelle have two fine boys.

Susanne had an incredible spirit and no one could get enough of her infectious laugh, her caring manner, and bright eyes. She would do anything for a friend. Our whole family misses her dearly, but we have an assurance that we will see her again. The suffering of losing a child can change you for the better if you let God work. We should never ask God "Why?" but instead we should ask the higher question of "What now?" God will reveal the "Why" in His time, and you will be blessed because you came to realize that everything in life happens for a reason. We should hold everything in an open hand to Him.

PROLOGUE

The sights and sounds of Africa: her vast plains of grass dotted with beast and bush; birds of unimaginable shape, size, and color flitting here and there, as if they had a plan, or as if they were part of a greater plan; dangerous game that would sooner eat you than waste time looking elsewhere; and elephants who don't want to be bothered, cape buffalo that think you owe them something, and lions that have an agenda far greater than your own. Giggles from bright-eyed native children, who gawk at the white man as if he were the first they had ever seen. Rivers, rains, mountains, wind, and sky; bush buck, stein buck, kudu, and giraffe. The hide and hair of Africa offers a striking mix of color splashed across the land like a cleansing rainbow. A land so rich it begs the mind to answer the nagging questions. But what does it matter? Sometimes you just accept the things that are.

Yet there are so many questions that remain unanswered that have to be addressed. What is the origin of species, and where did we come from? How long has the earth existed, and how was it formed? 1911 is a new age of scientific enlightenment in which men no longer have to live in the dark about such things and just accept a world described the only way the ancients, with their limited knowledge and understanding, knew how to explain things. The people of the Dark Ages lived in an insane world where, if anyone dared to challenge the powers of the Church, they were burned at the stake. Now, thanks to the courage of Darwin, we have been liberated and given a sensible alternative to the Bible, which I have skimmed but found quite unbelievable.

Now here I am on my last day in Africa before launching off on the grueling trek back to Chicago. Train and boat, boat and train—there will be plenty of time to ponder such things in my quiet time alone. Time to prepare for my reunion with my wife, Betty, the woman I thought would give me a family. But the tragedy of losing our ten-year-old son has threatened to ruin both of our lives. Just the thought of Betty gives me grief, and I wonder how I will cope once again with her depression that always brings me to the depths of the darkness of my own soul. If it weren't for these almost yearly visits to Africa, surely I would have been destroyed by her anguish. If not for my best friend, Lance, living in Nairobi, and for his wit and his adventurous spirit, I might have fallen into a hopeless depressed state as well.

Lance Miles, nearly ten years my junior, could be a younger brother, the brother I never had. We get along so famously. I think our love for Africa, a good cigar, a good woman, and a glass of brandy, not to mention the lust for adventure and of course the desire to answer the big questions about life, bond us like soldiers on a battlefield.

It seems like when I'm in Chicago I miss him more than I miss Betty when I am here. Is it because when I leave tomorrow I will leave my heart behind? Not with Lance, but under my favorite tree tucked under a rock, a safe place where it won't get hurt? No wonder David Livingstone had his heart buried in Africa before his body was taken home to England. I have told Lance that he needs to settle down and find a good woman to comfort him in his old age, but his reply is always the same: independence and freedom are far more precious than companionship. And with *that* I cannot argue.

I suppose the one thing I am looking forward to is going back to the classroom, where I can help mold young minds and challenge them to think critically. As usual, I will have to justify to the college my frequent absences. Admittedly, this time I may have stayed away a bit too long and am going back with far too little to show for my absence. But I know I am on solid footing with President Crawford, who has always supported my scientific endeavors here in Africa and who, given half the chance, would join me in a heartbeat, if for no other reason than to go big game hunting.

So now I am packed and ready, if not exactly willing, to begin the long trek back—and I say *back* because Africa will always be my *home*.

Chapter 1

REFLECTIONS

T he spotted leopard charged, leaping midair, and with her claws extended and her fangs exposed, let out a blood-chilling scream. I pointed my British double, slapping the trigger in a snapshot at her like a quail on the wing and dropping her still with a thud.

I awoke with a start, my heart pounding. The faint early morning light trickled through the open cracks in the window shade that bounced gently from the vibration. Another dream about Africa. I couldn't get the thoughts out of my mind, nor the dust out of my nostrils. A leopard might not eat you, but it would kill you dead just the same.

The rumble of the thundering wheels sang against the steel rails, clicking and clacking as the train car rolled along. It seemed like only seconds had passed since I had fallen asleep, exhausted by the grueling schedule of these past long months.

Anxious thoughts of home filled my heart with the growing anticipation of my reunion with Betty. Things had not been good between us since we'd lost our son five years earlier. The fact was I hadn't been able to handle her depression, and so I had found Africa as my first and best choice. I buried myself in my work, and if it hadn't been for my home in Chicago and my work at the institute, I might have taken up residence in Nairobi.

My greatest hope was that Betty would snap out of it. God knows I'd struggled with the thought of a permanent separation or even divorce.

Everybody suffers loss—heck, that's what life is all about—but you have to move on. Life goes on, and the things that fall along the way obviously change you, but they can never destroy you. Soon enough, these bones of mine will be rotting in some pine box and wearing a pinstriped suit cut up the back. And the person you so admired in the mirror will be long gone on the wind. That's why we have to make the best of each day and watch our step so it isn't our last. But depression, heck, get over it and start living. I say, don't try to add days to your life, but add life to your days.

I hoped I wasn't going home to more doom and gloom. Betty was too wonderful a girl for all of that. Just maybe I'd get a smile out of her for once. I could almost smell her hair, feel her touch, hear her voice, and see her beautiful brown eyes.

My comfortable residence in Chicago was a far cry from the harshness of the desert plains of British East Africa. But my summer search this year of 1911 had been lean at best. I say *summer*, but June, July, and August are winter in Africa south of the equator. Nonetheless, I was willing to pay a price to ensure that Darwin's theories survived, although much work had yet to be done. Considerable fossil evidence needed to be uncovered to convince the skeptics. I knew that Darwin had hit the target with his conception of the origin of species. Indeed, what a theory! It offered a brilliant alternative to the dogma of the religious fanatics, who believed in the far-fetched myth of a biblical creation. Surely if a god existed, he would have revealed himself long before now. Life didn't have to start out with magic, as the ancients thought; it could have evolved naturally over millions of years.

My pants lay neatly folded next to the bunk, and I retrieved my pocket watch, straining in the dim light to see the face. *Wow, 5:30 a.m. already. Guess I'll take a walk to the dining car to see if I can find some coffee.*

After sliding out of bed, I grabbed my safari shirt, slipping my arms into the sleeves, and then pulled on my khaki pants and put the suspenders over my shoulders. My bush jacket hung on a hook. I took the red scarf and tied it around my neck like a badge of honor, and then slipped on the khaki jacket with large patch pockets. These clothes were like pajamas; many a night on the plains they had kept me comfortable.

I struggled with the adjustment to wearing real clothes every time I returned from Africa, but Chicago winters were far too bitter for this attire. I tied up the laces on my low-cut brown leather boots—not those high-laced safari hikers, which fit like bedroom slippers—but I would have to save their soles for the plains. I chuckled to myself. *Save their souls. How many times have I heard that term?*

As I stared directly at a mirror across the room, I brushed my hair over with my fingers. *Not bad for forty-six years, if I do say so myself.* I stepped up to the mirror for a closer look. I had seen younger men who looked ten years older. My hair had barely a trace of gray. I leaned forward and scrutinized the lines in my face that showed the very beginning of crow's feet, and I pulled the skin tightly against my cheek. I had always felt good about how I looked: slender build, straight teeth, strong chin, and bold, narrow nose. I remembered my mother warning me that these baby blue eyes would melt the girls' hearts. The biggest part of who you are is in how you look, and who you think you are projects how others perceive you.

After exiting the stateroom and locking my private first-class quarters behind me, I headed down the narrow corridor.

"Top of the morning to you, Professor Rivers," said a young steward in a bold whisper. "How did you sleep, sir?"

I wrinkled my brow, trying to remember where I might have met this bright young man before. He couldn't have been more than fifteen years old. This fair-skinned, slender-built youth, very smartly dressed in an official company uniform, appeared to be standing post to keep second-class passengers separated from the first.

"I slept well. Thank you, Steward."

The boy put his index finger to his lips, challenging my volume as we stood just outside a stateroom door.

"Say," I whispered, "do you think there would be coffee brewing at this hour?"

"Not for the regular passengers, but for you, sir. I think I can find you some. Come along ... Follow me."

He motioned with his hand, and I followed him down the hall away from the first-class dining car. The kid walked proudly, as if he was leading a prized bull in a show arena. He stopped at a door marked *TRAIN STAFF ONLY* and then stepped inside.

"Professor Rivers," said a red-faced middle-aged man with wire-rimmed glasses and a ruddy complexion. "Would you like a cup of coffee, sir?"

"I told him I might be able to find a cup of coffee for him," the steward said.

"Oh, do come in. Let me get a clean cup."

As he spoke, I recognized the man, whose bushy, graying side-burns, thick eyebrows, broad chest, and puffy red cheeks were impossible to forget. He had taken my ticket when I'd boarded in New York.

"My name is Winchester Jiles, but my friends call me Chester." He held his hand out for a greeting. "I'm the conductor."

"Jonathan Rivers," I responded, taking a firm grip. "My friends call me John."

"Oh, everyone knows you, sir," he said, grabbing a ceramic cup that hung from a hook and pouring the steaming black brew from a pot that had been simmering on the coal-fired potbelly stove.

"And I am Jason Marshall," the young steward chimed in with a wide grin, exposing his straight white teeth. "My friends call me Jason."

"Tell me, good sir," said Chester, "I understand you have been on safari. What can you tell us about your adventures?"

"Oh, yes," I answered with a smile. *But where should I start?* I thought to myself. There was so much to tell, so much that I would have considered tedious that this poor guy would probably have considered a thrilling adventure. Maybe the vast herds of cape buffalo, or the massive bulls I had taken down. How majestic and menacing they were! Or the black rhino, their poor eyesight and nasty disposition making them even more deadly. Possibly the lions, or maybe my work would be of some interest. "I don't know where to start. What would you like to hear about?"

"I want to know about your passion," Chester said. "What is your passion?"

"Oh, well that's easy," I answered. "My passion is the Bengal tiger of India, secret and elusive, with its beautiful orange coat and thick black stripes. It's one prize that I long to hang in my trophy room. But that's another story."

"Dangerous?" inquired Jason. "What's so dangerous when you have a rifle?"

"Oh, yes," I answered, "quite dangerous, actually. India is a tangled country of thick bamboo, heavy jungle, and steep ravines that provide the tiger with perfect conditions to sneak around and kill. They don't as a rule consider men as food, but when they have been wounded in a fight or by some careless sportsman's bullet, or when they grow old and slow, they can turn to eating human flesh. And once they start, they quickly bring their toll of native victims into the hundreds. I have heard tell of many a sportsman who, after wounding a tiger, never lived to admire the rug and ended up on the tiger's dinner menu. One of these days I'll take a shikar, but for now I'm happy just to have bagged a bongo in Africa."

"What's a bongo?" asked the wide-eyed young steward.

"It's a trophy that old Teddy Roosevelt couldn't bring home from the overstuffed safari he put together for the Smithsonian Institution last year.

"I've never heard of it," said Chester.

"That doesn't surprise me," I said. "The bongo is a shy African antelope that lives in the deepest, thickest bush. Most people don't know this, but old Teddy just wasn't quiet enough, and he doesn't have good enough eyesight to sneak up on one."

"Did you say *shikar*?" the kid asked. "What's that?"

"Actually, safari means journey, and a shikar in India is the same as a safari in Africa."

"What's the most dangerous animal you have hunted?" asked Chester. "Here, take a seat."

"That question has been long debated," I began as we all sat together on the wooden chairs in the small office, "because there are lots of animals in Africa that will kill you, and there are lots of dead men who have been stomped by elephants, gored by rhinos and buffalo, and chomped by hippos and crocs. But probably the most dangerous to me is the lion. Their tail sticks straight up like a pole once they have been provoked, and they'll charge full bore. The only choice for the shooter is to stand firm and wait for a shot. You have to either kill the lion outright with a shot to the brain or chest, or die from your lack of nerve." I took the steaming cup from his hand. "Thank you, Chester," I said, giving him a nod before blowing the steam away from the brim. "The day I took my lion, one of my native Bushmen got mauled."

Jason's eyes lit up, and Chester sat forward in his chair.

"We had been tracking some buffalo when we surprised a small pride that was working on a zebra kill along the edge of some scrub trees about forty yards upwind. I took charge of the .500 British double rifle from my gun bearer to get ready for a shot. We were way too close for comfort, so we began to back away slowly to a safer distance. We had an inexperienced tracker named Mundo, and my gun bearer tried to motion to him, but he didn't see the lions or us. He crouched over, keeping his eyes focused intently on the buffalo track, and didn't see that we had begun to retreat." I paused to take a sip of my coffee, but it was still too hot to drink. "When we had backed off to within seventy-five yards, I stopped and held a steady bead on the big male who had quit eating and begun watching the native's every move. The other men with me were still back-stepping carefully so as not to make a sound.

"Suddenly the rest of the pride caught wind of my tracker and became agitated. Then he spotted them and stood fast, unarmed and watching the lions at a very uncomfortable distance. They charged without warning. I took a shot at the lead lioness but missed her clean, and Mundo began to run, drawing the full attention of the lions. I opened the rifle and dropped in a fresh cartridge.

"The big male lion, meanwhile, had turned toward the sound of the rifle shot and was now coming at us at a full charge. I stood fast, with the cat now heading straight on at just fifty yards away, and squeezed off my first shot at this magnificent beast, but my bullet grazed him just left of the chest. The three females who had broken off now disappeared out of sight, hot on Mundo's flanks, but the huge black-mane lion continued his charge toward our party without so much as a flinch. He had his sights set, and his big paws were pounding the ground at probably thirty-five miles an hour.

"I settled into the rifle, took a deep breath, a steady hold, and touched off the roar of the second chamber. The rifle bucked, and the bullet struck him square between the eyes at twenty yards. He went down like a rag doll, skidding in a puff of dust. Janga handed me the loaded rifle he was packing, and I handed him the empty double. Janga broke open the chamber, and I raised the new rifle, hoping to save Mundo, but at that moment we heard a chilling scream from the bush as the female cats caught him."

"Wow," Jason said excitedly. "What happened to him? Did he survive?"

"Hardly. The other native boys quickly tended to him and drove off the cats, but the reports were ugly. I had my hands full dealing with a four-hundred-pound lion, besides not being eager to witness the human gore. When I hired him, he told me he had experience as a tracker, but obviously he didn't have as much as he said. A seasoned man would never let himself get into such a position as that. We skinned the lion, then regrouped, taking to our horses that had been brought up from the rear, and headed back to camp."

"Have you hunted in Africa before this?" Jason asked.

"This is actually my third trip in five years."

"What sort of other trophies did you bring back?" Chester asked.

"I had a chance this trip at a very beautiful bull elephant with five-foot tusks, but he winded us before we could get in position. I did take a quality sable antelope bull, and one good cape buffalo. I brought back the trophy bongo, and a respectable kudu. While I was over there I shot three bushbuck, nothing worth a mount; nine impala, which I know seems excessive, but it all went to feed a local tribe; and a tommy, or Thomson gazelle."

"What kind of rifle did you say that you used?" Jason asked.

"A twelve-pound Holland and Holland .500 Nitro Express British double. That's a fifty caliber, with side-by-side barrels, double triggers for a faster second shot, and an open breach action. The cartridge comes loaded with eighty grains of cordite and drives a five-hundred-and-seventy-grain bullet that will break an elephant at the shoulder. That's what I use for the large game. I use a Springfield for my light shooting."

"Gosh," Jason said, his eyes wide with excitement. "Isn't a safari very costly, and doesn't it interfere with your work at the institute?"

"Well, son, actually, I really don't consider this trip to have been a true safari. All these hunting days were just little side trips where I could mix my work with pleasure. Someday, I'd love to take a true safari, do it up right, and go deep into the interior of Africa. You do know, then, that I am on staff with the Chicago School of Sociology?"

"Yes, sir," Jason said. "*The New York Times* said that you were, but I don't know exactly what you do there."

"You read the *Times* article, did you? Good man. But let me tell you, that newspaper must be hungry for a story. Not that I mind the attention, but everybody wants to talk about Africa these days. I'm a professor of social history. That's a part of history that documents how men lived in the past. My studies have mainly focused on anthropology, and I guess I consider myself to be an anthropologist more than a historian."

"They must pay you awfully well to be able to travel like this," Jason said.

As I put the cup to my lips and took a drink of the coffee that was now a bearable temperature, I caught Chester frowning at the young lad.

"Forgive him, sir. He's just a kid."

"Oh, no, that's quite all right. You see, my grandfather left me quite well off. I probably give more of my time to the institute than I actually get in pay. But my work there is rewarding, and most of these trips are all paid for by grants and such."

"Tell us about your work, Professor," Chester said.

"I run the science department at the college. I have a colleague in British East Africa with whom I am diligently searching for the 'missing link'—and we will find it! It's just a matter of time before someone discovers it, and Darwin's theory is proven."

"Did you make any findings while you were there, sir?" Jason asked.

"No, not this time. I directed some of the work in our most recent excavation sites and went over some bone fragments, but I don't think our current worksite is old enough for what we are looking for. I looked at some of the proposed future sites and helped map some of the drainages that we feel show promise. And, uh, I had several meetings with government officials to ensure our work there will continue."

I took a sip of coffee and felt a twinge in my stomach as I thought about the institute. *I hope I haven't been away too long. I think Dean Williams assumed I would have been back long before now.*

"What is this *missing link*?" Jason asked. "I thought Darwin's theories were accepted."

"Have you ever thought about attending a university? You seem like a bright young lad."

"Oh no, sir, I come from a destitute family. My father has long since passed on, and my poor mother died two years ago. She could never have afforded to send me to college. She was glad to see me graduate from the eighth grade. Anyway, I'm lucky to have this job with the railroad. I hope someday to become a conductor, just like Mr. Jiles."

I thought about this young lad and his potential. *What a bright shining star in a cold and dismal world.* Had my own son of our twenty-year marriage lived, he would have been around the same age as this boy. I had a pit in my stomach, thinking about my lost little boy, who had died at the age of ten, and the hole in my life that he'd left behind. *Dead and gone forever. What a damn shame.*

"How old are you, Jason?"

"I'll be sixteen next summer," he answered, puffing up his chest like a little banty rooster.

Just as I had suspected. My Johnny would have been his age.

"Back to your question of the missing link," I said in an effort to shake off my lingering grief. "This is the skeletal evidence between modern man and the ape-like creatures that we evolved from. We know they existed. But we don't have enough scientific documentation to prove the theory to the rest of this crazy religious world, with their ancient writings that are a mixture of myth and fantasy." I drained the last of my coffee cup.

"Would you like some more, Professor—I mean, John?" Chester asked.

"No, sir, I have taken far too much of your time. Your president, Jack Hastings, and I are close friends. I'm sure he wouldn't take too kindly to me keeping you from your work. I do appreciate your hospitality, and I'll put in a good word for you men with the boss."

"Well, thanks for sharing your adventures. Why don't you let me give you a warm-up in that cup and you can take it back to your stateroom. The dining car will be open at their usual time at seven-thirty."

"You talked me into it," I answered, holding out the cup for a refill.

"I'll get back to my post," Jason said and turned to head out the door.

"Thanks again, Chester. I hope we can speak again before I depart. And oh, what time can we expect to be in Chicago?"

"This New York to Chicago run is always on time. We'll be in at three o'clock sharp; you can set your watch by it."

I gave him a firm handshake to show my appreciation, then headed out the door behind Jason before it shut behind me.

"It was so great to meet you, sir."

"You know, son, you really should consider setting your sights a little higher," I said in a whisper, so as not to offend Chester on the other side of the doorway.

"What do you mean?" the lad responded.

"You are a bright boy with so much potential. All I will say is this, my son. Reach for the stars, and who knows—you just might catch one."

I continued down the corridor to my stateroom and then fumbled in my pocket for the key. I glanced down toward the boy, who had stopped dead in his tracks and appeared to be in deep thought. I nodded, making a gesture to bid him the morning, and entered my room. I let the door shut quietly behind me, then checked my watch again: 6:10 a.m. I had an hour and twenty minutes before breakfast.

A pitcher of water and a bowl were on the commode from the night before, with a little rail holding them secure in the corner. I poured the rest of the water in the bowl, splashed my face, and toweled dry. Looking in the mirror, I felt the whiskers on my chin. *I'll have to shave before the end of day.* My briefcase sat on the floor near the closet. *Maybe this would be a good time to go over some of my journal entries.* I sat down in the overstuffed chair bolted to the floor next to my bed.

What would Betty say about taking in a boarder? I had really taken a shine to this lad. Hard to remember a time when I had been so struck by a boy of this quality. *Johnny would have turned out just like him, had he lived. Oh my, how life takes twists and turns. How can I dare propose such a thing to Betty? I am sure she will think I have lost my mind on the plains of Africa. Oh my ... I wonder how she will be when I get home.*

After unlatching the case, I retrieved my journal and writing supplies as thoughts of Johnny came flooding back. I could see his little smile and feel his arms around my neck as he whispered, *I love you, Daddy.* The pit in my stomach forced a tear to drip down my cheek, and I quickly wiped it with my sleeve. *I still hurt inside, even though I always try to escape it—the loss of my little boy whom I will never see again. This god they speak about, who they say is so merciful and loving: if there is such a god, then he must be awfully cruel to take a little boy who had his whole life ahead of him. No one will ever be able to explain that to me. Nope, we live in a natural world, where things happen by chance and for no apparent reason. My only part in it is to be a disciple of Darwin, to try to convince the world that what he came up with is true, and to defeat the religious world.*

For the next hour, I tried to write, but this lad Jason kept creeping into my mind. I felt something pulling me to give the boy a chance. *This is insanity*, I thought. I couldn't explain it, but I could see this kid with me on the plains of Africa.

Chapter 2

MAKING MUSIC

As I went back over some of the entries from the last several months, I came upon the page describing the moment we'd stumbled upon the lions. Memories flooded my mind of the events of that day. I could smell Africa through my nostrils, and I could feel the chill of fear that had run through me after we'd spotted fresh lion tracks. The parched plains, heavy dried grass of the *wadi* (thick grass ravine), and the red dusty soil were etched into my senses.

I felt bad about the native tracker who'd lost his life in the hunt, but then their lives were very different from ours. They had to live with this kind of danger all the time. They placed great importance on human life, just as we did when it came to a neighbor or a family member, but they had a different view of death. When someone died, their ancestors were waiting to receive them. I didn't understand, so who was I to impose my values on them? Besides, everyone knew what Darwin taught about man's evolution. It wasn't that many years ago that these same natives were being bought and sold as property on the streets of the United States, and the practice was still accepted in certain parts of Africa.

I glanced toward the brown-felt wide-brimmed hat lying at the foot of my bunk. *Oh, Africa, why do you torment me so? When I am there, I miss home, and when I am home, you pull at me like a lioness dragging a dead gazelle. I haven't been gone but a few short weeks, and already I long to see you again.* I glanced at my watch and found it nearing the time for breakfast to be served, so I headed for the first-class dining car.

"Rivers!" shouted a familiar voice.

I turned and spotted a familiar face.

"Hastings!" I responded and then made my way to his table. "They didn't tell me you were on this train. What's the occasion?"

Hastings wore a shirt and tie, his hair combed flat over and plastered with hair grease. His dark eyebrows, pointed nose, strong chin, and piercing eyes gave a sense of why he held this important position with the railroad.

"Oh, just business as usual," he answered. "Actually, I am heading to Chicago to meet with the president of the Broadway Limited. They claim to have a new locomotive in use that's much more economical to run and that promises to give us more speed. He's a strong competitor, of course, but a good friend who wants to see me succeed. Won't you join me?"

"Delighted to," I responded, taking a seat at his finely set table.

A waiter appeared as soon as I sat down and handed me a menu. "Coffee, sir?" he asked, holding a finely polished silver pot.

"Yes, please," I said and turned the china cup over, setting it on the saucer perched on the white linen tablecloth. The coffee jiggled in the cup as the car waggled from the clacking rails.

"How about you, Rivers? You've been on safari again, haven't you? You'll have to get together with my friend Roosevelt so you two can boast about Africa together."

I smiled at the thought. "I hear he is going to make another run at the White House."

"He is a glutton for punishment. The Republicans won't have him, so now he is forming his own party, calling it the Bull Moose, for heaven's sake."

I humored him with a chuckle. Even though I admired the ex-president for his love of Africa, his politics left much to be desired. Besides, from what I knew about him, he had a reputation for taking long shots from over three hundred yards away and wounding animals. He prided himself on being an ardent conservationist and a sportsman, but he had a long way to go in my estimation. All this, together with rumors that he had killed nine white rhino when he only had permits for six, was quite disturbing in my mind. Even though the game was plentiful, I was convinced hunters ought to shoot only the number of animals they were permitted to hunt.

"How was Africa?" Hastings asked.

"Africa ... what a trip! I can't seem to get enough of her! They say Africa is a disease. Once you catch it, there is no cure."

"You must be married to a good woman to put up with your gallivanting. How is that beautiful wife of yours?"

I didn't say what I wanted to say. I admired Hastings for what he had accomplished, but we weren't the best of friends. You just don't share such personal things as your strained relationship with your wife with someone like that. We have mutual friends, and if you let a bird such as that go on the wind, there is no telling where it might land or what sort of eggs it might lay.

The waiter cleared his throat to get my attention, and I found him standing over me in his starched white jacket. "What can I get for you, sir?" he asked.

"I apologize, but I haven't had time to look at your menu," I responded, holding the card out at a comfortable distance to read the small print.

"Where are your reading glasses, Professor?" Hastings asked.

"I have never needed them, but I am noticing now that my eyes are straining."

"Forty-seven is about the time my eyes went," he replied.

I glanced up at the waiter, who seemed to be becoming impatient.

"Have the eggs Benedict," Jack encouraged. "That's what I am having."

"Excellent choice," I responded and nodded to the waiter, who nodded back before taking the menu card from my hand.

"You never answered my question. Is Betty okay?"

"Oh, she is fine. Actually, I'll know more when I get to Chicago."

"Didn't someone tell me you ordered a new automobile just before you left home last spring?"

"Betty said in her last letter that it's been delivered. I'm pretty excited about getting home to a new Rambler. Did you know they have a complete spare wheel on that car? No more having to change the rubber and patch the tires. You just pull the extra wheel off the side of the car, replace the flat one, and you're back in business."

"That's old Yankee ingenuity for you," Jack said. "I don't know why they didn't think about that earlier. Sure would have saved a lot of headaches for me over the last few years. How about Frederick Selous? Ever run into him over there?"

"I was in his camp once five years ago, but he was gone in the bush. I considered hanging around so he could meet me, but his headman said he might not be back for a week, so we moved on. I had hoped we might cross paths during my last two trips to Africa, but luck hasn't been with me."

"Have you read some of his books?" Hastings asked.

"I have. I find him to be refreshingly honest and delightfully knowledgeable. I have to credit him with his enthusiasm and an obvious thirst for adventure. Of course, he has enjoyed a time when Africa was at its peak. I have seen areas of Africa now that are being totally denuded of wildlife. I don't like what I see happening over there. More and more hunters are invading the land, and more and more guns are bringing down the game. In part, I blame men like Selous and Cunningham for trying to turn African hunting into their own private business. I know it's not hunters who are killing off *all* the game. The local natives and the white farmers should get plenty of the blame. But the way I see it, with every hunter who comes to Africa for the sport, it seems like so many of them are staying, and the place is becoming more and more populated."

"Excuse me, sir," the waiter said as he arrived with our meal. "Breakfast is served." He placed with precision the plates on the table in front of Jack and me.

"Jack, my compliments to the chef. This meal looks exquisite," I said, grabbing my fork and digging in.

"May I thank the Lord?" he asked.

"Certainly," I answered, unsure of what else to say.

As he prayed, I began to feel uncomfortable. Jack Hastings was someone I deeply admired and respected. How could a man of his position and seeming intelligence have been sucked in by this farce of a false god? Then he prayed for my reunion with Betty, and his words left me with a deep impression of his commitment to friendship and his love for others. He finished the prayer, then looked up with a sense of peace and carefully picked up his fork.

"How are Patricia and your boys?" I asked.

"Patricia is fine, although missing the boys now since they are both grown and gone from home. But our oldest is getting married soon. He is in love with an angel. Having never had a daughter, I will finally have a young girl to call me 'Daddy.' Patricia is so excited about the possibilities of grandchildren."

~~~~~~~~~

I spent the rest of the morning meal talking with Jack about such things as the stock market and politics. I must say, we had quite differing views on politics. He wanted to hear about Africa and my work at the institute. As the morning turned late, we retired to the lounge and had a smoke together. We gazed out the window of the train as we sped on to Chicago. I had grown accustomed to refined treatment, but the people onboard this train treated Hastings like a king. Anything he wanted was there at the snap of a finger; sort of reminded me of being in Africa with our native servants. Jack introduced me to some of his friends, and we engaged in quiet conversation on into the afternoon, when we sipped on champagne and brandy, snacked on caviar, and smoked the finest Cuban cigars.

Everybody wanted to talk about Africa, what with Roosevelt's high-profile visit and his book, *African Game Trails,* which had been declared Book of the Year the year before by the *New York Herald Tribune*. Then this young English lord named Churchill wrote about his African journey. Everybody had read the book by Colonel John Patterson, who wrote of his hair-raising encounter with man-eating lions. Heck, they had the lions on display in Chicago. Americans seemed to have quite a fascination with Africa. It seemed to be turning into a summer home for aristocrats. It made me think that writing a book about Africa could be a way to fame and fortune. But I wanted to go down in history as the man who proved Darwin's theory as complete truth and put to rest once and for all this nonsense of biblical creation.

"You ought to get a shave and a trim before you meet Betty at the station," Jack said.

"I suppose, but I really don't trust myself shaving on a vibrating railcar."

"I'll get it set up for you. One of my porters gives a great shave." Jack motioned to a man in a white jacket. "Steward, tell Anderson that my friend here needs a trim and a shave. When you find him, come back and get Mr. Rivers."

The steward nodded and hustled off, and Jack and I made more small talk for about ten minutes until the steward returned. I bade Jack my thanks for his company and then headed down the car to visit his barber.

"Have I got time for a shave?" I asked. "Are you Anderson?"

"Yes, sir. Mr. Hastings's personal barber."

"I'll be seeing my wife at the station, and it would be good to knock off some of this stubble to make myself presentable," I said, rubbing the whiskers on my chin.

"Oh, I agree, sir," Anderson said and stood up from the chair. He was dressed in a long white coat, hiding his potbelly, and his full white beard covered his wide face. He encouraged me to have a seat and then reached for a mug and brush, whipping it into suds.

I sat down, and he helped me recline in this makeshift barber chair, which hardly resembled the handsome brass and black leather barber chairs in the fancy parlors.

"Are you sure you don't want me to trim off some of this hair?" he asked.

"Not a chance, sir," I replied. "My wife would kill me."

He began by brushing my face with the warm lather. He then removed the leather strap from beside the chair and stropped the blade, bringing it to a sharp edge. He worked swiftly and quietly with the hands of a surgeon, scraping the blade across my face as the railcar gently swayed.

This makes me nervous, I thought, *knowing that any second that knife edge could slip and leave a gash in my cheek.*

He pulled up a warm, steaming towel and wiped the remaining soap from my face, then splashed me with manly cologne.

"How's that, sir?" he asked as soon as he had helped me sit upright.

I ran my palm over my chin to feel the results of his handiwork. "Very nice," I answered. "How much do I owe you?"

"Oh, nothing, nothing at all. I get paid by Mr. Hastings."

"Then here are two bits. I wouldn't have trusted myself. You should consider becoming a lion skinner in Africa."

"I don't think so," he said with a chuckle. "My wife would never let me go. And from what I hear, it's no place to take a woman."

"I can't remember when I have had such a fine shave," I replied and then added with a laugh, "Sort of like being skinned alive."

His comment about Africa being no place for a woman impressed me for someone who'd never been.

~~~~~~~~~

I made my way back to my stateroom to prepare for my departure and hopefully a civilized reunion with Betty. I fumbled through my briefcase and removed the letter from my journal that I had written to her on my last day in Africa. I wanted to recheck the spelling and to make sure it was all in order.

My beautiful wife, Betty,

How happy I am to have you for my life's partner. Thank you, my dear heart, for putting up with me and giving me so much pleasure in my freedom. I love how we complement each other, how we seem to pick the other up when the other needs it, and how you have always been there for me. It gives me such great joy to know that I complete you the way you complete me. Bone of my bone ... flesh of my flesh ... heart of my heart. If you only knew how I hate to be separated from you, even for an afternoon. My heart aches to see your big bright eyes, to smell your beautiful dark hair, and to feel your loving embrace. How I long to hear your laugh and share in your wit.

Oh, my precious one, the girl of my dreams, the target of my passion, the thrill of my emotions. Even though you know I will go away again, always remember this: your love consumes me.

Your loving husband,

John

I really didn't expect her to meet me at the train station. As I carefully folded the letter and slipped it back in the envelope, I thought about all that we had been through in our marriage. *I hope the letter doesn't seem too corny, because I wrote it from my heart. But then I know Betty. If she is going to give me her usual cold reception, this letter might never see daylight.* I remembered how she used to be. She was the kind of girl that would keep letters like this and save them for a blue day.

I checked my watch: fifteen minutes until our arrival time. *Seems of late her blue days are all that exist.*

I gathered my things and put them neatly together in my small leather attaché case. I knelt down on one knee, reached under my bunk, and slid the two rifle cases out, carefully placing them on the bed. I could never trust the railroad with this precious cargo. I undid the latch on the hard case, pulling the finely tooled Holland and Holland double barrel from the container that had been custom made from my own personal elephant hide. The engraving of elephants and leopards etched on the receiver in the blue metal was spectacular. I held the two empty chambers up to the light in the window and gazed down the barrels. They shone in the light, clean as a whistle, just as I had left them the day I set foot on the boat for America. I set the rifle back in the case and closed the lock, then slipped the leather straps from each case, one over each shoulder. I grabbed the attaché and started for the door, glancing back to make a final check of the room and spying my safari hat in the process.

My lucky hat, I thought, positioning it on my head. *That wouldn't have been so good.* Now I was complete, ready to greet my girl as I shut the door behind me.

"Looks like we will be at the station right on time, Professor!"

I turned and saw Jason making his way down the railcar. "Jason, you know that flower shop on the main street just out front of the terminal?"

"Sure do, sir," he answered with a huge grin.

"How long do you figure it would take you to sprint for that shop when the train stops and get me twelve big long-stemmed red roses?"

"I bet I could have 'em in ten minutes! But roses—those are quite expensive, sir."

"How long would it take you if I let you keep the change from this five-dollar bill?" I asked, pulling the crisp new bill from my overstuffed money clip.

His eyes brightened and his expression turned to one of amazement as I handed him the bill. "But, sir, I can get you a dozen roses for ten cents!"

"Jason, I want you to keep the change."

"I'll get 'em in three minutes flat!"

The train started to slow as it entered the yard, and we could hear the engineer letting the steam out of the great iron horse.

"Run along now," I said. "Betty will be waiting at the station."

Passengers had already begun to crowd around the exit. Jason, still in uniform, worked his way to the front of the line to be the first one out the door. I stood by a window to try to catch a glimpse of Betty and most likely my butler, Ralph. The train whined and hissed as it slowed to a halt. Then the doors on the car broke open, and the passengers burst out like a bunch of thoroughbreds at a starting gate. I held back and let the other passengers out first, hoping that the boy would end up a world-class sprinter.

After the crowds had thinned from folks starting to leave the terminal, I finally spotted her, this beautiful woman dressed in a handsome long blue satin dress, slit up slightly at the bottom to show off her petite ankles, which were laced into tall brown leather shoes with extended heels. The white collar contrasted beautifully with her beautiful eyes and flowing brunette curls that were covered by an elegant matching blue hat, rimmed with soft white lace. Her well-preserved, middle-aged attractiveness pleased me.

How foolish I was to go away from her. If only I hadn't been in love with two women: one being this one, so lovely, and the other being a continent full of wild beauty and adventure. If only she hadn't driven me to the latter.

I looked out to see if I could spot Jason coming with the roses, then I looked at my watch. That boy was pushing his three minutes. The last handful of people started down the steps to debark the railcar. I stepped behind the final man and emerged to see Betty smiling and waving to me. To my surprise, she came running across the brick pavement and threw her arms around my neck.

"Oh, God, how I have missed you, my darling," she whispered, her warm breath raising goose bumps on my spine.

I put my leather attaché down and held her in my arms. Her hair smelled just like I had remembered, and the familiar memory of her perfume intoxicated me. Her slim waist felt so tender between my hands.

"Are you home for a while now?" she asked. "Have you had enough of Africa for a while?"

"For a while," I answered. I glanced across the terminal and saw Jason sprinting toward the platform with a huge box in his arms. *What has that boy done,* I wondered, *bought the whole flower shop with one five-dollar bill?*

Betty stepped back for a moment. "Let me look at you, my big game hunter."

"I'll change when I get home, dear," I said.

I felt butterflies in my stomach as I gazed at her beauty, remembering that we were married and she was mine. I knew her age quite well, but she didn't look a day over twenty-nine. Her skin was soft, showing little signs of her real age, and her long lashes and bright eyes were piercing. She had delicate features: small turned-up nose, strong chin, high cheeks, and rosebud mouth.

Jason spotted me and began running in our direction, slowing to a fast gate as he approached. I turned and put my arm around Betty's shoulder, pulling my watch from my pocket and flipping open the face as he approached.

"Four minutes, son," I said as he drew near.

"Sorry, sir. The flower shop was busy. But I got two dozen for the price of one, so I bought four dozen. It was a flower sale, and I'm not one to pass up a deal!" He laughed as he struggled to carry all the flowers.

"Oh, John, you are so sweet!" Betty said. "They're beautiful." She leaned over and placed her feminine hand under one of the buds, gently lifting it to her nose and inhaling deeply. As soon as she had drunk from the rose's perfume, she looked up and gave me a smile, followed by a wink in a silent communication that only the two of us would understand.

I took the bundle from Jason and placed it in her arms. "Jason, I would like to introduce you to my wife, Betty. Betty, this is Jason, uh, Mitchell. He works for the railroad."

"You are close, sir. But it's Marshall—Jason Marshall."

I felt my face turn red. "I'm sorry, Jason. Forgive me, please."

"It is so nice to meet you, ma'am."

"Jason, would you have the resources, if I pay you, to look after my baggage and see that they are delivered to our home?"

"Yes, sir, I can!"

I pulled a printed card from my breast pocket. "This is my address." I reached for my money clip and pulled another five-dollar bill from it. "This should cover your expenses."

"But, sir, I still have your change."

"Keep it, my boy. I have already made arrangements for the cargo crates to be unloaded and taken to my taxidermist. The only things you need to deal with are my four trunks and five suitcases."

"I can take your rifles, too," he said.

"That won't be necessary."

"I'll have your bags there as soon as I can, Professor. It was a pleasure meeting you, ma'am." Jason tipped his hat as he turned and scurried off into the crowd.

"That is a pleasant boy," Betty said. "Where did you meet him?"

"On the train today," I said. "I had the same impression. He's quite a gentleman. Where is Ralph? Did he come with you, my dear?"

"He is waiting with your car."

"Did you bring my new car?"

"Are you anxious to see it? What kind of a wife would I be not to bring your new toy?" She laughed. "Come on. I'll take you home!" Betty hugged the roses to her breast with one arm, then reached for my hand. "I'll even let you drive if you think you can remember the way," she said, looking back with a silly smile.

We hurried across the train station grounds, rushing past the bustle of the crowds, and out the front entry onto the boulevard. I glanced down the sidewalk and looked up the street, and there stood Ralph next to my car. I held Betty's hand tightly, guiding her up the walkway as I gazed at the beautiful machine parked along the curb.

"That car is breathtaking!" I gushed.

"It's a beauty, all right!" she replied.

It was deep green, with a black canvas top, and the wide white-walled tires made it stunning.

Ralph stood stone-faced next to the car, wearing white kid gloves, a long white coat, and a driver's cap. He had graying sideburns, a wide mustache, and a pock-marked face. I had to chuckle to myself that he was always so serious.

"Good evening to you, Professor," he said. "It will be nice to have you home, sir. I should hope that Africa found you well." He held a cigarette to his lips and took a long drag, then blew the smoke out through his nostrils.

"Indeed, she did," I replied and then, after taking the roses from Betty, escorted her to the front passenger seat.

Ralph opened the back door for me, and I handed off the roses to him. I then slipped the rifle cases off my shoulders and tossed them in while he stood by, holding the door with his knee. As I came around the front of the car toward the driver's side, he looked confused.

"Don't just stand there holding the roses," I said. "Let's get this thing started. Give her a crank and get in." I stepped on the runner and slipped in behind the wheel. "Wow, it even smells new."

"Better hurry," Betty said. "Here come the boys from the newspapers."

"I'll talk to them," I said, stepping back onto the curb as two young reporters hustled down the street toward us with their flash cameras strapped around their necks.

"Let's go, John," she insisted.

"This will only take a minute."

"For heaven's sake, John, this will take you *thirty* minutes. I just want to go."

"Hey there, boys," I greeted them as they arrived out of breath at our car. "Here is your story," I said and reached for my attaché, which held the papers I had prepared during the passage across the Atlantic last week for just this moment.

"Come on, John," Betty said, "let's go."

"Sorry I can't give you an interview, but everything is there. I hope you understand. My wife is not feeling well, and I need to get her home."

"We understand, sir," said one kid while the other tucked his pen and paper back into his coat pocket.

Ralph leaned over, giving the motor a sharp crank, and the engine began to purr like a kitten.

I gave the throttle a couple quick revs.

Ralph's lower lip tightened as he returned to the car and plopped himself into the backseat.

"Can we get a quick picture, sir?" one of the reporters asked.

"Here, get a picture with me and my new car," I said, stepping back to the curb.

Betty rolled her eyes and shook her head as they snapped their box cameras. "Let's go, John, you publicity dog, you."

I tipped my hat and got back behind the wheel.

"Take me home, Nimrod!" Betty said and glanced at me, a wide smile on her face.

I had heard the term before but couldn't place it. "Where did you come up with that?" I asked, belly laughing as I let the clutch out and the car lunged ahead and out into the street.

"What? Publicity dog?"

"No, Nimrod."

"You mean you don't know who Nimrod was?"

"No," I said, curious. "Who's Nimrod?"

"Watch out for that horse and buggy!" Betty warned.

"Would you like to sit in the back with Ralph? Try driving from there, and I'd have to call you a backseat driver."

"Nimrod was Noah's great grandson. The Bible said he was a mighty hunter!"

"The Bible?" I snapped. "What Bible?"

"The Holy Bible, silly. I asked someone if there were any hunters in it."

"You be careful," I warned. "That book will turn you into a kook. And let me tell you, don't go believing that stuff about creation. It is nothing but a farce. I think the whole thing was written just to get people's money."

"My friend says—" She stopped suddenly, cutting the sentence short.

"Your friend says what?" I asked as I made a turn on Fifteenth and passed a slow motorcar. I could see people on the sidewalks turning their heads as we zoomed by in our shiny new car. "What friend?"

"I met this woman. Her name is Rose. She has been telling me about Jesus Christ."

"Sweetheart," I said in a loving tone and then exhaled slowly, "please don't get yourself involved in religion. You know how I feel about it. All I see is a crutch for people too weak to live life on their own and a bunch of rules that get in the way of living free. Promise me you'll avoid this Rose person."

"She is my friend. What do you mean, 'avoid her'? I love her company, and she makes me laugh. Don't I deserve a little happiness in my life? Certainly I haven't had much of that from my husband lately, running off to Africa every chance he gets."

I glanced up at the rearview mirror, saw Ralph sitting grim-faced in the backseat, and thought better of airing our dirty laundry in front of the hired help. "You're right, my dear. Maybe I am being a little overprotective." I patted her knee and then took a firm hold of the steering wheel with both hands. I turned to see her staring back at me tight-lipped with her puppy-dog eyes, as if I'd just taken a newspaper to her. "Hey, how about I change as soon as we get home, and you and I will pick out a fine restaurant and go out on the town?"

"Another night maybe. Seriously, Mae has been planning this evening meal for a month, I swear. The only thing she has talked about these last few days is making tonight perfect for us."

"That settles it. We're staying home. How's my Mae?"

"Still struggling with her knee, but she seems to manage."

As I made the familiar turn up the boulevard past the small park on the corner, I caught Betty watching the children as we sped by.

"All looks well!" I remarked, turning past the iron gate and onto the red brick drive. "The summer months have been kind to our yard."

How wonderful to be home, I thought. The house and grounds staff stood by the front entry, waiting to greet us. This was certainly a fine home, build in 1830 by my great-grandfather, Ryan Maxwell. My great-great-grandfather had been in the shipping business and had done very well before coming to America in the early 1820s. Through wise investments by my grandfather James Warner, he had built the family fortune in coal mining. The splendid Victorian mansion stood majestic against the late evening Chicago horizon. The finely trimmed lawn and the well-kept trees and shrubs accented the rich beauty of the home.

I brought my Rambler to a stop and set the hand brake under the archway of the circular drive at the front entry. Ralph hustled out the rear seat and opened my door. I went around to Betty's side and opened her door, taking her hand and helping her safely down from the car so that she wouldn't slip in her heels. I then greeted the staff and commended them on the condition of the home and the quality of their work.

Mae waited by the grand entrance at the top of the steps. She had been like a mother to me since my own mother had died while giving birth to a stillborn brother when I was only five years old. Mae had been my father's housekeeper and friend all these years until his passing six years ago.

Betty and I scurried up the steps. "Mae, you get younger every time I go away," I said and gave her a hug.

Her face was still as round as ever, packing extra weight that she had no intention of shedding. Her frizzy hair spiraled outward in tight, kinky graying curls, and when she smiled, deep dimples formed in her cheeks. She had a wide nose and thick lips, and when I looked at her face, all I could see was the mother who I loved.

"Oh, John," she said with a warm grin, putting her hands on her wide hips. "You have been shooting those bulls for so long. You're starting to become full of the stuff they leave in piles on the plains. I cooked your favorite dinner!"

"Don't tell me you made eland tail soup and wild bustard pie," I said, poking back at her wit. "I haven't had that since the Kikuyu threw a feast in my honor six weeks ago."

"John, you will never change," she said with her infectious laugh. "Come on in and get washed up, and you'll see what real home cooking is again."

"Do I have time for a hot bath?"

"Not hardly," she replied. "You've got time to splash some water on your face and wash up. Oh, but you can change out of those dreadful clothes." She laughed lightheartedly, probably knowing exactly how I felt about them.

I, however, was in no position to become impatient or angry with anybody. I had been gone for four months, and for them to accept me back with open arms seemed very good indeed. I needed to humor them with humility and love them with honor—something I had learned from the natives in the bush.

~~~~~~~~~~

I had just finished changing into suitable attire when I heard a motorcar coming up the drive. I peered out the eyelash window and saw Jason in an open cab flatbed truck, which was being driven by a teamster in a white coat, goggles, and hat. My bags and trunks were secured down with ropes. *Great! The boy has arrived just in time to join us for Mae's dinner.*

When I arrived at the front entry, they had already unloaded the bags and were untying the trunks from the back of the truck. I stood back while they set them neatly along the walk.

"Jason, hats off, boy, you have proven your resourcefulness. Can you join us for dinner?"

"I don't have to be back until tomorrow morning at eight when the train leaves for New York again, Professor."

"Then it's settled," I said. "We will have the pleasure of your company tonight."

"If you say so, sir," he said, settling up with the driver.

We started up the steps, and Jason paused to look back at the trunks.

"Never mind those," I said. "I'll have them brought up. Come along. I'll show you where you can wash up."

Jason's eyes were as big as saucers as he entered the grand entryway. He gazed up at the stained glass and glistening brass furnishings, then his eyes traveled over to the spiral staircase, and finally to the polished oak floor at his feet.

"After dinner I'll show you my trophy room," I said, "and take you on a tour of the house."

Betty, wearing another new dress I had never seen, greeted us in the dining room with a warm smile.

"I see you changed, my dear. That dress is beautiful."

"Flattery will get you nowhere, my darling. Jason, I see you found us okay."

"I was just on my way to tell Mae to set another place for dinner," I said.

"Oh, how delightful," Betty replied. "I will tell her. I think I have a clean shirt and a jacket that might fit you." Betty turned away to call one of our staff. "Jenny!"

Jenny, a young girl with a bright smile, walked briskly across the foyer. *Too bad about her crooked teeth*, I thought. She was adorable, otherwise. Her long red braids touched her shoulders, and her densely freckled nose and cheeks added to her charming appearance.

"Take Jason to the guestroom," Betty instructed. "There are some things in the closet that I am sure will fit him."

"Yes, ma'am," she replied and then directed her attention to Jason. "Come along."

"Jason," I said. "I'll be in my study through those double doors when you get changed."

"Dinner will be ready in about thirty minutes," Betty said, hesitating while Jenny led Jason down the hallway. "Why did you invite him for dinner without asking me?" she whispered.

"I'm sorry, dear. I guess I wasn't thinking."

"No, you didn't think. This was supposed to be a special night for us—just you and me. After four months apart, you would think we would be entitled to just one night to ourselves!" Her eyes welled up, and a tear rolled gently down her cheek.

"It *will* be special—I promise. You know how you've always wanted to take in an orphan? Well, he is an orphan, and I want you to consider him. I don't know why, but I have taken a shine to the boy. But listen to me! I am leaving this matter totally up to you. Whatever you decide will be fine with me. It just seems like such a waste for a boy of his caliber to be working on the railroad with no hope of any further education."

"You are an impossible man, Jonathan Rivers. You are gone all this time, and now you show up with some kid in tow. You may as well have brought home some orphaned lion cub. Honestly, John!" She paused to collect herself. "But I guess that's why I love you. Go and relax in your study, and I'll call you when Mae is ready."

I gave her a peck on the lips and turned to make my way through the double doors. The heavy slate and oak pool table that my grandfather had shipped in from England beckoned. Game heads dotted the room, and bookcases filled with scientific journals, anthropological and biological studies, encyclopedias, and reference material ran from the marble floors to the fifteen-foot ceilings. I began racking the balls for a friendly game before dinner. Just then Jason entered the room.

"Do you play?" I asked.

"Yes, I have played, but certainly not on anything as fine as this. Oh my goodness, that's some rifle collection!" Jason slowly approached the rifle rack displaying over thirty guns, which hung beneath a trophy moose I had bagged in upstate Maine. "Is this the .500 Holland and Holland you spoke of on the train?" he asked, pointing to the imposing British double rifle.

"That's it," I said, impressed with his memory.

"How about this one?" he asked and pointed to the rifle standing next to it.

"That's my .416 Rigby. Not quite as powerful, but she kicks like an angry mule, just the same. I actually prefer this 1906, 30-caliber Springfield action. It does everything you could ask for of a light rifle for the plains animals, and you won't have a black-and-blue shoulder after a good day shooting."

"And this one?" Jason asked as he pointed to another rifle in the long line of upright barrels pointing to the ceiling.

"That's a Swedish-made .375. Excellent rifle for lion. But see, it takes only a single cartridge. If you are going to hunt a lion with this, you best have someone backing you up in case you miss. Look at this one here ... this is a prize. I paid five hundred and fifty dollars for this 30-40 Blake bolt-action repeater." I removed the rifle carefully, holding it so Jason could look at the engraving, and then returned it to the rack.

The boy looked on with wide eyes.

"How about this one?" I asked, reaching out and taking the 30-40 Kraig rifle from its resting place. I opened the action to double-check it, and then locked the bolt closed. "This is the cavalry edition, a little lighter than the infantry rifle. I have never put a round through the barrel since buying it for sixty bucks from the government last year. Here ... you're right-handed, aren't you?"

Jason eagerly nodded with anticipation.

"Wrap the sling around your left arm and tuck the butt up tightly against your right shoulder. Lay your cheek against the side of the stock and focus on the front sight. Rest your left elbow on your hip, and don't grip it hard with your left hand—just let the rifle rest in the palm of your hand. Now when you are ready, take a full breath, let half out and hold." I waited a few seconds while Jason settled in. "Now squeeze the trigger until it breaks. Don't jerk it. That will upset your steady hold and throw off the bullet."

The hammer snapped as the firing pin slammed against the empty chamber, and Jason never twitched a muscle.

"You just took down a lion, boy. I don't like to dry fire them, but once or twice won't hurt."

We turned to see Jenny standing in the foyer with her black dress and white apron.

"Madam has asked me to announce that dinner is served," she said.

I took the heavy rifle from Jason and carefully placed it back in the gun rack.

"Let's eat," I said, tipping my hand in the appropriate direction.

As we entered the formal dining room, the smell of my favorite dinner filled the air. I pulled Betty's chair out to seat her.

"You can sit here, Jason," I said, pointing to a spot directly across from Betty.

I sat down at the end of the table, and Betty and I took our napkins from the table and put them in our laps. Jason, obviously overwhelmed by the number of utensils and the protocol of the meal, followed suit.

The white lace tablecloth was set with my grandmother's antique plateware imported from China. Two sterling silver candelabras were set with long white stick candles, and a fresh-cut flower arrangement sat in the center of the table. Our assistant cook, Tina, wheeled in a cart from the kitchen carrying a twenty-pound turkey, beautiful and golden brown. She was followed by a procession of servants offering up a mountain of mashed potatoes, brown gravy, sweet potatoes, and all the trimmings one would find on a Thanksgiving holiday.

Finally, Mae hobbled in behind them.

"Wow," I said. "Mae, you have done it, my dear. In my wildest dreams, I couldn't have imagined this would be my home-coming dinner."

"And you thought you would eat at a restaurant," she said with a laugh.

During the extravagant meal, Betty told Jason all about the fine art of dining, including the reason the table knife blade turns toward the plate (so as not to show aggression toward your guests). Nearly everything he said turned out to be funny, and at times I thought Betty might burst out of her skin with laughter. Somehow I felt this trip away from her had finally done the girl some good. She seemed to have a renewed spirit of vitality. I hadn't seen her this happy since before we'd lost our dear son. She had a twinkle in her eyes and a spring in her step that I hadn't seen in years.

~~~~~~~~~

After dinner, Betty and I took Jason on a tour of the mansion. She wanted to show him the grand parlor, and I wanted to finish up showing off my trophy room. Ladies first, of course, even though I knew Jason had to be dying to see my African mounts one by one. Betty had such a passion for decorating and a real eye for making our home beautiful. She had taken this old house and turned it into a thing of charm. Certainly I had nothing to do with it and had really taken very little interest outside the walls of my trophy room.

"Whose portrait is that?" Jason asked as he studied the painting above the fireplace mantle in the reception room off the main entry.

"That's my great-grandmother, Barbara Gardner Maxwell. She came to this country in 1820 at the age of seventeen and married my great-grandfather, Ryan Maxwell."

"She was beautiful!"

"As the story goes, she was kidnapped by pirates and had to be rescued by her father, John, just before they narrowly escaped a hurricane. She is the one who built this house. But enough," I said. "That's a whole story by itself. I know you want to see my trophy room."

Betty led the way down the hallway toward the east wing and entered through an archway of six-foot elephant tusks into my glorious room, of which my pride shone brighter than the sun. Jason stood in awe as he gazed at the lion skin rug sprawled out in the entrance, with the head attached and the mouth open wide and baring its angry fangs.

"Those big black monsters there are cape buffalo," I said, pointing to the mounts with curled horns that nearly hooked back on themselves. "Some of the largest ever mounted, according to my taxidermist," I boasted.

I pointed to each head individually and identified each animal one at a time: reedbuck, kudu, gemsbok, springbok, sable antelope, and wildebeest.

"Wildebeest?" Jason repeated. "He's a funny-looking character."

"That's right. He is actually an antelope. That one there, that's a Tommie, or Thomson gazelle, and there's a Grant's gazelle, an Impala, and of course you know that one," I said, pointing to the black-and-white-striped hide tacked on the wall.

"Zebra," Jason said and then pointed to a head hanging next to it. "What is that?"

"Oh, that? That's a warthog. They use those tusks for digging out roots, sort of like a pickax."

"You don't have any North American animals in here," Jason said as he glanced around the room.

"No, I didn't want to mix this theme with anything else. This is my African trophy room. The other heads that I am proud enough to display are like the ones you have already seen. They hang in other parts of the house where I have permission to put them. I glanced at Betty and gave her a wink, and she smiled back, knowing that she had set the boundaries.

"What about a giraffe?" he asked. "How come you don't have a giraffe?"

"No, not a giraffe. I can't bring myself to shoot one. There's no sport in it for me, Jason. Heck, you can spot them a mile away with those long necks. Some of those guys will shoot them, but I won't. I have seen more giraffe wounded because of misjudged organ placement. Fact is, I'd be ashamed to have one in my trophy room."

"Can't they see you coming from a long way off, too?"

"Oh, sure. A guy can justify whatever he wants. I just know for me it's not right. You see, a big game hunter is not an executioner. He is a person of high moral standards. He hunts cleanly, with precision shooting that doesn't leave the animal in agony. He has respect for what he hunts, and he pits his common senses of sight, smell, and hearing with the uncommon senses of the animals he stalks. He is courageous, but not foolish. Many a good hunter has taken unnecessary chances and been either gored, horned, trampled, or devoured by the very prey he was hunting, just because of poor judgment. These animals are not stupid. They live on the plains, and we're merely guests in their house. They use the winds for their advantage, and they can spot the slightest movement a mile away. See the way their ear has evolved? That acts like a cup that directs the sound straight to the ear canal. They can hear a twig crack a hundred times better than we can."

Jason seemed to hang on every word, digesting everything. "I know that one," he said, pointing to the spotted skin lying over the stuffed chair. "That's a leopard."

"Silent killer of the jungle," I said.

Jason turned and approached the full-mount lion with a long black mane. "I don't know what to say," he said and touched the taffy-colored fangs. "I just never imagined."

"This lion had turned into a man-eater and was terrorizing a local village. We just happened to be in the area and got lucky. Some say they start from the buttocks and work down the legs of a man, but I have seen them attack. They can put their whole mouth over a man's head and kill him instantly with one bite. Thirteen years ago, a man named Colonel Patterson from England was trying to build a bridge for the Uganda Railway and encountered man-eaters. All together, well over a hundred Indians were killed by these monsters before Patterson finally took 'em out. I did the same thing, but he got famous because he wrote a book."

"You're famous," Jason said.

"I know," I said. "I'm just waiting to choose my legacy. I don't want to be remembered for being a lion hunter as much as for my discoveries as an anthropologist. And that one—do you know what that one is?"

"I don't know. Is it another leopard?"

"That's a cheetah, and she can outrun my new Rambler."

"Wow!"

"Ever seen a footstool?" I asked, pointing to the elephant foot in the corner.

"Not like that one, Professor. Where did all these shields and spears come from?"

"They were purchased. Most tribesmen won't part with them, but sometimes you will find one willing to trade."

"Where are you going to put your bongo?"

"Very good. You were listening on the train."

"To every word, sir."

"I don't know exactly. I have a meeting with my taxidermist this week to discuss positioning. He will need to come over and view what I have so far. Then we'll map out a plan to work the new ones in. Well, have you seen enough?"

"I could stay here for a week."

"You and I still need to settle up on that game of billiards."

"Are you sure Jason isn't getting tired?" Betty asked, squeezing my hand. "He needs to be up early to catch the train."

"He's got time for one game of pool."

"You know," Jason said, "I saw a piano in the parlor. Does anyone play?"

"I don't think that piano has been touched in twenty years," I answered, "except by a dust mop."

"Mind if I try it?"

"Do you play?" Betty asked.

"Oh, just a little."

"I'd love to hear you play," she said, leading us down the corridor to the parlor.

Jason walked up to the grand piano that sat in the corner of the room. He reached for the dried flower arrangement sitting on the lid, protected by a knitted doily, and handed it ever so cautiously to Betty.

Then he lifted the lid, propped it up, and pulled up the cover on the keys, slipping it back to expose the ebony and the ivory.

"I've never played on anything like this before."

"Then you are about to," Betty said, handing me the flowerpot before reaching down to pull out the bench.

I wasn't sure what to expect as the boy sat down. *Maybe "Chopsticks,"* I thought. *A lot of kids his age play "Chopsticks," but even that is more than I know how to play.*

Jason spread his fingers out across the keys with precision, and then he began to play. The kid blew me away. He could play. He made that old piano dance as he started out with some snappy tune I had never heard before.

"What is that?" I asked Betty, who stood next to the piano, bouncing to the rhythm. "I've never heard it before."

"It's brand new, by some guy named Berlin," she said, talking over the tune. "It's called 'Alexander's Ragtime Band.' It's all the rage!"

"Can I have this dance, sweetheart?" I asked.

Betty came scooting around the piano and grabbed my hand. She had always been a great dancer, but she and I hadn't been out in years.

"Remember how we used to dance?"

"Well, we're dancing now," she answered, "and I would say we're doing a pretty darn good job of it."

The kid continued to play all the old songs. The staff heard the ruckus and watched from the hallway. We danced until we were out of breath and Jason was out of songs.

"Where did you learn how to play like that?" I asked.

"My mother played, and she taught me ever since I was a little boy."

"Ever considered going professional?" Betty asked.

"Not really," he said. "The thought of sitting around some smoky nightclub with a bunch of drunks doesn't exactly thrill me. I just like to play for the fun of it."

"Well, you play awfully well," I said. "Can you play some more?"

"Which ones do you want to hear again?" he asked.

"The old ones," Betty coaxed. "Play the old ones again."

~~~~~~~~~

We danced late into the evening, stopping only when Jason retired to his room. The familiar tunes sparked excitement, and I remembered all those nights spent alone in a tent on the plains of Africa. Betty and I made our own beautiful music together that night, and finally, in the dark quietness of our master bedroom as we lay peacefully next to each other, we had time alone to talk.

"That Jason is quite a boy, isn't he, John?"

"Indeed, he is."

"What were you thinking?" she asked. "Were you thinking you might invite him to stay on with us here and pay for his education at the institute?"

"There are ways that it wouldn't cost us a dime, as if we couldn't afford it anyway."

"If we adopted him, he would get free tuition, wouldn't he?"

"Probably a little early for that. We don't really know this kid that well."

"No, but I have seen enough to understand his depth. In just one night, I feel like I have known him forever. He has a spirit about him ... vitality ... and a joy. He brings a ray of sunshine to this old house that hasn't lived here since Johnny died."

"You're right. I don't want to see him go. Are we in complete agreement then?"

"Yes," she whispered quietly, as if in deep thought.

"Then it's final. In the morning at breakfast, we'll ask him to stay."

Chapter 3

THE BROKEN CASE

I awoke early and automatically reached for my African duds. But as I felt Betty's watchful eye from our bed, I realized my mistake.

"Oops!" I said, shrugging my shoulders and grinning and then grabbing my Chicago city clothes.

"Are you going into the office this morning?" she asked.

"I'm sure Williams is eager to hear about our findings, or the lack thereof. I won't stay but for a few hours, and I'll be home by early afternoon. You are getting up, aren't you? I think you should be there when I talk to Jason."

"Go ahead and wake him," she replied, "and I'll be along rightly."

I went down the hallway and knocked on his door, waiting for a response. After hearing nothing, I pushed the door and peeked in at the bed. The top comforter was pressed neatly over the pillows, as if he had never been in the room. The hands on my watch read 5:45 a.m. I wanted to alert Betty, but decided to make a further search before alarming her. I hurried downstairs and looked in on the kitchen staff, who were preparing the morning meal.

"Have you seen the boy? I asked.

They looked at one another and shrugged their shoulders.

The trophy room was the next logical place to look. If he was anywhere in this house, surely he was there. Discovering the room deserted left me puzzled. I decided to look in the study and there found the lad reading by a lamp.

"You are an early riser, aren't you?" I said, standing in the doorway.

"I'm used to it, sir. I find that I am just not able to sleep past five."

"What have you got there?" I asked, unable to see what the boy was reading.

"Just admiring your collection of Charles Dickens."

"Which book do you have?"

"*David Copperfield*, but I noticed that you have most of his titles."

"You impress me with your culture, son."

Just then, Betty arrived wearing a long white dress and looking quite beautiful. Her braided hair hung over her shoulder. "You are a live wire, aren't you, Jason? Up and ready to go at this hour. You must be excited to get back on that train."

"Not exactly, ma'am. I've been riding that train now for six months. It seemed fun for about the first week."

"Are you sure that working for the railroad is what you really want to do with your life?" I asked.

"No, not exactly, but it is a good job, and there is room for advancement."

"How would you feel about trying your hand at college and staying here with us for a while?" Betty asked.

"Oh, no, ma'am, I would never be able to afford such a thing."

"You don't understand, Jason. What we are offering is to pay for your education, and for you to stay on here with us while you are in school."

"Well, I would have to repay you, of course."

"Suit yourself, Jason," I said. "But you are of a mind to consider the offer, aren't you?"

"Oh, sir, it is more than I could have dreamed of, but it's more than I could ever repay. How could I ever ... ?"

"This is nothing you need to worry about right now," Betty interrupted. "Right now, the only thing you need to think about is cutting the ties with your old life and reestablishing yourself here as a college student."

Jason took a deep breath, and a huge grin appeared on his face. "I can't believe it!" he said. "But I'll still have to be on the train this morning to let them know what I have decided. And I'll have to go on to New York to get my things and cancel my room."

"Do what you need to do, Jason," Betty said. "But remember to bring only what is dear to you. While you're away, I'll shop for a new wardrobe for you so you can dress in the style fitting of a college student. I'll need to take some measurements before you leave."

"It's settled then," I said. "Shall we have some breakfast before I take you to the station?"

"Indeed!" Jason answered with hungry eyes.

During breakfast, Jason continued to amaze us with his wit. Mae had taken a shine to the boy as well, and when she found out he would be staying on, she howled with joy.

The time came for me to take him to the train station, and Betty bade him farewell from the front steps. As we stood on the steps, I pulled the letter from my coat pocket, placed it in her hand, and gave her a kiss on the cheek.

"You can drive, Ralph," I said, bounding toward the car.

Ralph's eyes lit up, and he eagerly got behind the wheel.

Jason had not a hair out of place and seemed to keep himself always looking good. His strong chin and narrow, pointed nose gave the boy a look of sharpness. A warm feeling came over me knowing that Betty and I would be able to help him make something of his life.

"I should be back in a few days if all goes well," Jason said. "I'll know better tomorrow, but I'll be able to wire you."

"Do you need some money?" I asked, reaching for my pocket.

"Oh, no, sir," he answered quickly. "My pockets are still stuffed full with the change from your ten dollars."

"If there is anything at all that I can help you with," I said, "you let me know."

Jason sat quietly a moment as we sped down the avenue. "I still have to break the news to Chester," he finally said, staring out the window. "I know he will be disappointed that I'm leaving the railroad."

"Chester is a good man. He'll understand."

"I have a half-sister living in New York," Jason said with a grim face. "We aren't that close. In fact, she is twice my age and married. But I'll need to tell her that my life is changing. I think she'll be happy for me."

The car rounded the corner as we headed down Main Street toward Grand Central Terminal.

"How are we doing on time?" I asked.

Jason pulled out his watch and opened the face. "Seven forty-five, sir. I'll be early!"

"What's going on there?" I asked after spotting a small crowd of women standing out front of the station. "Looks like a hen party!" I chuckled to myself.

"That is the women's suffrage movement," Ralph said.

"Oh, sure," I said, "that's what that is. What is this world coming to?"

"Why aren't those women home with their husbands at this hour?" Ralph asked.

"I don't know why they are in such a tizzy," I said. "If we give women the vote, it's going to ruin the country. They are just not educated enough to make intelligent decisions on such important matters as politics. If we ever did give them the right to vote, before you know it they'd be voting women into office, for heaven's sake."

Ralph drove the car past the crowd and pulled up to the curb.

"I'll be waiting for your wire, Jason," I said, reaching over the backseat to grab his satchel.

"I can't tell you, sir, what this means to me," he said and extended his hand. "I won't give you any trouble, I promise!"

I grabbed hold of his hand firmly, and our eyes locked. "I know you won't. I'll see you when you get back."

Jason walked briskly toward the terminal, and Ralph revved the motorcar as we pulled back out into the street. So much noise, traffic, and people—even at this hour of the morning, Chicago was nothing like the serenity of Africa. I couldn't even hear Ralph speaking.

"What was that you said?" I asked.

"Shall I take you on to the institute, sir?" he asked impatiently.

"Yes ... yes," I responded, trying to reclaim my thoughts.

These women don't know how good they have it in this country. If they could only experience firsthand the harshness of Africa. Then maybe they would see how good they really have it. Of course, I remained convinced Africa was no place for a woman whatsoever.

As we drove across town, I went over some of the reports to make sure I had everything together for my meeting with Williams. When I had departed four months earlier, he had held high optimism that the trip would yield some solid findings. There had been glimmers of hope, but now I had to present a report showing little progress. I had grappled with just such a possibility for the last several weeks, pondering how Williams and I might justify any future support from the institute and its investors. I knew that, like me, Williams stood firm as a disciple and faithful follower of Darwin. But still, he would need plenty of ammunition to maintain a loaded rifle to keep the skeptics at bay. The religious community continued to beat us back over our lack of evidence. I chuckled inside as I imagined how Williams would react to my hunting exploits. As someone who was against hunting, Williams believed in such things as reincarnation. He tolerated my *blood sport*, as he called it, because he respected my knowledge of science. But I knew he detested everything that had to do with big game shooting.

I had already sent the packing crates on ahead, addressed for delivery to myself at the institute. I knew Williams would be more than anxious to examine the contents. After readjusting my tie and lifting my hat, I brushed my hair flat, then made sure the brim on my brown derby was slightly curled. As I gazed up the hill, I could see the stone perimeter of the college.

"Be here at eleven-thirty to pick me up," I said.

Ralph nodded, and I tucked the papers back in my case and closed the latch as we pulled in front of the sandstone and marble buildings. I hurried up the front steps past a crowd of students hurrying to make their eight o'clock classes.

Just then, I heard a single voice call out from the crowd. "Professor Rivers!"

I turned to see one of my students from the previous year and slowed my step, allowing him to catch up. "It's James, isn't it?" I asked.

"Yes, sir. You remembered. How was Africa?"

"I just returned yesterday," I said, reaching for the half-opened door and holding it open while students streamed through the entry.

"Did you find it as successful as you had hoped?"

"Africa is always a profitable experience. How are your science studies going?"

"Science? Just fine, sir. I love it. It's the psychology I am struggling with."

"Take heart, lad. I struggled with it, too," I said and veered toward the administration office.

"I'll see you later, sir. I'm late for class," he said, disappearing into the crowd.

I stopped in front of an unfamiliar receptionist at the front desk.

"I know we haven't met, madam, but I'm Professor Rivers."

The young woman remained seated and gave me a half smile.

"Please inform Dean Williams that he will find me in my office."

"I believe he has been waiting for you, sir," she said and fumbled through her notes.

"I'm sure he has," I answered, turning toward the long hallway. I stopped and glanced back in time to see her standing with her back to me and opening a file drawer. "Miss," I said, getting her attention, "there should have been some shipping crates delivered to me in my absence. Would you have one of the interns check to see if they arrived safely?"

"Would you like them brought up to your office, sir?"

"Please," I answered before continuing down the hall.

I noticed Cassidy, my not-so-favorite colleague, approaching from the other end of the long corridor. I couldn't stand him. His little ego oozed from his nostrils, and it nauseated me. Some months before I had left for Africa, we'd had a nasty disagreement over curriculum at the institute in which he had downright lied behind my back to the regency.

I glared at him as he approached, and he glared back, smirking as he did. But neither of us greeted the other as we passed. *What a simpleton, with his thick wire glasses and weasely little walk!* I knew he was just jealous of my position and my authority, such as it was. I tried to shrug off the anger as I fumbled for the keys to my office, at the same time imagining him being mauled by a lion.

Once inside, I found my packing crates sitting in the corner of the room. *Oh well. Those interns don't have much else to do but scurry around the campus looking busy. They'll kill an hour or so until they figure out they have already been delivered.* I retrieved my hammer from the bottom drawer of my desk, then carefully began prying at one of the lids so as not to disrupt the contents. I wondered how much care had actually been taken with these boxes on their trip across the Atlantic. Some of the contents were extremely fragile, even though I knew most of them were nothing more than smoke and mirrors. I knew I would need something more to show for my time overseas other than just a few dead animals.

I heard a knock at the door.

"Come in," I said as Williams poked his nose inside.

"Rivers, it's about time you showed your face," he quipped in his English accent. "I was beginning to wonder about you."

"Glad to see you're happy to see me. Did you get my letter?"

"What letter? I got a short note in June stating that you had arrived, with no indication of when you would return," he said sharply. "Don't you know we have a college to run here?"

"Listen, Williams, we agreed in May when I left that I would be home the second week of September. Has something changed?"

"The regents are getting impatient with you, Rivers. We have contributors to consider."

"Well, you can remind the regency that I am one of their major contributors," I said, snapping back angrily.

"You know the problem with you, Rivers? You seem to take this institution and the important work we are doing here very cavalierly."

"Look here, Williams, you know better than anyone that I am trying to bring this college into the twentieth century. The work I'm doing over there will turn this school into one of this country's most prestigious institutions when I find it."

"When you *find* it? Sounds like you are returning empty-handed once again. Is that what you are preparing me for?"

I took a deep breath and then exhaled slowly, trying to hold my composure. "Brad," I said calmly, "I sent you a letter in late July from Nairobi. It detailed my itinerary and the progress we were making."

"It doesn't matter now. I never received such a letter. Maybe it would have helped, but I'm afraid even that might not have saved your program."

"What do you mean, saved my program?"

"You may as well hear it from me; you will find out soon enough. They have cut your funding."

"I thought you were supporting me, Brad."

"Supporting your work? Of course. Supporting your lifestyle? Not on a bet!"

"But Brad!" I pleaded.

He frowned, and his jaw hardened.

"I'll go to Crawford."

"You've always gone to Crawford, but it's too late. They've installed a new president in your absence. You won't get away with business as usual. This guy isn't a big game hunter. He was appalled to find out that you are killing in the name of science."

"That's not the nature of my project, and you know it."

"I think I know it, and I think you believe it, but John, your conduct away from your research is intolerable. Face it, you are a Renaissance man."

"What's that supposed to mean?"

"It means you are going in two different directions. You should have been born a hundred years earlier. Your antics are outdated."

"Outdated? What about Roosevelt?"

"What about him? He's washed up, too. He's damaged goods for the intelligent voter. Listen, Rivers, take my advice. You are a brilliant scientist, but you need to focus on your science and forget this horrid thirst for blood. It is indefensible!"

"Do you want to hear about the research?"

"Only if you have something significant to report. Well, do you?"

I sat speechless, staring at his face, not knowing what to say. Finally, I took the hammer off the lid of the crate and pounded the nails tight back through the wood.

"Just as I thought," he said, folding his arms across his chest.

"I can't share this with you right now, Brad. I need to cool off. I'm calling a cab. Will you be in your office in the morning?"

He nodded firmly without saying a word.

I turned to retrieve my hat and coat hanging on a hook, and then grabbed my briefcase from my desk. "I'll be here in the morning, after I have had some time to think." I opened the door, showing him the way out of my office, then locked the door behind me. "Have a good day, Brad," I said, turning to make my way down the long hallway. I remembered Cassidy's smirk and boiled with steam. He must have known what awaited me.

"Call me a cab, miss," I told the young receptionist. "I'll be waiting out front."

The halls were quiet now, with the students tucked away in their classrooms. As I walked outside, a fresh breeze began to blow and a light rain started to fall. The maple trees had not yet turned to their fall colors. The leaves rustled in the wind as the branches rubbed against each other. I stepped back under the awning covering the front entry of the building. *What is the matter with these people? What's happening to me? I have poured my heart and soul into this project for these people. The sheer stress of it has probably taken years off of my life. What a bunch of ungrateful—*

The cab appeared, rounding the bend and crawling up the drive. It had begun to rain a little harder now, so I ran down the steps, hurrying to get under the canvas top on the cab.

"Where to?" the cabby asked.

"Sixteen-fifteen Wilson Boulevard," I said, jumping in the front passenger side.

"Can I get the back door for you?" he asked, obviously indignant that I had taken the liberty of getting in the front.

"No, this will be fine," I insisted.

The driver shrugged his shoulders, let off the hand brake, and then gave the car some throttle. Only as the auto began to move off the campus did I begin to feel my shoulders loosen and my fists unclench.

"Hmm ... sixteen-fifteen Wilson," he hollered over the engine noise. "Isn't that the big white mansion on the corner?"

"That's the one," I said, shouting back.

"Will you be visiting long?" the cabby asked. He was dressed in a long white coat. "Do you want me to wait for you?"

"No need to wait," I answered abruptly.

We didn't speak as we made our way downtown past pedestrians, food vendors, horse-drawn carriages, trolleys, and cheap Ford Tin Lizzies.

"That's Wilson," I said.

"I know," he said and rolled his eyes, not knowing I had seen his facial gesture. "Do you know the owner well?"

"Yes, I know him very well," I replied, playing with him as I would with a fish at the end of a line.

"He is very rich, isn't he?"

"In what way?" I asked.

"What other way is there besides money?" he asked with a grin.

The car lumbered across Fifteenth.

"That's it on the corner, isn't it?" he asked, pointing with one hand and holding the steering wheel with the other.

I nodded, and he turned up the drive.

"You know," I said, "plenty of things make a man rich besides his money." I opened my billfold and thumbed through the collection of tens and twenties. I found a crisp new one-dollar bill and held it out in front of him. "But for those who don't have it, and for those whose only purpose in life is to seek it, they will never understand." I set it carefully in his opened hand. "By the way, you can keep the change," I said and hopped out of the cab. I looked up and saw Betty standing at the front entry.

"You're home early, John," she said as I walked up the long steps. "I can't say I'm not delighted."

The noise from the cab faded as it disappeared down the long drive.

"What's the matter with you, dear?"

"Oh, it's nothing."

"Don't you tell me that," she said, reaching for my hand. "I can read you like a book."

"Remember the problems I had with that Cassidy chump before I left?"

"Yes, but I thought you had that resolved."

"Apparently not, and the worst news is that President Crawford has left the institute. I don't know who this new guy is, but I am afraid he has been poisoned. For all intents and purposes, they have killed my program."

"I'm sorry, dear. I know how much it means to you. It will be okay. Don't worry about it. Let's get inside before we get wet."

Betty and I walked through the garden entrance.

"This has happened for a reason," she said. "I believe God has a purpose."

"Oh please. Not god. Please don't tell me you are foolish enough to have bought that."

"I believe there is something to it, John."

"Well, I am here to tell you there is nothing to it. Where was this so-called god when Johnny got sick? If there is a god, then why does he let innocent children die? Why is there so much evil in the world? If there was a god, then he wouldn't have forgotten about me."

Mae stood near the entrance of the kitchen. I caught her eye, but she didn't say a word.

"I can't talk about it right now. I need some time to myself to deal with this. Please!"

Betty let go of my hand, and I stormed off to my study.

I tossed my briefcase in a rage against the stone fireplace, tipping an oil lamp off the hearth. The lamp smashed against the oak planking and sent glass in every direction, and my briefcase broke open, strewing papers all over the floor. I slumped in my chair and rested my head in my open palms.

I heard footsteps and looked up to see Jenny scurrying to clean up the mess. "Leave it!" I shouted.

"But, sir," she pleaded, "the oil — it will damage the floor."

"Very well. Clean up the oil," I ordered, "but then get out."

My mind raced. The stress of being away and being torn between my two loves had been getting to me. Why couldn't those idiots understand? How would I break this news to my friend Lance Miles in East Africa? *He'll be devastated that the research money has come to an end. Should I fund the project myself?* Maybe I could find a less backward institution that would accept me. I'd had a hunch they were trying to force me out all along. I felt like Meriwether Lewis, without a boat to make his way up the Missouri. At least he'd managed to follow his dream, even if his life's frustrations had ended in suicide. I wanted to get out of town, but I had just come back to town. I wanted to be with Betty, but even she couldn't make me happy. What a mess I'd stepped in!

Chapter 4

A WEAK MOMENT

I tried to get some rest that morning but drifted in and out of sleep. Finally a soft hand touched my shoulder, and I looked up to find Betty's warm smile.

"Are you ready for some lunch, my dear?"

"Yes, I am," I said with a sheepish grin, hoping she wouldn't scold me for the broken briefcase and oil-splattered papers. "I think I have cooled off now."

Betty smiled back and shook her head. "I have a favor to ask of you, my darling," she said in her sweet little voice that always melted me.

"Name it, sweetheart. Your wish is my command," I said, not thinking of the consequences of any great commitments, but only considering my undying love for her.

"Are you sure?"

"Absolutely, darling. I mean anything — anything at all."

Betty scooted a footstool up next to my chair, placing her elbows on the big stuffed armrest. Then she put her chin in her open palms. Her sultry eyes pierced mine. She seemed hesitant, as if holding back for a few moments. Then she closed her eyes and began to speak softly. "I want to go to Africa with you. Will you take me to Africa?"

Shocked at the question, I paused to collect my thoughts, fearing that I might have just sold the farm. I really couldn't believe my ears. For each second that I considered the proposal, the more curious I became. What could have possibly provoked this woman to make such a ridiculous inquiry?

"You don't know what you are asking."

"Yes, I do," she replied.

"Why would you even consider such a thing?"

"Because I know you are going back. I can see it in your eyes, and I don't want you to leave me again."

"I have to tell you, darling, I know you. I know how you like things to be, and I can tell you flatly: you will not like Africa."

"How do you know?"

"Oh, sure, you might like Johannesburg, or Cape Town, but even the Nairobi streets will be too dirty and dusty for you. And where I go, I sleep in tents, and sometimes even on the hard ground. Things would be way too harsh for you."

"Maybe you don't know me." She sat up straight and put her hands on her hips.

"I know you, my dear. You are a city girl: prim and proper."

"I am?"

"That's right. You like your tea in china cups, your silver polished, and your napkins ironed. You hate snakes, bats, moths, spiders, and mosquitoes. You're not that fond of horses, and you always use a parasol, rain or shine."

"No, that's what you have made me into," she snapped. "Besides, I probably know more about horses than you do." She stood up and looked down at me sitting in my chair. "I'm stronger than you think. My daddy used to take me fishing when I was a girl, and he took me hunting once, too. He showed me a thing or two about shooting, but you have never included me in your world. You have never even invited me one time to go with you. I always stayed in the background, like a proper little woman. But I see my life slipping away, too. And I see us being torn apart by a place you won't let me see."

"I'll take you to Europe," I insisted. "We'll go to England, and you'll love it there."

"Africa. I want to go with you to Africa."

"Oh, Betty, please. I can't."

"You can't, or you won't? Or are you just afraid that I might steal some of your thunder?"

Again I paused, trying to respond intelligently so as not to hurt her feelings. All I could think of was all the men back in Africa who I had boasted to that I would never bring my wife. Maybe she was right. Maybe I was being selfish and wanted Africa all to myself. I cradled my forehead with my palms, wrestling with the dilemma. She didn't realize there were so many perils on the plains. The flies, ticks, and leaches, the sweltering heat and the choking dust, the torrential rain and the sloppy mud. I lifted my head and looked her in the eyes. "You will hate it over there, and you will want to come home." I shook my head, bewildered.

"It makes me wonder if you have a woman over there," Betty said.

"You know that's not true."

"Then give me a chance," she pleaded. "Try me just once. You can send me home if I don't measure up."

"You don't know what it is. You think it's glamorous, but it's not. There are lions and crocodiles that eat people. Where I hunt, a wounded animal can stomp you into the ground if you're not quick enough to get out of the way."

"I don't care!" she said, folding her arms across her chest.

I could feel myself softening at her insistence, but I tightened as I thought about showing up with her over there. I had joked often with Lance, the ardent bachelor, about those men who took their wives to Africa with them. What would he say if I showed up with mine? I had been so outspoken on the subject. Surely I would be a laughingstock among all the gentlemen at the men's club who I had been so blunt with. If only I had—

"You promised me anything," she said, interrupting my thoughts. "Now I dare you to hold up your end of the bargain."

Maybe this was one way of shutting her up. *I should just let her go over there and find out what it's really like. She'll be back here safe in Chicago, sipping tea and eating crumpets, so quick a cheetah couldn't catch her.*

This hadn't been the greatest morning of my life, and now it appeared the afternoon had begun to circle the drain as well. In a much weakened state, somehow I gave in.

"Okay," I mumbled. "Suit yourself." I couldn't believe what I was saying. "I guess I'll take you to Africa."

Betty squealed like a hyena, and Mae came hobbling into the room, wearing a curious look on her round face.

Betty ran to Mae, throwing her arms around her neck. "I'm going to Africa, Mae! John is taking me with him!" Betty stopped in her tracks and turned back. "When are we going, John?"

"I just got back yesterday. Let's hold our horses here. You know the planning that goes into one of my trips. We'll go in the late spring, after the rainy season."

Betty started in with a little tap dance, like they do on the vaudeville stage.

"Okay, settle down," I said, rising out of my chair. "All this excitement is getting to me. I think it's time for lunch, isn't it?"

"I'll have one of the girls pick up that mess," Mae said as she motioned to the papers strewn near the fireplace.

"No, I'll have to organize them later."

Mae stopped in the hallway in her blue flower-print dress and folded her arms. She squinted at me knowingly, no doubt wondering what the hell I was thinking. Then the three of us headed toward the dining room.

"Are you sure about this, my dear?" Mae asked. "Africa is a place people don't come home from."

"I'm sure of it, Mae," Betty said. "I've been thinking about it for a long time." She turned to me. "Did Jason get off okay this morning, John?"

I knew she was trying to keep my mind off the institute.

"That boy will do just fine. I didn't go into the station with him. I only dropped him off. The place was crawling with suffering women."

"What do you mean by that?" she asked, pursing her lips and glancing at me suspiciously.

"I guess they want to have a say in politics," I said with a shake of my head.

"And shouldn't they?" she asked.

"Are you sure you want to have this conversation right now?" I could feel my blood beginning to boil again.

Wisely she changed the subject again, this time back to Africa, and we sat down to have our afternoon meal. Thinking about Africa helped get my mind off of Williams.

"What about the rainy season?" Betty asked. "Is it harsh?"

"It lasts about three months, starting the last week of March and ending in mid-June."

"Is it bad?"

"Well, let me just say it's a nuisance. The rivers swell, and the plains turn to muck. Tents become saturated, your bedding and clothes are soaked, and as for dry feet — forget it."

"When in the spring will we go?" she asked, barely able to hold back her excitement.

"How about I take you on a luxury liner toward the end of April or the first week of May to England? We'll spend a few days in London and then catch a boat to British East Africa. By the time we arrive, we will have missed the rains, and the plains will be green and ripe for picking."

"What will we be picking?" she asked naively.

"During the dry season, the herds all migrate out to find water. When the rains come again and the plains are lush with grass, there is more game around than you can imagine. They're harder to find, mind you, because of the thick green foliage, but there are more of them. Then, as the winter drags on and the hot sun dries things up, they begin to congregate at the water holes. That happens in late July and August."

"Tell me about the luxury liner," she said. Her eyes sparkled in the light, and her cheeks became flushed pink with excitement.

"When I came home this time, I heard tell of a magnificent ship whose maiden voyage will bring it to New York this April. They call it the 'Ship of Dreams,' the *Titanic*. The accommodations are said to be of grand proportions."

"I'm just so happy to be going with you. I don't need extravagance, although I don't mind being pampered. But you'll see, John: I'm tougher than you think."

~~~~~~~~~

I rose early the following morning feeling more than ready to do battle with the dean of the college. While I was preparing some thoughts in my study, Mae had fixed a light breakfast. Betty looked bright and beautiful, as always, dressed in a long-sleeved black dress that made her slim figure stand out and revealed every curve.

We had met each other in our late teens. Our mothers were childhood friends, and they had dreamed about their kids one day getting married. Betty had harbored great aspirations to seek a career on the silver screen. She would have made it, too, if she hadn't fallen for me and decided to get married. Even after we were wed, she often spoke of it, but it would have meant a move to New York or even California, and the cards were wrong for both of us.

All these years I had carried the guilt of being the one who had killed her dream. She had never once tried to stifle me in mine, but I had kept her like a caged bird, not wanting to share her beauty but trying to keep it all for myself. Perhaps that was another reason why I had given in so easily to her request to take her to Africa. I loved her so much; I just wanted to protect her from getting hurt or falling ill. Even though I had all but abandoned her these past few years, a spark now flashed in our relationship, and the possibility existed that we could put it back together.

The front bell rang, and I sat waiting while Ralph answered the door.

"Telegram, sir!" a young boy said.

Ralph mumbled something, and I could hear his footsteps on the hardwood floor as he brought the cable into my den.

"It must be news from Jason," I responded as he handed me the paper.

Ralph nodded, then stood over me while I opened the envelope.

WESTERN UNION:

All is well. STOP. Will arrive Saturday. STOP.

"Is it from Jason?" Betty asked, standing at the door of the study.

"Yeah, looks like I should have given him a little more money so he could have splurged on a few more words," I said with a laugh. "He'll be here on Saturday." I got up and handed her the message.

"Do you want to talk about what happened yesterday?"

"I couldn't talk about it. I was too irritated. That Cassidy—what a weasel! And as far as I'm concerned, Brad isn't far behind him."

"But Brad has always been your friend."

"I know, but he has apparently abandoned me for some reason, and I intend to find out why. I have a hunch old Brad has always been a bootlicker. Now that my ace Crawford is gone, who as you well know has always been one of my greatest supporters, my old buddy Brad has dropped me like a dirty shirt." I turned to Ralph. "I'm ready to go, Ralph. Bring the car around."

He grabbed for his coat in the entry and disappeared down the hallway.

"What will you say to him?" Betty asked.

"For all I have done for that place, devoting my life, and now to be treated like dirt because they don't agree with part of the curriculum I am giving my students. I need to try to assess the damage and attempt to find out if there is anything I can do to repair it. I don't intend to indulge in the type of character assassination of Cassidy that he has taken the liberty to initiate against me. I need to try and reestablish Brad as an ally, and I hope to be able to set up a meeting with the new president. I'll fill you in when I get home, though I don't know when that will be. I'll put in a call to you, and you can send Ralph when I'm ready."

"No more hasty cab rides?" she asked with a smirk.

"No. I had to get out of there, and I wasn't going to wait for Ralph."

"Good luck, darling," she said, reaching out and putting her arms around me. "Just think about our trip to Africa and how wonderful it will be for us."

I kissed her cheek and let my nose linger at her neck. How lucky I felt to have this woman back. I grabbed my attaché as soon as I heard Ralph drive up to the front steps. "The worst that could happen is they might fire me. To save them the trouble, I might resign anyway and start my own institution."

"You're a survivor, John. You're my hero!" Her words reverberated in my head as I bounced down the steps to the waiting car.

As we drove across town to the college, I could feel the tension in my nerves. The reality of resigning my position put a knot in my stomach, and the thought of trying to start a school of higher learning would certainly be trouble. Besides, Africa was in my sights again, not building a college. I flipped the lid on my watch and looked at the time: 7:30 a.m. sharp. This would give me some time to unpack the crate and put away some of the things that were of no use to them.

As I sat patiently in the backseat, I concentrated on more important thoughts, such as Nairobi. Maybe with all this turmoil it would be good to get out of town again and head back to Africa. So what if we arrived in the middle of the rainy season? Still, I had to think about finding financial backing for my work. Not that I couldn't afford to bankroll the operation myself, but there were plenty of willing sources around to fund a project like this. I just had to look around, that was all. *Look at the kind of capital Teddy came up with from the Smithsonian and Andrew Carnegie*, I thought to myself. *I, too, have an abundance of affluent friends and associates*. Besides, there were plenty of men who owed me. Each had come with his hand out during lean times and was now very successful.

The motorcar turned up the long drive to the institute, and I grabbed my case. "I'll get a message to you on the telephone when I'm ready," I said, leaning forward so Ralph could hear me over the rumbling engine.

I watched for Brad and was happy not to bump into him as I walked down the corridor and slipped into my office undetected. Inside were the crates, just as I had packed them. I knew I had to sort through them to make some sense out of the contents, if for no other reason than for Lance Miles's sake. He had been such a good and faithful friend, and I knew he would be counting on me to keep the project alive.

The hammer rested on the lid, as if inviting me to pry the nails out. As I pried open the crate with a creaking sound, the smell of Africa wafted forth, filling me with beloved memories. Most of the things here were relics to display in my office. I had even tossed in a few things for Brad. I dug out the native figurines that were packed in the excelsior and had been carved from elephant tusks. I pawed through the stuffing and found the rhino horn I had traded to a Masai for my pith helmet. I remembered purchasing the helmet four years earlier from a catalog. I had always thought it looked way too European on me. I chuckled as I thought about how proud it had made that native to wear it, and how glad it had made me to finally be rid of it.

I fished out a tanned leopard hide I'd bought from a young native boy who hadn't had the faintest idea of how to skin one without putting holes in it. If only I had brought some of the fossils that Lance had insisted I bring. Obviously, I wasn't prepared to showcase our work yet, but I hadn't counted on running into this sort of homecoming. I gently lifted free from the crate the large twelve-inch-high ironwood carving of a bull elephant, which I intended to present to Brad. He'd told me once that when he died he hoped he would come back as an elephant. *Not a bad idea right now*, I thought, laughing to myself. I set it on my desk and then smiled as I thought that one should be careful what one wished for.

I leaned forward over the edge of the box and picked out the last few items: an arrow, spear tips, and a handful of stone tools that dated back more than 150,000 years. I examined them with care after laying them out in a row on the table. *Now prove to me, you Bible believers, that some god created Adam and Eve in the Garden of Eden, and that man did not evolve from monkeys.* How narrow-minded, how idiotic their perceptions to believe man had only been on earth at the most, ten thousand years.

I took a few minutes to sneak across the hall to use the plumbing, but as I grabbed for the door on the men's room, it burst open, hitting me square in the nose. I staggered back, then caught my weight on the backs of my heels.

"Oh, John, are you okay?" Brad asked. "Oh my, you're going to have a black eye there."

I couldn't believe it. All night I had dreamed about getting Brad in just such a position, but he'd gotten me first. I held the bridge of my nose, trying to ease the pain. "Gee, Brad, are you in a hurry?"

"Sorry, John. I was in a haste to see if you were in at this hour."

"I guess you have your answer," I said, squinting at him in pain.

"We need to talk, John."

"Wait in my office," I said. "I'll be there in a second."

"Are you okay?"

"Yes, I'm fine."

Like he really cared that I might be hurt. *If he cared about me at all*, I thought, *he would support what I am doing here at the institute.* As I used the facility, I thought how eager he seemed to have a conversation. I checked the mirror to make sure my nose was still on straight. I hadn't been hit like that since being run over by a wounded cape buffalo back in '08. *That old boy should have killed me, but he hit me with his shoulder and knocked me into a tree.*

I washed my hands, carefully opened the door, lest someone else fall to my same fate, and then waltzed into my open office. Brad was sitting on the edge of my desk, holding the carved elephant statue.

"Very nice piece, don't you agree?" I asked.

"Exquisite. Very fine workmanship."

"It's yours, Brad. I bought it for you in Nairobi from a Kikuyu tribesman."

"I'm touched, John."

"I've seen some crude ones, but this native had mastered the craft well."

"You know how I love elephants, unlike you, of course," he said with a hint of sarcasm in his deep voice.

"Just what do you mean by that, Brad?"

"Well, anyone who kills them must have a hate for them."

I couldn't believe my ears. Brad was throwing rocks at me right off the bat. I wanted to snap back, but caught myself and tried to think of how to handle his slashing attack.

"Brad, don't you agree that I have a deep love for Africa?"

"It would appear so."

"And don't you agree that I have a respect for her native people?"

"You have demonstrated that in the past," he said, frowning in a way that made heavy lines stand out on his face.

"And don't you agree that I am an advocate for protecting the wild places in Africa and thereby giving added protection to her wildlife?"

"Maybe," he said, setting the wooden elephant on the desk and folding his arms across his chest.

"Brad, I'm sorry that you will never know the thrill of the hunt. Hunting is not solely the act of killing an animal, and it's surely not mixed with hate. It's setting foot on their turf, pitting your senses against theirs. With all the new settlements going in, lions have to remain in check, and without the numbers of prides keeping the herds' numbers down, plains game could starve each other out in no time. They will either die a slow, agonizing death from starvation, or they will fall quickly and humanely to a sportsman's bullet. At least with a bullet they have a fighting chance."

"Not much of a fighting chance in my opinion, and I don't have the stomach for it, John. I don't have to like it, and I never will. But we need to talk about your position here at the institute."

"This has progressed further than you were willing to admit yesterday, hasn't it?"

"I am afraid so, John."

"Because I shoot animals?"

"You are simply not in line with this institution, its values, or what we stand for. Not only that, but the regency has agreed with the new president that they have no need for an anthropologist."

I couldn't believe my ears. "So is that it?" I asked.

"That's it, John. I'm sorry."

"Yeah, I can tell you are really sorry for me. You should be sorry for your other programs. When I leave here, I'll take my contacts with me, and you and I both know they have been the bulk of the support for this place."

"We had these discussions over the summer. They have anticipated and compensated for that."

"So give it to me, Brad. Lay out your cards."

"They have decided to let you keep an affiliation with the school, but they are bringing in a scientist to replace you in running the department, and they aren't supporting any more research."

"What sort of affiliation are you talking about?" I asked. "Is it a nonteaching position?"

"That's about the size of it," he answered as he folded his arms across this chest and nodded gently.

"You can tell them I'm not interested."

"It's not like that, John."

"I know how it is. They were hoping to appease me by giving me some title to keep my backers. All I ever wanted was to teach and to do my research. I don't need them, and I don't need this school. Sad thing is that the people who will suffer are the students."

Brad stood silent now, unable to argue.

"Who is going to break the news to Miles?"

"He works for you, John. He's your associate. He has never been part of this institute. You know that."

"My research will go on. You can stake your life on it, even if I have to bankroll it myself. But you know me, Brad. I'm a survivor. I have too many influential friends to count. There are plenty of people out there willing to invest in this exploration. I'm just disappointed that this college won't share in the victory."

"The new president wants to meet with you."

"Not interested. This man replaced me without even finding out for himself what kind of a person I am. Tell him whatever you want. I'll have my things out of this office by next week. One question: why did President Crawford leave?"

"I don't know for sure," he said. "I think he'd had enough. Just old and tired, I guess."

That didn't sound like Chuck Crawford to me. There had to be more to this than what Brad was telling me.

"You are a good man, Brad. Too bad you let them poison you. If you are ever looking for a job some day, look me up."

Brad started for the door, then stopped and turned, holding out his hand in my direction.

"Don't forget your elephant," I said. I folded my arms across my chest, and slowly his hand went to his side.

He took the wooden elephant from the table. "I wish you all the very best, John."

"I'm sure you do." I took the spearheads and stone tools and grabbed my coat.

"What do you have there?"

"Nothing, Brad. Nothing you are interested in." I exited my office, leaving him standing in the doorway, and walked down the long hallway to the main office.

"Would you call my home and summon my ride?" I asked the young girl behind the desk.

I then returned to my office, found an empty box, and began packing up my things. I felt anguish as I boxed up memorabilia from several years worth of work. It was like finishing the last chapter of a long book and then searching for another one to read. As I stood on the front steps waiting for Ralph in the chilly fall wind, I thought about what I would tell Jason. I had made a commitment to the lad to get him started in school. *And that is exactly what I intend to do.*

Chapter 5

JUST LIKE A PUP

The long months following that pivotal day in my life seemed to drag by. How do people live after succumbing to the age of retirement and idleness? The boredom of simple relaxation is enough to drive me nuts. If I hadn't been planning a safari and contacting potential investors, I wouldn't have made it. Jason had come to live with us and, just as I had promised him, had begun his studies in undergraduate work. Betty hovered over him like a mother hen. Her joy was obvious, and I had to admit that having him around brought life back in our home. When he wasn't studying or attending classes, Jason went with us to town to stock up on our supplies for the long-awaited safari.

"What is it that we still need to purchase here?" Betty asked as I went over the checklist in my study.

"Here is the updated list from our New York outfitter. Here are the items they are providing," I said and began to read from the list:

Camp supplies: *Bug netting, canvas tents, cots, canvas bags, folding chairs, folding tables, canvas wash basin, tea pot, pots, pans and grills, porcelain dishes, steel utensils, water tanks, copper boiler, canteens, tin cups, kerosene stoves, lanterns, tinder box and flint.*

Tinned goods: *Vegetables, fruit, nuts, coffee, tea, salt pork, honey, cheese, French brandy, whiskey, wine.*

Dry goods: *Cereal/beans/corn/flour/rice/yeast/hard tack/ dried fruit/sugar/salt/pepper/tar, spice-kit, sago, mustard, chew tobacco, cigars.*

Tent supplies: *Mousetraps, bedding sheets, wool blankets, pillows and cases, mats, rugs, canvas and tarpaulins.*

Maintenance: *Candles, soap, emergency medical kit, drug supplies, towels, rope, saw, auger, picks, shovels, axes, hatchet, hammer/nails, screws, punch, needles, threads, heavy thread, sharpening stone, oil can, pliers, wrench, screwdrivers, block and tackle, chain.*

Tack: *Four riding saddles, horse blankets, four packsaddles, halters, leads, spare stirrups, spare bits, spare shoes, assorted leather strapping and belts.*

"Here is what we have already purchased," I said as I continued to read:

Ammunition: 5 cases of 30-caliber 1906 Springfield, 5 cases of .500-.450 Nitro express, 5 cases 30-40 Kraig, 4 cases .416 Rigby, 10 cases 12-gauge birdshot, 4 cases of 00 Buck, 3 cases .275.

Supplies: Woolen underwear, lightweight cotton red-lined underwear (for sun screen). Towels. Extra motorcar parts, tow chain. Leather gloves, and shooting boots, knickerbockers, gaiters.

"And these are the things we still need to find."

Pith helmets, pants, shirts, jackets and socks, Butter churn, .275 Rigby rifle and hard case, one Colt .44 Magnum handgun with holster and ammunition. Eighteen skinning knives, electric torch, two compasses, rubber rain jackets and hats. Woolen mittens and sewing kit.

"Now, my darling, is there anything not listed here that we still need?" I asked.

"How come we need so many knives?"

"Every skinner gets three," I answered, "and we'll have at least six native skinners."

"Okay, well listen," she said, "I've read about the stream fishing in Africa and understand that it's fabulous. I'd like to take along some fishing gear."

"We'll be so busy I don't think you'll find time for that."

"Then I'll make time," she insisted. "Maybe when you're tucked away in your tent and reading your technical journals in the heat of the day, I will have time for myself to catch up on my childhood. I was once a pretty decent flycaster in my teens, and I'm sure it's like riding a bicycle. Once you have it, you never forget, and you never forget the thrill of the invisible tugging on the end of your line."

"Suit yourself. I've just never been one for the sport. You'll find out spending time along the riverbank in Africa is different from here, where it's peaceful. In Africa, you can't let down your guard, or you might end up being dinner for some croc."

"You're trying to scare me, John."

"I'm just telling you the way it is. Besides, I like to pursue game where I can see it and watch it, to stalk it using the wind and the silence of carefully placed feet. It is challenging to use the available cover and terrain to get close enough to take a bead, then take a rest, squeeze off the shot, hear the loud roar of the muzzle blast, and see your prey keel over dead from the slug. You really have to pit your skills against an animal that has adapted to its surroundings."

Betty rolled her eyes and looked away so I couldn't see the smirk on her face. "How about the butter churn?" she asked. "Do we really need that?"

"I saw a safari three years ago with a fresh cow and a butter churn, and they were always with fresh butter. It didn't seem like a luxury too extravagant to me."

"Have you thought about purchasing butter in Nairobi, mixing in an equal part of salt to preserve it, and putting it up in glass jars? Then when you want fresh butter, all you need to do is to work the salt out with water."

"I know how to do it. If we don't take a cow and we want butter, that's our only option. It just seems a little stupid to pay a porter to carry forty pounds of butter in glass jars when all we have to do is take along a cow and she carries everything. Then we get fresh milk and cream out of the deal, too. The real problem is that a cow usually ends up being lion food if we don't post armed guards. But we are planning on having other livestock, so we'll have to protect them at night with guns."

"Okay, I'll concede that you're the expert here, John. You just get me the fishing gear, make sure I'm not the one churning butter, find me a stream, and we'll call it even."

"Then let's go to town and see what we can do about crossing these last few things off the list," I said. "As for the pith helmets, we're going to have to order those out of a catalog. Are you sure you really want them?"

"I just think they look so grand," she smiled.

"Yes, all the greenhorns wear 'em. They show up by the hordes wearing their pith helmets."

"It's Africa, dear. Don't be so serious."

"See this .275 Rigby right here on the list? That's for you. It's a light rifle with good power and not too much recoil."

"I get my own rifle?"

"Well, you can't very well go to Africa unarmed, can you? It'll be well heavy enough for zebra, gazelle, or antelope, but pushing the limits on anything else you might want to shoot."

"Oh my! Fishing gear and a rifle to boot!"

~~~~~~~~~

I couldn't believe Betty was getting into the planning for the safari. We visited the sporting goods store that afternoon, and we purchased for her some fishing tackle odds and ends, plus the new rifle. I had the gunsmith cut the stock down to fit her shoulder. Jason didn't know it, but I already had in mind to present him with the Kraig rifle I had sitting in the rack at home. We looked at single-action large caliber pistols made by Colt. Instead of purchasing the .45, which I had seriously considered, I decided to go with the .44 Magnum, which was on my list. I liked the balance and the feel of it; it seemed to fit my hand better. I had a feeling it might just come in handy for protection in the bush.

We scrounged through my friend's store and gathered up nearly everything remaining on our list, except the butter churn and the electric torches. I picked out three very fine skinning knives. The total came to well over three hundred dollars, and I settled up with my friend, Buck, and we returned home for the evening.

~~~~~~~~~

"Betty, we still need to spend a day at the range," I said over dinner, "so you can get used to the feel of that rifle."

"Do you really think I'll be able to handle it?"

"I won't let you go to Africa unless you can."

"She can handle it," Jason said with his boyish smile.

Betty beamed at his confidence in her. "If you're going to leave me at home," she said, turning to me, "then I guess I better take the range serious. You wouldn't really leave me, would you?"

"You know I'll use any excuse," I answered with a sheepish smile. "After dinner, Jason, we'll take another look at the Kraig rifle. Remember the one I let you dry fire the night you first came to the house?"

"Yes, sir."

"Did you like that rifle?"

"Oh, yes, sir!"

"Well, consider it yours, and not just to use on the safari, but yours to keep."

"Oh, sir, I can't tell you what coming here to live with you means to me. I have a new lease on life, and now to be included in plans for Africa is just too much. I could have never dreamed this."

"I have to warn you, son," I said sternly, "this trip won't be all roses. There are all kinds of hazards and hardships on a safari. The reality of travel in such a remote place is that any one of us might not come home. Are you ready for that?"

"I guess there are dangers all around us, sir. Traveling about town in Chicago or in New York, we're all faced with the same stuff. I guess we just never know, do we?"

"I just want to give you fair warning, that's all."

"Has there been any news on our passage to Africa?" Betty asked.

"Oh, I guess I forgot to tell you. I contacted Cunard's shipping line and booked passage to sail on the *Mauritania*."

"I thought you were going to try for the *Titanic*," Betty said, "the one they call the 'Ship of Dreams.'"

"She's not set for her maiden voyage from England until the first week of April, and I want to get going. I thought you would prefer to go sooner than later."

"You're right, my dear."

"Here, let me show you the tickets." I grabbed my case from the hallway, unlatched it, and pulled out three boarding passes. "The date is March fifteenth. That puts us in England on the twenty-second, where we will lay over for five days. We then catch the steamer *Congo* for a twenty-eight-day trip to East Africa. We'll go by way of the Mediterranean Sea around the tip of Spain, and on to the Red Sea and Gulf of Aden. Then we steam around the tip of Somalia and south to the British East African Protectorate and the port town of Mombasa.

"What about the rains?" Betty asked. "Aren't we going to be in Africa too early and hit the rainy season?"

"We're prepared for rain. We'll be just fine."

"Where do we go from Mombasa?"

"From there, we catch the Uganda Railroad and take it four hundred eighty kilometers to Nairobi, where we'll meet up with Lance Miles, if he doesn't meet us in Mombasa. We'll make our final preparations there while staying at his modest home, a small farmhouse."

"How modest?" Betty asked.

"I suppose if it's too crowded, we could get a hotel in Nairobi, but remember I told you we would be roughing it. All in all, I have planned for three months in the bush, barring any unforeseen problems that might occur, of course. And if you decide that Africa is not for you after all, I'll put you on a boat, and Jason and I will see you in September."

"Well, let me tell you something, Mr. Smarty Pants," she said with a laugh, "that just isn't going to happen. The only way I'm coming home early is in a box."

I tried to laugh along with her, but the thought of that made me shudder. *This concept of death is the one thing in life that makes no sense at all. We are here one day, alive and vibrant, and the next day gone forever, never to exist again: dead, cold, and final.* "That's not funny, dear."

Her comment concerned me, and from that point on I really didn't trust that she really knew what she was in for. I knew I would have to keep impressing upon her the seriousness of what loomed ahead. I would try to toughen her up by taking her on long walks in the late afternoons.

~~~~~~~~

It was a clear and crisp December day when I took delivery of her .275 caliber rifle, which was actually a seven-millimeter, and I drove Jason and Betty out to the country to zero it in. Once again, the girl took me by surprise. Having to my knowledge never shot a rifle before, she jacked in the first round, threw the rifle up to her shoulder and fired off a round, hitting the target at one hundred meters offhand. I didn't want to seem too surprised, so I let it go. The .275 Rigby threw a slightly smaller bullet than the Springfield 1906 model, but at a higher velocity. I didn't want to encourage her to get in the dirt and take a rest in her skirt, but she got right down there and didn't seem to mind in the least. She fired off the rest of the magazine at the target slowly, one at a time, and then stood up after she had finished and brushed the dirt off her clothes.

"We'll have to get you outfitted with pants, sweetheart."

"I don't mind. I know I might not be able to wear this on safari."

The accuracy of this bullet impressed me when I put it on a rest and fired a three-shot group. But more than that, Betty impressed me as she hung in there with the rifle and never made a peep about the recoil. I knew for a fact that her shoulder would be sore in the morning, and I might have been looking forward to her complaining just a little. Apparently, I had never known her all these years. She seemed to be emerging as a person I liked a whole lot more. The closer we came to leaving for Africa, the more guts and gusto she seemed to possess. She continued to amaze me at every turn.

"Jason, are you ready to try out that Kraig rifle?" I asked.

"Want me to get it from the car?"

"Yes, but remember what I told you. Always open the action the minute you pick up a firearm. Make sure it is clear, and even when you find out it's empty, treat it like it's loaded. If I see you handling that thing like a broom handle and you point it where it shouldn't be, we'll put it up."

"Yes, sir," he said, walking deliberately toward the Rambler and then doing exactly what I had instructed him to do. He held the muzzle toward the dirt, brought the rifle over, and laid it carefully against the stump with the barrel pointed up. Betty stood downrange, studying her target before finally putting up new paper. I waited for her to get back off the range, and then I picked up the Kraig.

"This is a Lehman, 48 Peep sight," I explained. "It has adjustments for wind and elevation. See this graduated scale on the back here?"

Jason nodded as he listened intently.

"We'll zero this thing in for one hundred meters, and then you can set it at whatever range you want to shoot. This 30-40 cartridge packs a wallop, but you'll be pushing it to try anything over four hundred meters. We won't take any long shots like that. Long shots only wound game, and I just don't have the stomach for it. Hand me a cartridge out of that box."

Jason reached in and plucked out a shiny new loaded brass.

I set the rifle down across the stump and helped him get settled in on a good position. "Are you comfortable? Remember how I showed you how to use that sling to get a steady position? All right, go ahead and lay the round in the action and close the bolt, but keep your finger off that trigger."

Jason did just as I told him, keeping the rifle steady on the target.

"Squint your left eye closed, and with your right eye peep through that hole, center the front sight, and lay it on the black part of that bull's eye. Got it?"

"Got it, sir."

"Now it's time to zero that rifle. Are you ready to take a shot? Remember what I told you about taking a full breath, letting out half, and then squeezing the trigger?"

"Yes, sir."

"Now concentrate on that front sight," I said, "and squeeze it off."

Time stopped, and then the muzzle roared like a black-mane lion and kicked him like a mule.

I waited for the smoke to clear before I spoke. "Did you hit the paper?"

"I think so."

"Here is another round. Eject that empty."

Jason did just as I told him, and he shot two more rounds with similar results, then another three-round group at another target.

We cleared the weapon and all went downrange to get a closer look. He had placed the three-round group nearly one right on top of the other.

"You have a steady hand, Jason. That's some fine shooting for your first time."

I glanced over at Betty and saw she had a wide grin. I had made a bigger fuss over Jason's target than I had over hers, but her shooting actually amazed me much more. "I guess there is no sense in wasting ammunition unless you just want to make some noise. That's some fine shooting from both of you."

Betty seemed to glow from even that little bit of recognition. I didn't want to praise her too much, lest she become overconfident. If a person has too much confidence they won't take proper precautions.

"How was the kick?" I asked.

Jason rubbed his shoulder.

"How about this one?" I asked, pulling a 50-caliber round out of my pocket to show them the difference.

His eyes widened.

Betty came in to get a closer look. "That thing is twice the size of my rifle!" she said, marveling at the round. "Wouldn't that take your arm off?"

"Not really. The weight of the rifle actually makes the kick less than a bolt action. Well, sure, you don't want to shoot it in the prone position. You always want to either take a sitting position or shoot it offhand so your shoulder will give. Otherwise, I think it could hurt you."

~~~~~~~~~

Long shadows had begun to creep across the drive by the time we arrived home, where we found an unfamiliar horse and buggy parked just off our front steps.

"Who might that be?" I asked.

"It belongs to my friend Rose," Betty said.

"Oh great. Not that weird one, I hope."

"There is only one," she snapped, "and she is not weird, so be nice!"

"I'll try, but if she starts in on religion, just let me say, it's my house."

"John, you wouldn't dare be rude, would you? She's a very sweet woman, and she is my dear friend. So please, be on your best behavior. Will you promise me?"

"I'm not going to kick her out of my house, but Jason and I need to clean these rifles. Besides, she is here to see you, not me."

"Don't pull up too close," Betty warned. "Her horse is a little spooky."

"Okay," I said, slowing up the car. "Looks like she has him hitched." I eased the car up to the carriage and set the brake.

"Need any help with anything?" Betty asked as she jumped out of her seat.

"No. Jason and I will get everything. You go see your friend."

"Thanks, John." She bounced up the first couple sandstone steps, then stopped and ran back, throwing her arms around my neck. "I love you, darling. Thank you for this day!"

I looked back and saw Jason getting the rifle cases out of the back of the car.

"I love you, too," I whispered under my breath.

Betty scurried off and disappeared inside.

I started helping Jason with the rifles and the ammunition. "What did you think of Betty's shooting?" I asked, looking around to make sure she hadn't returned.

"She's good. She must do a lot of shooting."

"No. In fact, that's the first time she has fired a rifle."

Betty appeared at the top of the entry, standing with her friend.

"That must be Rose," I whispered. I noticed Betty had a pup on the end of a leash. "I'll have Ralph put the car in the garage. Jason, here, you take your Kraig and the .275, and I'll get the rest. We can leave this extra ammo, and I'll have Ralph deal with that, too."

As I walked briskly up the steps, I could feel the winter bite in the December air. "Whose dog is that?" I asked as I approached the women.

"Darling, I want you to meet my friend Rose. Rose, this is my husband, John."

"It is wonderful to finally meet you, sir. I have heard so many great things about you," Rose said. She appeared very intelligent, and possessed a look of sharpness that I hadn't expected. She had wild red curls, soft freckles, and a slim build, and wore an eggshell-blue dress that showed her figure quite smartly.

"Most people have," I said, tongue in cheek, as Rose responded with a chuckle. "This is my friend Jason. He's a student at the university."

"Let's go inside where it's warm," Betty said.

But what about that dog? I wondered. *How could she ignore my question? She knows how I feel about them.* "You're not bringing that mutt in the house, are you?" I asked.

"Oh, John, please," Betty said, rolling her eyes. "He's just a puppy. Besides, he's clean as a whistle."

"Well, he better be housebroke."

Once inside, Betty knelt down beside the animal and cradled his head in her hands. "Look at him, John. He's adorable. Look at these eyes."

The pooch had long floppy ears, saggy brown eyes, and a shaggy coat of liver and white.

"Yes," I said, "so what kind of a mongrel is he?"

"He is not a mongrel at all," Rose insisted. "He is a pure-bred spaniel."

"And what, pray tell, is he doing at my house?"

"Rose brought him over as a gift for our trip," Betty said.

"What?"

"Rose read how a dog is useful in the night for warding off predators and alerting sleeping campers to marauders."

I groaned. "They're a nuisance, and I have no use for one."

"What?" Betty asked sarcastically. "Marauders?"

"No!" I snapped. "Mongrels!"

"Jason, you would like one," Betty said, "wouldn't you?"

Jason's eyes brightened. He started to respond eagerly, then he looked at me and held back.

"What are you thinking, Betty?" I said. "You know how I feel about dogs." I had to admit the dog was kind of cute, but I would never admit such a thing to her.

"I want him, John," she said, standing toe-to-toe with me. "I think he is adorable, and he's smart, too."

Jason grinned widely, probably wondering who would win.

Once again I could feel myself cracking under the pressure of this brown-eyed beauty. Her long-lashed and sparkling eyes easily melted me.

"I guess I'm outnumbered." I said. "What kind of a dog is he again?"

"He's a purebred English springer spaniel," Betty said.

"Well, does he have a name? And let me tell you, the only reason I'm even considering this is because he's a hunting breed."

"His name is Buster," Rose said, "and he's fourteen months old."

"Rose sold him out of her litter," Betty explained, "but the family had trouble and asked Rose to find him a new home."

"Gee, thanks for thinking of us, Rose. How are we going to get him to Africa?" I asked, knowing full well that travelers commonly took their pets along with them.

"John, don't be silly," Betty snapped. "They have accommodations for such things."

"I know," I responded, "but it will cost us."

"So?" she said. "It's only money." She turned to Rose. "Can you stay for supper?"

"I really need to go," Rose answered. She glanced at me, her cheeks rosy, and I could tell she was trying to read me.

"It's okay," Betty said, "isn't it, John? We always have plenty. You know that, Rose."

"Well, I suppose," I responded, always a sucker for another pretty woman. "We'll be in the shop cleaning the rifles. Call us when we need to wash up."

I headed down the hallway with Jason close at my heels. I had given him instructions on how to break the rifles down and brush the barrels clean of any lead residue.

"Take good care of them, and they'll take good care of you. Remember, this rifle can be the difference between life and death in the bush. Keeping the barrel clean is what makes these things shoot straight. You let the lead build up, and the bullet tends to fly inconsistently. When you are facing down a lion or a croc, you can't afford to be wondering where your bullet is going to hit."

"How is this one?" Jason asked, handing me Betty's Rigby.

I pulled the bolt, held it up to the light filtering through the window, and looked down the barrel. The light glistened through the twisted rifflings that gave the bullet its spin, making it fly straight and true. "Very nice," I said, noticing Jenny standing at the door.

"Ma'am says that supper is nearly ready and to tell you to wash up, sir," she said and blushed, clearly enamored with Jason.

"Tell her we'll be right along."

We put the cleaning gear away and packed the rifles down to my den. Then we hurried along, washing up and changing into appropriate attire.

When I arrived at supper, Jason had beaten me and was already conversing with Rose at the table. I took my spot at the head, and shortly Betty joined us. Most of the meal had already been set out, but Jenny delivered the remaining dishes and then poured me a glass of wine.

"Enjoy it while you can," Rose said. "They are going to outlaw it, you know."

"I suppose the do-gooders will finally convince the government that this stuff is from the devil," I said, "but until then, I'll continue to indulge."

How bold, this woman, I thought. *She is a guest in my own home, yet she has the audacity to criticize me for drinking.* I began loading my plate, sampling tidbits as I went. I picked off a small piece of dark meat with my fingers and put it in my mouth. I looked up and noticed that the women were holding back, watching me.

"Rose would like to say grace, dear," Betty said.

I put my plate down, amazed at her nerve. Both women knew exactly how I felt; I made it crystal clear with my body language without saying another word. My mind drifted off to the African plains, and I didn't hear a word of Rose's prayer. When the women looked up, I knew it was safe to continue digging in.

"Might we allow our guests the courtesy of being served first?" Betty asked.

"Of course," I said with a sweet smile while burning up on the inside.

Betty had gone on the attack just to impress her friend. I sat quietly, trying to restrain myself. I felt like a second grader who had been put in a corner for speaking out of turn. Good thing this wicked old schoolteacher didn't have a ruler, or I might have gotten my hand slapped.

"Tell me about Africa," Rose said as she slowly put her fork into the roasted fowl and arranged the choicest pieces carefully on her plate as if she were creating a work of art.

"What would you like to know, ma'am?"

"Tell me about the animals. Are they really as dangerous as they say?"

"More dangerous than they say. They are less harmful left alone, but once you poke at them with the piercing crack of a rifle, their natural defenses take over. At that point, they tend to charge rather than run off. Those buffalo are used to taking care of their natural predators on their own. There are a lot of dead hunters lying under gravestones who were stomped after only wounding one. Sometimes the other herd members will defend a fallen comrade and attack the hunters who are approaching a kill."

"My dear, how are you going to fare?" Rose asked, looking at Betty with a furrowed brow and her freckled little pointed nose.

"I'm preparing myself," Betty answered. "I'm studying up on Swahili so I can converse with the natives."

"I didn't know that," I responded.

"Oh, yes, I found your notes lying about—and the listing of Swahili words you prepared."

"Give us a word," I said.

"How about *Mungu*?" she asked. "Do you remember that one?"

"Yes, that one means their god," I answered.

"What is the native concept of God?" Rose asked.

"Lots of them are Mohammedans," I said. "They pray to Mecca, and they won't eat wild meat unless it has been killed by having its throat cut by one of their priests. Or if they kill it, they have to recite a prayer."

"Where are you at, John?" Rose asked, nonchalantly cutting her food with her knife.

"Right here having dinner with you, Rose."

Betty gave me a frown, but I really didn't want to have a religious discussion with this woman in my own house.

"I know, sir, but what are your views on Jesus Christ?"

"My father always told me never to discuss religion or politics over dinner," I answered. "But if you really want to know, I think it's just a crutch that people who can't make it on their own seem to need. As for me, I am self-reliant. I think there is far too much evil in the world for there to be a god, not to mention all the cruelty exhibited in nature. No loving god would allow lions to attack and kill a baby elephant. I don't know. I see a world where there is no justice and nothing seems fair. And if there was such a loving god, he wouldn't allow such things."

"Life is not fair," Rose said. "In fact, did you know that Jesus taught us that life is not fair?"

"I'll admit by what I have heard that he was a great teacher, but a lunatic as well," I said with a chuckle, throwing it smack in Rose's face just to make her mad. I glanced out of the corner of my eye and saw Betty's grim face. "But I have never heard that he taught that life is not fair. If he claimed to be God, then how could this god of yours create a world where there is no fairness or justice?"

Rose seemed unaffected by my comment, and simply continued on. "If this life were only about our life here on earth, then God would have made it a place where everything was fair and just. But this life is not about here, but what comes after. Jesus said, 'So the last shall be first, and the first last: for many are called, but few chosen.' This is the most unfair statement that could have been made. When we think about being first in our life, then that counts for something. But for God it means nothing."

I had to admit that this conversation intrigued me to a point, so I advanced the question. "What did he mean by that statement?" I asked.

"He was talking about humility," Rose said. "Being first always gives a boost to our self-esteem. It goes directly to our ego, and it's our ego that separates us from God. But humility, repentance, and our final realization that life is all about God, and not ourselves, brings us to know Him. So the first shall be last, and the last, or the humble, will be first. But that is what creates life's ultimate dilemma, because life's quest is all about lifting ourselves, with money, power, and prestige, which tends to separate us from God's whole purpose.

Did you know that God uses everything in creation as an illustration to teach humanity, trying to reach mankind and bring us to Him?"

I had to think about that one. Being a teacher myself, I picked my words carefully. "But if a teacher teaches, and there is no one in the classroom to hear the lesson, what good has been accomplished?"

"To what are you referring?" she asked.

"For instance," I answered, "there are many times when an animal is killed on the plains by lions without a single witness."

"Who can explain the mind of God in every circumstance? For His purposes have eternal significance, and here on earth everything that we know is temporary, having a beginning and an ending."

"And that is exactly what I believe. I am a common sense type of person. I only believe in what I can see and touch. When you die, it's over, the lights go out, the mind turns off, and the music stops. There is no pain, no desire, no fear, and no memory of it, but only the quiet peace of eternal darkness and forever nothingness."

"Pretty frightening thought, don't you think?" she said with an innocent smile. "Where does your knowledge of this perspective come from?"

"From my own intellect and scientific knowledge," I answered.

"I can see you are a very wise man, with incredible insights into the world, much more than I possess. Even one of the greatest scientists who ever lived, Sir Isaac Newton, proved that energy is neither created nor destroyed; it simply changes form. This life is a series of crossroads and decisions, and we continually arrive at a fork in the road, wondering if we should step left or step right. A choice between good and evil, light or darkness, calm or storm, right or wrong, with every decision building one upon the other, every choice having the greater or lesser potential of being a matter of life or death. Many are called, but few are chosen. Think about that statement." She paused, perhaps to gauge my reaction. "The things that I know in my heart you don't understand."

"You Christians," I said, "you are all so narrow-minded when it comes to the world."

"Yes, I have heard that before," she said, totally unaffected by my jab. "But remember this: I didn't come to know Christ until five years ago, so I know your point of view all too well, because I lived it myself. But now I have a new understanding that broadens my horizon. Let me give you this challenge."

I shrugged my shoulders, not willing to commit to her nonsense.

"Look to the animals, sir. God is speaking to you through the lessons that they are teaching. You use their heads as a trophy to lift your self-esteem. Seek the Lord and His wisdom, for He is calling you, He is reaching out to you. Listen to the animals that He created to be your teachers in His classroom. Watch them and you will understand. For many are called, but few are chosen. In the end, everything will be gone: our money, our prestige, and our very lives will be lost if we are not careful. And that fits in perfectly with what you have told me that you believe. It is my hope that everyone would come to know the saving grace of the Lord, and that even you, John Rivers, would come to know God."

I sat silently for a few seconds to be polite, and then I changed the subject, turning to Jason and picking up the conversation surrounding his studies. Even though I tried to focus intently, Rose's words echoed in my mind like the trumpet from a bull elephant across the silence of the Serengeti plains. Somehow this woman had gotten to me, even though I could never allow myself to admit it. I continually tried to shake it off. I couldn't believe that this woman, Rose, whatever her last name, sitting in my own home, eating my food, had actually gotten to me. The prospects of eternal life might have been appealing, but giving my life to Jesus Christ ... appalling.

Chapter 6

THE GRAND OLD LADY

"I haven't been to England since I was a girl with my mama and my papa," Betty said. She was decked out in a long red dress and high-heeled, laced brown boots.

"It hasn't changed much since then," I answered. "Motorcars have modernized it a bit, but progress is slow to change what tens of centuries have created."

Ralph, seated at the helm of my Rambler, rounded the bend for the train station.

"You be sure and write me when you get to London," Mae insisted from the backseat.

"Oh yes, Mae," Betty answered. "I'll write weekly. But you better write us, too. We'll be looking forward to news from home."

I looked back to make sure the truck bringing our crates of cargo, trunks of equipment, and bags of clothing still followed behind.

Betty saw me looking back, and she looked, too. "I'm glad you were able to finance most of our trip through sponsors," she said.

"Faithful friends are hard to find," I replied, "and we are lucky to have them. I really thought my curator friend at the Smithsonian Institution would be interested in our safari. Unfortunately, he said they would be unpacking crates from Roosevelt's excursion for years to come."

"I'm so glad you were able to convince President Crawford to come along with us," Betty said.

"Chuck wanted to go, and it didn't take too much coaxing. He has always been an avid sportsman and a great supporter of my work. He is getting on in years but is still in great shape for sixty-five. I think he will be a wonderful addition to our safari. Besides, he is the one who knows several people like Andrew Carnegie, whose money makes up the bulk of our donors."

"You take care of this boy," Mae said, rubbing the top of Jason's scalp with her hand and messing up his hair. "I have grown quite fond of him."

He turned red as a beet and tried to fix the rat's nest by brushing his hair over with his hands. "I'll miss you, too, Mae," he said.

"You're in charge of keeping Buster on a leash, Jason," I said. "I started to make arrangements for him to ride in a crate in the baggage car. But since you know everybody on the train crew, I'll have you take care of that for me, okay?"

"Yes, sir," he answered.

"Betty and I will make sure the cargo and the luggage are properly handled. Here is your ticket," I said, handing it to him as the car pulled up to the front of the station. "We'll see you onboard."

"What about the rifles, sir?" Jason asked.

"See that crate marked *fragile*?" I asked, pointing to one of the crates on the truck pulling in behind us. "I spent hours packing that with excelsior, making sure they were well separated. I paid extra to get proper handling instructions all the way to London. For this trip, since we have so many rifles, I decided to go ahead and crate them. We won't pay duty in England if we leave them boxed up, but we'll pay a handsome fee when we get to Mombasa. I'm a little concerned about leaving them crated for a month in the salt air, but I have greased them down and I think they will be fine."

Betty leaned over and took Buster's face in her hands, rubbing her nose against his forehead. "You be a good boy now," she said, as if he could understand her. "We'll come visit you on the train." She stood and leaned into the car to give Mae a big hug.

"I love you, dear," Mae said, wiping her red eyes but missing a wet tear as it rolled off her round cheek. "Take care, and please be careful." She turned to me. "And you take care of her. Do you hear me, John?"

"Yes, ma'am," I answered, trying not to think of the terrifying consequences of anything less. "I promise to bring her back in one piece."

Jason held on to Buster's leash and reached into the car to give Mae a hug. He then shook Ralph's hand with a strong grip.

"Run along now," I said as Jason tugged on the lead and headed off toward the entrance, "and get that dog taken care of. We'll see you on board."

"Isn't that Dr. Crawford?" Betty asked, motioning in the direction of an approaching car that pulled up to the curb behind our luggage.

"Do you need any assistance, sir?" Ralph asked after closing the door of the Rambler.

"No," I answered, "I think we have everything under control."

"Then I will see you in the fall," he said, revving the motor and tipping his hat.

Betty reached out and touched Mae's hand as the car jerked forward, and down the road it went, spewing smoke out the tailpipe.

The drivers who had brought our luggage were removing the ropes from the crates and loading them onto a rail yard dolly.

"John!" Chuck shouted as he walked briskly down the brick sidewalk carrying his English pith helmet. He had a wide mustache that covered his upper lip, a wide face, and round puffy cheeks. His face was heavily wrinkled, which tended to show his age, and he wore wire-rimmed spectacles that he continually pushed up the bridge of his nose. He looked like a true greenhorn, carrying that pith helmet while decked out in a full set of khakis. "Are we ready?" he asked with a wide grin.

"I see you are," I answered with a smile.

"How do I look?" he asked, placing the khaki-colored hat on his head.

"You'll fit right in with the aristocrats in Nairobi," I said with a laugh.

"Isn't that the idea?" he replied. He turned to Betty. "Are you excited, my dear? This is going to be the trip of a lifetime for both of us."

I stepped away and paid the men who transported our trunks, then tipped the porters handsomely. Betty and Chuck were conversing on the sidewalk when I returned.

"Did you purchase that pair of field glasses we talked about last week, Chuck?"

"I did, and the German optics are quite fine. I have them here in my bag to watch the sights on the train."

"There will be plenty to look at, all right." I put my arm out for Betty to take. "Shall we go?"

Our trip to New York was quite uneventful. Betty acted like a schoolgirl filled with excitement and anticipation at every turn. She and Jason were getting along fantastically, like a mother and her son. I became enthused watching them together and seeing her emerge from the shell she had been in all these years since losing Johnny. My good friend Chuck Crawford and I spent the time watching the scenery and talking about the old times at the institute.

~~~~~~~~~

When we arrived in New York the following day, we met with the representatives from the Abercrombie and Fitch Company who were outfitting our safari. They showed us the latest red-lined cotton undergarments that had been designed to combat sunstroke by keeping out the ultraviolet rays of the sun. They reviewed for us all the latest drugs that had been incorporated into the medical supplies. Then they gave us a full listing of everything they had provided and showed us how every crate had been clearly marked with the contents.

We met with a corporate manager for the Ford Motor Company, who delivered a brand new Ford motorcar, compliments of Henry Ford himself. It had been made ready for overseas shipment, and we wouldn't see it again until we arrived in London.

That Ford, I thought. *What a character! He insisted that I take one of his cars with me.*

Cars were a new trend in Africa, and most safari guides were still clinging to the traditions of ground-pounding foot travel, mule, or bareback camel. I myself had not grown terribly fond of camel-backing. Because of the way they swayed when they walked, they made me seasick. Mostly cars were of little value in Africa, due to the condition of the terrain and the roads. But Henry had suggested it, and I had willingly accepted the challenge. Miles had a broken down jalopy in Nairobi, and parts were very hard to get. My plan was to leave the new Ford behind when we returned to Chicago in the fall, and I knew Lance would be ecstatic.

~~~~~~~~~

Finally the fifteenth day of March rolled around, and our little group found ourselves on the pier in New York Harbor, dwarfed by the breathtaking sight of the majestic *Mauretania*. The gulls screeched and sang their high-pitched song, trying to scavenge any tidbit of food they might find. The salt air smelled of the sea, and the smoke from the coal-fired boilers burned our eyes.

"She is gorgeous!" Betty exclaimed.

"I've seen these ships come and go," Jason said, "but I have never been up this close to one, let alone aboard one."

"I have made arrangements to have our bags sent on ahead," I said, "and checked through the baggage office."

"Let me take Buster to relieve himself," Betty said, taking the leash from Jason.

She stepped quickly off the curb and darted between a parked wagon and a team of horses. Buster let out a bark, and the two lead horses reared back. Betty let go of Buster's leash, and the horses came down, knocking her off her feet.

Buster scooted out from under their hooves, and I rushed in to try to grab Betty or the team. She tucked and rolled and somehow miraculously emerged unharmed from the dinner-plate-sized Clydesdales' hooves. She picked herself up and began to straighten out the wrinkles in her dress, brushing off the dirt from the street.

Jason called Buster, and he came running.

I settled the horses, then turned quickly to comfort Betty.

"Are you all right?" Chuck asked, holding her by the arm.

Betty tightened her lip, seeming perturbed at her carelessness.

I put my hand on her shoulder, trying to settle her. "Sweetheart, you scared the devil out of me!"

"I'm fine," she answered.

A crowd of onlookers began to gather around us, and she blushed.

"Jason, take care of that dog," I said. "We'll go check in with the boarding office."

"Do you have your ticket?" Betty asked.

"Yes, ma'am," he said, patting the front of his lapel.

"Okay," I said with a nod.

I took Betty's hand in mine, and we headed down the pier among the crowd. I could feel myself trembling as I thought about how she had almost been crushed by those horses. *This*, I thought, *is exactly why I didn't want to take her to Africa. What a way to start a trip!*

I noticed Betty favoring her right leg, cleverly trying to conceal her pain. "Are you sure you are okay?" I whispered so as not to embarrass her. "Did you hurt yourself?"

"I might have, but I'm not going to look at it here on the street. I'll wait until we are settled into our stateroom."

I didn't remember being married to this girl all these years. She had changed right before my eyes, but I didn't know when. The girl I knew would have demanded to be taken home and cancelled the trip.

We continued along the pier beside the massive black steel ocean liner, its side dotted with thousands of round head rivets and portholes too numerous to count. I looked up and strained to see the ship's funnels towering overhead.

"Quite a ship, don't you think, Chuck?"

"You know about her," he said, "don't you?"

"What's to know?" I asked.

"She's called the 'Grand Old Lady of the Atlantic,' and she holds the Atlantic Blue Ribbon for top speed. She is the fastest ship of her kind in the world."

There were long lines for second- and third-class passengers waiting to board. We continued past them, making our way to the first-class boarding office.

"Top of the morning, sir," a middle-aged man said behind the desk. He wore a white pressed uniform, with a mariner's hat perched squarely on his head. "Welcome to Cunard. May I see your tickets, please? And I'll need to see your papers as well."

I fished for the proper credentials and produced them.

"Ah, yes, the Rivers party. You have two adjoining first-class staterooms on our main deck."

"We have one more in our party who will be along shortly," Betty said.

"Here he comes," Chuck said, glancing down the pier at Jason pushing his way through the crowd with Buster at his heels.

"It says here you have a dog," the crewman said. "We have a special crew onboard here that has instructions to take all dogs to the kennel area. The animals are well cared for, believe me. We have a person assigned to exercise them every day, and you may visit our kennel at any time. I see you have quite a list of cargo here, including an automobile. Will you be staying in Liverpool?"

"Oh, no," Betty said, "we are going on safari in Africa."

"Wow, Africa! You folks be careful!"

"I know about her," I answered. "She is a wild and beautiful place. And I know all too well that she can kill you."

"Well, good luck to you, sir, and to you, too, ma'am. Oh, and may I say, it is a pleasure to have you sailing with Cunard Line. Here are your stubs. Show these to the bell captain, and he will escort you to your cabins."

We started up the covered gangway, then paused to wait for Jason to show his ticket and clear the boarding office. Buster saw Betty and pulled on the leash, dragging Jason behind. The dog nearly turned inside out, wagging his tail as he approached her.

"Good boy," she said, reaching down and patting Buster on the head. "Is he okay?" she asked, directing her attention toward Jason.

"He's fine. Not a scratch on him."

Betty took the leash, and we started up the ramp.

"Welcome aboard!" said a man with a gold leaf crest on the front of his hat and bright polished double-breasted brass buttons on the front of his coat.

I tried to show him my stubs, but he wrinkled his nose and waved them off.

"For the lady," he said, handing Betty a pink carnation. "And how might your names appear on the ship's registry?"

"Professor Jonathan Rivers," I said. "This is my wife, Betty, Dr. Charles Crawford, and Jason Marshall."

"Yes, oh yes, here it is. First-class state rooms, three-sixteen and three-seventeen. Steward!" he called.

A young man came forward, took the keys off the hook, and handed them to the young steward, who motioned for us to follow him.

"I can take your dog," another man said as we passed. "They are not allowed in the rooms, ma'am."

Betty handed him Buster's leash and then caressed the dog's head, and we climbed the grand staircase to find our state room.

The steward opened the door to reveal our accommodations, and Betty couldn't get over the lavishness of the stateroom. I had to admit to the extravagance as well, and for this ship to have been in operation for near on five years now, the room seemed brand new. Quite spacious for a ship, it had beautiful hardwood floors and pink-and-blue flowered wallpaper. There was a large double bed, with a heavy red comforter and large fluffy down pillows. There was an ornamental table with an oil reading lamp in the center and two cushioned chairs. Natural light filtered through the room from two round portholes that were draped with flowered curtains.

This was a powerful testimony to the effectiveness of the ship's officers and the crew, and to the leadership from the Cunard Line itself and the obvious pride they instilled in their workers. I didn't know their president personally, but if my first impressions proved out over the next week, I knew I would have to contact him to give him my compliments.

Once inside, Betty sat on the bed and pulled up her skirt to look at her knee.

"Oh, sweetheart, you did hurt yourself," I said, examining the gash and reddish bruise on the side of her right knee. "You could have torn something. Does it hurt?"

Betty pointed her toe and flexed her long, beautiful leg. "I wanted to cry," she confessed, "but with all those people watching, I would have rather died."

"We better have this looked at by the ship's doctor," I insisted.

"No, it's fine, really. It's just a scrape."

"Then let's order up some ice packs," I said. "We don't want to take a chance with any injury. Once we get to Nairobi, we are going to be putting plenty of miles on these legs, and they have to be in good shape."

~~~~~~~~~~

We were pampered day and night the following week with gourmet dishes, vintage wine, and fine Cuban cigars. Betty and I liked to take romantic midnight strolls around the promenade deck and verandah. She enjoyed bundling up in the cool night chill, sauntering, feeling the wind on her face, and asking me questions about Africa. She always said that dreams come true for those who have the courage to stick to them. I could feel a peace in her soul now as we were getting on to her dream.

After arriving in Liverpool Harbor in England, we picked up some additional odds and ends from a sporting outfitter there in London and then transferred all of our cargo and supplies to the ninety-foot steamer, *Congo*. I wondered from time to time how this would all work together with my ardent bachelor friend Lance, with Betty being the only woman in a safari full of men. I hoped she knew what she was in for.

Then we sailed for nearly a month, chugging our way across the Mediterranean to the Suez, Red Sea, and Indian Ocean, on toward Africa. Jason went down with a nasty case of the influenza early on in the trip, but somehow the rest of us managed to avoid its scourge. As the days passed, our excitement grew. I had to admit Betty's enthusiasm seemed contagious, and my anticipation for our arrival at Mombasa grew in intensity, surpassing anything I'd felt before.

Chapter 7

AFRICA AT LAST

B y the end of that long month, we began to feel like caged animals—a feeling I knew all too well from my many trips to this strange land aboard slow-moving steamers. The heat of the day became stifling, and we tried to escape it by sitting in the shade and using the winds blowing off the Indian Ocean. Then, on the late afternoon of the twenty-fifth day of April, I spotted Mombasa at the far end of the shoreline as we approached the motherland.

"That's her!" I shouted, springing from my canvas lounge chair and pointing enthusiastically. "That's Mombasa!"

Betty stood to attention and trained her eye to the spot. "Oh finally," she replied. "I thought we would never get here."

Jason and Chuck jumped to the rail, and Chuck put his German optics against his eyes, scanning the landscape.

The sun had begun to drop on the horizon, and I could tell we would still have to spend one more miserable night on this old scow. I held on to the likelihood that my friend Lance would be here to meet us. I hadn't really insisted on it, but I had written and shared with him our itinerary, and he had come down from Nairobi to meet me here on past occasions. Having never met Betty, his curiosity might get the best of him.

As our little steamer pushed its way into Kilindini Harbor, the sweltering heat of the equator day finally began to cool. We glided slowly among the jagged coral reefs to a deep-water anchorage about a hundred yards offshore from the deserted British government customs shed. Native merchants paddled out in their small boats, holding up their oriental wears for us to see, trying to coax us into parting with our money.

Captain Sherman stepped out on deck to check on the commotion. "Are you of a mind to indulge them, or are they simply a nuisance to you?" he asked. His hair was rustled and windblown, he hadn't shaved for about five days, and his khaki shirt had a permanent sweat stain down the front.

I hadn't had much time to really talk to Captain Sherman over the last month, being so occupied with Chuck, Betty, and Jason, but the captain was an old salt of a character for sure.

"We'll have plenty of time for trinket buying," I answered. "Right now, we have plenty of stuff onboard to worry about, and we don't need anything else.

Captain Sherman stepped to the rail and shouted, "*Jambo, maridadi sana, Bwana, hapana kwenda manyatta!*"

The natives happily put their belongings away and paddled off toward the shore.

"What did he say?" Jason asked.

I tried to translate quickly in my head from Swahili to English. "Okay, let's see. He said, 'Greetings, your things are very beautiful, but the Master wants nothing, so please go home now.'"

Jason's eyes sparkled at the magic of the place and the language, and I could only imagine what thoughts were rattling between his ears.

~~~~~~~~~

After dinner, the four of us sat on the deck and watched the glow of the African sun disappear. The palm trees dotted the delicate coastline, and the smell of smoke drifted offshore from native cooking fires. We could hear the faint sounds of singing and laughter gently floating across the water. I looked over at Betty, and she had a perpetual smile etched on her face.

"Are you happy, my dear?" I asked.

"It is a dream come true, my darling," she answered.

"There is as much work ahead as there is adventure," I cautioned.

"*Mimi nasikia*," she answered.

I chuckled. She had just told me in Swahili that she understood.

~~~~~~~~~

The ship's cook prepared a light breakfast for us in the morning, and the crew organized our luggage in a pile on the fantail of the ship. We had cleaned out our staterooms and packed up the rest of our belongings the day before, and everything seemed ready for transfer, including our cargo crates that had been unlashed and made ready for the government inspection.

Our Tin Lizzy had been shipped by a freight line that wasn't due in Mombasa for another fourteen days, but delays were only a small inconvenience and always part of a trip like this. After a long day of choking heat, during which we dealt with fumbling porters, outlandish government customs fees, the language barrier, reckless rickshaw drivers, and overzealous Indian merchants, we finally found our way to the cool and comfortable accommodations of the Manor House Hotel.

There we dined in style, relishing the lofty ceilings, thick concrete walls, cool drinks, and gourmet lunch. We hadn't been pampered like this since leaving London. Although I was a little disappointed at not being greeted by my faithful friend Lance, the four of us made small talk in the hotel and ventured out into the streets of the town later on after the noonday heat had subsided.

In the early evening, Betty penned out a letter to Mae and made it ready for mailing. "Would you like to read the letter I am sending home?" she asked. She sat at a writing table that overlooked the large open veranda and boasted a view of the blowing palm trees. We could see the backsides of the native villagers and hear the faint noise of children playing.

"Let's see how you did," I answered with an encouraging tone.

Betty eagerly unfolded the letter and passed to me the three pages of parchment with beautifully and precisely written script.

"I am always amazed at the beauty of your handwriting, my dear!" I commented as she smiled sweetly with pink-flushed cheeks and handed me the letter. I settled back in the overstuffed easy chair and reached for my reading glasses.

April 25, 1912

My dearest Mae,

Finally after a month of steam travel we have arrived safely in Mombasa in British East Africa. The morning news reached us about the tragedy at sea involving the Titanic. How grateful we all are that our journey did not fall to this horrible misfortune, and how much our hearts go out to those who are suffering the loss of loved ones.

This land is more beautiful than I could have imagined. Tomorrow we will board a wood-fired steam train for Nairobi, another 330 miles northwest of here. The natives are very friendly, and John met some of his black friends here who were his porters on past trips. Jason is doing fine now, after being quite ill with influenza on the boat. His affection for Buster has grown immensely, and the two are inseparable. Honestly, Mae, that dog goes everywhere with him. On the boat Buster slept at the foot of his bunk every night. But I will never forget how you insisted that it was good for a boy to have a dog.

John has great anticipation for his reunion with his colleague, Lance Miles. We received a wire this morning from Nairobi that he has secured a native hunting guide, a safari camp headman, a cook, and porters. The men who we met here at the Manor House Hotel are returning home and have given a good report as to the condition of the game on the Serengeti. The word is that the rainy season swings on a ten-year pendulum here and we are on the backswing of the five-year sweep of the very driest year.

Today we went on a tour of the old fort Jesus, built here by the Portuguese in 1593 and dedicated to the Savior. It is now used by the British Military as a store and a central jail. We also toured an ivory warehouse, where we saw possibly the greatest ivory collection in all the world. There were tusks of all sizes and shades of brown to white, the only remnants remaining of these poor fallen beasts. I was struck by the thousands of elephants who have given up their lives for the sake of man's passion for carved ivory.

Knowing how you love to shop, I longed so for you to share this experience with me today in the marketplace. Mae, the shops are full of beautifully ornamented oriental gowns. The jewelry shops are many, bursting with rare bits of jade, chipped rubies, Mediterranean pearls, and South African diamonds. And the children here will steal your heart; the Swahili word is "motto." Their big eyes and round chubby faces have the effect of causing my soul to melt. They come in droves to beg and to appeal for my favor; thus so far I have been an easy mark for them.

Tomorrow we will catch the train at 9:00 a.m., and now we are all very tired from the long day's activity. I will seal this and get it into the hands of our captain to mail from Liverpool when he returns in short order. I will write you more from Nairobi and continue to write throughout our safari.

Best regards, and our love to you all,

Betty, John, and Jason

"That is a very nice letter, dear. Let's seal it and post it, and we will make sure it gets in the hands of Captain Sherman in the morning."

"I think I will turn in for the night," she said with a laugh. "It has been a long day, and I am sure we will be up with the birds tomorrow."

"You thought right, my dear. I will need to ensure that all of our cargo boxes have made it to the flatcars and have been properly secured. Tomorrow we are African travelers, and I know how anxious you have been to wear your safari duds. I might suggest that you lose those skirts for your khaki safari breeches and bush coat."

"Oh?" she said, shrugging her shoulders and wrinkling her cute little nose. "Don't forget, I am still a lady. I'll make the transformation, but in due time. Don't forget about Mary Kingsley, Florence Barker, and the many others who have followed them. All of these women have worn skirts into the bush. Not that I intend to do that, but I expect to be treated like a woman, even if I am wearing breeches. I intend to make my first impressions in Nairobi when we are received by the governor and his wife. I am looking forward to meeting your game warden friend Blaney Percival, who you have so often spoken about, and of course Lance. After that, when we have organized and settled everything, then I will be content to don the khakis. But you never get a second chance to make a good first impression."

"Indeed," I responded, "that's a good one. I never thought about it like that before."

~~~~~~~~~

We were ready to go at seven o'clock the next morning, and the four of us left the hotel to take our first-class reservation onboard the railcar for Nairobi.

"That's quite a silly looking train," Betty said.

I had to agree, even though I'd never thought of the train as looking silly. The locomotive was stubby, with a long, narrow stack. But I had seen it many times, and to me it had become normal looking.

"Sure," I agreed, "it's not a locomotive like back home, sleek and beautiful, but it's very functional here in Africa."

"There's a photograph of Roosevelt riding on the front of this train in his book," Chuck said.

"Oh, yes," I answered, "I have ridden there. Are you interested?"

"Absolutely!" he responded enthusiastically.

"Hey, John!" a man shouted from the train car. I turned to see my old friend Wayne Pusser standing in the doorway of a car two down from the one we had been directed to board.

"That's my friend Wayne," I explained to Betty. "Stay here. I'll be right back."

I slipped away and headed toward his smiling face as he stepped from the train car among the crowd of black faces.

"Wayne, it's great to see you!" I said, grasping his hand tightly.

"I had no idea you would be back here so soon."

"Didn't Lance tell you we were coming?"

"Oh, Lance. I haven't spoken to him for a couple of months."

I could tell from the tone of his voice and the look in his eye that something was wrong. "What is it?" I insisted.

"What is what?"

"Why haven't you spoken to Lance? The two of you are like brothers."

He tightened his lip and paused in deep thought. "It's nothing. We have just had a difference of opinion, that's all."

"So you will patch things up then, right?"

He shrugged his shoulders, and I looked for an opportunity to change this difficult subject, not wanting to get in the middle of their problems. I couldn't help wondering what might have come up between Lance and Wayne. Lance was so even tempered that I knew it just couldn't be anything he'd done. Wayne, on the other hand, I had never trusted. Even though he always had a smile on his face, there was always much more cooking behind the scenes.

"Then you haven't heard," I said. "We are going on safari."

"Who is the woman, John?" Wayne asked, looking toward the railcar where Betty was waiting for me.

I remembered my conversations with Wayne over the years about bringing American women to Africa. The place was full of European women, most of them not very comely, but both Wayne and I had done our fair share of ridiculing lesser men who'd brought their wives with them.

"Oh, her?" I said, trying to hide my embarrassment. "That's my wife."

Wayne smiled and gave me a wink, helping me to recall our many conversations.

I could feel a lump in my throat. I had just been humbled, and the cat was now officially out of the bag.

He looked again toward Betty and grabbed the handhold. "Have a good safari, chap," he said as he took the step and jumped onboard the second-class coach.

As I took the walk back toward Betty, it struck me how awkward our conversation had just been.

"Who was that?" Betty asked with suspicion in her voice.

"Oh, just an old friend of mine, that's all."

"Old friend, is he? I noticed you didn't introduce me."

I tried to look nonchalant, as if nothing had happened.

"Well, obviously I've never met the man, but I don't like him."

"What do you mean, dear?"

"I don't like the way he looked at me, that's all."

The train whistle blew, and we watched out the window of our first-class accommodations as the landscape began to move slowly. The deafening rumble from the steam engine echoed through the coach as the train labored, pulling the cars away from Mombasa. There were frequent stops throughout the day to reload from wood piles and take on water from huge black water casks. The Uganda railroad was pulling five luggage vans, two cargo flatcars, and nine passenger carriages. It clattered along the rails as it strained up the long pull from sea level to the three-thousand-foot-high plateau of the green hills of Africa. Smoke and embers billowed from the furnace, keeping the steam bursting at the seams of the funny little locomotive. Then in the evening they announced to the passengers that we had to stop in Samburu for urgent repairs to the engine.

"How long of a layover did he say this would be?" Betty asked in a disgruntled tone.

"He said ten hours," I answered.

"At least maybe we can get some sleep in our sleeper car," she said.

"I don't know how to break the news to you, my dear, but there is no sleeper car. What you see is what you get. Besides, they will be up there banging and hammering on that engine all night."

"You must be joking," she said.

"Betty, there is an alternative. We could get out and walk the remaining one hundred and thirty miles."

She smiled quaintly at my poor attempt at humor.

"Ladies and gentlemen!" a steward shouted from the head of the carriage. "We will be serving a first-class dinner on the veranda of the Samburu station in one hour, compliments of the rail line. We apologize for the bother and hope that our delay will be only a small inconvenience. The engineer has your utmost interest and safety in mind while correcting this small problem with our locomotive. We pray for your patience and thank you in advance for dealing so graciously with our troubles."

Chuck leaned over the back of my seat and whispered, "This better be one fine meal."

There with the other first-class *inmates,* the four of us dined together at an intimate table, set under a draped canvas, where we were served a fine five-course meal. The meal began with eland tail soup, seared buffalo steak with wild mushrooms and herbs, boiled wild asparagus, native posho, wild rice, baked guinea fowl stuffed with celery and bread crumbs, and a lukewarm native brew that had a very strong skunk taste.

"This is buffalo? It's good!" Jason said as he chewed on a big piece of roasted meat. "My mother used to love to eat good beefsteak, but we never had it much."

"My mama, too," Betty said. "We always ate pretty well. You know, John, I really do miss her."

"What was she like?" Jason asked.

"Oh, where to start?" Betty mused, setting her fork down on her plate and putting her index finger to her cheek. "You would have loved her, Jason. She always had a preference for boys. Not that she didn't love me, but I was an only child. I know she always wished I had been a boy."

"Was she pretty, like you?" Jason asked with a wide grin.

Betty smiled, and her cheeks became flushed. "I don't look anything like her. I look like my papa. She was very pretty—thinly built with fiery red hair."

"Was she like you?" Jason asked.

I had to chuckle to myself at his question, considering Joan's fiery disposition. I was grateful that my wife wasn't like her mother.

"I don't know. Sometimes I don't know what I'm like. I thought I was a lady once—high society, afternoon teas—but I don't think that's me anymore. My dear sweet mother had a thing for horses. My papa took care of them, but Mama was the horsewoman. I think she had a secret desire to make me into a horsewoman. I like to ride, but look, if you gave Mama an afternoon ride in the country, she was in heaven. A wiry, short-tempered Irishwoman from the old country, she came to America as a young girl with my grandparents. She never had much till she married Papa."

"What about your papa?" Jason asked, digging for more, hanging on Betty's every word.

"A devoted husband and father. I still don't know how he put up with her all those years. He used to take me fishing. Those are the times I remember. I think he went fishing just because she didn't like to go."

I thought about the sparring matches I'd engaged in with Betty's mother, who had always possessed strong opinions. I had to confess that I didn't miss her a bit, something I would have never told Betty.

"How long has she been gone?" Jason asked.

"Papa has been gone twenty years, and Mama—let's see, six, no—seven years now. The only blessing is that she went before I lost Johnny. If she hadn't already been dead and gone, I know that would have killed her. Heck, it almost killed me."

"Are you over him now?" Jason asked.

I was surprised how far Jason was willing to push Betty, and I wondered how she would handle the question. I knew she wasn't over Johnny. But life went on, and Betty crawled into her shell and wouldn't let anyone in after our son's death. I tried to reach her time and again, but her depression had driven me all the way to Africa. I cut off another piece of the medium-rare buffalo, putting the tender morsel into my mouth. It melted like butter.

"No," Betty said, shaking her head and closing her eyes, "you never get over losing a child. But I can at least talk about him now without crying." Her eyes welled up, and a tear rolled down her cheek. "My mama loved that little blond-haired, blue-eyed boy. She would take him riding when he was just a little squirt of five years old."

"I've never been on a horse," Jason said.

"Never been on a horse?" Betty asked in astonishment. "What do you mean, you've never been on a horse?"

Jason shrugged his shoulders and held up his hands. "I don't know, I've just never been on a horse. Guess I'm a city boy. Some people grow up with horses, and other people grow up with pianos."

"Well, we're going to fix that," Betty said. "I have to confess, it's been years since I have been on a horse, but it's one of those things you never forget."

"What about things?" Jason asked.

"What do you mean?" Betty asked, wrinkling her nose.

I, too, was confused by the question.

"The important things, the ones you never forget. Everybody seems to have something different that's important. What's important to you?"

Betty paused as she considered her answer. She looked at me, and I figured that I would top her list.

"People," she answered. "My mama always put great value on things, probably because she never had anything much as a kid growing up. But the older I get, the more I see that things don't matter too much at all. What about you, Jason?"

"Hmm," he said, pausing to cut another piece of meat. "I guess I value adventure. Riding a train from New York to Chicago seemed exciting before I met you."

"Well, Jason, if it's adventure you value, then you came to the right place," Betty said, looking over at me with a smile for approval.

I smiled back in agreement.

Chuck started to speak, but went silent, chewing his food and smiling along as if he agreed. It made me wonder what thoughts might be bouncing around in his head.

~~~~~~~~~

We sat outside the train car after dinner and watched the sun go down while Jason threw a stick for Buster.

"I have an uneasy feeling about Lance," I said.

"What is it?" Betty asked.

"When I saw his old friend in Mombasa, there seemed to be a definite chill that fell over him when I mentioned Lance's name."

"What do you think it is?" she asked.

"I don't know. Maybe it's nothing," I said, convinced that I didn't have the whole story.

I couldn't stop thinking about it and wondering why he hadn't shown up when we landed. His cable seemed to be a good sign of his diligent work on our plans for the safari, but deep inside I had an uneasy feeling.

We spent the night trying to make the best of the hard, narrow seats. Not exactly first class accommodations other than the blankets. The blankets smelled like they had been used to saddle camels. Well, not quite that bad, but one might get the picture that I had been none too pleased by this untimely delay. Between the tinkering of hammers and the jabbering of the native mechanics, there was no room for any sleep. How envious I was to see Betty, Chuck, and Jason sleeping in the twilight of the moon, which gleamed through the window. They were out like snuffed candles. Even Buster, snug and warm and curled up in the corner, had it up on me.

Somehow I must have finally dozed off, because I awoke to the morning sun peeking over the horizon, with its pink glare dancing off the clouds.

"All aboard!" the native conductor shouted.

I could hear what sounded like the tossing of wood sticks into the boiler fire.

Betty and Chuck began to stir, and she poked her head out from under the blanket.

"What time is it?" she asked, stretching her neck and pulling the blanket around her. "This thing smells like—"

"I know," I interrupted, "like camel sweat."

Betty chuckled and smiled, shaking her head up and down in agreement and holding her nose. "How did you sleep, Chuck?" she asked.

"Like one of those English pretzels," he said, sitting up and stretching his back. "This should make my cot in the bush feel like the Waldorf Astoria."

"Oh, you better take Buster off the train," she insisted. "Quick, before we leave."

I bounced up, Buster sprang to his feet, and we dashed to the door.

"Can I relieve my dog?" I asked.

The conductor nodded his approval and then pointed to a spot beside the terminal shack.

"Quickly! Quickly!" he demanded as I tugged Buster out of the carriage and ran for the place the conductor had pointed me to, where Buster began to sniff.

The engineer began motioning me to get back aboard.

"Hurry up, Buster," I grumbled as he found a bush and lifted his hind leg.

Before he was through, I sprinted for the train.

The engineer gave me a hand signal, and then the whistle blew. Steam burst from the port housing on the thrust cylinder, and the train lunged forward. I called to Buster, and he came running. I gathered him up and tossed him aboard. Then I grabbed a handrail, stepped on the iron runner, and swung aboard.

"You like to call 'em close, don't you, dear?" Betty said as the ground began to disappear under my feet.

"Better late than never!" I said with a laugh. "They wouldn't have left me. The engineer just wanted to see me sprint. This isn't Chicago. I knew he wasn't going to leave me behind."

~~~~~~~~

Later on that morning, they served hot coffee and rolls. Our eyes were glued to the rolling hills as we searched for signs of game. Then in the distance we saw the breathtaking sight of the snowcapped Mount Kilimanjaro poking above a circle of clouds and looking like the fluffy white lace collar of a lady's finery. Now we began spotting herds of zebra, gazelle, and wildebeest dotting the open glades. Betty's excitement, Jason's wonderment, and Chuck's quiet enthusiasm formed the perfect complement to my old-hat confidence.

It saddened me to see how the herds had dwindled even in the last six years since I had first set foot on this wild plain. I had never realized how delicate a place my beloved Africa had always been, and I could see her changing right before my eyes. The hordes of novice sportsmen, white farmers, and natives trying to feed their tribes could not continue to chop away at her wildlife before it would disappear from the landscape altogether. It seemed that even the meager attempts of the British government to curtail the gunfire by putting a price on the game could not stop the relentless slaughter. There were far too many who felt that wildlife was a scourge to agriculture that needed to be eradicated. And the game wardens were helpless to stop the greedy poachers, who were desperate to reduce the skins of these animals' backsides and to turn the tusks of the old monarchs into cash for their own coin purses.

My companions glued themselves to the windows, watching the terrain unfold as we neared the end of our trip. On our last stop before reaching Nairobi, I made arrangements with the engineer to allow Chuck and Jason to ride on the cowcatcher bench. I liked to call it the bug-catcher bench. Of course, there existed the unwritten rule that if a trophy rhino, big jumbo, or black-mane lion appeared, the engineer would stop the train and let someone take a crack.

"Is that Mount Kenya, John?" Betty asked as I turned to acknowledge her. "It almost looks like a backdrop."

We sat gazing at the scenery in the silence of the moment, while the countryside moved under us.

Then a smile came to her face. "By the way," she said, putting her arm around my neck as we gazed out the window, "thank you, my darling, for bringing me on this trip."

I reached over and kissed her on the neck.

"I bet those boys are cold up front," she said and reached for a wool blanket to wrap around herself. "There is actually a chill in the air, quite a difference between the lowlands and here."

"Yeah, well, they were prepared for it," I answered.

"Oh, look!" she squealed. "Giraffe! My first ones!"

I squinted to see them, but those critters were so far off across the plains they were hardly noticeable. "How did you spot those? You must have eyes like a hawk. Look, you can barely make them out against that line of mimosa trees. They must be two thousand yards away."

Betty sat up in her seat, clearly proud of her accomplishment.

"We'll be in Nairobi soon," I said, "and you will enjoy meeting Lance."

"How is the farm doing?"

"Growing coffee and tobacco is a difficult proposition here. He just runs it for the owner, but the labor is cheap, so they survive. It's only because he so desperately loves Africa that he has found a way to stay here. He could have been a professional hunter, but he found this farm, and for the most part it consumes him, notwithstanding his anthropological pursuits, of course."

Betty remained focused on the giraffe until they were undistinguishable, and then she turned and settled back into her seat, continuing to gaze out her window.

~~~~~~~~~

The hour passed by quickly, and suddenly Nairobi stood over us like a vulture. The train pulled into the station house, and the engine released a huge burst of steam, as if exhaling from her exertion. I craned my head to look over the crowd of onlookers and catch a familiar face in the crowd. There were black men dressed in white men's clothes, and natives in traditional dress. White men were barking orders to porters who were getting ready to load shipments bound for Uganda. Kikuyu women had their burdens balanced delicately on their heads.

Nairobi hummed with activity unlike I had ever remembered it. The afternoon sun shone high overhead through the broken clouds, taking the chill off the morning. The streets were still wet, and the air smelled of fresh rainfall thick with humidity.

Chuck and Jason appeared, holding their heavy jackets over their forearms.

"How was the ride?" I asked.

"Just marvelous!" Chuck answered.

Jason gawked at a group of young native women whose bare breasts were exposed.

"Get an eyeful, Jason," I chided him.

He squinted and looked away, and his face turned red as he grinned sheepishly. "You didn't tell me about this. Hey, did you guys see the giraffe?" he said, skillfully trying to change the subject.

"You're not getting out of this that easy," I said and laughed. "What are you looking at, boy?"

"Oh, John, leave him alone," Betty said, attempting to rescue his pride. "Weren't the giraffe beautiful?" she said, handing Jason Buster's lead.

Jason reached down and began rubbing Buster's sides, and the dog panted and wagged his tail.

Then I heard a familiar voice from the crowd shouting my name, and I turned to see Lance smiling at me and making his way through the mob. He was dressed sharply in clean and pressed khaki breeches and a khaki bush coat with patch pockets and epaulets on the shoulders. He was clean-shaven, and his hair nicely trimmed. Ten years my junior, he had dimples when he smiled. His dark eyes, slender nose, and pointed chin gave him a look that would have captured the attention of any woman I knew. I never understood why he wasn't the kind of man to carouse the bars at night. He definitely had the look.

"It's about time, you scoundrel!" I shouted back at him. "I thought for sure you would have met us in Mombasa."

"I really tried to get away. Believe me, I wanted to, but first my friend who works on the train couldn't get me a seat. You know me: if I can't finagle a free ticket, forget it. Besides, I am behind in my work on the farm and have had so much to do getting ready for this safari, juggling the harvest, and making arrangements to get away. I needed to tend to business."

I felt a tad suspicious, remembering my conversation with Wayne. I wanted to take Lance aside immediately and call him on it, but I decided to let this play out. Besides, I didn't want to throw cold water on a gleeful reunion.

"Well, it's great to see you. Let me make these introductions. First, this is my wife, Betty."

"Finally, after all these years, and all the stories. You are as beautiful as your husband has boasted!" He took her hand and kissed it, classy as always.

Betty stood silently, her cheeks turning pink as she batted her long eyelashes.

I knew instantly that she would be taken in by him, as most people were. He had a down home country warmth about him that made you want to get closer.

"And this is my long-time friend, Dr. Charles Crawford."

Chuck reached for his hand, and the two held a firm grip.

"It seems like I know you after all these years working with the institute and after all the correspondence I have received from John with your name always listed on the top of the heading as college president."

"It's my pleasure, of course, but please, you can call me Chuck."

"Chuck it is, and this must be Jason."

"Yes, sir," Jason said. "Jason Marshall."

"Can you shoot?" Lance asked.

"I can shoot."

"Are you ready for this safari?"

"I think so, sir."

"Okay then, let's get one thing straight right now. Do you know what it is?" Lance had a curious look in his eye that I knew meant he was giving the lad a hard time.

"Yes, sir. I mean, no, sir."

"You can quit calling me, sir," Lance said with a laugh, and everyone joined in. "The railroad said there would be a ten-hour delay. Goodness, they were right on, weren't they? I woke up early and got down here at six a.m. sharp, expecting you to be here, and they sent me home."

"Sorry for the delay," I said.

"Nonsense. What can be done?" Lance said. "Listen, I had my men bring both wagons, and I brought the motor lorry. I'll have M'culay round up the cargo and the crates and bring them out to the farm. There should be room on the lorry for your handbags."

"There is one small crate that I have been watching like a hawk. It contains all my rifles. Do you think that one will fit on the truck?"

"We'll make it fit. You guys wait here, and I'll fetch up the help." Lance turned and trotted off around the corner of the terminal.

"Well, John!" spoke a familiar English voice.

I turned to see Sir Winston Roberts smoking a pipe and dressed in a fine white suit with a wide-brim straw hat. "Back so soon?"

"Good to see you," I answered with a smile and reached out to shake his waiting hand.

"I see you have brought your family with you. Are you immigrating?"

"Oh, no, just on safari this time."

"Doing it up right, aye? Well, good hunting to you, sir." He hesitated, as if struggling with his words, and then nodded to me subtly, encouraging me away from the others.

I had suspicions that he was about to give me hell for bringing my wife on safari, but I knew he lived here with his family. So I was puzzled about what he was about to throw at me.

He stepped away discreetly, leaving the door open for me to follow him to a vacant part of the brick pavement. "A bit of advice, if you don't mind," he said in a low tone, pausing again and rubbing his chin, as if not knowing exactly where to start.

"Yes," I said, "what is it?"

He took his pipe from his mouth, crossed his arms, and closed his eyes as a cloud of sweet-smelling smoke rose from his lips. "In the future, regarding Miles, it would be well advised to choose your company very carefully."

"What is that supposed to mean?"

"You'll find out."

"Tell me. What has happened?"

"I don't need to. You will find out on your own. Good day, sir. Enjoy your stay."

"Hold on," I said. "We were supposed to be received by the governor and his wife. Do you know anything about that?"

He slipped his pipe back between his yellow teeth and caught me with a piercing stare. Then he tipped his hat and abruptly disappeared into the crowd, leaving me flatfooted and standing alone.

I paused for a few seconds, shocked by the reception and trying to regain my composure. I turned and saw Betty laughing with Chuck as Jason held Buster on the leash.

"Are you ready?" I called to them, still burning inside. "Let's go!"

"John," Betty said, "I was hoping to shop for something to send back for Mae."

"There'll be time for that," I snapped.

"All right," she replied sharply. "I just asked."

"Oh, darling, I'm sorry. It's just that . . ." I paused as I considered sharing my concerns about Lance. "Oh, never mind. Lance only lives ten miles out. We'll be back. I promise."

Chapter 8

BOUGHT THE FARM

"That's it," I said, pointing to the rifle crate, "that one right there!" Lance's man eagerly jumped aboard the freight car and removed the ropes from the crate.

I leaned over and spoke to Betty in a low voice. "I'll feel better when those are unpacked and racked up in Lance's farmhouse."

The native slid the crate off the edge, and two other men lifted it and carried it across the train yard to Lance's waiting motor lorry. Other men eagerly hauled luggage bag after bag, while we stood and watched. Betty and I jumped in the front seat, with Lance behind the wheel, and Chuck and Jason sat atop the pile of baggage, while Jason held tight to his mutt.

"Hang on back there," Lance said. "This thing rides like an un-broke jackass." He revved up the engine and then turned to me and laughed. "Do you think you brought enough luggage?"

He let out the clutch, and the lorry lurched forward, taking us down the dirt main street of Nairobi.

The town, I thought, could have been Dodge City fifty years ago. It felt good to be back, and I was looking forward to seeing some of my old friends, although I hoped that I wouldn't be too humbled when they met Betty.

Lance skillfully maneuvered his jalopy in and around the snarl of rickshaws, camels, and oxcarts, which were loaded down with commodities coming in from the outlying farms.

"So how was your ride on *The Lunatic Line?*" Lance asked, looking over with a wide grin.

"It gets you there," I answered, "but that's about all you can say."

"Is that really what they call it?" Betty asked, wrinkling her cute little nose.

"No, not really," Lance answered with his same wide grin. "Most people call it *The Lunatic Express.*"

Betty smiled and shook her head. "So," she said, addressing Lance as if challenging him to pull her leg once more, "what does the word *Nairobi* mean?"

"It's the Masai word for cold," he answered.

Betty caught my eye for confirmation, and I shrugged my shoulders, not knowing the answer.

"How can that be?" she asked. "It's really never that cold here, is it?"

"No, not really," he answered, "but the town is named after the Nairobi River that flows out of the ice-capped mountains."

"Really?" she asked.

"Gospel!" he replied, raising one hand off the wheel.

"How about the fishing?" Betty asked. "I've always heard there is some great fishing around here."

"You like to fish?" he asked.

"I brought my stuff," she answered.

"John, you don't fish. How'd you get a girl that fishes?" He kept his eyes glued on the road, trying to miss the potholes as we made our way through the outskirts of town. "We'll take you up to the Ewaso Nyiro. There are some beautiful fishing spots along that river. It's been awhile since I fished it, but you'll love it up there. In fact, you are gonna love this place. You're gonna fall in love with Africa, just like your old man."

"How's Blaney?" I asked.

"Still fighting the poachers, as always. Never a shortage of work for a game warden around here. I told 'em you were coming to get permits this week. So we'll probably drop in on him tomorrow. There's something I didn't tell you, John, something I wanted to keep a surprise."

"Oh?" I said. "What is it?"

"I bought the farm."

"No!" I said, surprised at the news. "That's great. How did it happen? I thought old man Stewart said he would never part with it."

"Yes, well, old man Stewart died, and his kid just wanted the money. He made it affordable, so Esther and I made him an offer." There was a definite pause in his voice, as if he had just let the real cat out of the bag. He looked over out of the corner of his eye to gauge my reaction.

"Esther?" I asked in an inquiring tone. "Who is Esther?"

"Would you buy that she is my sister?" he asked with a sheepish grin.

"No, I'm not buying that one," I answered.

"Okay, John. I didn't know how to tell you, but I got married."

"Well, good grief, didn't you think I would be ecstatic for you? Congratulations, Lance. This is wonderful news! I brought some French wine with me from London. When the cargo gets here, we'll have a celebration. Why didn't you tell me? Why didn't you bring her to the station? Why didn't you — ?"

I stopped dead in the middle of the sentence and thought about what I was asking. Then I remembered Lance's friends. I glanced at Lance and could tell there must be more to this story. Then the pit in my stomach grew larger as I began to wonder if he had actually gone and married his sister. He talked about her often, saying how much he wanted her to come and visit. *Goodness, I hope he didn't go and marry his sister,* I thought.

"There is the farmhouse, Betty," Lance said, changing the tone of the conversation. "You are going to love it here. We have all the conveniences of home."

Lance slowed down on the rough road to keep from tossing Chuck and Jason off the back of the truck as he turned into the long driveway. There were rows and rows of stubby coffee trees on both sides. The servants gathered at the front of the house as we pulled up, and the brakes squealed on the truck. Jason jumped off the back and helped Chuck down, while Betty and I crawled out of the cab.

One of the servant women stepped off the porch and approached. She had a long white skirt and beautiful black curly hair that fell just above her shoulders. She had a striking smile, with beautiful, straight white teeth that contrasted sharply against her dark skin. I tried to remember if I had seen her here on the farm before, but my memory failed me. Surely if I had seen her before, I would have remembered.

Lance walked to her and took her by the hand, then turned to face us. "John and Betty, I want you to meet Esther."

I felt my jaw drop, but did my best to hide the shock on my face, acting as if I could see nothing wrong with a mixed marriage of a white Anglo-Saxon man and, I must say, a quite lovely African woman.

"How did you meet?" I asked.

"Oh, there will be plenty of time for that. Let's get you unloaded and settled in." Lance looked out into the yard, where Jason was walking Buster. "Jason!" he called.

"Yes ... yes," Jason stuttered, obviously trying to contain the word *sir*.

"You can let that dog off his lead now and let him run. He's gonna have to learn he's got space to roam now. You ain't in Chicago anymore."

"Okay, Mr. Miles," Jason yelled, "whatever you say!"

"Hey," I said, "you always had a jumble of hounds running around here. Where are they?"

"I'll have to get some more, I guess, because they ran off a few months ago, and they didn't come back."

As we followed Lance and Esther into the farmhouse, I felt a little relieved that Lance had not married his sister. But then it hit me why all of our friends were giving him the cold shoulder. We walked into the farmhouse, and immediately I could tell the place had received some long-needed attention from a woman.

"What a beautiful place you have here," Betty said.

"Nothing like your home, I'm sure," Esther answered.

"You know what?" I said. "I've only been in this house one time, back when Stewart lived here, but I remember it being a little rough."

"Yes," Lance answered, "he never was much for keeping a house. Come in and have a seat."

We moseyed into the parlor and got comfortable on the stuffed chairs, which were covered with animal skins. Chuck came in behind us and found a space on the sofa.

"Who did you get for an elephant guide, Lance?" I asked.

"I found the best. Remember Janga?"

"Oh, sure," I said, "he was with us two years ago. Last I heard he took off in the Belgian Congo."

"Yep, well, he came back. I guess he ran into a little trouble with the law over there. I talked to Blaney about him, and he had gotten word to keep his eye on him. But he's still the best darn tracker in the territory."

"Without a doubt. How did you find him?"

"He just came here on foot about six weeks ago. Said he wondered when you would be back in Africa. I told him we were heading out on safari in a couple of months, and he begged me to go along."

"Who else did you get?"

"Mostly new faces, but I managed to latch onto Bamira for a head cook."

"That's fantastic. I remember those meals in the bush. And his bread—oh, Betty, remember how I told you about Bamira's raised bread? I can smell it now! Oh, and Chuck, he's the one I told you about who roasts those clay birds. Wait till you taste them. What about a headman? Are you planning on letting M'culay run the camp and the porters?"

"I can't spare him. He's the only one I can depend on to run this farm in my absence. I would love to have him on safari, and believe me, he would love to go. But he knows he has to stay behind."

"So who did you get?"

"I had a good friend who was a professional hunter who got busted up pretty bad last fall by a wounded elephant. Before they could get him in from the plains, he got gangrene in his knee and lower leg and they had to take it off. He just darn near met his maker on that one, but he decided to go home and convalesce in Holland. I've always been very impressed with the order of his camp, and I always attributed it to his headman. His name is Willie. I spotted him uptown a couple weeks ago, and he agreed to sign on. He's energetic and meticulous, and he likes to keep everything in order. But there's nothing wrong with that."

"Sounds like you've done well, Lance. What about my gun bearer from last year? Is he still around?"

"Yes, I got him working on the farm now. Actually he has turned into quite a mechanic, and I doubt if he will go on safari with us. I found another good tracker and gun bearer, and he can guide as well. His name is Tomba. He doesn't speak much English, but he's got an excellent reputation for finding game. I got a camel string coming in from up north, I bought some extra mules, and I hired on the best skinner in all of Africa."

"With all this livestock," I warned, "we better hire on some armed guards to watch them at night."

"Don't worry. I've got it covered."

"You men can talk all night about safari if you like," Esther said, "but I think what Betty needs is a good hot bath and some clean clothes."

"Oh, my dear," Betty said, "you are a sweetheart. I can see we're going to get along delightfully."

"Esther has a big dinner planned, so why don't you folks go ahead and get settled in. Chuck, I'm gonna put you and Jason up in the guesthouse, and John, you and Betty can stay here in the spare room."

"You mean your old house, right?" I said. "You call that the guesthouse now? Anyway, first things first. I have got to break into that rifle crate and make sure everything survived. Where do you want me to do it? Out in the shop?"

"That's great," Lance said.

"I got a peek at them in Nairobi when those vultures skinned me for the duty. Do you believe that? The price went up from just last year."

Lance summoned one of his servants in Swahili, and the man immediately disappeared out the doorway. "I believe it," he said. "Did you know they raised the elephant permits again?"

"No, not again! What are they now? I'm almost afraid to ask."

"Eighty-five American dollars," he said as I shook my head in response. "I'm having my guys haul that box out there for ya."

"Come on, Chuck, you're probably anxious to see how yours fared, too."

We made our way out to the shop and saw Jason and Buster exploring down by the edge of the pond, which was nestled among the lush green fields and wide open straight rows of coffee shrubs.

Lance called out to one of his men in Swahili, telling him to keep an eye on the boy and his dog.

"By God, it is good to be back here, Lance," I announced, taking a deep breath of Africa through my nostrils.

"It's good that I never left," he answered with a smile.

As we walked into the shop, I could see that nothing had changed. I had to chuckle to myself; Esther had probably done nothing more than poke her nose in the doorway. The shop still had the broken and upside-down chair in the corner that Lance always said was a project he had been meaning to get to. The bench was littered with tools, nuts and bolts, nails, and oil cans. It had a dirt floor, which meant it never had to be cleaned. In the rafters hung the horns of animals of many shapes and sizes. There were dried skins on the walls, most of them suffering various degrees of hair slippage thanks to the rainy season.

Lance pried open the crate with a bar, and we tugged at the excelsior that separated the rifles packed from Chicago. I wanted to bring up the marriage, but I didn't feel comfortable. Besides, anything I might have said would have only caused a rift between us, and Lance and I had shared such a special friendship I didn't want that to happen. There were so many questions I wanted to ask, but I thought it better for him to approach the subject than me. It was as if there was an elephant in the shop, but neither of us dared to point him out. Still, it was clear to me that he had a big problem.

"These rifles are in beautiful shape," Lance said. "That heavy grease was a great idea. Hey, let me get you some rags and solvent."

"I've always hand-carried them," I said, "but this time I took a chance. I talked to the outfitter, and he told me this is always how they crate them. It was kind of nice because we didn't have to lug them around and worry about them all the time. How much time do we have before dinner, Lance?"

"Oh, a couple of hours, at least."

"It's not like they need the bores cleaned. It's just the outside. This shouldn't take us too long."

Lance headed out the door.

"Hey," I shouted just before he disappeared, "if you see that kid out there, tell him to get his rear end up here and give us a hand."

As he walked away, I looked over at Chuck, who had begun making space on the workbench and laying out the rifles. We made eye contact, but neither of us said a word, both knowing exactly the other man's thoughts.

~~~~~~~~~~

We had a beautiful dinner that evening. Skeptical of Esther and her motives, I wanted to hold back. But with her personality, it was difficult not to be drawn in. She had the gift of warmth, which seemed contagious. Her laughter was infectious, her wit was exhilarating, and her compassion and ability to listen nearly matched those of my lovely wife. I did keep my commitment and located the French wine from the too-numerous-to-count crates of cargo. And we relaxed that evening outside on the verandah, listening to the sounds of the rain on the roof and watching the sun through broken clouds as it sunk low in the sky. After the men-folk among us enjoyed a few of those Cuban cigars, we finally retired.

I heard Betty stir next to me in the bed. "Can't you sleep?" I whispered.

"I was almost asleep," she whispered back. "Can't you?"

"No, I just can't stop thinking about those two and the terrible mistake I think Lance has made."

"I'm glad you qualified your thoughts as your own," she whispered in a barely audible voice, "because I don't happen to feel that way at all. And if that is how you think, then you are nothing but a bigot."

"But how are they going to fit in?" I whispered louder.

"All that doesn't matter, and it doesn't matter what you think. You've seen how they are. They are in love, and that's all that counts."

"Tell that to their children."

"Shush! They're going to hear you."

"Okay," I whispered, "but life is going to be very difficult for both of them from here on out."

"Oh, John, it's not your problem. Put it to rest. If you dwell on it, if you breathe a word of how you are feeling to him, you will kill your friendship and possibly ruin this safari, too. What do you think your mammy would say?"

I paused, considering this beautiful black-skinned woman who I loved so completely, who had been like a mother to me all these years. "I think she would be realistic."

"Well, I think she would approve, and if you don't, you better get it in your head right now to make a change of heart. Don't hurt them. They are precious, wonderful people, and they are looking for your approval. You are his best friend in the whole world. At least you can decide right now to give him what he is so desperately searching for. Everybody else in town has turned their back on him, and he is expecting the same from you. I think we should put this whole issue to bed."

"You're right, my dear. These are all things I hadn't considered. Honestly, darling, it takes a woman to see this. I'm so lucky to have you. If you weren't here, this whole thing would have blown up in my face, and I would probably be staying in town with the rest of those idiots."

"You're darn right you're lucky to have me, and you're lucky to have me on this safari. Now shut up and go to sleep."

~~~~~~~~~~

Finally, after a month and a half of solid travel, I experienced my first good night of sleep. I woke up naturally, with the sunlight filtering through the crack in the open curtain, and I could hear laughter from the other part of the house. I lifted my arm and patted the empty bed next to me, realizing that Betty must have been up and dressed. I rolled out of bed and threw my safari duds on. It felt good to once again don this khaki African garb. As I opened the door, I was blasted with the smell of bacon and Lance's homegrown coffee. Betty, dressed in her khaki breeches and safari shirt with epaulets on the shoulders, sat in a chair at the kitchen table.

"Looking pretty sporty there, kiddo," I commented, not having seen her in this attire since the day we purchased it in Chicago all those many months ago.

She gazed up at me with a beautiful smile, her flowing curls full and lush, and I almost had to pinch myself to make sure I wasn't dreaming.

"You are looking as beautiful as ever!" I said, reaching down and kissing her on the cheek.

"Are you hungry, John?" Esther asked.

"Famished is the word. I slept like a baby."

"I slept well, too, darling," answered Betty.

"It's a good thing you got up when you did," Lance said. "I told Blaney we would be by this morning to purchase those permits, and if you hadn't rousted right quick, we were getting ready to roust ya."

"How do you like your eggs?" Esther asked.

"I like 'em cooked," I said with a laugh.

Esther giggled at my wit. "I know, silly, but really," she said, putting her hands on her hips.

"Break the yokes and cook 'em hard," I answered. "Where are Chuck and Jason?"

"Oh, they've been up for hours," Lance said. "They had breakfast, and Janga took them out exploring. Took that little dog with 'em, too."

Esther poured a cup of steaming black coffee and placed it on the table in front of me. "Now don't burn yourself," she cautioned as I put the cup to my lips.

The aroma of that fresh-roasted coffee, straight from Lance's crops, filled my nostrils. This well-run farm—so self-sufficient, with good help and sitting on beautiful land—had always taken me. It gave me great peace to know that now Lance stood at the helm of the operation and was making a true go of it.

I gazed out the window at the flat-topped trees dotting the rolling green hills on the horizon.

"John," Betty said, "are you listening?"

"No," I said. "Were you talking to me?"

"Yes," Lance said, somewhat indignant. "I asked if you're interested in doing some fossil digging."

"You know what, Lance? I think I need a break from it this time, if that's okay with you. I'm still licking my wounds after getting burned by the institute. It's not that I won't go back to it and throw myself heart and soul into my work again, but I need to take a serious break."

"I don't have a problem with that, John. I'm with you, buddy."

"I am really looking forward to getting on with the safari," I continued, "camping out in the bush, sitting around a campfire at night, sleeping under the stars, reading some good books, watching my gal fish in a stream, having some great conversation with my friends, and stalking some of the world's finest game."

Esther set the breakfast on the table in front of me with a warm smile.

"Esther, if this is how you cook, why for heaven's sake did we hire someone to do the cooking on this safari?"

"I thought we were going on safari to relax and find adventure," she said and laughed. "There ain't much adventure in cooking. Actually, I don't do much cooking here because I have a staff, but I gave them the day off."

Just then we heard footsteps on the front porch, and in came Buster with his tail wagging.

"Oh, he shouldn't be in the house," Betty said.

"No, no, it's okay, really!" Esther said. "He's welcome. He is a delightful little character. Besides, if he is going on safari, he needs to feel like he is part of the group, too."

"Where have you two been off to?" I asked as Jason stepped through the front entry.

"We just took a little morning hike," he replied.

Chuck stood in the doorway, looking a little worse for the wear.

"How are you doing, Chuck?" Lance asked.

"Well, I can tell you this: I am not fifteen years old anymore." He dragged himself across the floor and collapsed in a chair. "Imagine trying to keep up with that."

"Did you pack that shotgun with you?" I asked.

"Right," Chuck said, "only because Lance insisted that I take it."

"Some of my help spotted a lion marking his territory off the end of that last coffee field out toward the southeast quarter," Lance explained. "I don't think those lions would bother a human if they go unprovoked, but you never know how cranky they might be or if they might just be having a bad day. You have to be armed if you're going to be on the outskirts of the farm. I'm glad Janga went with you because it's not a good idea to go alone. Look, that's why I hire natives. They've grown up here, and they have a sense about it."

"So what kind of pistol is that one you have there, Lance?" I asked. "I don't remember you as being a pistol man."

"It's a .45 Colt. I picked it up in Mombasa last summer. Always wanted a big handgun like the ones they carry in those Western books."

I glanced at Betty, who had a big grin. "Boys and their toys," she said, shaking her head at Esther, who put her hand over her mouth to keep from laughing.

"Yes, well, you girls will be happy to have us packing some heat, like this here, when we are out pounding around in the bush," I said and patted my .44 resting in my holster. "A forty-four Magnum, or a Colt like that one of Lance's there, will kill a lion outright if he's hit right. And if not, he'll think twice, and you've got five more quick shots where that one came from."

"Hey, I heard tell about a semiautomatic that John Browning put together last year for the U.S. government," Chuck said. "Supposed to be quite a pistol from what I hear."

"Yes, it's the .45 auto Colt, model 1911. I inquired about bringing one along, but my gunsmith steered me away from it. He thought the casing was a little light for effective use against anything over here, and after looking at the cartridge, I had to agree. Besides, I guess it's very temperamental, and they are still working the bugs out of the design."

"If you're done with your breakfast," Esther said, "I'll take your plate."

I slid back from the table, handing her my empty dish. "That was quite a breakfast."

"I told Blaney we would be in around ten o'clock," Lance said. "What time is it?"

I removed my gold pocket watch from my shirt pocket and flipped the lid. "It's nine-thirty. Guess we better get scooting."

~~~~~~~~~

Lance's native kitchen help took care of the cleaning up, and we all hurried to get ready for the ride into town. When we stepped off the front porch, Lance had the motor churning on his jalopy.

"Should we take Buster with us?" Jason asked, standing with his pup at his heels.

"No, he'll be fine here," Lance answered. "Hey, Janga!" he hollered across the yard.

I looked up and saw my old hunting partner making his way toward the truck. "Janga!" I called and then greeted him in Swahili as we shook hands. "*Jambo rafiki!*"

"I am guide-man, *Bwana*," he said with a grin, showing his broken front tooth. "I am finally big man."

"*Ndiyo* (yes) *ndiyo!*" I said.

Lance rattled off Swahili so fast at Janga I could barely keep up with his words. I was pretty sure he told him to watch the dog while we were gone, that the dog loved to fetch, and that if he tossed the stick, the dog would be his friend for life. Then we all piled into the truck, and a moment later we were lumbering down the driveway and hitting the main road. We bounced along, watching the scenery, and Lance managed to miss most of the bad holes in the road.

"Stop the truck!" Betty said.

"What is it?" Lance asked. "Did you see something?"

"Right there," she said. "Back up. Are those sable antelope right there?"

"Where?" I asked.

"Right there!" Betty said in an exasperated tone as she pointed across the open glade, squinting and gritting her teeth. "See that tall brown grass along those flat-topped trees? Are they all female, or is that big one in the group a ram?"

"I don't even see 'em," Lance said, disgusted. "How did you know they were sable?

"Hey, my husband has a whole trophy room full of these animals."

Chuck had his binoculars up and was scanning the area. "Yes, that one to the far left is a ram for sure."

"Well, we're not going after them right now," Lance said. "Let's go see Blaney about the permits first."

"Old Blaney," I said with a smile, "he'd understand if we shot a sable without a permit, wouldn't he?"

"Oh, sure, right after he locked you up and threw away the key," Lance said. "My goodness, lady, you've got a set of eyes there. I'm taking you hunting with me."

137

"You can't have her," I said. "I set my claim years ago. He's a nice sable, isn't he, Chuck?"

"Here, Betty, take a look at him in my glasses. He's your animal. You spotted him."

Betty took the field glasses, trained them on the antelope, and steadied them with her elbows resting on her knees.

"I still can't believe she spotted those," Lance said.

Esther, sitting in the middle of the front seat between Lance and Jason, shrugged her shoulders.

"You want to have a look, Jason?" Betty asked.

"Yes, please!"

"Here, take these," she said and handed him the glasses.

Lance waited while Jason homed in on the herd.

"You ready, boy?" Lance asked, revving the motor with the throttle.

"Okay, let's go," Jason answered.

Lance let out the clutch, and the truck lurched forward, once more taking us down the dusty road in the growing heat of the morning. The wild flowers were bursting forth, ushering in the close of the rainy season like a great curtain on the stage at the end of a play.

~~~~~~~~~

The Nairobi streets were bustling with activity, and Lance wove in and around horses, the town folks on bicycles, and a smattering of mule carts. We made our way to the British Protectorate headquarters and Game Department. We pulled up to the modest government building just as a group of men were stepping from the awning-covered boardwalk, folding papers, and stuffing them into their coat pockets. Black men with British rifles slung over their shoulders followed behind them.

Lance pulled the truck next to the edge of the street and shut it down, and the tailpipe backfired, shooting an echo down the street. People inside the headquarters rushed outside, and those already on the street stopped and stared. Other men crouched low as they took cover.

Then Blaney emerged, pushing people aside as he tried to fight his way through the doorway. "Lance, is that you?" he shouted in his deep, gruff voice. "What in the hell is going on out here?"

At 5'8" and 220 pounds of solid muscle, Blaney was built like a fireplug. Pushing fifty, with skin weathered from years spent in the sun, he had thick gray hair and a thick brow that nearly touched the top of his nose. His face was pockmarked, and he had a pronounced scar on his chin. He wore a khaki shirt with green-and-gold-striped epaulets on the shoulders and red embroidery over the left breast pocket, which read *Game Warden* in English and right below it *Matokeo Ya Utafutaji* in Swahili.

"I guess I need to keep a better eye on my mechanic," Lance said.

I laughed to myself, knowing that Lance didn't know the first thing about tuning up a truck. My old gun bearer had probably tuned it correctly, but Lance had messed it up trying to tinker with it.

"You really know how to give somebody a heart attack," Blaney said. "Well, come on in."

We followed him inside past the crowd of men who were waiting at the front desk.

"Sorry to make you wait, boys," he said as we pushed our way through the Dutch and French men standing in the lobby, "but these folks here are ahead of you. They had an appointment."

If looks could have killed, we would have all been dead. We followed Blaney Percival past the reception area and into his private office.

"Have a seat," he said, pointing to several hard benches that faced a broad wooden desk. He took a seat behind the desk in the captain's chair. "John, it's been oh, what, a couple of years now, hasn't it?"

"Yes, you were off in the bush when I came here last year."

"Yep, that was last June, and I was out chasing a bunch of renegade Shifta from Somalia. Those scoundrels wiped out nearly fifty bull elephants before we got 'em corralled. I'll tell ya, they are a murderous bunch. I'm lucky to have my men because I don't get much help from the government's police force. Heck, I get more help from the professional hunters who are out in the bush."

"You sound bitter, Blaney," Lance said.

"Nah, just frustrated, that's all. It's hard when you're fighting a losing battle. The game is disappearing, and it seems nobody cares. In fact, some of them are happy about it. It's not the sportsmen; it's the poachers and the farmers. Sorry, Lance. I know you're a farmer, but you know I'm right. Well, enough of my troubles. You didn't come here to hear me bellyache. How are you, Esther? Is that old man of yours treating you okay? Good thing Lance married you when he did, because I was next in line. So ... who do we have here?"

Esther's cheeks turned pink as she blushed.

"This is my wife, Betty, and this is Jason, not my son, just a friend. And this may as well be my father, Dr. Charles Crawford."

Blaney's dry and wrinkled face had lost its youth and was showing the long years of working beneath the scorching sun on the plains of the Masai Mara. His nose revealed signs of heavy drinking, obvious by the red tone from the underlying veins.

"Fancy to finally meet the mystery woman," he said in his gruff voice. "Ever since I knew you, you've been telling me you had a wife. But let's get down to business. Lance filled me in on most of your plans. Sounds pretty ambitious. You know some parties are beginning to use autos."

"Yes, we know," I said, "but we decided to keep our safari somewhat pure. We do have a vehicle, but we plan to do our hunting on foot or horseback. We might do some scouting in the vehicle, but that's all."

"John, what's the matter with you?" Lance protested. "You know we can't use my old truck. That thing is on its last leg. Besides, you heard it. We'd scare off half the game in the countryside with that thing."

"Yes, well, what you don't know, my good friend, is that I have a brand new Ford Tin Lizzy coming here, due to be delivered by the end of next week."

"Why didn't you tell me?"

"I wanted it to be a surprise."

"What about camp meat?" Blaney asked, clearly trying to get us back on track. "You're gonna need extra permits for gazelle and antelope to sustain that size of an entourage."

"Lance and I figured it might take as many as two animals a week to keep our porters and staff fed."

"That might be a little high," Blaney said. "You know most of those boys won't eat anything more than posho."

"That's true," I said, "but they prefer to eat meat."

"I'll grant you permits for six a month, and that's just for camp meat. That will allow you to shoot ewes and cows, but for gazelle and antelope only, nothing else. Now what sort of trophies have you decided on?"

"Everything but giraffe," I said.

"I can get you the permits for giraffe. Are you sure?"

"Do you want to take one home, Chuck?" Lance asked.

"No, I don't need one," he said.

"They do make a beautiful wall hanging," Blaney said.

"I will never kill one," I said firmly. "They are not a trophy to me. Besides, we're after horns, Blaney, the biggest and the best."

"All right, you know all the cats are considered vermin, and you don't need a permit for that."

"I know, but we won't shoot them just to kill them. We'll take only trophy lion and leopard, and if we have to, we'll shoot in self-defense."

"Let's see, then. You want permits for elephant and rhino—both black and white—buffalo, kudu, eland, hippo, sable, zebra, wildebeest … What else?"

"We'll be in bongo country part of the time, and we'll want permits for that."

Blaney had his nose to the page and looked to be doing the math. "Didn't you get a bongo last year?"

"Sure did," I answered.

"I don't see many of those come through, unless you have a pack of hounds."

"We don't have hounds," I said.

"How much are the permits for elephant and rhino?" Lance asked.

"Don't worry about it, Lance," I said. "I'm paying the freight." I turned to Blaney. "Give us permits for an elephant each and two rhino. Then we'll take the regular allotment allowed for everything else."

"Are you including Esther, too?" Blaney asked, raising his thick brow.

Lance looked over for my approval. "She's going as a member of the safari. She'll shoot, too."

"Can you shoot?" Blaney asked with a slight smile.

"I can shoot," Esther said.

"Okay then, let's see here ... everything times six then, eh? Okay, rhinos and hippos are the equivalent of fifteen American dollars each, and you are limited to two each. Elephants are eighty-five, and remember, no cow elephants or bulls less than thirty pounds per side. Buffalo are ten each, and you can take six bulls. Everything else you can take six, except greater kudu, bongo, and sable, which you can have five. As for your camp meat permits, you can take doe, cows, or ewes. The zebra is the only one we are still giving a four-bit reward for their hides. Are you sure I can't talk you into some giraffe?"

"I'm sure," I answered.

"Okay, let's see what the damage is." Blaney buried his nose in the paper as he scribbled down the numbers. "Looks like just the elephants are five hundred and ten, and with all the rest we're talking a total of ... shoot, are you ready for this?"

"Shoot away!" I said.

"The total is sixteen hundred and fifty bucks."

Lance whistled in amazement.

"I figured that first-class railway charge from Mombasa was steep," I said. "What was it? Eighteen cents a mile times three hundred and thirty miles? I thought fifty-nine dollars and forty cents apiece was outrageous. But I figured that's about what our licenses would be, so it's really no surprise to me." I looked over at Jason as I stood up and then reached into my pocket, pulled out my money clip, and laid out seventeen crisp new one hundred-dollar bills on Blaney's desk.

Jason's eyes nearly popped out of his head. "I've never seen that much money in all my life."

"You boys know the drill here," Blaney said. "Jason, you and me are gonna take these ladies and show 'em something out back of the government post. Come on." He turned to one of his assistants. "Wilson, will you see to it that you or someone else takes care of that other safari party that has been waiting at the front desk? I'll be back in about a half hour."

I knew the routine well. Blaney had a habit of taking first timers out to the cemetery to show them what making reckless choices on safari will get you. We followed the bulldog out the back door, down the alley, across the street, and down the block. We walked about half a mile to the edge of town to an iron gate, which led to a fenced graveyard. Blaney trod softly and reverently through the gravestones to a section that was clearly separate from the hundreds poking above the ground.

"Esther and Betty, I brought you out here to show you this. Jason, you get up here too, son," Blaney said in a stern voice. "You see these graves? These are well-intentioned folks who came here for the adventure of their life. They were all seeking fulfillment, every one of them, but what they got ended all their dreams. Lots of these are just grave markers because the survivors buried their friends, what was left of 'em, right where they died in the bush. Anyway, see here? This one right here? Killed by lion. And that one? Gored by rhino. They go on and on. Mauled by leopard, chomped by hippo, stomped by buffalo, charged by elephant, eaten by crocodile. Or look at this one over here," Blaney said, stepping past the first row. "This man here was a personal friend of mine. I sold him permits two weeks before. I brought him out to this cemetery and tried to impress upon him the dangers, but then just two weeks later we planted him right here cold in the ground. I showed him every grave and gave him every warning, but I buried him just the same when they brought him back strapped over a jackass, fatally wounded in a hunting accident. Let this be a lesson to you. I don't want to see anybody come back here after you have bought the farm.

"Don't let your porters handle your firearms; that's why you hire experienced gun bearers. I know John has taught you how to handle a weapon and not treat it like it was a broom handle. Make it a rule right now: either your gun bearer or yourself, but that's it. Remember what I'm telling you right now. Most of these animals will leave you alone if they go unprovoked. But those darn buffalo are so unpredictable. Sometimes they run at the sound of a shot, and other times they will charge headlong. Make your first shot on old Mr. Buff count. If you don't, his adrenaline will take over, at which point you can fill 'em full of lead and they just won't die. After that, it's the same with lions, elephants, and rhinos. Well, they are just plain nasty all the time."

The women were very solemn, hanging on Blaney's every word, which was reassuring. I had sensed Betty's exhilaration and eagerness to get going, and now I felt confident that she would take Africa a little more seriously. I knew how she felt about death. Heck, I knew how *I* felt about death. The thought of it terrified me.

As I studied the cold grave markers, I tried to visualize the people sleeping in the ground, dead and gone for all eternity, never again to flicker like a light. Why did life have to be so terrifying? Why did life have to be so complicated?

We followed Blaney back to his headquarters, and no one spoke a word. The air was heavy. Still, I was glad that he had brought Betty and Jason out here. Maybe it would save their lives.

Chapter 9

THE SNEAK

Later that evening, after enjoying a beautiful meal prepared by Lance and Esther's personal kitchen staff, Betty and I sat out on the open-air veranda to enjoy the cool air and watch the rose-colored sunset in the western sky. Betty penned a letter to Mae, and I read from Roosevelt's acclaimed book, *African Game Trails*. But I didn't have my heart in his book. There were good insights about the game and all, but reading about someone else's adventure didn't really thrill me when I knew what lay ahead of us.

"I am finished with my letter," Betty said. "Would you like to proofread it for me?"

"Certainly," I replied, thankful for the opportunity to close Roosevelt's egotistical volume and set it down next to my chair. "Two pages. My, I didn't know there was so much to write about since your last letter."

"I promised her I would write, and I am keeping my promise," she said, handing me the pages of script.

I reclined in my chair and let my eyes settle in on her words.

April 29, 1912
Dear Mae,
Today has been our first glorious full day on our dear friend Lance Miles's farm in the lush green hills of Nairobi. There is so much to tell you I don't know where to start. John and I were pleasantly surprised to find his friend, who has been a devout bachelor ever since John

has known him, got married during John's short absence. Mae, I have to tell you that I took an immediate liking to her from the very first minute I met her. She is an American girl who was born of Negro descent, became orphaned at a very young age, and was raised by a white family in New York. I know you would have taken to Esther as I have just by her soft, well-spoken disposition and her loving, graceful attitude toward others. Here I thought I would be a rose among the thorns for this entire safari but am now pleasantly surprised to be sharing the vine with another woman in the party.

I hope you enjoy the small gift I have enclosed. It was just a little something that John and I picked up in the marketplace. It was the first chance that we had to go shopping in Nairobi after spending a horrid amount of money on big game permits. No one told me that safaris were so expensive. So far Jason is having the time of his life running free in the wide open green fields with his dog.

Today we met with an old friend of John's who is the local game warden here. We had a sobering experience when he showed us a graveyard where they bury fallen sportsmen. He gave me a stern warning to be careful on safari, and I have taken his words to heart. Your lecture is still ringing in my ears, and I wanted to tell you that you have my attention now, and not to worry.

The rainy season has left this place the most luscious green you can imagine. John said to enjoy it now because it quickly fades to brown during the dry months. This is, John said, the very best time here for a safari because now the rivers will begin to recede and the country will be full of wildlife. I have already seen my first giraffe, and we spotted a herd of sable antelope today. John wants to wait to get away from the farm before we start hunting in a couple of weeks. Until then, we are going to relax and get recharged and make our final preparations for our trip. I am still looking forward to receiving my first letter from you, my dear. You must be teaching me patience.

Until then, my dearest Mae, we love you and we miss you.
Betty

"Are you sure you want to talk about all the dead hunters that have perished as a result of their own stupidity?" I asked. "I mean, she has always been convinced that one of us is going to be eaten by a lion or something over here. I don't think we should feed her fears or make them worse than they already are."

"Exactly why I mentioned it," Betty replied. "I know she is home fuming with worry, and I'm trying to impress on her how careful we are all going to be."

"I can appreciate what you are trying to do, dear. I'm just not sure this is the best way to go about it."

"If you don't like the letter," Betty huffed, "I'll tear it up and start over!" She folded her arm across her chest and slumped back in her chair.

"I'm sorry. I didn't mean to hurt your feelings."

"No," she insisted, "give me the letter. I'll start over. Give it to me right now."

"No, the letter is fine. Really, it's a good letter. I think you are right about her. The fact that you are assuring her that we are going to be extremely careful is exactly the right thing to do. I just hadn't thought of it that way, that's all."

Our conversation was cut short when Lance and Esther joined us, followed by Jason and Chuck.

"Where have you been?" Betty asked.

"We took an evening walk down toward the river," Lance said. "Chuck wanted to visit the Kikuyu huts."

"I would have gone," Betty said.

"John, don't go getting me in trouble now," Lance warned. "You said you wanted to stay behind and relax."

"I confess, dear, that's what I told him."

"You have to take me tomorrow, then."

"We're getting up early tomorrow," Lance said, pausing and suddenly looking sheepish.

"Oh?" I said. "Why is that?"

"Well," Lance said and then paused again.

"We're going to church," Esther announced.

"*Church*?" I asked in disbelief. "Lance, what have you gone and done now? You haven't gone religious on me, have you?"

Lance glanced at Esther and then back at me. He frowned awkwardly and squinted. "Don't fret, old buddy. It's just church. Come along if you like."

"No, I won't come along," I said in a huff. "I have seen my friends fall for this nonsense one at a time. It sickens me to see how weak they are, how they can't live their lives under their own power, how they need a crutch. Don't let them suck you in, too."

Esther obviously didn't know what to say. She smiled politely and left the room without making a peep, leaving Lance standing by himself.

"Well?" I demanded. "Don't you see how even the English language shows the similarities between the words *crutch* and *church*?"

"We are retiring for the evening," Lance said, looking away and turning to leave. He paused in the doorway. "Our crutch starts early, and anyone is welcome."

I could see Betty about to speak up and caught her gaze with mine. She wisely said nothing.

"I'm turning in, too," Chuck said. "All this fresh air and altitude makes me sleep like a baby.

Buster curled up in a ball at Jason's feet, and I could see by the flickering candlelight that his eyes were growing heavy, too.

"Jason," I said, "take that mutt and hit the rack, boy."

Betty and I sat quietly in the still darkness of the African night, neither of us saying a word to the other. Then finally she got out of her chair and motioned for me to follow her to bed.

~~~~~~~~~~

I awoke abruptly the following morning to the sound of Lance revving his Chevrolet lorry in the drive. I heard the motor race and then began to lag under the weight of the vehicle, and I listened as the noise faded while the truck put distance between it and the farmhouse.

"Are you awake, my darling?" I whispered in the dimness.

There was no response from my slumbering princess.

I waited a few moments and then asked again. Once again, she did not respond, which was odd, considering she was a light sleeper. I rolled over, expecting to whisper in her ear, only to find the bed empty.

That sneak! How dare she deceive me and run off with them!

I leaped out of bed and threw on my clothes in the dim early morning sunlight peeking through the window. In a rage now but trying to control my temper, I hurried out of my room, only to find the house empty and quiet. I found a handwritten note on the table in the front entryway.

John,
Have gone to church with our friends. I didn't want to wake you because I realize how tired you have been. See you when we get back.
Love, Betty

"That little conniver!" I hissed aloud. "That little sneak! How dare she defy me! She is here because I allowed her to come, and now she has the gall to throw this in my face. When she gets back, I am going to give her a piece of my mind!"

I crawled back in bed and tried to sleep, but my heart began to race and my mind churned. The more I thought about what she had done, the more my blood boiled. I finally decided to get up and take a walk down to the river.

The birds were singing as I approached where the coffee rows ended and the lush green grass of the open field began, and I found a Kikuyu trail leading toward a grove of trees down along the river. I entered the heavy brush with my .44 Magnum long Colt hanging heavily from my waist, the barrel touching my right leg as I walked. It gave me a feeling of confidence and protection. The early morning air felt cool and crisp in my face, and the rolling hills still concealed the approaching sunshine. I paused to watch the brightly colored birds dart from tree to tree. Then I recalled my studies of Thomas Henry Huxley, who remained convinced that birds had evolved from dinosaurs, a theory I found quite compelling. As I tried to stay focused on my thought, I kept hearing the horrid words of Betty's friend Rose, who had told me that all creation teaches a lesson about life and points to a creator.

Hogwash—to the core, I thought, feeling my temperature rise again. *What possible lesson other than evolution could a creature teach to anyone?*

After emerging in an open glade, I found a log on the riverbank and sat to watch the morning's activity. I spotted a bird known as a "honey guide," a literal nod to its chief claim to fame. The honey guide will practically take a man by the hand and show him a beehive, because the bird knows the man will break into it to get the sweet prize and then there will be plenty for both. Nearby were starlings, doves, and a flock of pinkish-gray finches with pink tails. I spotted one of the most beautiful birds in all of Africa, the Lilac-breasted Roller. Then a small group of snipe, with their peculiar-looking long curved beaks, worked the shoreline, looking for insects. Warblers and larks danced on their wings and sang their tunes, along with robins and thrushes, which filled the airways with melody. There were so many birds flitting about me it would have been impossible to count them. They were like a river that flowed down from the unknown before passing on, never to be heard or seen again.

There seemed to be no order to life; everything happened at random. Suddenly the songbirds dispersed in a panic, and I looked overhead to see a large hawk floating on kite-like wings high above the Athi River. I correctly identified it as a fish eagle, much like the American bald eagles I had observed along the shores of Lake Superior.

A strange feeling of déjà vu came over me, sending a chill up my spine. It was as though I was reading from the pages of a book that described a scene I vividly recalled, one that I had no business recognizing. At that very instant when I felt like someone had their hand on my shoulder and was controlling my very destiny, the eagle folded its wings and made a dive straight for the water, splashing hard and then emerging unscathed with a fish in its talons. Had I dreamed this moment before? I wrestled with the image and tried to cast it from my mind. I wanted to run but knew there was nowhere to hide. There seemed to be no mistake that the helpless fish, impaled by the raptor's talons, symbolized my life.

How stupid could I be for falling into this religious trap? My anger, first projected outward, turned inward. Not one more second would I indulge in this nonsense. I imagined striking a match and then stood back to watch the image of the moment shoot up in flames before falling to the ground in harmless ashes. After gathering my feet under me and brushing the dust from the seat of my breeches, I regained my composure and made my way back toward the farm-house, following the same trail for about a mile.

As I backtracked, I spotted a pugmark from a lion next to the very footprints I had left on my way to the river. Not terribly large, the footprint likely belonged to a lioness or a young male. I was surprised I hadn't noticed it on the way down, because I always watch the ground for tracks. I continued a few more steps and found that the lion had walked on and off the trail. I then spotted a place where its paw print had been left squarely over my shoe print. Now there was a reason for concern.

I froze in my tracks. I could detect the distinct odor of blood and musk from some sort of beast. Then came a chilling roar, and I knew I had stumbled upon a fresh lion kill. But the brush stood so very thick along this riverbank that I could not see through it but for the narrow trail.

I reached down and unsnapped my holster and quietly cleared the .44 from the leather. After carefully checking to make sure each cylinder contained an unfired round, I grabbed the hammer with my thumb and cocked it back.

I had to be right on bad boy, probably less than twenty feet. I figured him to be a lone male, since lionesses always hunt in groups, but a young male could be out on his own. I could hear him tearing at the flesh from his breakfast, and the thought that he might be concerned that I perhaps would want to join him did not thrill me.

Slowly and methodically, I placed one foot behind me, putting an additional three feet between us, then trained the pistol in the direction of the noise, just in case a charging lion came bursting through the bushes.

My heart felt as if it would burst through my throat, and I kept thinking that I had never shot a big cat with a pistol before. I hoped I wouldn't have to find out if one would actually stop a lion at a full charge. I found a fork in the trail that headed west, and I turned and made haste, giving the lion plenty of room for which to finish his banquet in peace, then I beat feet on back to the farmhouse.

Upon my return, I found Chuck had begun making preparations with Lance's house staff to rustle up some morning grub.

"I think I found the lion Lance said his boys spotted last week," I said, laying my hat on the chair and taking a seat at the farm table.

"Where is he?" Chuck snapped.

"Down by the river. I walked right up on him coming up the edge of that thicket and heard him crunching bones."

"Well, let's go get that kitty cat," Chuck said, raising his bushy brows. "He's probably still there."

"He is gonna stay there, too. You'd need a pack of hounds to get him out of that brush pile. You've seen it. It's a tangled mess of thorny brush that just ain't friendly to a soft-skinned mammal such as us. Besides, it's too risky. He would either spook early and we would never get a shot, or he would try to defend his food and we would end up way too close for comfort. They get real cranky and protective when they think someone might take their grub away. Anyway, I am starved. What's for breakfast?"

"You're going to pass up a trophy lion just to feed your belly?"

"Nah. He's no trophy, believe me. I saw the track, and if it isn't a lone lioness, then it is a juvenile male. Hardly worth our trouble, Chuck."

"Are you sure about the track?"

"I'm sure. I've seen plenty of 'em."

"Are you sure I can't talk you into it? You can bet they don't want him hanging around this farm."

"Yes, I'm sure. I don't want to be gone when my little missy returns. You know that little sneak ran off with them to church this morning?"

"I wondered where she was," Chuck said. "I thought she was with you. What about that Jason boy? He should have stirred by now."

"I'll bet he went off with them to church," I said.

"I took a little morning walk myself, and I heard the truck depart. I never checked his bunk when I got back here, but this is getting pretty late for him to sleep."

"What about this dog, Chuck? Where was he when you got back?"

"He was right here in the house, and he should have been sleeping at the foot of the kid's bed."

"Go find Jason, Buster," I told the floppy-eared mutt. "Where is he, boy?"

Buster wagged his shaved-off tail and went sniffing on down the porch toward the bunkhouse before veering off toward the pond.

"I'll check the bunkhouse," I called back to Chuck, who stood watching from the porch. "I'll be right back. Come on, Buster. He's in his bunk, boy."

Once inside, I found his bed flat as a board. *That kid must have gone with 'em, too. What sort of corrupt ideas were they trying to put in that boy's head?* For the life of me, I couldn't see why he had gone. I remembered being dragged off to church as a kid. I swore when I grew up I would never set foot in another church until the day I got married—and again on the day they buried me.

It really impressed me that this little dog would make a search at the first mention of Jason's name.

"Come on, Buster. He isn't here," I said, heading back to the farmhouse with the dejected pup at my side. "You're right, Chuck. He's gone. But you know that boy hangs on to that woman of mine like she is his mother."

"You know, John, I think that's a good thing. You shouldn't be complaining about Jason's loyalty. There are worse things. Besides, he doesn't have a mother of his own."

"You're right. Let's have some breakfast, my friend."

Out on the open-air verandah, M'culay served up scrambled eggs and a side of seared warthog.

"This is living, aye, Chuck?"

Chuck rolled his eyes and took a deep breath with his nostrils, smiling in utter ecstasy.

The pork melted in my mouth, and the eggs were done to perfection. I sipped the hot coffee and wondered how things were back in Chicago with the hustle and bustle of city life.

Just then a rifle shot rang out. Chuck swung his head toward the north end of the farm, where the shot had come from, before returning his gaze to me and wrinkling his brow. I started to speak, but a second shot ran out.

"That came from the end of the farm," Chuck said. "Who would be hunting here?"

"No one, as far as I know, Chuck. How far do you figure that came from?"

"Fairly close, just up that first draw. Maybe a mile—maybe two at the most."

"After breakfast we'll mosey up there and have a look-see," I said.

I tried not to gulp down my breakfast, but my curiosity had certainly gotten the best of me. As far as I knew, none of Lance's hands had a rifle. And if he had given someone permission to hunt, he hadn't told me. I drained the rest of my coffee, washing down my last bite of breakfast.

Chuck had already found his rifle.

Then my ears perked up at a familiar noise approaching from the south. "Listen, Chuck. That's Lance and his crew coming home from town."

Chuck cocked his head and lent a leading ear as he tried to home in on the faint hum. "Boy, you got better ears than me." He squinted, then nodded his head. "Yep, that's them."

The noise grew in volume with every second before we finally spotted Lance's truck bouncing and pitching along the road.

"Just as well. I'm sure Lance will want to investigate those shots with us."

I went back inside to get my hat and coat, and there Betty's pith helmet hung on the hook next to mine. I thought about her cute little turned-up nose, her soft voice, and loving touch. How could I be mad at her for such a thing as a viewpoint? Here we were in Africa to experience the time of our lives, the safari of my dreams. There wouldn't be another one to take its place, nor a better time for Betty and me to repair our relationship.

I resolved right then and there not to get mad over this religion nonsense, which would only ruin our trip. I could encourage her in the future to stay clear, but to publicly scold her in front of our dear friends would not be a wise move. I plucked my hat and coat from the rack and walked out to the front steps to greet our party.

I counted heads as the truck made its way down the drive. When I noticed Jason absent from the car, a chill came over me. I scurried off the porch and approached the truck as Lance pulled up to the farmhouse.

"Where's Jason?" I yelled over the noise of the motor to the blank faces of the returning threesome.

Lance switched off the motor, and all went silent.

"He didn't go with us," Betty said. "Isn't he here?"

"No, we thought he was with you," I said.

"There he is!" Chuck hollered, pointing off the end of the porch. "Isn't that Jason?"

I could see someone far off in the distance, about five hundred meters away. He was waving and yelling something.

"What's he saying?" Betty asked.

"I don't know," I said. "Listen."

All ears were tuned toward the horizon as Jason paused, cupped his hands over his mouth, and shouted, with the sound of his voice coming to us after a short delay.

"What did he say?" Lance asked.

"He said something about a lion," Betty said.

"Come on," Lance said. "Let's go!"

"Wait a minute," I insisted. "Let me get my Springfield."

Lance had the truck turned around and the motor running when I made a dash for the vehicle. Lance revved it up, I jumped in with the rest of them, and off we went across the grassy field and onto a dirt path along the edge of his coffee field. We hung on as Lance pounded the potholes and plowed his way on toward Jason, who stood waiting for us. As we got closer, I could see Jason holding the 30-40 Kraig. I felt my blood boil.

"What's he doing with that rifle?" I asked.

Betty put her hand on my thigh and looked in my eyes, melting me with her calming gaze. "Don't be too hard on him," she said. "Give him a chance to explain himself."

"I'll give him a chance, all right," I answered. "This better be good."

As he raced to intercept us along the trail at the edge of the field, the dust began to rise in a cloud behind him.

"You know I'd appreciate it if you wouldn't walk through my coffee plants, boy," Lance shouted over the motor as soon as we pulled alongside him. "What is it, anyway?"

Jason could hardly speak. "Lion," he said as he gasped for air. "I shot a lion!"

I leaped off the truck, took hold of his jacket lapels, and brought him face-to-face with me. "Just what in tarnation do you think you are trying to pull here? Who said you could take this rifle out alone?"

"I spotted a lion, sir. I tried to find you, but you were gone. Everybody was gone, so I took the liberty."

"Jason, you don't have enough experience for this," I scolded. "Where is the dead lion?"

Jason looked down at the ground and kicked a clump of dirt.

"You hear me, boy? Where in the hell is the dead lion?"

His face turned pale, and I could see beads of sweat forming on his brow. "I don't know, sir."

"What do you mean, you don't know?" I snapped.

"I'm pretty sure I might have hit him, but he disappeared into a ravine."

"Oh great," Lance said, rolling his eyes, "now we have a wounded lion on our hands!"

"What is the matter with you?" I said. "What were you thinking?"

"I don't know. I was walking up from the bunkhouse when I saw him right down there in the lower end of the field, and I didn't … I mean … I guess …"

"Yeah, you weren't thinking. I told you before: you don't take a shot on a lion unless you know you can put him down, and nobody goes hunting here in Africa alone. Do you understand me?"

"Yes, sir."

"Now that we have that settled, how far off was he when you shot?"

"The first time?"

"Yes, how far away were you?"

"Maybe two hundred yards, I guess."

I gritted my teeth, trying to control my anger. "I told you a long time ago I wouldn't tolerate wounded game." I took a deep breath and exhaled slowly. "All right, let's go see if there is any blood."

I angrily jumped in the truck, leaving Jason standing in the dirt.

"It's okay, Jason," Betty said. "Don't worry."

"No, Betty," I said. "It will not just be okay. Jason, get in the truck now, and give me that rifle."

He opened the bolt, ejected the round from the chamber, and handed it over, then dragged himself up to the truck and took a seat beside Chuck. The thought crossed my mind that I was being too hard on the boy, but I didn't care. My blood was boiling, and it felt good to release some of the pressure. Only later did it occur to me that all

158

this anger had been pent up since Betty's little sneak, and now Jason was taking the brunt of my ire.

I glanced at the boy out of the corner of my eye as the truck bounced along the edge of the field. He looked like a beaten dog, and no one in the truck dared speak a word.

"That's it," Lance said, bringing the lorry to a stop at a wide ditch across the road. "That's as far as we can go."

"Let's go," I ordered. "Show us where you were when you took the shot."

"Like I said, I spotted him when I was up by the house. He was sauntering along, making his way on towards that big flat-topped tree right down there. So then I got the rifle and headed down across the field, but I didn't see him anymore. I figured he might be plumb gone, but I came across the field and went through that draw right over there just to have a look-see. It's a good poke through there, but then it opens up again when you get through that heavy bush. Then I found his track, so I followed him out. And then I spotted him. I'm pretty sure I can find the place."

"No, you better be damn sure you can find that spot. Listen to yourself, Jason. You have no business out here hunting lions. There is a big difference between courage and stupidity, and hunting a lion by yourself is plain stupid."

Jason let his shoulders slump and hung his head.

"Girls, you stay in the truck," I said. "Betty, here's the Kraig rifle."

"How long will you be?" she asked.

"How far away is this, Jason?" I asked.

"It's a ways, sir."

"Esther and I will head back for the house and wait for you there. It's getting pretty warm to be sitting out here in the sun for an hour or so."

"Hang on to that rifle," I said. "You know how to use it. If there is a wounded lion running around here, you just might need it." I turned to Lance. "Here," I said, passing him the big six-shooter from my holster, "take my hog leg."

"Don't need it," he said and reached under the seat of the truck, fishing free a double barrel twelve gauge shotgun. "I always keep it here for emergencies. It's loaded up with buckshot."

We all piled out of the truck and started heading down the field, leaving the girls seated in the truck.

"I wish you had those hounds back at the house now," I said.

"This isn't the best situation, that's for sure," Lance said, shaking his head.

"Maybe we should get Janga to give us a hand," Chuck said.

"We'll find it," Lance said. "John and I have been doing this a long time."

"We'll just walk back," Betty called to us.

"Can't you drive the truck?" I asked.

"Of course I can drive the truck," she answered, sliding up to the driver's seat.

"I'll see you back at the house then," I said.

"John!" called Betty as I had gotten only a few steps from the truck.

While the others continued toward the field, I returned to her side.

"Be careful," she said, "and don't be too hard on him, John. He's just a boy."

"Oh, Betty, for heaven's sake!"

"I mean it, John. Go easy on him. Do you hear me?"

I looked across the field and saw Chuck putting his arm around the boy and telling him something.

"I'm just trying to impress upon him how important this stuff is. If he wounded a lion, then that is a problem."

"Then deal with it, but show some compassion. Teach him about it, instruct him on what you expect, but don't beat him up. Now here," she said, holding out the Kraig, "you give him back his rifle and show him how to do it right."

"No, you keep it."

"We won't need it. We're just driving a half mile back to the house. This rifle means a lot to that boy. Besides, you're going to need the extra gun. You can teach him discipline without breaking his spirit."

"I have no intention of breaking his spirit."

"Then put yourself in his shoes. How would you feel right now?"

I considered her point of view and decided that she had the edge on me. Reluctantly, I took the Kraig from her. "You ladies be careful." I turned and hustled after the others, now fifty yards ahead.

As I walked, I thought back to my childhood and the day I killed my first whitetail deer in upstate Illinois. I was fourteen years old and proud as punch of this little two-point buck. It had been just me and my father on the hunt, and our mood was joyful. I had a lever action 30-30 Winchester, and when I had jacked the last shell out, I pointed the rifle to the ground and pulled the trigger. The rifle went off with a blast, throwing rocks and dirt clumps in all directions. My dad jerked the rifle out of my hands, his jaw set tightly, and I feared he might wrap that rifle around a tree. He gave me hell like I had never seen, and as I thought about it, I realized I was lucky to be passionately involved in the sport.

Chuck still had his arm around the boy; he was probably telling the kid what a schmuck I was. I threw the second rifle sling over my shoulder.

The motor on the truck revved as Betty's face grimaced while she pulled on the wheel trying to get it turned around.

I turned and called to her, "Need any help?"

"No, I got it," she shouted over the motor.

After I'd caught up with the others, we hiked down to the place where Jason said he'd first spotted the lion. I knew it had to be a juvenile. Maybe the same one I had run into down by the river. If he'd shot a young lion, I knew that I would have a hard time controlling my anger. I thought about my hike to the river this morning all alone. I had actually modeled something to the kid. Could I expect him to do something differently from what I wasn't willing to do myself?

"Here is the place where I picked up his track," Jason said. "There's my track. Oh, and here is the lion track—right here."

I leaned over, expecting to find a housecat track.

"Holy smokes," Lance said, "look at the size of that pugmark."

"That's no lioness, and that's no juvenile," I said, laying my hand to the ground and stretching my fingers across the width of the track. "That's a monster."

"Did he have a black mane?" Lance asked.

"It looked dark on the tips of the hair, but it didn't seem exactly black."

"Well, this is a big boy, that's for sure," I said. "We'll track him out, but gentlemen, let's be careful. Here, Jason, take the Kraig."

"Are you sure?"

"You know how to handle this thing. We have done it enough. You remember."

"Yes, sir. Safety on, slung over my shoulder muzzle up, or in hand muzzle down, finger out of the trigger until I'm ready to shoot. And the most important thing: it's not a walking stick, a broom handle, or a toy. It's a rifle, so respect it like one."

"And if it ain't loaded, treat it like it is," I said, handing him the rifle and then digging into my pocket for the extra cartridges. "Anything else?"

"I know," Jason said. "You said you can never take a bullet back once it leaves the barrel, so don't let it leave unless you know where it's going, right?"

"Good stuff. Now let's go get him, boys, but watch your ass."

As we followed the big cat, his tracks appeared to grow in size. We continued through the bush, picking up a track here and there, along with Jason's boot track in the rocky and dusty hardpan. As difficult as it was, I wondered how Jason could have possibly followed the tracks by himself. Had I not been still smoldering with anger, I would have complimented him.

"This is the last track right here," Chuck said, standing at a point where the cat had come across a rock shelf and then entered a patch of dense grass. "Do you see any more?"

"This cat won't change his direction much," Lance said. "You can keep going along the same line and usually pick up his track again. Besides, look here. See how the grass is flattened right through there? Keep on it. That's our cat."

We picked our way through the thick grass about forty yards and back out into a big open area, where we spread out, trying to pick up the track again.

"Keep a sharp eye," I warned. "He won't give you much warning if he decides to charge."

"Here it is over here," Jason said, pointing to a big pugmark in the dirt. "Right over there on the other side of those trees—that's where I shot at him. And when he ran off, he took to the south right through there."

"Come on then," Lance said. "Let's go down where you last saw him and see if you hit him."

"Yes, we're wasting too much time here trying to track him," Chuck said. "If you're sure about where you shot, then let's go."

"It's right down there," Jason said.

"Okay, I'll lead the way," I said. "You just point me in the right direction. But keep your voices low from here on out, watch your step, and try not to crack any twigs."

Jason pointed with his finger to the exact tree he wanted me to walk towards. The sun had risen high overhead, and I could see heat waves rising from the grasslands.

"It won't be raining today," I said as I grabbed the Springfield slung over my shoulder and paused to open the action to double-check it. I closed the bolt and then continued on, carefully watching the placement of each step. *This is what I live for,* I thought. *This is who I am: a predator on the hunt.*

I had watched these lions kill. They were cunning and crafty, and they were savage, ruthless, and courageous, with little compassion, even for their own. Going against a lion was the ultimate experience, but going against a wounded lion was another thing altogether. Doing this without a pack of hounds bordered on stupidity.

Jason grabbed my shirt, and I turned, briefly startled, to see what he wanted. "This is the place," he whispered. "When I shot, he was standing right across there against that edge of brush. There's my empty casing by that rock right over there."

A gentle breeze blew off the plains, blowing in our faces, and it felt reassuring to know we were downwind, just in case any life lingered in this beast. I took a deep breath through my nostrils, trying to imagine what I might smell if I were a lion. Then we made our way quietly to the spot where Jason claimed he had hit the lion. I didn't expect to find any evidence at all.

"Here's his track right here," Chuck whispered.

"Look here," Lance said, crouching on his haunches just ahead of Chuck. He reached down and picked up a small red-stained fragment of bone between his fingers. "There's a lot of blood here, too. Looks like he's hit pretty good."

"And his track leads right for that donga," I said.

"*Donga*?" Lance whispered. "Don't you mean *wadi*? A donga, that's a Zulu name."

I nodded in agreement, but he knew what I meant.

"What is it?" Chuck asked.

"It's the name for a ravine or depression that carries water in the rainy season," I explained. "Because it stays wetter than the rest of the surrounding soil, the grass flourishes. It can grow up four to five feet high, making a perfect place for a lion to hide. A donga—well, okay, a *wadi*—can be especially dangerous because a lion will hide and wait, then get you when you least expect it."

"What's the plan here, John?" Lance whispered.

"Obviously, we are playing with fire," I said in a low voice, "and I don't like it. I don't want to see anybody get hurt. Jason and I will cross over back there, where the grass is thinner, and come up on the other side. Then you and Chuck take your time and pussyfoot up along the edge, but keep a sharp eye. The grass isn't too thick anyway, and this wadi ain't that wide. But we'll keep you guys in sight, and we'll try to stay parallel with you. Lance, you know how to spot him. He'll look like a dim yellow smear amidst that yellow-brown grass. But don't take any chances with him. If you think you can get a shot at him, let him have it."

"Judging by that hit," Lance said, "he isn't going to be in a real good mood."

"If you see him first," I said, "give us the high sign. We'll do the same."

I motioned to Jason, and we crept to the opening and crossed the ravine quickly, stepping lightly in the mud. We scrambled up the far bank without a sound and came up where we could make eye contact with Chuck and Lance. Cautiously, we inched our way up the edge of the gully. Our eyes strained to catch any movement, and we kept our ears peeled, listening for the slightest noise.

Suddenly, the brush exploded below us, and my heart nearly jumped out of my throat. I threw up my rifle, expecting to see a charging lion, but only a grouse flew out of the bush, setting his wings and gliding gently across the prairie to safety. I turned back to Jason, rolling my eyes and putting my open palm over my heart.

Jason exhaled slowly and then smiled and shook his head.

As soon as I had gathered my composure again, I continued combing the grass with my eyes.

Lance and Chuck were fifty yards to the south, sneaking along like a couple of old hound dogs. Chuck had his rifle up at the ready, and Lance had the twelve gauge long barrel backing him up.

I loosened my red bandanna and unbuttoned my khaki shirt in an attempt to escape the heat. My tongue began to stick to the roof of my mouth, and I thought about how a cool drink might taste right at this moment. I couldn't be sure if the heat or just my nerves were getting to me.

The tension built with every step, and I could feel the hair rise on the back of my neck. I sensed that at any moment this shark could strike the bait. The only problem I could see was that we were the bait. Now I'd never met a worm I didn't like, but maybe that was why I never got into fishing much. Merely thinking about sticking that hook through it and getting worm juice all over my fingers left me cold.

Just when my mind had wandered completely away, I spotted him crouched in the grass. I blinked, trying to bring the image into reality and trying to make sure my imagination hadn't taken over. The lion suddenly appeared right before my eyes.

It was crouched and ready to strike just twenty yards away. I caught Lance's attention, giving him the high sign, and they froze in their tracks. The motion of my hand must have set the old boy off, and he moved, straining to get up, but then settled back down. A chill went up my spine.

I reached back and grabbed Jason firmly by the arm with my left hand, bringing him forward and then stepping back just behind him, all the time keeping my rifle trained on the beast.

"Okay, son," I whispered in his ear, "he's your lion. You claimed him. Now finish it."

Jason licked his lips and squinted, examining the situation.

"Hurry up," I whispered, "before he decides to charge!"

Jason brought the Kraig rifle up to his shoulder in a deliberate motion, sighting down the barrel.

"Take him right between the eyes," I encouraged.

He took a breath, letting half of it out, just like I had trained him. He began steadying the rifle, resting it in the palm of his left hand, his right elbow down against his chest. This kid had nerves of steel. Either he didn't understand what great danger we were in, or he had courage that would have made his victim jealous.

I brought my Springfield up on the target, just in case.

Finally, after what seemed like an eternity, he squeezed the trigger sufficiently to make the rifle discharge with a thunder that shook the ground. The blast hit my ears so hard at such close range that it covered the sound of the bullet slap. The shot echoed through the hills, and smoke rose from the end of the barrel.

Jason recovered from the recoil and quickly jacked in a second round, bringing the rifle back up on target.

I tapped his arm to get his attention and then gave him a hand signal not to shoot again.

The lion quivered for a moment, then collapsed in a heap.

Jason let the rifle down from his shoulder and started to take a step toward the lion, but I grabbed the back of his shirt and stopped him short.

"Hold on there, son," I said. "Give him a minute. Let's make sure."

Lance and Chuck stood their ground at the ready, waiting for a glimpse of the fleeing savage. I held a bead on him, ready to deliver a second blow should he try a move. My arm held steady under the weight of the Springfield as the seconds turned to minutes, until finally I could see that the big cat lay dead. Just a couple more seconds to be sure: time was always a friend in this situation. You could never be too patient. The cat would be dead a long time, and there would be plenty of time to admire him. Too many a novice hunter had rushed in to admire a kill when no kill lay dead to admire.

I had made an acquaintance, an English gent who'd arrived three years before in Nairobi. Lance and I had met up with him at the club. He'd come to Africa on what he'd referred to as a holiday. A very educated man, he had shared my interest in Darwinism, and his knowledge about hunting had quite impressed me. He was the last person I had expected to see arrive back in town one week later with a personal undertaker appointment. We buried what remained of him after his tangle with a wounded lion on the Masai Mara.

What a waste. What a shame. One moment he had been a vibrant, intelligent man, full of life, wit, and animation, and the next he had been extinguished in stillness and emptiness. What sense could anyone make of death? The finality of it was as intriguing as it was challenging. To contemplate her was to reach into the heavens and grasp at a star. Both were quite impossible.

"Now, Jason, easy does it," I whispered, reaching down and picking up a hefty stone. I wound up and gave it a toss. The rock flew perfectly toward its target, hitting the brute with a thud that brought no response. "Okay, let's hold on, Jason."

"Is he dead?" Lance shouted from across the wadi.

"He's down, and he looks dead," I yelled, "but we're going to give him a minute just to make sure."

Time stood still as we waited quietly for what seemed like forever.

Then I gave Jason a nudge to move up, and we crept forward cautiously to the edge of the tall grass.

"Back me up, Jason. I'm going down the bank right here. Keep your Kraig on him. If he shows any signs of life, let him have it."

I watched the animal's side for any ripple or movement in the hair as I struggled to make my way down the bank without turning my back to him. The eyes of this old boy were strangely penetrating, and I studied them to check for a sign of life.

Once at the bottom, I approached him while holding the Springfield stretched out at arm's length. I nudged his head with the end of the barrel. I had my finger on the trigger, ready to send a bullet to his brain if I had to. I really didn't want to put another hole in him if I didn't have to. Besides, this old boy belonged to Jason, and if I had to deliver the final kill shot, it would just take the edge off his victory.

Not completely satisfied with one tap, I reached out and touched the end of the barrel to his open eye. There was no response.

"It's all clear!" I shouted back to the others. "He's dead as a mackerel!"

Everyone came running at the news. Jason threw up a cloud of dust as he nearly fell down the bank while trying to get to his lion.

"Congratulations, son," I said. "He's a beauty." I put my hand on his shoulder and looked him square in the eyes as Chuck and Lance approached. "Next time you see a lion that is minding his own business and you get the idea to poke a hole in him, for heaven's sake, find me, would you?"

Jason responded with an eager nod.

"And if I'm not around, then wait for me. Do we have an understanding?"

"Yes, sir."

"Oh my gosh!" Chuck exclaimed. "That is a beautiful lion."

"I think that's the one we've been seeing," Lance said. "It's good to get him out of here. There are plenty of places for a lion to roam here in Africa. We don't need them hanging around these farms, especially mine."

"Should I head back and get a skinner?" Chuck asked.

"No," I said, "since this is Jason's first lion, I think he'll want to skin it himself. I'll walk you through it, son, to make sure you don't put any holes in the hide."

Killing a lion was like taking possession of a soul. It was a magical thing that anyone who had never done it could never understand. This lion, in all of his power and authority as the king of beasts, had the right and ability to kill you and devour you anytime he pleased. But death over him was power to the one who claimed him. There would now always be a connection between this young man and this ferocious creature of ultimate courage. This boy didn't know it, nor did he understand it, but he would forever be changed by this event.

"Let's get him rolled over," I said.

All four of us tugged on the big brute until we were able to maneuver him so that his belly was turned up and exposed. After unsheathing the razor-sharp skinning knife from my belt, I made an incision in his skin along the underbelly, careful only to cut through the skin and not the gut.

"Jason, this is how you use the blade. See how I am laying it flat against the flesh? Then you pull the skin like this and slide the blade along the edge, and you'll undress him. But be careful not to cut the skin. Carl Akeley is a master taxidermist, but he doesn't like it when there are too many holes in the skin. Here, Jason, take over, son. I'll walk you through it."

Jason took the blade and started slowly at first, but as he progressed he began to get the hang of it. There were a few difficult spots where I took the knife to help him skin the tail and paws, but for the most part the boy did the whole beast all by himself. I took over and lopped off the head, deciding to finish up the job around the lion's ears, eyes, lips and nose when we got back to the farm. We rolled up the hide and tied it in a bale, and then helped Jason to get it situated on his shoulder. Then we gathered up the rifles and trudged back toward Lance's farm.

Jason labored in the warm afternoon sun under the heavy weight of the bundle. He huffed and puffed, but not once did I hear a moan or a hint of frustration out of the boy. I sensed that if anyone would have dared to try to take the prize away from him, there would have been a dogfight. His steps were slowing and his shirt was now drenched with sweat. As we approached the farm, the two women hurried down from the porch to greet us. We paused to wait for them, and Jason labored to shift the heavy weight on his shoulder.

"You got him!" Betty said. "We heard the shot and figured you had him."

"Who got him?" Esther asked.

Betty studied my face, hoping for a hint. But Jason's smile said it all. He had a grin that could have touched his earlobes.

"You did it, Jason," Betty said. "You got your lion, didn't you?"

"One shot right in the head with his 30-40," I said. "The old boy lay waiting for us in the tall grass just like I figured he would. He even gave us a growl, just to warn us that he was ornery."

"He was hit pretty hard," Lance said.

"Yes, that's right," I said. "When Jason skinned him out, he had a broken front shoulder."

"Even at that," Jason said, "he went about a mile before he settled in a ravine."

"Look at you," Betty said. "Did those men make you carry this all the way in from the bush? John, help him with that thing."

"Put it over there in the short grass by the house," Lance said. "We'll get Willie to have someone flesh it out and salt it." He turned and shouted in Swahili to a servant standing on the porch.

"Can we roll him out and have a look at him?" Betty asked.

I hated to admit it, but this lion appeared to be one of the biggest I had seen. I couldn't bring myself to tell that to Jason, not yet anyway. I didn't need him going and getting a big head over it. When Janga arrived with a skinner, he made a big fuss and said it looked like the biggest lion he had ever skinned. Jason beamed from ear to ear, and I wanted to take the edge off his excitement. But somehow I couldn't bring myself to do that, either.

"You boys get washed up now," Esther said. "Dinner will be set in about a half hour."

"I'm as hungry as a lion," Jason said, poking me in the ribs to get me to laugh at his poor sense of humor. "Thanks, Professor. I know I done stupid, but thanks for going easy on me. Thanks for letting me finish him."

"I'm not going to rehash this thing," I answered. "We all make mistakes. Luckily, this one turned out okay. But that's how we learn— by correcting our mistakes. I'm impressed with you, Jason. You're humble and willing to change, you're inquisitive and ready to learn, and you're obedient and eager to please. On top of that, Jason, I'm impressed by your courage."

"Thank you, sir. That means a lot to me. Do you really think he's a big lion?"

"I know he is, son. You should be really proud of it. But wear it with humility and dignity, and other sportsmen will respect you for it."

"Yes, sir."

"Let's have dinner."

Chapter 10

SHUNNED

B etty and I took a walk after dinner to clear the air over her morning excursion. I didn't tell her exactly why we needed to talk, but I knew she had a pretty good idea that I wanted to confront her about attending church. Neither of us said a word as we strolled along the lane. The sun stood just above the hills, and the evening air smelled sweet.

"You should have come to church with us this morning, darling," Betty said, trying to break the ice first. "It was fun."

"Don't be ridiculous."

"John, it's not that bad, really. Must you be so close-minded?"

"This is the second time I've been scolded by you today. Frankly, dear, I'm beginning to wonder if my mother raised me properly."

"I'm not saying you're a bad person."

"Then what are you saying?" I asked. "You chastised me over my feelings about Esther, too. Okay, maybe I was wrong, and maybe you were right about both of them. But I'm telling you, dear, you're wrong about religion."

"You're entitled to your opinion on this one," she said, shaking her head and letting her hair flow. "I won't be mad at you for not believing. I won't even talk to you about it if you don't want me to."

"That suits me fine, Betty, because you know who I am. You know about what I stand for. I am a naturalist, down to the very fibers of my flesh and bones, so don't talk to me about some higher intelligence. If I know anything, I know the universe and I know the world. I have studied it, and I have asked myself all the same questions you are asking now. The only answer to any of these questions that makes any sense at all is the one I have found. If I were to try to throw religion in the equation, I'm afraid, well—"

I didn't want to admit it, but religion had the potential to make everything I had ever worked for go up in smoke. I had put so much of myself into my work and had literally placed my reputation on the line for something I believed in, yet there was always this god thing that threatened it. But I had studied under some incredible men in my life, men whom I admired for their intellect and their willingness to seek intelligent, tangible answers to the big questions in life. Something I could put my finger on, not some mystical thing that amounted to the chasing of rainbows and shadows.

"What?" I asked, not catching Betty's comment after letting my thoughts drift.

"I said, what are you afraid of, darling?"

"Afraid?" I snapped. "I'm not afraid of anything. Just don't preach to me, okay?"

"I just told you I wouldn't. Isn't that good enough? Listen, John, I love you. You know I do." Betty reached down and took my hand in hers and then looked up with those gorgeous brown eyes. "Thanks for bringing me here to Africa."

"I'm glad you're here. I admit I had some reservations, but only because this place is so severe. I have for so long secretly wanted to share this place with you. I just never figured ... I mean, I ..."

"Spit it out, sweetheart. You never figured I could handle it, right?"

"I guess that's it. I thought Africa was a little harsh for you."

"This isn't too harsh for me."

"Not this place, I know. But where we are headed isn't exactly the lap of luxury. I'm warning you, and I have warned you from the beginning. Life on safari is tough. It's intense, hard work, and full of hazards. Not to say we won't have a great time, but I want you to be prepared for adventure."

"I will be—you'll see. I'll make you proud to have me with you."

"I'm always proud to have you with me."

"I'm so happy now, John."

"It took us a long time, didn't it, baby? I mean, for so long we were distant partners after losing Johnny."

"I'm sorry I had such a difficult time dealing with his death. You know it wasn't you. I just wanted to escape the hurt. I wanted to crawl away and disappear. I know I haven't been there for you for a long time, but so help me, John, things are going to change. You'll see. I want to be your companion, your lover, your friend. I want to be a part of your life and rekindle the passion we once both enjoyed. I want to heal like you have, and I want to be happy again."

"Here is what I did to cope, Betty. I believe grief is a process of letting go of the person who is gone. Lots of people run from the hurt and try to hold on, because that seems a little easier. Letting go of them is what causes the grief and the anguish, but unless a person is willing to let go and truly grieve the loss, then no healing can take place. By holding on, the wound stays open and festers. We can get stuck in our grief, and years later we are no better off than the day it happened. I decided a long time ago that I couldn't change the past, and so I was gong to make the best of a bad situation. But it was only when I let Johnny go, not his memory. I stopped trying to hold on to *him*, which is what causes all the anger and frustration. Once I realized I couldn't bring him back, I began to heal." I paused to reflect. "You've come a long way already, Betty. I never thought I would see the day when you would actually want to take an active part in my life."

"No, you mean you never thought you would see the day when you would let me come with you to Africa," Betty said with her cute little smile.

We continued down the road while the sun began to set on the horizon. The sky shone a brilliant red, and the birds chirped and sang as if they were serenading us with a love song. Life felt good. Life seemed wonderful.

~~~~~~~~~

The following morning we found ourselves busily organizing our equipment and trying to break the loads into sixty-pound bundles so our porters could carry them on their heads. Betty had brushed

175

her hair out and had it tied in pigtails. She wore a pair of khaki jungle pants and a bush shirt with extra pockets and epaulets on the shoulders.

Each porter had been assigned a number corresponding to his load, with a description of its contents. Betty carefully recorded each item, while Chuck and Lance tied them with twine.

Our headman, Willie, had made it plain that we were not to load up on the bundles and try to go over the weight limit by cutting down on the numbers of porters we had to hire. As Lance put it, Willie had great experience with shoestring safari men trying to stretch their trek past the point of what they could afford. As we went through the crates, we did find items that Willie thought we wouldn't need. We had purchased extras of everything, including tarpaulins and tents, which only added to the weight, but he insisted we would never use as many as we had purchased because it appeared that the rains were pretty much done for the year. Really heavy units, including extra munitions and food stores such as flower, sugar, rice, and beans, we would pack into the wagons.

"I hear a car coming," Jason said as he tipped his head, trying to listen intently.

"I wonder who that could be," Lance said. "Nobody visits this farm, at least not since I got married." He put his bundle down and stood with Jason to watch the road leading to the farm.

I could see two men in a Chevy making the turn down the long driveway.

"That looks like Pete Wesley from the railway office," I said, remembering that I had dealt with him on a number of occasions over cargo issues.

Esther stood on the porch behind us as Lance walked out to greet the men at the driveway. They pulled up and shut down the motor, restoring the farm to its former stillness.

"Hey, Pete," Lance said. "How are you? What brings you out this way?"

The men spoke not a word, but gave him a cold look, as if he were a second-class citizen. They both wore dark clothing, which contrasted with the nearly white hair poking out from beneath the derby perched on Pete's head. Pete had a slender build and appeared to be in his early fifties. He had thick wire-rimmed glasses that he pushed up his nose as he spoke and a gray mustache that hung down over his lower lip. The other man was younger, maybe in his midthirties, a husky kid, obviously trying to be like Pete, but clean-shaven with a silly looking derby that didn't fit his personality or his oversized head.

"John Rivers, how are you, sir?" Pete said. "I have a delivery for you at the station."

"Is it a big package?" I asked.

"As big as a car," Pete said.

"How about that, Lance?" I said, laying my hand on his shoulder. "It sounds like we got ourselves a Tin Lizzy."

"Is it all assembled and ready to go?" Lance asked.

"Oh, she's rearing to go," I said. "I cranked her up before we left Chicago, and she purrs like a kitten."

"Can you guys give us a lift?" Lance asked.

"We can give you a lift, John," Pete said, "but your friend here will have to find his own way."

Lance's face turned crimson as he pursed his lips. Out of the corner of my eye, I caught Esther standing on the porch with her hands clasped beneath her chin and her eyes closed tightly. Was she praying?

"What's your problem, Pete?" Lance asked between gritted teeth. "Get off that buggy right now and come down here and tell it to my face. Let's settle this thing right now!"

"I don't need to tell you a thing," Pete said. "You know good and well the problems you have created for yourself, and my broken jaw isn't going to solve any of your problems."

"Maybe not, but it might teach you a little something about respecting a lady."

Pete looked ready to unleash a storm of vitriol. "If—"

But he was cut short by the other man, who grabbed his shoulder and whispered in his ear.

Pete sat up straight, regaining his composure. "Come along, John, if you like. Otherwise, we will expect to see you later."

"I would prefer to bring someone with me," I said.

"Anyone but him," Pete said, glaring at Lance.

"Would you men like a cup of hot tea or coffee and a fresh biscuit?" Esther asked softly from the porch.

"No, thank you," Pete replied.

"They're just out of the oven, and our Jamaican stock is fresh roasted." Esther made her way off the porch and approached the vehicle. "Maybe, dear sirs, if you took the time to get to know me, you would find out why your friend Lance has been taken in by a Negro woman."

As she spoke, her voice appeared to have a calming effect on the men. The scene took on a surreal feel as I watched it unfold.

"We'd love to, ma'am," the younger man said from the passenger side of the vehicle.

Wesley stiffened and turned sharply to glare at his partner.

"I didn't catch your name, sir," Lance said, reaching across Pete's rigid frame to glad-hand the man.

"Douglas French," he said. "Come along, Pete. Let's have some coffee and a biscuit."

French jumped out of the Chevy and came around to offer a handshake to Esther, who greeted him with a warm smile. He towered over her as he removed his derby, revealing thick dark hair flattened with hair oil. His fair skin contrasted sharply with his dark eyebrows and deep blue eyes.

"Is it Doug or Douglas?" she asked, smiling with her white teeth and taking his hand.

"It's Doug," he said. "I have always heard tell of this farm. It is as beautiful here as they say."

"Everything on this farm is beautiful, Doug!" Lance said, putting his hand on the man's shoulder as they started up the steps.

Doug paused to look back at Pete, who had remained in the vehicle. "Are you coming?"

Pete fumbled for a response, his arms folded tightly.

Esther stepped through the front entryway, leading Doug with the gayety of a princess.

I expected Pete to stay in the Chevy, red-faced and arms folded, but here he came. I couldn't believe my eyes.

"Come in," Esther said, "come in, please, and make yourself at home, Mr. Wesley. Will you have coffee or tea?"

"I guess I could have a cup of your coffee," he replied.

I caught Betty's eye, and she made a curious face as she leaned over and whispered in my ear, "So what is this hyena doing here amidst the meerkats?"

I didn't know how to explain what had just happened. People didn't have a change of heart like that, not without a good reason. I shrugged my shoulders, careful not to let anyone see our silent communication.

"Lance, that's quite a lion rug there," Doug said. "Where was that fellow taken?"

"John and I took him off the Rift Valley in o-eight. He's a fair lion and one I have always felt good about, but he wouldn't hold a candle to the one that boy took off the lower end of my farm yesterday."

"No kidding," Doug said. "This boy killed a lion yesterday?"

Jason beamed with pride and a confidence that I hadn't seen in him before, and Pete managed a smile, despite himself.

"Tell us the story," Doug said. "How'd you get him?"

Esther interrupted the conversation just long enough to direct her servants to pass out the coffee from a silver serving tray.

Jason continued to amaze me with his wit and vibrancy. As he sketched out every detail from the point at which he first spotted the animal, outlining his mistakes with lighthearted humor and not painting me out to be too great a villain, he held the men on the edge of their seats, leaving them hanging on his every word.

Storytelling was an age-old craft handed down through the generations from ancient times, when men used to wear animal skins and sit around a fire telling of heroic warriors, family ancestry, and great adventure. Their myths were overstated and exaggerated, told and retold, growing by the years in the minds of the tellers. It was, of course, one of the reasons I could never swallow the accounts of the Bible. Who knew what literary liberty had been taken while editing those manuscripts over the years in order to change the story into something seemingly incredible just so people might put money in a plate.

My goodness, how could anyone ever buy a story of a man parting the sea to free his enslaved people, or a virgin having a child, or a man walking on water? Let alone the biggest farce of them all: a man coming back from the dead after being hung on a cross. No, I didn't need all that magic to know that the world is an incredible place, a place so unbelievable that man has to invent stories to explain how we got here instead of coming to terms with the fact that it happened naturally without someone's magic wand.

"Can we show 'em the hide?" Jason asked at the conclusion of his story.

"Let's finish our coffee first," Betty said. "Esther, you need to tell them how you and Lance met. It's a Cinderella story, truly."

Pete tried to inconspicuously reach into his pocket and check his watch.

"Oh, they don't want to hear that," Esther said.

"Esther, no please, we would love to hear the story," Doug insisted.

"Tell them from the beginning," Betty encouraged.

Esther looked toward Lance for approval, and he gave her a silent nod to proceed.

"We've known each other since we were children. Lance was twelve, and I was eight. His father worked for my father in New York in the steel industry. You see, my mother and my father were white and could never have any children of their own. They rescued me from an orphanage when I was six. I always knew I was different from the other children, but my mother told me to ignore people's prejudice and just forgive them. She said I could never do anything about somebody else's problem and that all I could control was how I felt about them. She told me to never become angry with the failure of others to rise to your expectations.

"Our parents were close, and we both thought of each other more as a brother and sister. But one day we had a school dance that I had my heart set on attending, and Lance's mother arranged for him to take me. From that night on, I had a secret crush on him, but I knew he was out of my league. We lost touch after my father passed away, and my mother and I moved to Minnesota to be near her family. I stayed with her and cared for her with my aunt until she died ten years later of tuberculosis. Mother always said that family is the most important thing, next to our relationship with Christ.

"After her death, I moved to New York, where I pursued a career writing for a newspaper, and there I started a small street mission to save the lost. Finally, last fall I decided to make a trip here to Nairobi to start up a mission for the natives. Then, low and behold, when I got off the train, I came face-to-face with Lance.

"I never had a clue he would be here in Africa, and it seemed so strange to travel halfway around the world and find the love of your life. We had always denied what we had always known, and after I'd been here in Africa for just three short weeks, we were married. We knew it would be a bold move and that a lot of people wouldn't approve, but we knew that somehow our love would prevail. We decided it didn't matter who loved us; we would love them. Lance is still working on it, right, honey?" She caught his eye and gave him a cute little smile.

As Esther spoke, I looked around the room and tried to assess the attitudes and thoughts of each person. Pete's body language, with his arms folded across his chest, spoke volumes about his continued reluctance to accept Lance's marriage. I knew Pete was probably thinking about what his buddies back in town might say about coming inside and having coffee with us. Doug sat on the edge of his chair, hanging on Esther's every word, eager to get to know her, and was obviously taken by her black beauty and meticulous manner and speech. I could tell that Betty remained guarded about Doug's reactions and was waiting for the other shoe to drop. I knew she had very little trust that either man had accepted Esther, and I had no doubt she was ready to pounce on either of them should any part of this conversation go sideways.

"Tell us about your safari plans, John," Doug said. "The whole town is abuzz about it. You're not planning on taking that new Ford motorcar, are you?"

"That's the plan," I answered.

"I hope you brought lots of extra rubber tires," Pete said. "I'm afraid you're gonna spend more time fixing flats than it will be worth."

"I considered that," I said.

"You'll be cussing Henry Ford by the end of the first day," Pete said with a laugh. "I'm warning ya. Why don't you just take along a good horse? You'll be much happier."

"Oh, we have plenty of good horses," I said, "and we don't need the motorcar. But Henry Ford insisted."

"Oh yeah," Pete said, laughing once again. "I suppose Thomas Edison sent you along with some light bulbs, too."

"I'm serious," I said. "This car was a personal gift from Henry Ford."

"You're kidding," Pete said, dropping his jaw. "You're not kidding, are you?

"No, I'm not kidding," I said. "Henry Ford is a personal friend of mine."

"Well, we had best get along," Pete said, obviously still skeptical of whether or not I was pulling his leg.

"Thanks so much for the hospitality, Esther," Doug said with a wide grin that appeared sincere.

"John," Pete said, "can I give you guys a lift to town?"

"Does that mean Lance?" I asked.

"Sure does," he answered.

"Can I come, too?" Jason asked.

"It will be tight," Pete warned. "But sure, come along. We'll all squeeze in."

~~~~~~~~~

When we arrived in Nairobi, the railroad crew had just unloaded the Ford from the flatcar.

"Isn't she beautiful?" Lance said.

I jumped in on the seat and set the right lever all the way up, which was the spark advance, and then set the left lever down to give it just a little throttle. "Go ahead and give her a crank, Lance!" I knew I had to be ready on the spot with the spark to prevent a backfire that could break Lance's arm.

He put his back into it and gave it a quick jerk.

"I told you she'd start with one crank," I said.

"She purrs like a kitten, John," Lance said. "And look at that tread. It's got good rubber on it."

"She's even got a spare wheel, Lance," I said.

"We're gonna be in business," Lance said, "aren't we? There's a gross of extra tires and tubes, a jack, plenty of gas cans, extra oil, and spare parts."

"All compliments of the Ford Motor Company?" Pete asked. "How well do you know Henry Ford, anyways?"

"Oh, I've known him for years," I said. "I tried to get him interested in Africa, but he's got plenty of pursuits to keep him busy."

"Have you got a spot to hold on to that other crate right there, Pete?" Lance asked. "I'll send one of my boys along first thing in the morning to fetch it."

"We'll hold on to it for ya," Pete said.

"Couple more days prep," I said, "and we are off on safari."

"What have you got left to do?" Doug asked.

"Finalize our porters, settle up on the camel string, and load the wagons," Lance said. "We're still breaking up the loads, but we should have it all done day after tomorrow."

"Camel string?" he asked. "I've never heard of a safari using camels here in Kenya."

"Lance has a friend who brought them down from the north," I said.

"You'll have to hire armed guards," Pete said, "or else feed them piece by piece to the lions."

"Maybe," I said, "but my guess is that the lions won't bother them because they only eat what they are used to."

"Don't count on it," Pete said.

"We'll have armed guards," Lance said. "I have a few last minute things to get resolved on the farm before I take off for the bush, but everything looks to be on schedule."

"Lance, will you accept my apology for how I treated you?" Pete asked, extending his hand with a sheepish grin.

"Apology accepted," Lance said, taking his hand in a firm grip.

"I hadn't met her," Pete said. "I didn't know. I guess I let my prejudice get in the way of my common sense. She's a delightful woman, and I can see why you fell in love with her. Can you forgive me?"

"It takes a big man to say that, Pete," Lance said. "I can't tell you what this means to me, and I will always respect you for it."

"You men be careful out there," Pete said. "Have a great hunt, and watch over your women. It can be mean out there, but then I don't have to tell you that."

"We will, Pete," I confirmed.

"And don't let old dead-eye show you up!" Doug said, shaking Jason by the shoulder with a wide grin.

"We'll try to keep him humble," Lance said and laughed. "Grab those extra tins. I've got fourteen six-gallon tins of petrol at the farm. Let's stop by and give these to Philip so they're ready for pickup tomorrow morning."

I stayed behind the wheel while Jason and Lance lashed the extra tins on the back of the jalopy. They piled in the car, and off we went, both Pete and Doug waving from the train station.

I couldn't believe what had just happened. I saw an ugly disposition of hatred and resentment turn mild and sweet, with little or no explanation. I couldn't wipe the vision of Esther appearing to pray on her front porch, and I knew that if I had asked her, she would have attributed it to her god. It made me afraid to ask, but I knew that was exactly what she would say. But I wondered still: Had I just witnessed a miracle? Surely this was not on par with the parting of the Red Sea.

Chapter 11

THE WILD BLUE YONDER

As the first light filtered through the shadows of the acacia forest and glistened on the early morning dew, it made the tips of the grass sparkle like diamonds. Thursday morning had arrived, and finally, after all of the long months of preparation, our safari was about to begin. It was the second week of May.

There were six camels loaded with three hundred pounds each, sixty pounds more than a good packhorse. We had sixty-five good Somali and Kikuyu native porters who had been assigned loads and were ready to go. Lance, Esther, Jason, and Betty were saddled up on four of the eight steeds we had handpicked for the trip, while Chuck and I were ready to start off in the Ford. We had two mule-harnessed wagons loaded down with the heavy equipment, too heavy for our porters to lug, and the camels had already begun their groaning and crying like spoiled children.

We had been up early and eaten a hearty breakfast, and Lance's cooks had put together box lunches for us for the trail. Our gun bearers and guides waited anxiously for the signal from Willie, our safari headman, to give the word to roll out. It all seemed so strange, as if it were not really happening, the adventure of my life. I didn't dare pinch myself, for the fear that I might wake up in Chicago sitting behind some desk.

Lance rode up next to the motorcar, and his white horse had flared nostrils and wide eyes. He tried to hold tight the reins to control the mare, which was obviously spooked by the humming gasoline engine. "I think we are ready to go, aren't we?" he asked.

"We're ready," I said, "only I'm not too sure about the camels. Maybe I've just never been around them before, but the more I think of it, I'm afraid all we are doing is taking lion bait with us. Besides, they make such an annoying noise. I don't see why we didn't just get extra mules."

"Now come on, John. We've already discussed this, and I thought we had it settled. You know those were a gift from my friend up in the northern territory as a tribute to my American friends. He'll know if we don't use 'em. Heck, he sent them along with native handlers. I think that would be a real slap in his face if we don't use 'em."

"All right then," I said, shrugging my shoulders.

"I'll give Willie the word," Lance said, tugging on the reins and spinning his horse around.

Jason and Betty rode up as we were getting situated in our seats, with Buster following along behind Jason's horse.

"You be careful with that dog," Betty said. "Don't let these horses step on him."

"How about we take him with us in the car to start out?" I suggested.

"Here, Buster ... here, boy!" Chuck said from the front seat, coaxing the dog into the car.

Buster eagerly jumped into his lap.

"How does it feel to be sitting on a horse again, dear?" I asked.

"Like old times," she answered. "Makes me think about Mama."

We heard Willie yelling to the safari, and everybody responded at once, the porters lifting their bundled loads and chop boxes, the camels giving mean, dirty looks and lamenting and moaning to their camel boys, who rallied to bring the humpbacked animals to their feet.

Ahead lay Africa, her parched plains, harsh heat, drenching rains, night chill, choking dust, and soupy mud—hardship, danger, adventure, joy, and tragedy, all rolled into one.

Oh, if only there was a god, I thought. *Now might be a perfect time to pray. But as for me, hardly.*

My eye caught Betty sitting erect on her horse, and I thought how I loved her so. The thought of not bringing her back alive from this safari crossed my mind, and a shiver went down my spine. I worried whether or not I had made the right choice in bringing her here.

"Jason, you keep your eye on her!" I yelled as they trotted by to take up the head of the march.

Jason nodded and sat up just a little higher in his saddle, taking on the new responsibility.

"How many miles will we cover today?" Chuck asked.

"Oh, I suppose we'll be pushing eighteen or so. Lance wants to head northeast toward Mount Kenya and the Athi River. From there, we'll head toward the Tana River Valley and wind up on the east side of Mount Kenya. It's a good hundred-mile push till we hit the Tana, and then we'll loop north and hunt elephants along the plains and the east side of the foothills of Mount Kenya. We're in no hurry. This first leg of the safari should take us about a month. Then we'll head on into the northern territory and the equator country.

We sat in awe as the porters passed, lugging their load on their shoulders and singing merrily their strange Somali tune.

"How 'bout we jump in front of the mule carts, John?" Chuck said. "There will be a lot less dust."

"Yes, I know, but Lance and I agreed the Lizzy would take up the rear for the first day. After that, once we are in game country and the safari has a day under its belt, the car can move up. We can even head out on some side excursions. It's what we agreed to."

Chuck shrugged his shoulders, not wanting to disagree.

~~~~~~~~~

The first day's march left me feeling fulfilled. The scenery was typical of Africa, with her grassy plains, dotted acacia trees, and thick mopane (mo-poney) forests. We saw plenty of animals, and each time Chuck quickly trained his field glasses on them to identify any potential trophies. This part of the African scene had been heavily shot for ten years now by the hordes of tourists seeking to get a quick kill; thus the trophies here were few and far between. That was the main reason why we were pushing far into the interior of the African bush.

The Lizzy proved to be a successful ride, not having to negotiate anything too difficult as we motored painfully slow across mainly flatlands. We had made about eighteen miles when, toward the late afternoon, we saw the party gathering up at what I assumed was a suitable campsite. I goosed the motor and ran on ahead of the end of the long line of porters, on past the camel string, and approached Lance and the others getting off their horses. Betty turned to see us coming and gave a big grin as she rubbed her bottom with both hands.

"It has been a long time since I've been on a horse for six hours!" she shouted.

Willie began barking orders to his lead camp men. They scurried off, helping others to drop loads, and then they quickly dispersed like ants and began to make a city out of the flat spot Willie had selected. Lance brushed the dust off his breeches after handing his lead to a horse boy, who quickly led the horse away. I shut down the Ford's purring engine, bringing a welcome silence.

"We did well today," Lance said. "There's plenty of game here, too. We can try a hunt in the morning if you want, or we can push on for another day."

"I'd like to get to some kudu country before we start a hunt," I answered.

"We'd have to go all the way to the Ewaso Nyiro River," Lance said. "That's a good two hundred and fifty kilometers from here."

"Well, maybe not that far. But you know, Lance, there's plenty of good kudu ground in the hills around the Athi River, and that's just a couple of days away. I think we should push on at least a couple of days before we fire up the guns."

When Buster spotted Jason making his way toward the car with Betty and Esther, his ears perked up and he leaped off the back of the Ford and sprinted for his boy.

"We'll keep our eyes peeled in the meantime," I continued, "but I'll guarantee you won't find any fifty-inch kudu here in the tourist belt."

"I know what we decided," Lance said. "I'm just getting anxious, that's all."

Chuck eased off the passenger seat and stretched his back. "How was the horse ride, Jason?" he asked.

"He took to it like a duck to water!" Betty answered, grabbing Jason's shoulder as the boy sported a big grin.

Meanwhile, as we talked about the day, our camp boys were split into work parties, some gathering wood for the fires, others cutting thornbush to make a *boma* (camp perimeter), and still others setting up our tents. The camels and the horses were tied safely inside the protection of the boma to insulate them from lion attacks during the night. Every porter had a job, and in what seemed like a matter of minutes, the fires were lit and the table and chairs were set up. Washbasins were filled with warm water, and clean towels were provided for us. Willie clenched his teeth, tugging on a corkscrew that popped as it separated from a bottle of wine, and he began filling cups set out on the table covered with a white linen.

"Sit, *Bwana* (Master). Sit, *Memsahib* (Mistress)," Willie said as Betty and I stood waiting to eat. "Has been long day for you. Bamira serve dinner now."

Betty and I took a seat, then Chuck and Lance pulled up chairs, each grabbing for a tin cup, and we sat around the table, sipping wine and discussing the events of the day.

"Where is Esther?" Betty asked.

"She's with some of the natives," Lance said, "translating Scripture into Swahili. The woman has been devoted to explaining the Gospel to them since she first set foot in Africa. She told me that coming on safari would only increase her efforts."

I started to make a comment, but as my lips began to form disdain for the Bible, I noticed out of the corner of my eye Betty's piercing gaze, which told me to hold my tongue. I stopped short, knowing Lance's heartfelt love for his wife's work. Moreover, I had come to respect Betty's wisdom in matters of the heart.

"Did you see that rhino track we crossed today?" I asked.

"Looked like a cow and a calf to me," Betty said. "But did you see the zebra and wildebeest?"

"Beautiful," I answered.

Just then, Esther approached the camp and without a word quietly took a seat next to Lance, giving him a kiss on the cheek before glancing around and offering her warm smile.

"Amazing how these animals have evolved and adapted to their environment, isn't it?" I remarked.

"Evolved?" Esther asked. "What do you mean, *evolve*?"

"Are you sure you want to discuss such matters?" I answered, knowing I had the upper hand when it came to arguing, since I had all the evidence and all she had was her faith.

"So make your point," she said, folding her arms. "Explain *evolve*."

I had not seen this side of Esther before, and it made me sit back for a moment to consider her intent. At the same time, I couldn't help admiring her spunk.

"Evolve is a term that needs no explanation," I said.

"Then tell me, John," she said, piercing my soul with her dark eyes, "do you not agree that the zebra is the main food source for the lion?"

"Yes, I suppose I would have to agree with you."

"And would you not agree," she continued "that, because of the zebra's coloring, they are much easier for the lion to spot at night?"

"Yes, I would have to agree that the zebra sticks out like a sore thumb on the African plains in the moonlight." I felt as if she was trying to lead me down some primrose path that went nowhere.

"Then tell me, good sir, if the zebra has evolved into the lion's main food source over millions of years, why, pray tell, has his coat not evolved into a more suitable color that would protect him?"

I thought about her question, but I stood at wit's end. Admittedly, she had stumped me, and I didn't have an answer for her. I thought for a moment and then offered one plausible explanation. "The zebra did adapt to their surroundings," I said, "but now those surroundings have changed."

"Nice try," she said and smiled.

"Their stripes might tend to confuse the lions when they are grouped together," I suggested. "The lion doesn't know where one stops and the other begins."

"That's a thought," she said, seemingly amused by our sparring, "but let me tell you, from God's perspective, everything here on earth is put here for His purpose. Each creature gives a silent lesson about God and His glory, for the benefit of all who have the ears to hear and the eyes to see. He intended for the zebra to live here as well as any other animal on the plains, including the lion. He created the zebra to be the main food source for the pride, and that is why he gave them a coat suitable for a stalk."

"And tell me, dear, what do the zebra tell us about this god of yours and His glory?" It was my turn to stump her.

"This animal teaches a story about sin and judgment," Esther answered. "Can you see it?"

"No."

"The zebra is actually a white horse, which represents God's purity stained with the sin of man," Esther said, her white teeth sparkling. "As the zebra clearly demonstrates, even a little sin stains him from his nose to his tail. It's a stain not easily seen in man, but it's there on the zebra for all to see. Every line represents one of man's sins and gives us a total picture of how many sins man is accountable for. The lion represents God's judgment of man. In our blindness we ask, why did God make their life so miserable here on the plains of the Serengeti? God says that, as teachers of humanity, they are held to a higher accountability and they must pay for man's sins here on earth. As for man, he will pay for his own sin in eternity, unless of course he has a savior."

The pomposity of her statement, combined with its implied judgment of me and my supposedly sinful nature, made my blood boil. "What about your skin, Esther? Are you saying that you are stained with man's sin?"

Her eyes softened, and she answered me with a soft voice that could have melted butter. I had been sure she would react in anger, but her grace shined true. "Here is how it works, John. God loves humility, but he hates pride. He tests humanity in every way possible, and so he uses the evils of sin as a consuming fire to strengthen His saints. Sort of like cooking fires: they can burn you if you use them wrong. You see, what Satan intended for evil, God meant to strengthen us through our suffering.

"It's like pruning a good apple tree. The tree sees his branches cut off, but the farmer prunes it so that the tree might bear good fruit. I may have to live with dark skin, and I may struggle my whole life living in humility among white folks. But in the end, my ability to keep this humility and live in peace and harmony as a black woman who serves God will bring me far greater blessings in eternity than any earthly pride to be white. Now, I'm not saying I'm proud to be black, because that would bring me face-to-face with the same sin, but I am talking about true humility—the kind of humility it takes to find God in the first place."

The group went dead silent as her words echoed in our ears like a clap of thunder in the mountains. No one spoke a word as we sat quietly and sipped our wine.

"Smell that dinner cooking?" Lance asked, finally breaking the ice. "I'm starved."

"What do you think Bamira has brewing for our first camp meal?" asked Chuck.

"He started working on tonight's dinner yesterday at the farm," Esther said. "I think he cooked up a pot of stew, and if you've never had Bamira's stew, you're in for a treat."

~~~~~~~~~

We sat around the cooking fire for a while after dinner, and the men told the women adventure stories from past hunts. Esther and Betty listened politely, but Jason hung on every word, lapping at them like a thirsty dog. The African night brought a welcome relief from the day's scorching heat. It also drew out numerous animals that in the day had stayed hidden in the shade of the thornbush. Over the crackling of the flames, we could periodically hear a hyena laugh or a zebra squeak. We could also hear the groans of a lion off in the distance and were comforted that he remained far away. Our camels and horses presented inviting pickings for a hungry pride. Every night we could avoid an encounter with a marauder out here in the plains of Africa was like a gold piece in a piggy bank.

"I'm ready to retire," Chuck said. "How about you?"

I pulled my watch from my pocket to check the time. "Yep, me, too. It's nine-thirty. We'll be up early again and on the march too soon. Come on, kiddo," I said after standing up and taking Betty's hand, "let's get some shuteye."

"Good night, everybody," she said. "See you in the morning."

As we stepped away from the flickering firelight, I gazed up at the vast array of stars. "My goodness, Betty, just look at the universe. Isn't that incredible? You sure don't see 'em like that back in Chicago, do you?"

"Makes you wonder what's out there, doesn't it?" she answered. "Where is the Big Dipper?"

"No Big Dipper. You grew up in the northern hemisphere. There is no Big Dipper here."

"Oh, you're right," she answered with a big smile that shone in the light from the campfire.

"I almost decided to study astronomy," I said. "It was a toss-up between that and anthropology. I'm glad I followed the path I took, but how fascinating the sky is! I often wish I knew more about the stars. Maybe I'll decide to be an astronomer in my next life."

Betty chuckled as she ducked under the fly of our tent. As I stood gazing up at the sky, I could still hear Esther's words echoing in my head. If it were true, if this god really existed, why wouldn't he just show himself? Why did he have to make life so difficult? Why did he have to remain so silent? Why did he have to leave men lingering for answers? I ducked into the tent, took off my boots, kissed my wife, and fell fast asleep.

Michael D. Neil

Chapter 12

BEAUTY LOST

I awoke with a start. I had an eerie feeling something was dreadfully wrong. I listened intently for any noise that might be out of the ordinary. I held up my hand, but I couldn't see anything. The firelight had stopped flickering against the side of the tent, and there was a ghostlike silence. Why was I so spooked? More importantly, why had the fires gone out?

Suddenly out of nowhere came the roar of a lion, followed by a bloodcurdling scream.

I grabbed my Springfield lying beside me and leaped out of bed.

"What is it, John?" Betty asked.

"I don't know, but I intend to find out. Wait here!"

I threw on my pants and slipped on my boots. When I threw open the tent flap, Lance had just emerged from his tent, rifle in hand.

"Sounds like it came from down there," he said in the darkness.

"Those damn fools let the fires go out," I growled. "If anyone's been hurt, somebody is going to pay hell."

"I'm going with you!" Jason said as he ran from the lower end of the camp.

Chuck followed, breathing hard, at his heels.

"No, you guys stay here and guard the tents. And Jason, get your finger off that trigger. We've got a lion in camp, but let's not make it worse by adding a madman with a rifle."

Lance put his finger to his lips, then motioned me to follow. The weight of the Springfield in my hand gave me a measure of comfort.

I clicked the safety off and then snapped it back, just to make sure. I thought of the famous Bible verse, "Yea, though I walk through the valley of the shadow of death, I will fear no evil: for thou art with me; my rod and my staff they comfort me." I didn't know who'd written it, and I didn't know if I had even quoted it correctly, probably not. But I knew one thing: my rifle sure comforted me now.

"Sounded to me like the noise came from down there by the camels," Lance whispered.

We crept cautiously toward where they were tied off, careful not to make a sound, and as my eyes began to adjust to the darkness, I could see the camels' eyes, wide with terror. Their legs were stiff, and the ropes were taut against the ties. A dark pool and a drag mark revealed the obvious fate of someone.

Lance reached down and touched the wet mark, then rubbed it between his fingers. "It's blood," he whispered.

Just then a branch cracked over our heads, and a chill went up my spine. I jerked my rifle up, my sights trained in the direction of the noise.

"*Tafadhali, usifyatue!* (Please, don't shoot!)," a frantic camel jockey said, clutching at a branch.

I took a deep breath and tried to relieve the knot in my throat.

"*Simba ... simba!* (Lion!)," the camel boy shouted and pointed toward the drag mark.

I took a step in that direction, but stopped after Lance put my arm in a vice grip.

"No," he warned, "this is suicide. There is nothing you can do now except let them have their meal."

"Are you crazy? I heard a scream, and I think they got one of our boys."

"No," Lance said, "that was a camel scream. I knew it the minute I heard it."

"No," I said, trying to recreate the sound in my mind.

"Yes, that was a camel. Look here."

One of the hemp ties hung limp among the tethered camels, frayed and broken at the end.

The camel boy leaped out of the tree and picked up the broken rope in the darkness. "*Rafiki yangu* (my friend)," he said.

I could see only the whites of his eyes. I reached out and put my hand on his shoulder, trying to comfort him. "*Pole rafiki yangu* (I am sorry, my friend)," I said.

The hideous laughter from hyenas began to echo across the plains, and we could hear lions growling as they began to defend their dinner.

"Let's go get some sleep," Lance said and then stopped to issue an order when he saw Willie approaching. "Hey, let's get some men over here on these fires — now!"

"You better find out who let these fires die," I demanded, "and this better not happen again!"

"Yes, Bwana!" Willie turned and began rattling off Swahili, gathering his forces like an invading army.

As we walked back to the tents, men scurried to rebuild the campfires.

"Now I'm thinking it would have been a good idea to post armed guards around the animals," I said.

"We've already thought this through," Lance said. "Would you rather lose an animal or duck stray bullets all night? Besides, the lions wouldn't have come in if they hadn't let the fire go out."

"Who was it?" Betty asked, emerging from our tent and running to meet me.

"Oh, it was just one of the camels," I said. "Our camp boys fell asleep and let the fires go out. But Willie knows, and it won't happen again. The excitement is over. Let's get some shuteye around here. Morning will come soon enough."

~~~~~~~~~

I slid out of my cot and slipped on my clothes at first light, hoping not to wake Betty.

"Should I get up?" she asked.

"I'm gonna go find that camel carcass and take some revenge on a lion."

"I'm going with you!" she said, bouncing from her cot and dressing in a flash. She grabbed her rifle and then checked the action.

I threw open the tent flap and started to march on down toward the place where the camels had been tied.

The camp boys were up, and Bamira had breakfast going. I grabbed a couple of muffins and poured us some coffee. Betty and I stood with our rifles slung over our shoulders, hurriedly sipping our coffee while the steam from our cups rose like dancing ballerinas.

"I hope the lions didn't get Lilly," Betty said.

"Who is Lilly?" I asked.

"When we left yesterday, Moodu, one of the camel boys, introduced me to his pride and joy. She is so lovely and gentle. He called her something like *Lyeily*. I thought she was so beautiful. I called her Lilly. He told me to scratch her ear, and she kissed me on the cheek."

"Chances are pretty slim the lion singled her out," I said, hoping to comfort her.

"I hope so. I just hope ..." Betty paused in silence without finishing her thought. "I'll know her. She's the only one with a red harness."

"Are you finished with your coffee?" I asked.

She nodded.

"Come on. Let's go."

We made our way to the place where they had been tied the night before, but all the camels were gone. The single broken rope still hung from the tether. We could see the blood and the prominent drag mark, as well as a good-sized lion track in the dirt.

"The camel boys must have taken them for a drink before today's long march begins. Let's follow this drag," I said, pointing in the direction of the skid mark.

Following the trail didn't exactly require the skills of a master tracker. We had gone about a hundred meters when we came to a place where the lions had devoured the camel. Nothing remained except a few scraps of camel hide and a pile of green stomach contents. Lion and hyena tracks littered the area.

"Here's where they ate most of it. Look here," I said, pointing to the lion track. "Let's follow him. See here where he dragged the remains of the carcass, trying to keep it away from the hyenas?"

We continued about a mile when Betty spotted vultures circling a baobab tree. We approached cautiously, so as not to spook anything.

"If you get a chance at something," I whispered, "even a hyena, take the vermin."

Betty gave me a puzzled look and wrinkled her nose. "What about the curse? I thought it was bad luck to kill a hyena."

"I don't know if I swallow all that hogwash," I answered.

Then we spotted a horde of vultures working on the remains of the carcass. Despite our best attempts to be secretive, they spotted us and flew from the leftovers in a thundering cloud. The lion was long gone, and the camel had been dismembered far beyond any recognition. Its scattered, picked-clean bones resembled nothing of a majestic camel. We looked for the head, but I figured the hyenas had probably carried it off. Betty, scouring the area like a detective at the scene of a murder case, walked toward the base of a tree.

I moved cautiously, making sure not to let her out of my sight, and stepped over another bush. As I did, I kicked something with my foot and nearly tripped. I looked back to see the obstacle, and there lay the nearly unrecognizable tattered skull of the camel, still wearing the remains of a broken red harness.

"What is it?" she asked, surprised at my clumsiness.

"Nothing ... nothing but a rock."

"Nothing, you say? Don't toy with me, John."

I groaned.

"John?"

"Okay, it's a camel head, if you must know."

"Tell me it doesn't have a red harness!"

"I wish I could."

Betty's eyes welled with tears, and her lip began to quiver. "This is what I was afraid of all along."

"We'll give her a proper burial if you like," I said.

"Those thieving scoundrels—I'll kill every last one of them, so help me, John." Betty's face turned red as she gazed down at the torn head of her camel friend. "Moodu must be sick to lose her. I don't understand it, John. Why? If there is a God, why does He allow this sort of thing? She was so beautiful ... so ... oh damn!"

"You're asking me? Fat chance of me explaining that one to you. It's just nature—cold, cruel, impersonal nature. There is no god thing about it, as far as I'm concerned, only random chance. The poor damn camel got in the way of a lion, that's all."

"There has got to be more than that," she said through tears. "I can't explain it, but there has to be more. I just don't understand it, that's all."

"I don't see what there is to understand," I said. "It's life and death. No less, no more. We better get back before we miss breakfast."

Betty and I hightailed it back to camp. I felt relatively unaffected by the death of the camel. But I could see it in Betty's eyes and hear it in the vibrato of her voice as she fought to contain her grief.

So what? I thought. *A camel dying means one less crying baby to keep me awake at night. Maybe it's one less mouth to feed, and maybe it's a few more pounds for the porters. Should I care? Would I say, good riddance? Surely not, I should hope, and if that is my attitude, what sort of wretch am I? Do I deserve a place in the natural order of things? Why can't I share in this tenderness of heart with my life partner? Why am I so cold and so dark?* I had known for years that I couldn't outrun my grief, and yet I had always tried to stay one step ahead of its open jaw. How might life have been if my son hadn't died? What joy would he have brought to Betty and our marriage? When I looked on the face of Jason, I couldn't help wondering what might have been.

Betty's footsteps echoed mine as we traversed the African bush together. Her heavy breathing reminded me of the intimacy we shared. I stopped dead in my tracks, pausing to catch my breath, and then embraced her, just to smell her hair.

"What is it?" she asked.

"Can you feel it?" I asked.

"What?"

I closed my eyes and inhaled deeply the African morning, gathering as I did the fragrance of the red-flowered wild aloe, the bloom of the whistling thorns. I kept my eyes closed and listened to the music of a thousand birds feeding across the vast forest canopy.

"I can't believe we are sharing this together. How often I have wished secretly you could be here! Yet I was certain you would never come, and certain I would never find the courage to allow it."

"Well, I am here now, and that's all that matters, isn't it?"

"But can you feel it?" I asked, hoping that she would catch the vision.

"I don't know," she said, closing her eyes.

"It's the pulse of the blood that pumps through her veins, Betty. Africa is alive!"

"I hear it, but it doesn't take away my pain," she said. "It doesn't fill the void left in my heart. How could you have left me all those years when I needed you the most? Don't you know how it hurt me, John? Don't you know how much I needed you?"

"I knew. Believe me, I knew. But I had to deal with my own pain in my own way. I wanted to run away, and you wanted to be alone. I couldn't take it. Everything around me reminded me of his smile and his laughter. In that old house he is everywhere. I could hear his voice and his footsteps, and the hurt always remained. When I looked into your eyes, I saw his. Africa seemed like the only thing that could ease my pain. Here everything made sense. I could focus on something else besides my troubles. Every time I came home, I lived with a pit in my stomach, waiting for the chance to escape again. I know you must have thought our love was drifting. I have to admit now, looking back, our love was dying, and I didn't even realize it. I had contentment in Africa, and I just couldn't get enough. Can you ever forgive me, darling?"

"I will. I do. I already have. And oh, by the way, John, I can feel Africa, and now I know it, too."

I grabbed her in my arms and kissed her lips, lingering for a moment to share the passion.

Her arms slipped around my shoulders, and her finger caressed the hair on the back of my neck.

"You're my best friend, Betty," I said, pulling away and looking deep into her eyes.

"Better than Lance?" she asked with a chuckle.

"Way better than Lance."

We laughed, then I took her hand and we walked back to camp, our rifles slung over our shoulders, our feet kicking up dust, and our hearts flying high, like a couple of school children who'd just kissed on the playground for the first time.

As we approached the *boma* (camp perimeter), we could smell the sweet aroma of sizzling wild hog in the layer of smoke that hung low over camp.

Jason spotted us and came running, with Buster hot on his heels. "What did you find?" he asked.

"A mutilated and dismembered camel," I said. "But we missed the banquet, all except for a few uninvited guests." I reached down and gave Buster a rub of the ears.

"Bamira cooked up the pork scraps for Buster," Jason said.

"Grab a plate," Lance said. "There's fresh wild boar and muffins. Did you find the lion?"

"No," Betty said, "just a pile of vultures."

The camp boys were finishing up packing the last of the tents and loading gear into the chop boxes.

"Runner!" Willie shouted, pointing toward the grasslands.

There in the distance I could see a dark figure, probably six hundred yards off, making his way toward our camp.

"Who would it be?" Betty asked.

"Messenger," Willie said.

"I hate this," I said. "It always makes me think somebody is bringing me bad news." I took a bite of bacon, and the salty taste permeated my mouth. "Wow, you don't find bacon like this at home, do you?"

"How far will a runner like this one go before he rests?" Chuck asked.

"He probably curled up on a tree branch during the night," Lance said, "but I'd guess he can run twelve hours. See that water cast over his shoulder?"

"What tribe is he?" Betty asked.

"Oh, he's a Somali," Esther said. "He's got to be."

My anticipation and apprehension grew as the runner drew closer.

"I hope nothing has happened on the farm," Lance said.

"I hope nothing has happened at home in Chicago," Betty said.

Some of our men began to run from camp to meet the runner and escort him back. Everyone looked on solemnly without saying a word.

My mind began to race with possibilities. I looked toward Lance, and the color had gone out of his face. Betty looked up and wrinkled her nose.

Moments later, the runner came waltzing into camp scarcely out of breath. He broke his stride and walked the last few yards to our cooking fires, where we stood finishing up our breakfast. Mumbling in Somali, he handed a bent and wrinkled envelope to Willie, who glanced at the addressee before handing me the letter.

"Betty," I said, "looks like it belongs to you."

"Is it from Mae?" Betty asked. She took the letter as if it were a precious jewel, cradling it in her palms like a mother with a newborn. "Hope it's not bad news," she said, looking up and batting her precious long eyelashes. "She is probably answering my letter I sent her from London."

Lance pulled a glistening ten-inch skinning knife from his belt, handing it to her, and Betty carefully slit open the envelope, pulling out the folded letter.

"How much do I pay him, Willie?" I asked as the runner stood waiting.

"You can start by offering him some breakfast," Lance said. "Then you can pay him whatever you think he is worth. But remember, if it is too much, our porters will be mad, and if it is too little, we probably won't get him or anyone else to come out here again."

Willie nodded to confirm Lance's advice.

"Then I won't pay him," I said. "Here's a pocketful of change. Willie, you pay him."

"Oh, John, it's a wonderful letter," Betty said. "Do you want me to read it out loud?"

"I'll read it after you. Go ahead and savor every line."

"She says she misses me," Betty said. "Oh, John, I miss her, too. I didn't realize how much, but I do miss her so." Betty's eyes moved over the creased pages as she consumed the words like a wild dog. I noticed that Willie had taken the runner aside and begun counting out coins in his eager hand with a wide grin across his face. Bamira brought him a tin of posho and some strips of pork belly.

"Keep your eyes peeled today for trophies," Lance said. "If we get a chance at anything good, we'll take it. Then tomorrow morning we'll start the day out with a hunt for a kudu. How does that sound, John?"

Jason perked up with a wide grin of his own.

"The camp boys have consolidated your personal gear from your tent," Lance continued. "It's right over there in that duffle."

As Bamira and his boys broke up the cooking fire, I made ready the Ford and put my things in the car.

"Here's the letter, dear," Betty said, handing me the page. "Enjoy. I think she wrote this letter before she got my letter from London."

"You be careful on that horse," I insisted. "You hear me?"

Betty leaned over and gave me a kiss on my neck, then turned and headed off in a hurry toward the makeshift camp corral where we had kept the horses overnight. She paused and glanced back with her cute little smile. I took a seat in my Ford, unfolded Mae's letter, and then eased back in the soft cushioned seat to enjoy her words like a big ice cream soda.

My dearest Betty, and John and Jason, too,

Yur Mammy Mae dint know how much empti there would be here after you left. I think sometimes this big old house shurr be full of spooks. My heart aches for you when I member all the laffter we shared in here. I dont mean to throw cold juice on yur time with John and Jason cause I do hopes you are having a nice time of it in Africa. I juss pray that you wont daside not to come home to me when you are done.

I em so lonely here I even fine myself eager for the iceman ta visit. Oh yea, hes the same one we laffed at with the personality of a dead duck. Member how we use to laff that his product matched the tempature of his soul? Well, I ackshualy got him to tawk the other day when I did telled him how lonesome it is here for me. He told me bout his family, an I foune out that he an his wife loss a son lass year to some sickness I culdnt say. Anyways, he telled me he was lonely, too, and we tawked a bunch. He says hes really shy an its hard for him to make frens. Funny how along we thought he was a stick in the mud an he was juss fraid to speak out. Sure is funny how we think we got him all figgerred out when we dint know nothin.

Rite now Mammy Mae prays ever day that God will watch over you and keep you safe an even since you only been gone a week maybe since when you get this letter youd be deep in Africa. Please member all what Mammy tells ya bout bein safe, my dear heart. If anything ever happen to you, I wood surly die in my heart. You know, baby cake, my lammy pie. I hope the days will pass fast for you in all you aventure, but member my days move here like a snail. If I stay bussy an keep my mind on my work at dustin and keeping up this house, what I know you like it seems better for me and I know you be home afor I can say lickety-split.

Take care, my darling, an give some of my love to my John and to Jason.

Till then and soon, love always,
Yur Mammy Mae

I chuckled to myself as I tried to ignore the bad grammar, misspelled words, and lack of punctuation. It was hard to hold back the professor in me. But this was what made Mae so precious. She wasn't in any way pretentious, but was still self-confident in her own way. She had sent this letter off knowing it had flaws, but it didn't matter. I knew these words came straight from her heart, and if they had been perfect, they wouldn't have come from her.

Betty came walking back across the camp toward the Ford, and I jumped out to meet her.

"What is it?" I asked. "I thought we were going."

"Oh, they're still saddling up, and it'll be a few minutes yet. Did you read the letter?"

"Isn't she something?" I said.

"I do miss her, John. But tell me again that we'll be fine, that you won't let the rhinos get us, that some lion won't haul us out of our tent feet first and devour us."

Finally, I thought. After all my preaching, it had finally sunk in.

"I guess that's what they say," I responded. "Feet first: who would figure? Somehow it seems out of character for a lion. I think they will grab you wherever they can and then bite the top of your head."

"Thanks for the reassurance, John. That's what I'm afraid of. I know their character. They are killers, and they love it. They don't worry that they might be ruining somebody's day. I just don't want them to ruin mine."

"Betty, you stay close to that rifle and stay alert. We'll be fine — you'll see. We don't exactly have any other choices, unless you want to go back."

"I'm not saying I want to go back, unless you want me to. I think you're just trying to scare me with that lion story."

"I don't want to scare you, but I'm glad to see that you are finally taking this all very seriously. We're not going back, believe me!" I gave a little smile and a chuckle to keep her spirits up.

She looked up with those big beautiful brown eyes and batted her eyelashes.

"Hey," I said, "here comes Willie with your horse."

Betty turned quickly to catch a glimpse of Willie, then kissed me again and ran off to greet him.

Wow, I thought, watching her backside as she trotted off, *what a beautiful woman I have to love*.

Chapter 13

MORE THAN THIS?

O nce again, Chuck and I took up the rear of the march. The thought of entrusting Jason to watch over my wife, who was my most treasured possession, kept rattling in my head, and it gave me a pit in my stomach.

Our porters looked like ants trailing back to their colony while carrying bits and crumbs they'd found at a Sunday picnic in the park. They were a dedicated lot, carrying out their task with very few complaints. Without their help, we wouldn't have been on safari at all.

"What do you think about me riding horseback tomorrow with Betty?" I asked. "You can drive, and Jason can ride shotgun."

"That's fine if you would rather be with her than me," Chuck answered, tongue in his cheek.

"Actually, I would prefer it if Betty would ride in the car with both of us, but I know that will never happen. I may as well try to wrestle a bull elephant; it would be easier than getting her off that horse."

Chuck sat silently, clearly thinking about my proposal. "Maybe *I* wanted to take a horse for a while," he finally said.

"Too bad we can't find a place to park this hunk of bolts," I said. "We could cover it up with sticks and pick it up on the way back in two months."

"Why would you say that?" he asked.

"Because it's been easy going until now, but just wait. We are going to be fighting this thing and cursing it before this safari is over. That's my prediction."

"Oh, I suppose," he said, "but I am really starting to appreciate this ride. I say as long as we can keep the wheels turning, we should have it with us. Besides, if somebody gets hurt, this car will be nice to have. You just never know."

"So what do you say, old chap? Will you be okay for a couple of days without me?"

"You'll owe me," he said and laughed. "I don't know about having to spend a couple days alone with that kid."

"I always do!" I laughed to myself as I thought back to our work at the college. Every time Crawford did me a favor, like finding me a substitute professor or another grant to continue my work, he would have this attitude like I owed him something.

I looked ahead and tried to figure out why our safari had slowed to such a snail's pace. I kept trying to hold back the speed on this bucket of bolts, and then I noticed something holding up the line.

"What's going on up there?" I asked. "For heaven's sake, what the hell is the holdup now?"

Only about half of the porters were visible to us because the front of the line had entered the heavy trees and brush, about two hundred yards ahead. Suddenly men tossed their loads and began scattering like a flock of quail.

"Get your rifle, Chuck!"

He responded instantly, reaching over the backseat for the blue steel and bringing it to the front, where he quickly checked the action.

A cloud of dust rose from the edge of the trees as Chuck brought his rifle up at the ready.

"Okay, here he comes!" I yelled as I reached down and cut the engine.

The car went silent.

"Don't let him turn," I said, "but watch out for the ..." I felt my jaw drop.

"It's a rhino!" Chuck exclaimed.

"Of course it's a rhino! Shoot him, damn it! But watch out for the porters!"

Chuck lined up on him, taking a rest across the front windshield of the Ford.

"Hold it!" I said.

"Why?"

"It's a cow with a calf," I said.

Chuck lifted the barrel of his rifle, pulling off the shot, and the rhino trotted harmlessly away from our troops.

"Looks like everybody is okay," Chuck said as the calf ran behind his mother like a little puppy with an oversized set of shoes.

"She's no trophy," I said. "Take a look at that pathetic horn. Besides, that little one is probably a future hulk. There just isn't any sense in shooting her if you don't have to."

"If you kill her," Chuck said, "you would be killing the little guy, too."

We sat in awe while the locomotive steamed by pulling the little caboose, which was kicking up a cloud of dust. The pair finally disappeared into the bush again.

"Wow," I said, shaking my head, "the only thing missing was the bellowing smoke pouring out of her stack."

Just then Lance broke out of the trees in a full gallop on his horse, looking like Paul Revere and shouting wildly.

"Hey, crank this thing and let's get up there!" I yelled.

Chuck jumped out, and we fired up the Ford. He then came running back around and jumped back in his seat, hanging onto Buster's collar. I popped the clutch and spun the tires in the soft red dirt, tossing a trail of sand and dust behind us as we lurched forward.

"Come on!" Lance shouted in a panic.

My heart pumped. Something terrible had happened to Betty.

"She gored one of our porters and stomped another! Bring the bandage kit!" Lance jerked the reins on his horse, spinning her, and then galloped off full bore, kicking up dirt as he went on toward the porters.

Some of the men began climbing down out of the trees, and as we approached, others were picking up gear they had left strewn in haste. I saw Betty cradling the head of a black man bleeding from the groin, and Esther clung to the arm of another who struggled while she tried to help him to his feet. I hit the brakes as we pulled up and came skidding to a stop.

"I'll get the kit," Chuck said.

I jumped out, running for Betty to render assistance. Blood covered the black man from the tear in his side.

"We've got to stop the bleeding," Betty said in a panic, "or we'll lose him!"

Chuck ripped open the kit and came up with some clean cotton towels. "Here," he said, "hold this on the wound."

"What about his innards hanging out?" she screamed.

"I don't know," I answered. "I'm not a doctor. Push them back in!"

"Oh, John, help me!" she pleaded.

Esther arrived and spoke Swahili to the man, who managed a faint response. She looked up with her big brown eyes, tears coming off her cheeks. "This is a man who accepted Christ just last night at our talk around the fire," she said.

"We're losing him," Betty said as the man's eyes rolled back and his feet began to kick the dirt.

"I suppose that makes everything okay," I said to Esther, "because you think he's saved."

Esther looked up with her gentle, loving eyes that could have melted the heart of a rhino. "If that gives me peace," she answered in her soft voice, "why should that matter to you?"

"It doesn't matter to me," I responded, "except that it keeps getting shoved down my throat. And now I have to worry about who is going to carry this man's gear."

"John, stop it—right now!" Betty said. "I know there's more inside of you than that. For Pete's sake, a man has just died here. Try to show a little compassion."

Right then I began to rethink my thoughts. I couldn't have been as cold and dead inside as I made myself out to be. Could this be a sour note that prevented others from singing along with me? I realized I had no idea where I might be headed into eternity, but I felt safe to utter these silent questions to myself. If only the Bible had been written more scientifically and not like a fairytale.

I knew that Darwin had stumbled upon something brilliant. There had been nowhere to turn for man until Darwin had developed his theory of evolution. And now the very foundation of man's faith had been shaken. When the missing link was found from monkey to man, the final kill shot would be delivered to this quivering beast called religion. It would be a shot heard round the world, and to whoever found the missing link, there would come inevitable fame and fortune.

How desperately I longed to be the one to pull the trigger, to shake people like Esther to their senses, to bring them out of their dream world. But what did they see in life that I couldn't? Was it possible that I refused to look at life from their backward perspective? Or did they just have their heads so far in the clouds that they were in a fog? I was thankful that I didn't need such a crutch to stand on my own two feet. Man had created religion ages ago for weak-minded people who had no self-confidence. It was a mere ploy to control them and take their money.

I had seen people die before on a number of occasions, and each time it had left me with a feeling of desperation, loneliness, and frustration. This was finality so cold, and so chilling, the mere concept of it begged for an answer. Now this bag of human bones that might have been a husband or a father lay silent. Just moments before he had been alive, and now, as if a candle had been snuffed out, not even the smoke lingered in the stillness.

I caught Betty's eye, and a tear came sliding down her cheek. We looked toward Jason, who was tying the reins of his horse to a scrub tree.

"Go be with him, John. I don't want him here."

"You're right. He's got plenty of time to get wounded by death."

I stepped away and cut him off before he could reach the dead man's side, putting my arm around his shoulder and guiding him in a one-eighty.

"What's going on?" he asked. "Who is it?"

"It's one of the natives," I answered.

"Is he okay?" he asked, struggling under my arm as I tried to hang on. "Let me go."

"No, Jason, he's dead," I said.

The boy stepped back with a determined look in his eye. "What happened?"

"He took a rhino horn," I explained.

"Is it anyone I know?" he asked. "I want to see."

"Well, you're not going to. The queen has spoken."

"The queen? What queen?" he asked. "Oh, you mean Betty?"

"That's right, Jason," I said.

The mere mention of her name took the fire out of his fight, as if I had just doused him with a bucket of cold water. He turned and began walking away in the direction of his horse. I stood there, not knowing what to say or how to comfort him. I felt like a blocked writer grasping for words to fill the next page. I felt so stupid that I hadn't been able to convince him not to look, but at the first mention of the queen, he had transformed from night into day.

But what could I say to him about death that would bring this young lad to any greater understanding than what I possessed? A life had ended, and for all intents and purposes, it looked from my perspective to be over for a very long time. I had no hope in an everlasting life, and maybe I was fine with that. It just made it hard to explain, and even tougher to share any sort of a message of hope with anyone.

I ran after him and grabbed his shirt. "Jason, she only wants to protect you."

"I know. She's a good mom. She's all I have—and you too, John. You're like a father to me."

I could feel a lump in my throat, and I tried to shake it off like I had done so many times before. "Jason, you're like a son to me, too. And if my son were here, I wouldn't want him to look on the face of death, either."

"But what does it all mean, John? Where do you think we go when we die?"

"Into thin air, I guess. Where does a flame go when you blow out a candle? Is there anything there? I think you linger on in the memories of the people who love you, but as for anything else, who knows? Their book says, 'Dust to dust, ashes to ashes.' As far as I can see, when the show is over, the curtain closes and the music stops. It's a natural part of life. There is a time to live and a time to die, and when you reach the end of the road, the horses tire and the cart comes to a stop. As for me, I think once around is elegant and complete."

"That's pretty depressing, isn't it?" Jason said. "I love life, and I don't want it to end. There has to be more than this. There just has to be."

"I wish I could tell you there is, Jason. I wish I could give you a glimmer of hope. Hey, just ask that religious fanatic, Esther. She'll fill your head with all sorts of weird stuff. It's a great story, but I can't buy all the syrup, or the thought of losing my freedom and submitting to all those rules. All that sugar coating is nauseating to me. I don't know about you, but if that's what it takes to have eternal life, then they can keep it. I am who I am, Jason, and I don't intend to change at this point in my life."

"I don't know, John. Esther seems so very sincere. She really believes in what she is saying, and it seems like she knows something. She has a glow about her."

"Let me tell you a thing or two. There is no scientific proof for any of that stuff. Life is natural, not supernatural. There is no logical approach to her thought process. It seems like it's all backwards. It's all smoke and mirrors as far as I'm concerned. I think she has jumped off the deep end and doesn't know how to swim, so she is trying desperately to convince everyone around her to jump in too so she won't look so stupid. Her philosophy doesn't hold any water. I'm just sitting back on the shore, waiting for her to shout for help—and she will, believe me. They all do. It's only a matter of time before she sees her faith in this madness as a chasing of the wind, and when she does, I'll be there."

Jason stood in silence, wrinkling his young brow and hanging on my every word as if I offered true nuggets of wisdom that he should collect and carry with him in his pockets. It gave me a good feeling to have such an important and positive influence on him. I felt as if I were on a mission to save him from being poisoned by eating the wrong berries in the jungle. It seemed like all the fanatical Christians I knew never had any fun. They wouldn't get drunk, or let loose with their tongues, or have a good laugh at anyone else. They were a bunch of stuffed shirts who sat around reading their Bibles, and that seemed like the only time they had any fun—or at least pretended to. Still, my answers seemed so shallow, and even to me, death felt hopeless and tenuous, and our time here on earth far too short.

"You okay?" Jason asked.

"Yeah … why?"

"Oh, I don't know," he said. "Will we make camp here?"

"No, I think we'll go on," I said. "Not that we are cold-blooded, mind you. But the natives will prefer to deal with this matter in their own way. We'll probably load up the remains on an oxcart and make headway toward the next camp. But we'll do whatever Willie wants."

I glanced over at Betty and Esther, who were standing arm in arm as the natives wrapped the man in a blanket.

"It really isn't safe out here, is it?" Jason asked.

"You just figured that out, did you? That's why they call it adventure, my lad. What good would it be if this place had no danger?"

"I like adventure," Jason said, "but I'm not crazy about dying."

"I don't intend to have any of us die, either. Not to say the threat isn't real. That's why we stay alert—and keep a loaded rifle handy. That's why we're damn careful. Just make sure you're ready for the next beast. You watch yourself, Jason, because I don't intend on leaving any of us here on the plains under some pile of rock."

~~~~~~~~~

We sat around the fire after dinner that evening and sipped wine. We tried to avoid discussing the tragedy, but it weighed heavily on everyone's mind. The blazing fire danced and crackled, and I slid back from the heat. Willie eased another log onto the coals, sending tiny red sparks into the night sky.

"It almost looks like you can see patterns in the flames," Betty said as she sat close to me. "Don't you think so?"

"They say if you stare long enough into the flames," Lance said, "you can see the faces of your dead ancestors."

"Sometimes I think I do!" I answered.

"Oh, look," Betty said with a laugh, "I think that's Mama, with her fiery red hair, hot temper, and warm smile. Oh, too late. She's gone, all burned up, nothing but ashes."

"Ashes to ashes, you know," I replied.

"Tell me more about your mama," Jason said.

"Oh, my mama ... what can I say that I haven't already told you?" Betty sat back and put her index finger to her cheek. "You would have loved her, Jason. I think as we discussed before that she always had a preference for boys. She always loved my papa, despite their differences, and I know after he was gone she missed him terribly. They met in school, and they got married when she was just sixteen. I think he was seventeen."

"Wow," Jason said, "I'm almost old enough to get married."

"That was then," Betty said. "You need to think about getting an education before you think about starting a family."

"Oh, I suppose," he said. "I suppose I would have to look for a girl first, and finding one out here in the bush might be a little tough."

Everybody burst out in laughter at his comment.

"What about trying for kudu in the morning?" Chuck asked. "Those hills to the west look promising."

"We can try a hunt in the morning," I said. "We'll send the porters on ahead to the next camp, hunt for a few hours, and then catch up. What do you think Willie would say? I am getting the itch to get shooting."

"Okay, I'll concede," Lance said, turning and then raising his voice so Willie could hear. "Willie!"

"Bwana?" he answered respectfully as he approached us from across the camp.

"We're going to make a hunt in the morning for kudu," Lance said. "What do you think?"

I sipped the last from my wine glass.

"Willie hunt hills before," he said. "Good sable. Many, many kudu track. But never we see. Kudu like ghost here."

"It's set then. Everybody in agreement?" Lance paused and searched our faces for dissenters. "Get us up early, Willie, and make sure Bamira has breakfast ready. Oh, and have him pack us some food for the trail tomorrow. Two more days and we'll be in some fair elephant country.

"Two years ago I talked to some boys who took hundred-pounders off the herd twenty miles north from here. I've heard tell of bigger bulls, too, but they are really wary and smart. They have been shot at now enough in their seventy-year lifespan, and they get pretty cagey. You gotta watch 'em, though. They see men as a fly on the wall, a nuisance to smash under their feet. They have watched enough of their friends die to rifle fire that they are angry with men. Most adolescent males grow up seeing their masters killed by men, and remember, elephants never forget."

"If we're getting up early," Esther said, "then we should consider going to bed, don't you think?"

"Come on, everybody," Chuck said. "Let's hit the sack."

~~~~~~~~~

Morning came way too early. My eyes, it seemed, had just closed when Willie spoke through the big netting in the darkness of the tent.

"Time to rise, Bwana."

"It's morning already?" I asked.

"If Bwana want kudu," he answered.

"Then I want kudu."

I could hear the wooden joints in Betty's cot begin to creak as she stirred. "Already?" she asked. "What time is it?"

"I don't know, but if Willie says it's time, it's time."

We dressed by lamplight and made ready our rifles and our gear. As we were eating, Jason finally emerged from his tent and joined us, his hair disheveled. Betty tried to flatten it with her hands like the loving mother she wanted to be. I sipped my coffee and gazed off at the lush dark hills standing magnificently against the hue of the approaching day. They were all that stood between us and a ghostlike bull kudu.

As we made our way across the grassy plain and trudged toward the base of the mountains, the horizon burst forth with the orange fireball sun. Janga led, while Betty and I followed close behind him. Lance and Esther trailed us, followed by Chuck and Jason. Behind them came a small collection of necessary gun bearers, skinners, and packers. Janga halted and spoke to Lance in his broken mixture of English and Swahili.

Lance listened carefully, waiting for him to conclude. "We'll split up here," he said. "Chuck, you come with Esther and me. Jason, you tag along with John and Betty. We'll take Janga with us, and John, you take Temba."

"Temba, not hardly. Janga is my man."

"Don't you remember when we hunted with Temba two years ago and took the Oryx off the Mara?"

"I remember," I said.

"He's a good guide," Lance assured me. "He knows these mountain kudu."

I had to wonder why, if he was so good, Lance was taking my favorite guide. But I had to bite my tongue because I knew this was only our first day out. We had months of hunting left, and there would be plenty of time to hunt with Janga. I was amused that Lance wanted to get a jump on things and take the best chance to score first.

"If you get one down," he said, "wait ten minutes and fire two quick shots, then follow up with one shot after thirty seconds."

"Same as always," I said. "Did you think I'd forget?"

"No," he said and chuckled. "You guys take that draw right there, and hunt to that flattop plateau. We'll head for those rocks. We'll drop under the face and cross that side hill to the green scrub trees. Then we'll meet back here around noon."

I gazed at the hills and tried to evaluate them quickly. I couldn't help feeling like the one Lance had taken for himself was somehow better: flatter and a bit more open, and probably teeming with kudu. "Sounds good to me," I said, biting my lip again so as not to make it sound like I was growling like a dog over a bone.

"Temba tends to hunt fast," Lance said, "but he's good."

"I know," I said. "You don't have to remind me."

"Good luck then," Lance said, "and hunt up a trophy."

I had to stop myself from laughing out loud at his insincere remark. As I watched them trudge off, I tried not to let my jealousy ruin my first hunt on this safari. But I remembered well what it was like to hunt with Temba. I felt he was overeager—and somewhat careless. But that had been four years ago; maybe he had settled down.

Temba nodded, turned, and then revved up his legs, leading the pack.

"Can you believe what just happened?" I said to Betty, trying to talk under my breath.

"No, what?" she answered.

"We just got hornswaggled by Lance!"

"How?" she asked.

"I think he took the best hill—and the far better guide, too."

"Deal with it, John. Don't let it ruin our day."

I turned away, realizing she wasn't going to put up with my whining. Maybe a guide could learn a lot in four years.

We began to pull the slow grade to the approach of the hill, and gradually the tsetse flies started buzzing.

Betty swatted at the little pests as they began to attack. "Where are these foul things coming from?" she asked as she took a swipe at several flies buzzing her head.

"I think they hole up in this thick underbrush, and we're stirring them up."

"Look out!" she said, jumping back and hitting at one of them.

"Here, lift your collar up." I slung my rifle over my shoulder and lifted the collar of her jacket up with my fingers. "Do you have a bandanna?"

"Yes," she answered.

"Get it out and take your helmet off."

She reached in and pulled the red scarf out of her pocket.

I folded it in half and then tied it around her hair, letting the tail end tumble down her neck before tucking it under her collar.

Betty swatted at her arm, defending herself from the flying bugs. "You never told me about these. Do they bite?" she asked as I buttoned her top button.

"You're darn right they bite," I said, trying to fend them off. "You can get sleeping sickness, and it will kill you."

"It will kill you?" she asked, incredulous. "Jason, you better do the same thing with your bandanna."

Just then I felt a tap on my shoulder and turned to face Temba.

He took his finger and ran it over his lips. "*Temba vumbua tandala ... njÓo!*" he whispered and then motioned for us to follow.

"What did he say?" Jason asked.

"*Vumbua* means find by chance," I whispered. "*Tandala* is kudu, and I think *njÓo* means to come. *Kuja* means come, but in this context I think *njÓo* means come. Basically, he wants us to shut up and follow him."

"*Tandala?*" Jason asked, repeating the word under his breath as he tied a bandanna around his neck to ward off the flies.

I nodded yes and then put my finger to my lips. "Let's get away from these flies," I said, grabbing Betty and taking her up the hill.

Betty's gun bearer stayed close to her, following like a shadow. Even though my British double was heavy, I didn't trust my native to carry it. I let my gun bearer carry my Springfield and have it ready for me, just in case I needed another loaded rifle. It seemed incredible to me that the tsetse flies had no effect on the natives at all. Thankfully, none of us had been bit, but the natives treated them like they didn't exist.

Temba maneuvered in and around the labyrinth of brush and sticker bushes as he made his way on up the steep hillside. I tried to show Jason how a great hunter would walk in the bush so as to avoid cracking twigs and alerting game of our presence. Temba stepped quickly, never once looking down, always with his eyes ahead, yet never stepping on a dry twig and never missing a fresh track in the dirt. Somehow he kept one eye to the ground and one eye ahead, the latter searching for a piece of horn, a twinkle of an eye, or a flash of an ear.

We had gone about an hour when we heard a shot echo through the hills coming from the direction of the other party. We all froze in our tracks, waiting for any animals to bolt. I pulled my watch from my pocket, flipping the lid, and it read seven thirty-four. If they had one down, they would probably make a single-kill shot, then it would be another ten minutes for the signal shot.

"Let's wait for the signal," I whispered.

Temba made his way to the edge of a hill, where we crept out on a jumble of rocks overlooking a deep gorge. We had escaped the attacks from the tsetse, and Betty took the bandanna off from around her head. We bellied up to the rocks, and Jason and I took a rest on the overlook with our rifles at the ready. Beneath us lay an open grassy meadow about one hundred and fifty yards to the bottom tree line. A gentle breeze blew from beneath the rocks and up into our faces, and the sweet smell of thorn blossom filled the air.

Then in the east corner I spotted animals in the bush about a hundred and seventy-five yards off. I nudged Betty to alert her, and she pointed them out to Jason.

"*Mbarapi* (sable antelope)," Temba whispered.

We sat poised, waiting for a big bull sable to show himself in the open, where we could poke a hole in him. But the echoing gunfire had spooked them, and they were shy about coming out of the bush. Finally, after we had sat in suspense for several minutes, one of the cows stirred up the courage to emerge at the edge of the clearing. We held our position as one by one they stepped out single file into the clear.

"Looks like they're all cows," I said. "Let's wait. Maybe there will be a bull."

Ears up, noses in the wind, every step perilously on the edge of flight—the small band of antelope began munching on the new shoots.

I looked at my watch. Nine minutes had passed since we had heard the single shot. I watched the twelve sable cows, knowing they would scatter as soon as the ten-minute shot rang out. They stood unprotected about a hundred yards straightaway broadside.

"Can I shoot one?" Jason asked.

I furrowed my brow and shook my head, no.

"Why not?" he whispered.

"Why do you want to shoot one of those?" I asked. "There's no trophy there."

"I just want to shoot something," he insisted.

"When we get back to camp, you can shoot a wine bottle," I said. "How's that? But let's leave these poor ladies and their children alone."

Jason looked at Betty and tightened his lip.

"There'll be plenty of time for shooting," I said, "but let's be choosey, okay?"

Jason conceded, nodding in agreement.

I checked my watch again. Eleven minutes had passed since hearing the shot.

"*Hapana dalili* (no signal)," Temba said, "*Tandala* (kudu)." He slid backward off the rock ledge, keeping his head down to stay concealed from view of the antelope.

"Don't spook 'em, Jason," I cautioned.

"Why don't you let him take that lead cow?" Betty said. "She's probably barren."

"Not in the middle of a kudu hunt. If he just wants to shoot something, I'll let him take a tommy or a grant on our way back to camp this afternoon. I want to get him a fifty-inch kudu; then he'll have something to brag about."

Temba motioned again for us to come along.

Betty put her hand on Jason's shoulder and smiled.

Temba continued his relentless attack on the hill, and suddenly we heard something crash through the bush, snapping swigs and pounding hooves before fading away quickly into stone silence. Temba began searching the ground until he found tracks.

"*Kongoro tandala* (old bull kudu)," he said, pointing to the set of prints heading down the hill.

"Shall we track him?" Betty asked.

"*Nyata* (follow stealthily)," I said.

"*Hapana ... hapana, Zunguka* (no ... no, go around)," he said, pointing up the hill and then taking off again for the high country.

"Stay with him, Jason," I said. "He knows where he's going."

"I don't know if I can keep up with him," Betty said.

"I know. That's why I'm letting them go ahead. Besides, I'd just as soon Jason had first crack at a kudu."

Temba stopped and looked back to acknowledge that we were staying behind.

I motioned for him to take Jason and go.

"What's Temba up to?" Betty asked. "I'm surprised he didn't follow the tracks."

"He's working the winds," I explained. "He's going to circle above it. These animals are used to running from predators that track them. They always go for the high ground, especially these cagey old bulls. He'll head downhill to get a jump on whoever is chasing him, just to get up a head of steam. Then he'll circle and go right back up the mountain to try to shake his pursuer. It always works with leopards and lions. But Temba knows the tactics. He'll be right on him when he tries to sneak back up the hill."

"I don't know if I can keep up," Betty said, "but maybe we should."

"Oh, let 'em go. That boy needs to get some of the vigor run out of him. We won't let them get too far ahead."

We tramped the grade, following the two sets of man tracks with our native gunmen following behind us. I had to believe that Jason was in seventh heaven: just he and Temba on the trail of a *kongoro tandala*. As we scrambled up the rocks and through the brush, the morning began to heat up.

"I'm glad we didn't try to stay with them," I said, pausing to catch my breath.

My gun bearer had not yet broken a sweat.

Reluctantly, I gave in and traded my British double for the light Springfield, and he took the rifle from me with a wide grin. No doubt he thought that I couldn't carry my big rifle and make the hill—and that I was soft. I had always felt comfortable with Janga as my gunman, but now he had been promoted to a hunting guide and I had to let him go. I just wished I was hunting with him now.

As we neared the top, I began to look toward the open areas to get a glimpse of Jason and Temba moving up ahead on the hillside, but they were nowhere to be seen.

"Let's find a spot to watch the open area below them, just in case this brute catches wind of them and makes a dash downhill. Besides, I don't want to keep going on and ruin their chances by blundering in and spooking their kudu."

I led our small band across the brushy hillside to the edge of a wide draw where we could watch some open country. We had just settled in when a shot rang out from the crest of the hill and echoed down across the rolling dale, bouncing two and fro between the green hills.

Betty's eyes sparkled with excitement. "I hope he connected," she said.

Just then another shot filled the canyon.

"Okay," I said, "let's go. That should be the kill shot."

I tried to pinpoint the origin of the second report. I checked my watch, knowing that Jason still had his from his train riding days and that Temba knew the signal. Even if he forgot, I figured we could get to them in less than ten minutes. I had nothing but pride for my little gal, who hung in there with me every step of the way as we hurriedly made our way toward the spot where I figured the last rifle shot had come from.

"I hope he got a nice bull," Betty said, fighting to speak and catch her breath at the same time.

"If it's the same mammoth that made the track down below," I said, "then he's got himself a dandy."

After cresting the hill, we continued to follow their tracks, picking them up from one surface to the next: grass, brush, sand, rock. A piece of heel, a bit of toe—this one was Jason's, that one was Temba's. We had gone about a half mile across the plateau when I found a shiny new empty brass casing nose down in the dirt.

"If he connected with a trophy bull, he'll want his brass for a keepsake," I said, plucking it out of the sandy soil and holding it so it glistened in the sun. "His first kudu."

Our gun bearers started to fan out and look for their tracks.

"Bwana!" Betty's man said, pointing over the hill and down a long open draw.

I came close to have a look, and I could see that Jason and Temba had been on a dead run. I motioned for him to lead the way.

Just then the silence was broken by a shout from Jason about two hundred yards below us. "Betty, down here!" Jason yelled, waving his arms so we could see his head just above the scrub bush. "I got him! He's a bruiser!"

I checked my watch and saw that it had been exactly ten minutes. I gestured to the native to let him know I was going to make a signal shot for Lance and Chuck.

"Hold your ears, dear," I said and then turned and shouted back to Jason, "I'm gonna signal Lance!"

I held the rifle barrel up and, resting the butt on my hip, fired off two quick shots, then counted to thirty and fired off a third. "Now let's have a look at this beast."

As we approached the lad, he had a grin that could have surpassed the Cheshire cat in the story of *Alice in Wonderland*.

"You couldn't bring him down with one shot, eh?" I jabbed.

"Nope, he was so big it took two. Actually, he did go down on the first shot, but he got up and ran another hundred yards. Then he stood broadside, and I shot him again, finishing him off."

All I could see were the monstrous corkscrew horns glistening in the sunshine. Temba had already rolled the entrails from the carcass and disposed of them in the tall grass. It always amazed me that a native like Temba could work over a carcass and not get blood above his wrists.

"He's a beauty, all right," I said. "I've only seen one bigger, but this one should measure out a good fifty-five inches, maybe more."

"This thing is as big as a moose!" Jason exclaimed.

"Well, not as big as a moose. But I shot a Rocky Mountain elk a few years ago in Colorado, and these mountain kudu are every bit as big as one of those."

"Can I pack the head back to camp?" Jason asked.

"Oh, I don't think you need to do that," I said. "There are plenty of natives to handle the heavy work. Besides, they will be offended if you try to take their job away from them. They won't understand. They will end up resenting you for it, and it's not worth it. Besides, Janga will be along shortly with the rest of his crew, and they'll have this skinned, quartered, and packed out to the oxcart by the time we get back for lunch."

Temba stood proudly over the kill.

"*Mteule* (one chosen for great skill)," I said.

He puffed up his chest.

"We came out on that bench right there," Jason said, pointing up the hill. "Temba motioned me to watch, and we had not waited for more than ten minutes when the kudu came in the clearing. I shot just like you taught me, John. I figured to hold a bit high in the midsection behind the shoulder, then I squeezed off the round from a perfect rest across the forearm of the rifle."

"Hold the details, boy. This will be a wonderful campfire story. Chuck and Lance will revel in it like a rare beefsteak."

Temba began peeling back the hide with a razor blade that glistened in the sunlight, and we gathered up our rifles. I tipped my hat, and Temba gave me a nod, acknowledging that he knew we were departing and would meet him and the other natives back at camp.

~~~~~~~~~

By the time we caught up to the rest of the safari later that afternoon, Bamira had a big iron pot of eland tail soup simmering over the cooking fire. This native continued to amaze me with his ability to create tasty delights fit for the Western palate. Mostly their simple diet had no appeal whatsoever, but he knew from experience how to spice things up for his European and American clients.

We had broken our first fresh elephant tracks, left by a herd of twelve to fifteen, but we were much more excited about it than our elephant guides, who described the herd in Swahili as a nursery band of mothers and juvenile females, with several *totos* (babies). The one promising bull track in the bunch fell far short of the monarch tusker we were looking for.

After a hearty dinner, we watched the sun set and had a few well-deserved drinks around the campfire. Lance hesitated to tell us about the big sable bull he shot at and missed. Then Jason told the story of his magnificent kudu hunt as the men among us puffed on our cigars. I had to hand it to the boy: he had a knack for a story, and he avoided the boasting common to young men. Even though he had been victorious, he kept the focus of his success squarely on the shoulders of the expertise of Temba and never once took any of the glory for himself.

I liked that in a lad. Funny how, even though I liked this posture and felt so very much that it was the right way to behave, I had never once been able to match the trait personally. It was strange how virtues eluded me, even though I knew what was right to do. To act accordingly was quite another thing altogether.

"My tent is calling," Chuck said, sipping the last drops from his wineglass and then handing it to the native steward.

"Tomorrow we'll be in elephant country," Lance said.

"What's the biggest tusker to leave Nairobi this past year?" I asked.

"They say Bill Judd's party took a good one several months before you arrived. Supposedly, it was some rich Swede and his son. So the story goes. They tracked him for three days, and he charged them before they even fired a shot. Old Bill said he never saw a crankier bull than that one. He kept coming after they took cover, and the kid hit him with a frontal brain shot. I guess he went down like a two-ton sack of grain—to their relief."

"Remember that old bugger you and I killed on the Thika River four years ago?" I asked. "That one was one tough old bird, I'll tell you. Or else you were one poor shot. I was worried he'd figure out where the shots were coming from and stomp us both in the dust before you could put him down. By the way, what did you ever do with those tusks?"

"I traded them to one of my neighbors for a plow two years ago," Lance explained. "He came by and took a shine to them and wanted to trade me something, so I took him up on it."

"I'm turning in," Chuck said. "All this talk about elephants makes me want to get plenty of rest for tomorrow."

"I'm going to our tent, too," Esther said. "That climb took the soup out of me. I'm sitting here fighting to keep my eyes open."

"Tell Willie to keep his camp boys on these fires and keep 'em going," I said. "These lions are hungry around here, and they aren't picky about their food. By the way, Lance, have there been any reports of man-eaters since Patterson's fiasco at Tsavo?"

"Yes, we have them now and again. But you know Africa was a much wilder place fourteen years ago than it is now. The railway has done a lot to bring civilization. There's one thing old Colonel Patterson never said, but I heard tell that at least one of those lions had a busted canine tooth."

"That would explain a lot, wouldn't it? How many people do they figure those maneless rascals ate before Patterson brought the whole thing to rest?"

"Well over a hundred. But they never did get a final count because a lot of them were natives that nobody knew. When they ended up missing, nobody reported it."

"What do you mean, *maneless*?" Jason asked.

"For some reason," Lance answered, "those old males up in the Tsavo region don't dress up with the big, long, hairy black manes."

"They look like a bunch of girls," I said. "But guaranteed that don't make 'em any less ferocious. Those boys have always had a bad reputation for having a taste for human flesh."

"Won't the lions out here get you?" Jason asked.

Just then the camp boys showed up with armloads of wood and tossed them onto the fire, sending glowing embers into the sky.

"Oh, they'll get you all right," Lance said. "Don't ever count them out. But those Tsavo beasts have probably eaten more than their fair share. Maybe they are trying to prove their manhood because they look like girls."

Jason burst into laughter, and we all laughed along at the thought.

"Unprovoked, these prides will keep to themselves," I said, "and eat what is natural for them."

"Oh, sure, unprovoked," Betty said, "but we're provoking them just being in their territory."

Just then we heard the low guttural roar of a lion off in the distance.

"Speak of the devil," Betty quipped, "and he shall appear."

"That's a Bible verse," Esther said, getting out of her chair. "It's first Peter, chapter five, verse eight. Be sober, be vigilant; because your adversary the devil is like a roaring lion, prowling about, seeking whom he may devour."

"Yep, the lion is the closest thing to any real devil, that's for sure," I said with a laugh, knowing the comment might hit a nerve with Esther.

"So there you go, John," Esther said. "You said it." She settled back in her chair with the flickering firelight against her face. "The lion is God's way of showing us how Satan is. The Scripture says that he prowls around *like* a roaring lion seeking to devour someone. But remember, he is *like* a lion; he is not the lion. The lion is Christ himself, but Satan always appears like an angel of light. You can never trust him or deny his power to deceive you. All the power Satan has is handed to him by people. We should always remember that he is out there waiting, trying to deceive you and convince you that he is good, that wrong is right, that darkness is light. That is where Satan's power lies: in his ability to twist things and deceive us. There are two lions in Scripture: the lion of Judah, who draws men to God, and the other, the prowling lion, who drives men to God."

"Oh come on, Esther," I said as my temperature began to rise. "This charade has gone on long enough. This is the twentieth century. We are scientifically enlightened about the natural world. We don't need anything supernatural to help us understand the natural. There is no hocus-pocus or black magic; it's just nature. We began naturally, evolved naturally, and occur in a naturalistic state. We are no better than, or less than, any other animal on the planet. We are nothing more than a predator that is higher on the food chain."

"If that's what you believe," Esther said. "You are certainly entitled to your opinion, but you are missing such a wonderful part of life. Life is all about perspective. What you see is what you get. You can choose to ignore many aspects of it. But just because you ignore them, doesn't mean they don't exist."

"I don't ignore anything that is natural," I snapped, "what I can smell, taste, touch, hear, or see—things that are real."

"What is reality?" she asked. "Do you mean to say that only the things of the physical world are reality to you?"

"They are the only things that matter to me," I said. "And if they don't matter to me, then as far as I'm concerned, they are only imagined."

"What about emotions?" she asked. "Are they real, or are they imagined?"

"That's a silly question," I answered. "If they are only imagined, then they are neurotic."

"What about your fear of the lions. Is it real or is it imagined?"

I glanced at Betty, and she smiled, probably figuring I had gotten in over my head.

"You'd have to ask the lion to be sure of that," I said. "I can only fear and respect him. He is the one who decides the level of my respect. I can be wary, smart, and alert, and yes, I will fear him, and my fear is real. I have only but one offensive weapon against him, and that is my courage."

"So I'll ask you again: Is your courage real or imagined? Does your courage originate in your body, your mind, or in your heart?"

I wasn't going to admit that she might have something here. I knew she was trying to get me to paint myself into a corner. But I was clever enough to see that my emotions began first with my imagination. I supposed there was really no difference between that and acknowledging God. But I would never admit that to her.

"Well, John," she said, "have I stumped you?"

"Not at all. Never! My courage is real. Ask anyone who knows me."

But I had to wonder how much courage it would take to speak up for something that you believed in that no one else could see. I would sooner have faced a charging lion than try to convince someone like me that there was a god.

Esther just smiled, no doubt confident she had planted a seed with me.

But I was determined to dig it up and toss it into the fire. "I'm turning in," I said, looking around for the camp boys. "Hey, Willie, tell your guys to keep these fires going. I'll sleep much better knowing those lions hate fire."

I took Betty by the hand and led her to our tent. I hated to lose, but I wasn't certain who had come out the victor. I guessed time would tell whether my courage was real or imagined. That would be for me to know and for her to find out. And as far as her god . . . no way.

Chapter 14

THE CURMUDGEON

I awoke at the first sniff of the camp boys putting the morning grub together. Maybe the walk from yesterday had caused me to sleep like a log, but for the first time I woke up feeling rested and ready to go. I began to rustle around in the still-dark tent to find my clothes.

"Are you getting up already?" Betty asked.

"We'll have our first small taste of some elephant country today, and I feel like a kid with a shiny nickel in his pocket just around the corner from a soda shop."

"Oh, John, you don't need a nickel to make you feel like a kid. But it's not even light yet."

"Go ahead and sleep for a while. I'm going to watch the sunrise and write in my journal. You know I never intended for this trip to be all play. I intend to get some work done."

As I stepped out of the tent, I could smell wild boar roasting over the cook fires. The eastern sky glowed light pink just above the distant mountains. I spied in the firelight a gleaming cup hanging from a nail and poured freshly brewed coffee from a steaming pot. After adjusting the sling on my British double, which was hanging heavy on my shoulder, I headed down the trail toward some jagged rocks overlooking the wide green plains. The grasslands were dotted with tommies, grants, wildebeest, and impala grazing just out of gun range, and I found a perfect place to sit and ponder as the morning dawned.

I remembered Darwin's statement in his epic book, *Voyage of the Beagle*, where he'd said that any person fond of natural history could enjoy great walks in England, where one could always find something to attract his attention. But, he pointed out, in the fertile climates such as Rio, teeming with life, the attractions were so numerous that one was scarcely able to walk at all. *I wonder what Charles Darwin might have thought about East Africa.*

I opened my satchel to retrieve my journal and began to jot down my impressions of the flora and fauna. As I wrote, I impressed myself with my scientific intellect and imagined how even Darwin might have praised my brilliance. A termite caught my eye as it made its way across the dirt before dipping into a depression made by an animal track.

Suddenly, my heart pounded as the image came clear of a big round lion pugmark in the soft red sand. I took a closer look, leaning on my British double for support, to determine just how recently the owner had pressed it.

I was less than fifty yards from camp, but the reality of a marauding lion was truly worrisome. The print looked so fresh I could imagine steam rising from it, like it would from a hot iron on a damp shirt. I scrambled to my feet, dropping my writing implements, and then grabbed a long, cool breath to clear the pit in my stomach. Just how close had this intruder come while reconnoitering our tents?

"What's going on, John?" Jason asked, making his way from camp.

"Where's your rifle?" I demanded. "Don't leave camp without your rifle, son. See here?" I said, pointing to the track. "We had a marauder in the night. Looks like an old male sniffing for an easy meal."

"We need to show these to Willie," Jason said.

"We will, but he'll come to the same conclusion. These are fresh, probably made in the last several hours."

"Look here," Jason said. "He even took some steps toward us, and then he backed off and continued on over that way."

"That's what I mean," I said. "You need to keep that fire-stick close at hand. It doesn't do any good back in your tent. The problem with these old boys is they have huge catfights for control of the pride, and the loser leaves injured. Then they are tossed out of their harem in a weakened condition, and they have to start hunting again on their own, something they haven't had to do since they were in their prime, because their ladies have been taking care of them. All they had to do was sit back and wait for the girls to make a kill and then bully in and take it away. Gazelles and antelope are too quick for them now, so they start looking for easy prey. Once they get a taste for the two-legged pig, they go and make a nasty habit out of it."

"Two-legged pig?" Jason asked. "What do you mean?"

"That's what the natives call human lion prey: two-legged pig."

Jason smiled and shook his head. "So this big old lion is just lonely and hungry, isn't he, John?"

"Pretty much. Speaking of hungry, how about let's go get us some breakfast from that four-legged pig so we can get scouting for a tusker." I gathered my writing things, and we walked back to camp.

~~~~~~~~~

Later on, before the morning heat began to swelter, we broke into hunting parties and left camp with a plan to meet up that evening ten miles ahead toward the Rift Valley. We were just on the edge of good elephant country, but it felt good to check every inch now so as not to pass up a real trophy. Lance agreed to let Betty, Jason, and me have Janga since his skills as an elephant hunter were a mite better and he spoke a bit more English.

The Ford had begun to be more of a hindrance than an asset for bush travel. We were constantly worried about getting it stuck in the sand or coming to a ravine where we wouldn't be able to pass. There were worries enough on this safari without anything additional to throw in my knapsack. I knew I would have to give a report as to the success or feasibility, but my report so far would not be a glowing one. As for today, I would have liked to have been carefree on horseback or on foot to concentrate on getting a trophy, but we had to always consider moving the Lizzy to the next camp. I had hoped to find a native to drive her, but so far coaxing one of them to learn to drive — or even get close to it while the motor churned — had been difficult. There was also the possibility that they might run her off a cliff. But I was beginning to warm to such a scenario.

Betty would not concede to ride in the car and insisted on remaining in her saddle. My only hope was to find a suitable place to park this bucket of bolts so we could continue on horseback and hopefully—or maybe not so hopefully—retrieve the Ford later in the afternoon after scouting for a trophy elephant.

As we made our way toward the foothills, there appeared to be plenty of signs all right, but the tracks belonged mostly to young adolescents. According to Janga, we had found just another bunch of women and their kids.

"What do you think about all the elephant spore?" Jason asked, approaching the motorcar after tying his horse to a branch.

"Oh, there are plenty of elephants around here, but we're looking for that band of bachelor bulls. When Janga finds 'em, he'll know. The ones we're looking for are a bunch of bulls working on their last set of molars, far past their prime. Lots of times they'll hang out with young bulls that aren't quite up to the challenge of taking on a big bull in his prime to take a mate.

"The prime bulls are big and strong, but the big trophy bulls, the ones we want with the huge tuskers, are content to be solitary and out to pasture. The young bulls follow them because they are in the same boat with nowhere to go. The strong breeding bulls don't take kindly to young'ns or old tired monarchs taking a shine to any of their ladies. It's sort of nature's way of giving those young boys a role model to look up to. Their mothers kick 'em out of their families when they are about five years old so they will go and learn how to be a bull. So it's the old boys who raise the young boys and show them the ropes."

"Their mothers kick 'em out that young?" Betty asked, rolling her eyes. "How do you know these are ladies, Janga?"

"*Toto* (baby)," Janga said, pointing to a small elephant track. "This is *mamke* (mama) and *toto*." Janga's eyes widened, and a big grin came over his face. "Here, Bwana," he said with renewed excitement. "This one we look for. Him tusker!"

I leaped off the Ford and ran toward the massive elephant track. The huge smooth-heeled impression gave us all a sure sign of a prized bull. The spoor appeared to lead east, toward the foothills, and at the edge of the clearing forty yards from the parked Ford lay an enormous pile of steaming fresh dung.

"Can we catch up to them?" Jason asked.

"We're not far behind him," I said, "but we'll never see him riding in this contraption. All this spitting and sputtering is making far too much noise. I'm sure they can hear us coming five miles away."

"With him ears, Bwana," Janga said, "he hear noise for twenty mile."

"Then why are we driving this thing?" I asked.

"Now we found track," Janga said with a wide grin, showing his yellow teeth, "so we shoot motorcar with gun."

I took my rifle off my shoulder and leveled it at the Ford.

"No, no, Bwana. Janga make joking."

We all got a good laugh at Janga thinking I might really follow his directions.

"I think we can park the motorcar, Bwana. We continue on foot from here."

We picked out the necessary gear to finish the load for our porters while the late morning sun beat down on us like a refiner's blast-fire. I knew this would be an exhausting march for Jason and hoped that Betty would be up to the task.

"We will leave the horses behind with the horse boy," I instructed. "I intend to track this bull for several hours, just to see where he is headed. We might find out he is close at hand. If there is no sign of him, then we will take it up tomorrow where we leave off. I think we should make a serious effort to catch him, even if it takes us three days."

Betty seemed reluctant to respond.

"This is a quality bull," I assured her. "Did you see that smooth heel? That's the sign of a true curmudgeon."

"What's that?" Jason asked as he loaded his pockets with extra rounds.

"It's an old guy," I answered, "with a bad temper who doesn't like being around people too much. Let's get going. Time's a wasting."

~~~~~~~~~

Janga led us into the trees toward the foothill of the Mau Mountains. We trudged for the next hour through the heavy timber, following the elephant spoor along a trail forged over the centuries by the great herds. The mighty trees towered high overhead, and the bushes under the canopy choked the ground, making it impossible to penetrate anywhere but where the elephants had gone before. The thick forest shaded out the sun, and the air felt cool and damp. The immense mimosa trees stood straight and tall, towering aloft, spreading their graceful branches. Everything was decorated with green hanging moss, like tinsel hanging from a Christmas tree. Each time we came upon another dung pile that looked like loaves of bread, Janga kicked it to test the freshness. I thought for a moment he might try to taste the stuff. He continually checked the wind by tossing into the air a small handful of wood ash, which he carried in a cotton pouch on his belt, to make sure we were still downwind from the mammoth.

Janga was the master elephant tracker, constantly on the stealth, creeping effortlessly through this labyrinth, always encouraging, but often scolding us as well to be silent. There seemed to be no rhyme or reason to the tangled trails left by the elephants. Where the brutes had fed and rested, wide areas had been trampled for many yards around. Now and again we would have to cross through swamp ground where the beast had sunk up to his belly in muck.

We came to a cross trail, and Janga began fidgeting as he searched desperately to pick up the spoor again. A fresh group of elephant tracks had covered over the track of our round-heeled brute.

He picked out the biggest track among them and shrugged his shoulders. "Good bull, but not our bull," he whispered, motioning us to follow in silence.

The long-nosed and big-eared beasts had incredible smell and hearing. He pointed to the track and nodded in the affirmative with a wide grin to let us know that we were still on the trail of the old curmudgeon. Pay dirt, so to speak—sort of like when miners hit the gold vein deep in the ground after digging months on end.

Janga instructed Betty and Jason to walk in the elephant tracks so we could avoid breaking sticks. Elephants actually made less noise walking in the bush than a man because their huge feet expanded as they pressed the ground. The twigs and branches tended not to snap.

The adventure of the hunt was in the anticipation of the kill, and not so much the kill itself. Each nerve ending tingled at the thought of capturing this monarch of the jungle and claiming his immense power as ours. Just to imagine standing over him, to be the first man to conquer his supremacy, touched on ecstasy.

Janga tossed another handful of dust aloft. Every sense had to be alert now. We had no idea how close he might be. I held tight to my double barrel again, feeling its comfort. I pointed to Betty's gun bearer and encouraged her to pack the rifle herself if she could. I lifted two extra rounds from the loops on my belt, loosening them for easy removal for a follow-up shot should I need one.

Suddenly a deep elephant growl drifted through the trees, and my heart began to pound in my ears. The sound reminded me of sitting in my easy chair at home in front of the fire with a tabby purring on my lap. My blood veins stood on edge, my spine tingled, my throat turned dry.

I glanced back at Betty, who looked frazzled. She tried to stuff her frizzed hair under her hat, pulling her pith helmet down hard on her ears. Her shirt looked as drenched as mine from the exertion.

I placed my hand on her shoulder for encouragement.

She set her jaw tightly, and I could see the veins in her neck.

I had to laugh to myself. What would the society ladies back in Chicago say if they could see her now? Never in all my life had she looked more beautiful to me than she did right now.

Our stealth intensified again, but still we were unable to see the elephants due to the extreme denseness of the surrounding cover. We were mere yards from the herd but still did not know if our old bull stood among the band. As we inched ever closer on our haunches, we strained for a glimpse of gray or brown wrinkled hide.

Betty grabbed my shirttail and gave a sharp tug, and I wheeled around in alarm. She calmly pointed through the trees toward a thin spot in the underbrush where an elephant foot stood just sixty yards straight away.

We froze in our boots, and I held my breath as I reached slowly to take Janga's shoulder. Once again I felt deflated knowing that she had showed me up again. Wouldn't you know she would be the one to spot the first elephant? The foot moved, and another immediately took up the space. Janga motioned us to lie flat in the elephant trench at the center of the path.

Another set of feet moved in and out of the small opening, and suddenly we saw the forest giant we had been following. Still unaware of our presence, the huge old bull stepped out from behind cover, preceded by his glistening white sabers nearly dragging the ground, likely pushing well over a hundred and fifty pounds per side.

His head remained hidden behind a tree trunk, and I lifted my double, waiting patiently for a head shot to his brain. I let my thumb snap the safety off and then clicked it back just to check. I could feel beads of sweat forming below my hat brim. I didn't dare move to see where Betty and Jason were now; I kept my total attention trained on the task at hand. I knew I could take a heart shot if I had to, but elephant hunting required much more precision than that. The bullet had to be placed precisely in the small brain, or the massive beast could kill us all. Even though he would be dead, he wouldn't know it, and he could do so much damage before he expired. But I saw no feasible shot. Not yet, anyway.

Janga held his position, confident that I wouldn't be stupid enough to let a shot go that would only make the critter mad. The small band of elephants were feeding peacefully, purring back and forth like kittens as they cracked small branches. The others were moving now, and I felt sure there would be an opportunity to bust the huge tusker just about a hand span in front of the ear hole as soon as he came out from behind the tree. I would have to be patient.

I counted eight, nine, and then ten elephants move across the opening and progress on ahead through the trees. The brush cracked, and the noise echoed under the forest canopy as they forced their way through the undergrowth. Still, the old monarch held his ground. I wanted to move to get a crack at him, but I knew he would hear me. Then the old bull turned and moved out of sight behind another grove of trees.

Betty eased up close to my ear and whispered ever so softly, "You should have shot him before he left."

I didn't dare answer her and instead tried to hold back my anger. *I bring her out here on my turf, and suddenly she is trying to tell me how to hunt! Me—the expert game hunter! Why, I'll drop this beast with one shot just as soon as he makes his move in the open. Just you wait and see, little lady.*

I shook my head ever so slightly and frowned to let her know of my displeasure with her trying to push me. I wanted to speak, but these elephants were all ears. With a dozen or so in this bachelor herd, that meant twenty-four great big ears, all up and tuned to listen for human tones.

Elephants didn't have many predators other than man, but they were always wary. In fact, elephants had *no* other predators but man, although some lions would take *totos* (baby elephants). I wasn't sure even a cranky old rhino would take on an elephant. I had heard tell once of an elephant killing a rhino, but never the other way around. For some reason, elephants were social and rhinos weren't. *It would be a worthy pursuit*, I thought, *if a man had an itch to study elephants. There would be a lot to learn from them and about them.*

My thoughts were broken when Janga rose slowly to his feet. The elephants had put some distance on us and had moved from the heavy brush to the trail ahead, which was several hundred yards away. Janga checked the wind again, and then he began to proceed in abundant caution. The trail started to gain elevation, and the jungle thinned with each footstep up the side of the mountain.

Our party included ten in number: us three, Janga, the three gun bearers, and the three porters carrying our gear. Janga told the porters to sit and wait here for us to return, smartly aware that any extra feet involved in the stalk would only serve as a hazard.

We continued to stay behind Janga, and when he stopped, we stopped. A half mile ahead we found where the herd had broken through the trees and had taken up a march on toward the mountain. I knew we still had a chance to catch them in the open because the wind continued to drift in our favor. The trail began to level out, and the bush thickened again.

We could hear the elephants talking amongst themselves as we tried to get in close to catch a glimpse once again. Now we were even closer than we had been before, but for some reason the whole herd had stopped to rest.

Janga moved cautiously, straining for a position to catch sight of the big tusker. We had moved off to the edge of the pathway to take cover behind some trees, when suddenly the air, which had been gently flowing down the mountain in our face, brushed the back of my ears.

I held my breath, knowing we were way too close for safety to be winded by this rogue curmudgeon.

Then, like a baseball hitting a plate-glass window, the serenity of the forest was shattered by a thundering bellow from the nose of the bully bull. As Roosevelt had put it so eloquently, *the beast who had a serpent between his eyes for a hand.*

The ground began to shake, and the trees started to shiver. A second later the bushes exploded in our faces as the massive bull with ears like sails appeared out of nowhere like a steaming locomotive.

With not even a second to raise my rifle, I leaped clear from his path, dragging a fistful of Betty's jacket, thankfully with her still inside it. Again the monster screamed his trumpet song, sending a chill up my spine.

I spotted the fleet-of-foot Jason leaping to avoid the polished sabers of this prehistoric creature. The animal roared past our position, and Jason disappeared in heavy brush hidden from our view, blocked by the giant rear end of the monster.

I pushed Betty aside and raised my double, hopeful for a fleeting shot, but thornbush and scrub *mopane* (mo-poney) tree were all I could see. The earth shook as the bull stomped the ground, hoping no doubt to take out his aggression on Jason.

Betty squealed a sorrowful and desperate moan at what we both knew would be a certain end for the boy. "Kill it!" she screamed. "Shoot it!"

I knew my bullet had no chance. Besides, I couldn't be sure where the kid had gone. From this angle, it would only serve to make the beast madder and possibly turn his attention toward us — and we had no better cover. *If I could only turn him*, I thought, *maybe I would have a chance at his head.*

Betty sobbed and screamed again, "Kill the elephant, John. Shoot him!"

"I have no shot, Betty!" I screamed back.

Another loud roar cut the air, causing my toes to curl in my boots, and like an exploding volcano, the elephant fled the scene of the crime, crashing through the trees at twenty miles an hour.

And just like that, dead calm descended on the forest before I had been able to throw even one chunk of lead. The trees hung silently, as if in sorrow, and I dared not move, knowing the anguish that lay ahead for both of us.

Janga crawled out from cover and cautiously approached the spot where Jason lay motionless under a pile of dead trees. Betty covered her eyes and wept uncontrollably. I held her in my arms to give some measure of comfort. I could hear her mumbling something under her breath, and it struck me that she might be praying to her god for a miracle. But I knew the horrible reality that we were both about to face.

Janga reached in to take the boy's arm and try to pull his limp form free from the tree.

"Stay here," I said and sat Betty down on a log.

Her shoulders were trembling.

I let go and ran over to lend some assistance. As my steps closed the distance, I could see the boy twitch. It was the same quivering motion I had seen so many dying animals make after receiving a fatal rifle shot. I recalled a native I had seen stomped by an elephant once, his skull having been flattened, and I expected to see more damage to Jason's body.

Just then Jason blinked and lifted his head. "What happened?" he asked groggily.

Betty burst from the log toward us.

Jason grabbed branches and began fighting his way out from beneath the pile of trees, which had been knocked down by the feeding elephants. My heart sang. My whole being leaped with joy. I felt like that old grand piano in my parlor, with Jason playing on me one of his favorite tunes.

I was certain there had to be some damage to the boy that would cause us some difficulty in returning to camp: maybe a broken back or a leg or two, which would cut our safari short and possibly send us all back to America.

As Janga and I dragged him out from under the bush pile, I couldn't believe such flimsy sticks had saved him. There just didn't appear to be enough stout protection here to support a stomping elephant.

"Are you okay?" Betty asked, still trying to gather her composure and wipe the tears from her face.

"I don't know. What happened? The last thing I remember is being chased by that gray monster, and I thought he got me."

"You fell down below these trees," I answered, "and he couldn't get to you. He stomped enough to kill a hundred men. But I guess you finally frustrated him, and he took off."

"I must have passed out, because I don't remember a thing. All I remember is seeing that big bugger on my tail and then tripping over a branch."

"Well, you're damn lucky, boy," I said. "That's quite a bump you've got on your noggin. Here, let me help you up."

Janga and I pulled him to his feet.

"Are you hurt anywhere?" Betty asked as she brushed the dirt off his shoulder.

Seeing how the boy had nearly ruined my life, I could feel my joy turn to anger. "Don't you remember me telling you not to try to outrun an elephant?" I scolded.

"Not rightly, sir."

"Well, let me tell you again. The only protection you have out here from one of these curmudgeons is a six-foot tree trunk and your rifle. Next time, use them. Do you hear me, boy?"

"John, for heaven's sake," Betty said. "Don't you think the boy has learned enough for one day?"

"I'll ease up on him when he's in the grave. Until then, I'll keep pounding the both of you with the things that will keep us *all* alive out here. Remember, this safari was your idea, so don't give me any grief about the way I choose to keep you safe. Now let's head back for the horses."

"Aren't we going to go after him?" Jason asked.

"Don't you think you've had enough adventure for one day? Besides, we'll never sneak up that close to him again today. He could be five miles away by now. We know he's here, but he won today. Let him have his victory; he earned it."

No one spoke a word as we trudged along the elephant trail back to where we had left the horses and the Ford. We stopped along the trail and had lunch under a spreading mimosa tree. Chirping monkeys high aloft leaped from branch to branch as we ate biscuits and dried meat. Betty sat close to Jason, as if trying desperately to hold on to him. I felt thankful that the boy hadn't perished, because I knew his death would have pushed Betty over the edge.

I had never been able to understand her so-called depression. Why couldn't she just buck up? From what I could see, life was hard, and anyone who was going to live it had to come to grips with that. I thought back to hunting moose in the state of Maine several years earlier. The weather grew harsh, and the whole party's spirits became cold and damp. That might have been the closest I had ever come to being depressed. But she seemed to be caught up in a whirlpool without an oar to get her out.

All she needed was a little dose of personal fortitude, some backbone. Maybe I needed a little more compassion, but I just didn't have the patience for it. As far as I was concerned, it was all self-absorption and self-pity, and I just didn't have time for it. If someone couldn't stand on their own two feet, then they best get up and get going, because the herd was coming and they were going to get trampled underfoot.

"I have God to thank for Jason's safety," Betty said, putting her hand on my knee and speaking with a soft voice.

"Huh?" I said, still in deep thought. "Oh, right."

"Yes, I prayed to Jesus that He would spare him," Betty said, "and He did."

"Right," I said. *It always comes back to this*, I thought to myself, *doesn't it?*

~~~~~~~~~

After packing up and returning to the car, we moved on with the others toward the next encampment, where we had high hopes of getting in some good elephant hunting. I hoped Betty hadn't lost her enthusiasm. I would be waiting and watching, because if she gave me even the slightest indication that she might not be ready to go, I would need to push her right back in the saddle, lest she lose her nerve.

We were eager to relate our story around the campfire, and to listen to the exploits of the others. But I knew Esther would jump on this incident with Jason and chime in with my wife, being sure to give their god the credit, and I just didn't want to hear it.

Then, out of nowhere, I heard Rose's voice echoing in my mind, as if I were sitting across from her at the dinner table back in Chicago. *Look to the animals, sir. God is speaking to you through the lessons that they are teaching. Seek the Lord and His wisdom, for He is calling you, He is reaching out to you. Listen to them and watch them, and you will understand.*

But where was the lesson here?

"Ah, hogwash," I whispered under the purr of the Ford, trying to shake my shoulders like a dog returning to the shore after swimming after a stick. "Hogwash!"

Chapter 15

HUMILITY

W hen we arrived at camp, Chuck greeted us with a bottle of whiskey. "We're celebrating!" he said with an enthusiastic smile.

Buster came running behind him and nearly spooked Jason's horse.

"Did you get an elephant?" Jason asked as he struggled to hold the reins and settle the mare before he greeted his dog.

"Whry-no," Chuck said with a guttural laugh. "And it's a beaut. Come on. Get off that car, John, and have a look at this horn."

Jason and Betty handed off their horses to the horse boys, who were waiting to take them.

"How'd you get 'em?" Jason asked, scratching his dog behind the ears.

"Oh, no," Chuck said, "you know the rules. Stories have to be left for the evening fire pit. But for now you can come and admire my rhino horn."

As we walked to his tent, he reminded me of a little kid skipping his way to the first day of school to show off a new pair of shoes.

"Quite a weapon, wouldn't you say?" he asked, wrestling the horn with a grunt to lessen his back pain.

At the first sight of it, I knew the rhino was a very respectable trophy, but certainly I wasn't going to tell him that. "I've seen bigger of course," I said, feeling the guilt of an outright lie and struggling with the effects of my green envy.

"Oh yeah?" Lance said as he approached. "Where?"

"Back in o-eight in the foothills of Kilimakiu. I think it was the Fredrickson outfit. Yeah, that's right. They brought in a rhino that would make that one look like a pup."

"Funny, I don't remember that one," Lance said. "Frederickson you say?"

"Yeah, well ... this is a nice rhino all right, but I'm just saying that I've seen bigger, that's all."

Chuck manhandled the skull with double gray sabers into position to show it off.

"Could you imagine carrying that around on your nose?" Jason exclaimed

"He was probably glad to see you, Chuck," I said with a laugh, "in hopes that you would put him out of his misery."

"No," Chuck countered, "he wanted to put *us* out of our misery, and he wanted to do it using this horn."

"Is it a good story?" Betty asked.

"I don't know," Chuck said, laughing. "I haven't told it yet. But hey, it's time to celebrate. Here, have a swig."

He retrieved the whiskey bottle that he had set on the ground, grabbing it by the neck, and Jason reached out for the bottle and grabbed it.

"Hey, sonny," Betty said, "ease up there."

"He's okay," I said. "Let him alone."

Jason glanced at Betty, and she wrinkled her nose and shook her head.

As he started to hand the bottle back to Chuck, I spoke up. "Here, take a gulp," I said, pushing the bottle back toward him.

Jason closed his eyes, tipped it to his lips, and took a short swig.

"Stop it, John," Betty said. "You know I don't like that."

Jason pulled the bottle off his lips and tried not to cough.

"Now look here," I argued, "one little sip ain't gonna turn him into a lush."

Betty's face turned red, and she stomped off toward our tent, but not before scowling at me.

"Was it something I said?" I asked with a big grin, hoping to get a good laugh out of the guys.

We all looked at each other like schoolboys who had just been scolded by the teacher, and then took turns snorting on the whiskey. The kid coughed and nearly choked, but the men among us never skipped a beat.

"So, besides the Fredrickson party," Chuck began, "have you ever seen a black rhino bigger than this?"

"Oh, sure," I answered.

"Well, Lance says he has never seen one bigger than this," Chuck said. "Right, Lance?"

"Well," I said, "old Lance, he's been too busy farming to notice any real trophies."

Lance rolled his eyes when Chuck wasn't looking and gave me a wink. He knew exactly what I was up to.

"Let's get cleaned up for supper," Lance said as we separated from Chuck and Jason.

"Hope she has cooled off some," I said as we walked toward the tents.

Lance shrugged his shoulders. "Nice rhino, right, John?"

"I've never seen one bigger," I said and laughed.

"How was your hunt?"

"Listen, we tracked a tusker, all right. I almost had a shot, and Jason—we damn near brought him back strapped over his horse. We were just getting in position when the bull charged us outright. Jason got saved when he fell beneath a pile of broken trees. We thought for sure the elephant got him."

"You didn't fire a shot at him?"

"No, I didn't have a shot, and he almost killed us, too."

"Then he's not spooked that bad, is he?"

"Probably not."

"Is he worth going after?"

"Oh, sure, he's worth going after, all right," I confirmed. "He's worth a five-day march if we have to."

"Bamira has been holding back supper for you guys," Lance said. "I'll tell him we're ready to eat."

"What's on the menu, Lance?"

"You'll see."

~~~~~~~~~~

As we sat around the folding table, which was draped with stained off-white linen and set with elaborate but chipped fine china, we dined on wild rice and roast kudu, cooked to perfection. We paused before partaking to listen to Esther give thanks to her god for our safety and for the meal. It struck me as I chewed on the tender pieces of kudu that Esther might have an interesting perspective on the elephant attack, and for some strange reason I felt compelled to ask her. But I also knew I didn't want Chuck jabbing me for being anywhere near interested in her point of view.

"I think we should go after the monarch you guys tangled with today," Lance said. "I talked to Janga, and he thinks that if we want a trophy bull, we should stay with him.

"Couldn't we find one a little less grumpy than this one?" Betty asked.

"Hey, we could leave the women behind," Lance said.

"Okay," Betty said, "but I don't intend to be left out."

"It could end up being the march from hell," Lance warned.

"Why do you say that?" Chuck asked.

"Because he's probably one day ahead of us right now," Lance said, "and by the time we have put down two days, he will have put another day between us. If anybody here wants to stay behind, we'll make this the main camp, and the rest of us will head off after the bull."

"Well, I for one am exhausted from the hunting we have done so far," Chuck said. "I could use a few days' rest. I'll be perfectly happy lying around camp. I'll take care of Buster and catch up on some reading."

"How about you, Jason?" I asked. "Are you up for it?"

"Seeing as this old boy nearly ground me into the dirt," he answered, "I wouldn't mind going after him just to settle up."

"Esther, what's your pleasure, my dear?" Lance asked.

"I'm with Chuck. This has been a stretch for me so far. I could use a few days' rest. I'll stay behind and sleep in, enjoy the solitude, and listen to the birds sing."

"Betty, will you stay behind?" I asked, hoping that she might agree and give me a little break from the responsibility of constantly looking after her.

"And miss this adventure? Not on your life, mister. You know me better than that."

Or did I? Something had definitely clicked for this woman. She would have never agreed to tag along with me in years past. I had always secretly hoped she would take more of an active interest in what I did, but I had always been forced to go it alone. I guess I had become accustomed to going it alone, and now this new woman stood in my way.

"I would like it if you would stay behind with Esther," I said.

Betty folded her arms across her chest and tightened her lip. "This is my safari, too."

"We're going on foot. No horses. Get it? And we won't wait for stragglers. You'll have to keep up."

Betty set her jaw tightly, her cheeks burning red. "I'll keep up."

"I'm only afraid that—"

"Afraid that what?" she snapped. "You just worry about yourself."

"We'll talk about this later," I said.

I knew I wouldn't get anywhere with her discussing it in front of everyone. On top of that, my mammy didn't raise no fool. I knew when not to go poking sticks at a rattlesnake ready to strike. I could tell our discussion had ended, because I had seen the same look in her eyes before.

~~~~~~~~~

The western sky blossomed like an orange-and-pink flower as we finished our evening meal.

"Is it story time?" Chuck asked, excusing himself from the table.

There had been tension in the air during the whole meal. Betty had eaten without saying another word, apparently still smoldering from our argument. She rose up and eagerly encouraged Chuck, likely sensing that his story would rub salt in my open wound. She knew I had never killed a real trophy rhino because I had told her many times about my utmost desire to take one.

As we settled into the canvas camp chairs surrounding the small campfire, Chuck said, "Tell us about your elephant, John."

"Not mine," I said, "Jason's. Let him tell it."

"To tell you the truth," Jason answered, "I don't remember much about him. Betty, you tell it."

Her face brightened. She was obviously touched by his confidence in her. She looked to me for approval.

I gave her a nod, and then she began.

Her eyes sparkled as she revealed every fine detail, carefully choosing her words so as not to leave any stone unturned. The inflection in her soft voice, the carefully chosen pauses, and her facial expressions had me hanging on every word. The intensity of her account made me forget that I had actually been there, too. Her rendition tasted like warm chocolate cake with creamy icing.

I glanced around at her audience, first looking toward Jason. His eyes were like pinpoints trained on a target. Lance gripped the corner of his chair tightly, his fingers turning white from the pressure. Chuck sat on the edge of his seat like an Irish setter pointing a rooster, waiting for it to burst from the bush, and anticipating the blast of his master's shotgun. And Esther, well, Esther sat as she always did: peacefully, with a quiet calmness in her spirit that I could never seem to explain or quite put my finger on. When Betty had finished her story, we were all amazed.

"Now I wish I had gone first," Chuck said, laughing. "At least I would have been the warm-up for the main event."

"Oh, Chuck, I have so looked forward to hearing your story," Betty said. "It will be wonderful."

"If it hadn't been for my good friend Lance," Chuck said, "I wouldn't have bagged this rhino. He was off about three hundred yards when he first spotted him."

"Wait, Chuck," Lance interrupted, "you have to start at the beginning."

"Oh, sure," he said. "Well then, when we left you this morning, we headed east toward the Kikuyu village where we heard the faint drums and saw the smoke column last evening. Temba thought we might get a lead from the local tribesmen on an elephant herd. So we made our way on down toward the valley floor through the scrub trees, hoping to intercept the camp. Temba found out from the tribesmen that the elephants had not been seen in the low country since the rains. They told us about buffalo in the area—and about a pesky lion they wanted us to rid them of—but as for elephants, the chief said the territory was empty.

"Temba thought we should make a proper scout anyway and said that he had seen them in this vicinity in years past during the dry season. He said he didn't trust this tribe and thought they might be trying to trick us into leaving their hunting grounds.

"Let me suggest not entering that village without proper trinkets. The children there are quite obstinate, and we had to tear ourselves free from their little fingers and hands grabbing at our pockets. Our pathway led us on forward and deeper into the bush. A couple of hours later we spooked a band of cape buff, and had we not been looking for elephants, Temba might have agreed to let us lay one down.

"We had high hopes of making contact with a fresh dung pile or a round-healed elephant track, but as the day wore on, our spirits waned. My legs felt like noodles fresh from a boiling pot, and my lungs like the wind from a bellow weary from a blacksmith's fire. The clock had struck, and as our day's hunt stretched out, Lance spotted a dust cloud to the north. All the time I had been thinking zebra, but Temba knew something, and we hustled along to investigate the puff trail.

As we approached the area, a flight of gazelle bounded aloft, as if flying on wings, and Temba, confident we had located the source, advised that we should break off the search. But Lance insisted we continue our pursuit to end the mystery and to make sure we had properly homed in on the source. On down the way we spotted dust again to the east, now encouraged that our gazelles had gone west. Lance had from the beginning called the possibility of rhino feet stirring the cloud, and Temba didn't argue.

"Foolish me, I became adamant that we should turn back, but Lance bowed his neck until we found ourselves staring at the armored brute just three hundred yards to the leeward. He must have sensed us with his hearing, because the wind did not allow him a sniff, and with his poor eyes, there was no way he could see what or who we were.

"The rhino made a charge of half the distance and stopped abruptly to evaluate us again. He stood poised at the brink of another charge that would bring him face-to-face. Lance stood at the ready with his rifle trained on the beast.

"At his encouragement, my gun bearer handed off my four-fifty, and I cranked home a waiting round. We had no real feeling of safety, because this brute could close a hundred and fifty yards in a matter of seconds. But Lance reassured me that he would back up my shot. I took a steady bead and held a half breath to settle my hold. Just the sight of his breathtaking horn made me unsettled, afraid I might miss the chance to take this prize, but I calmed myself to ensure a hit to end him. I squeezed the trigger, and my rifle barked.

"Lance stood by my side as our solitary prey stood poised to strike. I held my breath, not knowing if I had been on the money. I ejected the spent brass and drove another home, my trigger finger ready as I held a tight bead. Then I caught sight of his knees wobbling, then a sway, and finally he buckled under the immense weight of his form and went down in a pile.

"With one hot lead from the barrel of my four-fifty, his bitter disposition had been concluded. Of course, as we speak here relaxing around this fire, our men are dealing with the hide and packing out the meat to the Kikuyu villagers, meat enough that they will feast for a week indeed."

"That was a wonderful rendition," Betty said as she switched the subject. "Now, Lance, will we be getting an early start in the morning?"

"Are you really going with us?" I asked.

"Yep!" she snapped.

"No talking you out of it, is there?"

"Nope," she said, folding her arms tightly across her chest in defiance.

"Okay then," I said, "we will be getting an early start."

"Then I'm going to put a few things together in a chop box," Betty said.

"Oh, no, we won't be taking enough porters for personal gear, just the clothes on your back. We'll toss some grub together and take some bedrolls. But that's it!"

Betty raised her eyebrows and stared at me with her big brown eyes, obviously not sure if I was serious.

"Believe me," Lance said, "you'll be glad by the second day that we packed light."

"You can bring an extra pair of socks and a clean pair of shorts," I said, "but that's it. We'll have gun bearers and trackers, but the few porters that we decide to take along will be carrying lightly loaded grub boxes. The less feet we have on this march the better."

"Then I'll be heading for bed," she said, getting up from her chair. "And you had better get some rest too, Jason. You had a big day."

"Yes, ma'am."

"I'm turning in, too," Chuck said. "I'll be up in the morning to see you off."

"And I'll be headed the same as well," Lance said, "as soon as I meet with Willie so he can put together what we need. Esther, are you coming?"

"No, dear, I think I'll stay up and enjoy the fire for a while, if that's okay."

"Suit yourself," Lance said as he headed across the camp to find Willie.

"Aren't you turning in, John?" she asked.

"Not quite yet," I said as the other members left for their tents. "I wanted to hear your perspective on something, but I want your assurance that this is a private conversation."

"What is it, John? You know I wouldn't betray you. Is it a question about God?"

"How did you know?"

"Because I know you, John. And it's okay. I won't tell anyone. I understand that you are trying to protect your pride. It's for this very reason that Nicodemus came to Christ in the night to ask him if he was truly from God."

"Who was Nicodemus?"

"He was a Pharisee, a member of the Jewish ruling council. You see, the religious leaders of the day rejected Jesus as the Christ. Even though it was predicted in their Holy Scripture and by their ancient prophets, who had said the Messiah would come. But they were filled with pride and self-righteousness. They were certain that if God were to bring the Christ, he would come first to them, not to the sinners and the lowlifes such as the shepherds and tax collectors."

"And what did Jesus tell Nicodemus?" I asked, skeptical but curious.

"He said you must be born again to enter the kingdom of heaven."

"Well, I wouldn't know about that," I said, trying to hold my voice down so no one could hear. "But what I really want to know is what lesson the elephant teaches about God."

"First, let me ask you, why are you asking?"

"Betty has a friend named Rose, and today I heard her voice echo in my ears to look to the animals for a lesson. But I don't know what they are saying."

"How did this voice come to you? Did you hear it?"

"No, it was as if my own thoughts came into my head, but then I could hear Rose's voice as if she were sitting with me in the Ford. I have never experienced anything like it before. It gave me a chill as if she was there, but I knew she was half a world away."

"Tell me, do you believe in the spirits?" She paused as I contemplated the question. "Do you believe in angels?"

"Of course not. I mean, I never have, nor do I think I am ready to begin."

"Here it is in a nutshell, John. We think we live in a natural world, and when supernatural things happen, we tend to discount them or pass them off."

"I suppose we do, Esther."

"You were hearing the voice of the Spirit," she said with a warm smile. "I think that's where you need to start from."

"I don't know about that. All I want to know is about the elephant."

"Yes, the elephant. I heard the story from beginning to end. As I listened to Betty, it crossed my mind that you would be asking."

"Really?"

"Yes, and I had to give it a lot of thought, and I prayed that God would reveal to me the answer."

"Now wait a minute. You mean to tell me that you actually knew I would be asking you about the elephant? Come on. Really?"

"I'm not going to lie to you just to make you believe," she insisted. "If you find faith, it has to start from a firm foundation of truth."

"So what was your conclusion?" I asked, wondering why she was so reluctant to answer my seemingly simple question.

"Are you sure you want to hear this?"

"Yes!" I said, trying to hold my voice down.

"I just wanted to make sure, because what I am about to tell you, you cannot take lightly. This has been revealed to me by the Holy Spirit and given as a message for you to hear. So if I tell you this thing, you must take it to heart."

I had to admit that most of me wanted to get up and leave without hearing what she had to say, but something else stood in my way. Maybe my own stubbornness or desire to be in control spurred me on, but by darn, I had come to ask, and now I would not be denied.

"Do you agree?" she asked, her warm smile glowing in the orange firelight.

"Yes, please tell me. I am listening."

"First off, what does an elephant mean to you, John?"

I was taken aback by her question and pondered it a moment. Finally, I spoke, choosing my words carefully. "He is most of all powerful. I would describe him as awesome, noble, majestic, and vicious."

"You have spoken wisely, John. And how does he conduct himself?"

"In what respect?" I asked, wondering why we had to go through this twenty-question routine when I had asked a straightforward question and had expected to get a straightforward answer.

"How does he conduct himself in the African bush?" she asked.

"He is not a predator. He minds his own business and takes care of his families."

"The bull elephant is like a shepherd watching after his sheep, is he not?"

"I would say so."

"When a wolf threatens his flock, is the shepherd not there with his staff to drive it off? He uses his power for the good of his flock. He will not hunt you down like a bear or a lion, and he will steer away from you to avoid direct contact. He is elusive, even though he is very large and easy to see. But he leaves behind small traces that he has recently been near. He is the greatest big game prize of them all, and when you bag this trophy, you will be humbled by his majesty, his nobility, and his awesome power. For that, my dearest, John, is the key to finding God." She stopped abruptly and sat silently.

My mind scrambled to try to understand what she had said, but I had drawn a blank. "So … what you are saying is that the elephant is the key to humility."

"No, what I am saying is that humility is the key to finding the shepherd. And the elephant can teach us what it means to be humble."

"And what about Nicodemus?" I asked. "Did he come to believe in Christ?"

"We don't know for sure, but he spoke up and defended Christ in front of the Jewish leadership. And after Christ died on the cross, he assisted a man named Joseph, who was a secret disciple of Christ, in burying Jesus in the tomb. Surely anyone that close who had witnessed His death and then the resurrection could have become a believer, but the Bible never says for certain. It is God who gives us this gift of faith, by His grace. We are blinded to the things of the spirit until the appointed time, and then the veil is lifted."

"I think if I had been alive then," I said, "it would have been a lot easier to believe."

"Perhaps," she answered, pausing for just a second, "but perhaps not. Would you have been as willing as Matthew, who was doing very well financially collecting taxes, to give up everything and follow Christ when he called?"

"How well was he doing?"

"Very, very well," she answered.

"I don't know." I thought how curious this whole conversation had been. I expected her to pounce on me and pound me with her religion. But she seemed more interested in my point of view than in selling hers. I still didn't understand how, if this Christ really did exist as their book claimed, it wouldn't have been easier to buy into this story as an eyewitness. And I did not for sure see how my weakness could lead me anywhere.

"Good night," I said. "Will I see you in the morning?"

"Possibly."

"Thanks for sharing your insight," I said and left for my tent.

My head was spinning. I couldn't understand why this all seemed so difficult. I had great pride in myself as being an intellectual, someone who could understand difficult concepts. But why the Bible seemed to speak in gibberish and why the concepts of the supernatural were so difficult to grasp was beyond me. I didn't seem any closer to an answer now than I had been before. And somehow, I was just fine with that.

Chapter 16

THE MARCH ON THE MONARCH

I t seemed my bones had barely hit the sack when I found myself rising for the day. Betty was up, dressed, and ready to go. I hoped she knew what she was getting herself into. I had been on an elephant march one time before, and it took toughness. Now we were going with Temba, and goodness, that man could flat pick 'em up and lay 'em down. Even though I knew Janga would rein him in a bit, Temba was a concern. Our only saving grace was that we all packed into the Ford and brought Chuck along to drive the Lizzy back to camp after we had driven the car as far as we could take it. It was a tight squeeze with the five of us, but it saved us a lot of walking as we followed the natives up the narrow trail.

When early afternoon came, we said goodbye to the Ford and sent Chuck back to camp to stay with Esther. Then we trudged up the foothills to the place we had left off the day before. Temba and Lance marveled at the size of the elephant track, while Janga quickly determined how to follow the spoor. We took a short lunch break and then headed off across the side of the mountain in pursuit of the elusive monster.

When putting one foot in front of the other, a man has time to ponder many things. There is the scenery, of course, and one is occupied with the obstacles in the bush. But plenty of thoughts cross the mind. Esther's words dripped in my mind like rain leaking through a roof in a rainstorm. I tried in my mind to move the tin pans to catch the drips in order to make some sense out of what she had said. Near as I could figure, these things of the spirit, as she referred to them, made no sense whatsoever. The more I tried to understand, the more I became frustrated. I considered myself an intelligent person, a man of reasonable intellect, a likeable person, a decent man. But trying to buy into spiritual things left me cold indeed. I understood the concept of humility. I could even put it in my mouth. I just couldn't swallow. Maybe I equated humility with cowardice, like hiding behind apron strings of a mammy. I despised a coward. Weakness made me furious. This humility concept wasn't working for me. If god existed out here, then he would have to find me first.

My legs grew numb as my feet pounded the red dirt of the African bush. The sun baked the ground, and my mind wandered to days past and much more pleasant times.

~~~~~~~~~

I had met Lucy for the first time on the train from Mombasa five years ago. She had blond hair and great beauty. She wore white cotton lace and crimson chiffon. Like a delicate flower blooming in the desert, she sat quietly, traveling alone and looking out of place next to the European roughnecks around her.

"Is this seat taken?" I asked.

She looked up, batting her long eyelashes.

I might not have asked if things had been better at home in Chicago, but I knew how strained my marriage had become. I couldn't talk to Betty anymore. She had withdrawn from me in every way. I felt as if I were married to a missing person. She was someone I didn't know anymore. I still loved her, but not the person she had become. I loved the person I used to know.

"There are plenty of seats," she said in a sultry voice. "Why would you want to sit here?"

"Because you look as lonely as I feel," I said.

She returned her attention to the pages of her book, and I took it as an invitation to have a seat and slithered in next to her. The wheels on the train clicked to their rhythm as we moved across Africa in the heat of the equatorial afternoon. Neither of us said a word. I sensed by her absorption in the novel that she had no interest in the scenery.

"Is this your first time in Africa?" I asked.

She looked up from her book and let out an impatient sigh. "No," she said, sticking her nose back in the pages.

Clickity-clack, clickity-clack, clickity-clack.

The seconds dragged until they were minutes as I watched Africa speed by the window.

I spied a band of giraffe nibbling from the tops of an acacia in the far distance. "Have you seen giraffe before?"

"Many times," she answered, not raising her eyes from her story.

"What are you reading?"

"Look here, sir," she said, looking up and piercing me with her bright eyes, "can't you see I'm busy? Why are you bothering me?"

"I don't mean to be a bother," I said indignantly. "I just thought you looked like you needed a friend. Excuse me." I started to get up, but she put her hand on my arm.

"It's okay, you can stay."

I stopped and abruptly sat back down.

"Is this your first time in Africa?" she asked. She had gorgeous straight white teeth and soft blond curls.

I felt a flutter in my chest as her piercing blue eyes nearly stopped my heart. "No, this is my second trip," I said.

"Have you come to hunt?"

"I will, but my purpose here is science."

As I described my work, her eyes intensified and she seemed genuinely interested. I felt like I had found a jewel in a sand dune. The exchange of thought and ideas between us became intoxicating. She lifted the hardback, then closed it gently on her lap, saving the place with a bookmark. As she did, I noticed she had an expensive diamond and wedding band on her left hand.

"What does your husband do?" I asked.

"He is a professional hunter. We have a home in Nairobi. But you're right: I don't have very many friends here. He told me to meet him in Mombasa two weeks ago when I came in from England, but he never showed up. You might know him. His name is Allen Rogers. Oh, and I'm Lucy."

"And I am Jonathan Rivers."

Actually, I did know Al Rogers. At least I had met him. He was truly quite a popular character in this part of Africa. Quite arrogant, too.

"Instead, he sent one of his servant boys yesterday to tell me I should go on to Nairobi and he would be there in four weeks. Four weeks! Can you believe that?" A tear rolled down her cheek and caught on the corner of her trembling lip.

"I wish I could—"

"No, there is nothing you can do," she said. "There is nothing anyone can do."

I knew the feeling of being ignored in a relationship, how painful she must have felt to be alone with no companion. Not that I wanted Betty's companionship. In fact, at that very moment, it was good to be separated from her.

"Do you have children?" I asked.

"No, we don't have any children," she said with a tight jaw.

I knew that to probe further would put me on thin ice.

We made small talk the rest of the afternoon, and then we parted company. I didn't see her again until after we had arrived in Nairobi the following day. She caught my eye in the railway station, and I approached her, thinking she would bid me a polite goodbye. She glanced around to make sure no one saw her, and then she stepped close to speak in my ear with her warm breath.

"I could use some company for the next couple of weeks if you have the time. I'd like to hear some more about your work."

I didn't know how to respond. She had caught me quite off guard. I took a gulp, stepping back to admire her gorgeous frame. This thirty-year-old flower had just invited me to partake in what I could only imagine. And here I stood, thousands of miles away from Betty, who would be none the wiser. She reached for my hand and slipped a piece of paper into my palm, then turned and walked away without so much as a wink. I looked around to see whose eyes might have spotted the exchange, but none were upon me. I eagerly unfolded the paper in a quiet, inconspicuous corner and found an address scribbled in pen. Part of me wanted to throw it in the trash, but the other part stuffed the note in my shirt pocket.

Our meeting would be the first of six to take place over the next five years. I always upheld her honor, and mine as well, even though I knew she didn't have the most honorable intentions. There were nights afterward that I wished I had not been so principled. I had seen her last year for the last time, just before leaving Nairobi to go home to Chicago. She told me they were separated, and I knew she wanted another husband. She offered to let me stay with her for the week. I had to admit now that I had found her poise and beauty sorely tempting, but I was content for never having indulged.

Now I felt I was the luckiest man in Africa, for I had a companion who took an interest in the things I loved. I could honestly say that I had stood on the edge of infidelity and that, if someone had brushed me with a feather, I might have fallen into trouble. The memory of Lucy's beauty still haunted me. But when I looked into Betty's eyes, I felt thankful for what I had.

~~~~~~~~~

I could feel Betty panting against my back as we trudged along in the afternoon heat, our feet the only conversation, the sweat soaking my shirt from the inside. I grabbed my canteen from my belt and took a welcome swig. I wanted to pour some over my head but held off from wasting any. I still held out hope that we might cross a clear creek. I looked over my shoulder at Betty to check on her, and she gave me a reassuring look of determination.

Throughout the day we passed a number of what might have been considered trophy animals, and I began to estimate the numbers: sixty impala, twenty Kongoni or hartebeest, sixty zebra, eighty wildebeest, ten sable, fifteen duiker, two eland, and a pair of giraffe. But we had made a pact—the elephant or nothing—and we had no intention of being sidetracked. The elephant was the aim, and we would not be denied, short of Janga and Temba losing the track, and that just wasn't going to happen.

My legs began to feel like rubber, my head light from the heat. Temba showed no signs of slowing down or needing to take a break. I stepped forward, grabbing hold of Lance by the shoulder, and he slowed to lend an ear.

"Tell them we need a break," I whispered. I looked back again, and Betty and Jason had now lagged behind about twenty yards.

Lance gave me the high sign and did a quick step to catch up to the guides. We had been on this march for nearly four and a half hours since leaving the Ford at noon. Janga stopped and came walking back toward me with a curious look.

"We want to *uwa tembo* (kill elephant), no?" I said. "Is not that the *fikira* (idea)?"

"Yes, Bwana!" he said with wide eyes.

"Well, I'm afraid you're going to *uwa* (kill) one of us first if you keep going."

"Janga get *tembo* (elephant), Bwana," he said with a wide grin.

"Yes, yes," Lance said, "but we are *dhoofik* (tired) and *njaa* (hungry)."

"We'll rest for a bit," I said, "then have supper and go one more hour before making camp for the night."

Lance rattled off the plan in Swahili, and Temba nodded his approval. The porters gathered around, and Lance rummaged the grub box and began passing out food like a bank robber sorting out the loot.

"How many days do you think before we can catch him?" I asked Janga, who gloated over the food box.

"Him no fraid. Him go slow now and not run. We *kuta* (find) him *kesho* (tomorrow) maybe, or who know?" Janga said with a shrug. "But we *kuta tembo* (find elephant)." He put a piece of dried meat between his teeth and winced as he tore the jerky with a firm grip.

"If we can get him today," Jason said, "what did we stop for?"

"Because these old bones said *stop*," I said, grinning and giving the kid a slap on the back of his head.

Just then we heard a growl from a lion, which set us on edge and ended our horseplay.

I snapped my fingers, and my gun bearer handed over the British five hundred.

Janga held his finger to his lips, and both Lance and Jason followed my lead and took up their rifles.

The brush at the edge of the clearing moved about eighty yards away, and Jason brought his rifle to his shoulder. Then a big male lion ran out from the trees and stopped in his tracks, scrutinizing us with his piercing eyes. He opened his mouth and let out a shallow grumble.

Lance reached over and pushed the barrel of Jason's 30-40 toward the ground. "Let's wait and see what he does before we make our presence known to every creature in the countryside," he whispered.

The sun glistened off the lion's black mane as he looked over his shoulder at a lioness joining him. She, too, fixed us with her gaze, as if to say, "Who invited you to the party?"

We stayed frozen like a covey of quail at the end of a pointer's nose, and the lioness slinked off in the bushes, leaving the big male on his own.

In the eerie silence of the moment, I felt as if I were standing alone before God Himself. The lion, the king of beasts, had piercing eyes, and his presence was terrifying. A voice from within told me not to succumb to this foolishness, but the power of the lion continued to dampen my soul like a stream of water. I felt afraid, afraid that I might be losing my grip on reality, afraid that everything I stood for might somehow evaporate into thin air.

The lion let out another roar and then turned and crouched on us, as if ready to charge.

I lifted my double barrel and took a steady bead on his forehead.

Temba held out his hand for me to remain steadfast.

The weight of the heavy barrel grew to a steady burden, the pressure of my waiting trigger finger a lingering temptation.

Temba, of course, was showing great restraint and wisdom. It was best to wait until the last possible moment before sending an echoing report down the valley. Our elephant had not been spooked, and taking an unnecessary shot now could surely mean several more days of tracking. The lion's tail swished in the air, a sure sign he could strike at any minute like a coiled diamondback. I could feel a bead of sweat trickle down the center of my back, and my forearm began to quiver under the stress of holding the weight of the rifle.

In that moment it felt as if time stood still. I took a quick glance around at the stone faces of my companions, their breathing halted and their eyes frozen. I looked back to the lion, who now stood colorless. I felt as if I had stepped into another dimension. My hands and feet were numb.

All at once the lion spoke to me in the voice of an angel, who said, *I am the Lion, the one who was sent for your salvation. You know it is true. You know what you have denied. And you know what you must do.*

I took a deep breath just as the lion took a step forward, and suddenly the color returned to my surroundings and everything was as it had been. The lion turned and bounded off, leaping over a dead tree and disappearing in the bush.

Betty exhaled as I dropped the muzzle of the heavy rifle toward the ground. Lance had a stunned look of relief, and I let down my rifle, struggling with the reality of what had just happened.

"Did you hear … ?" I began and then stopped short, not knowing how to finish the question.

"Did I hear what?" Lance asked.

"Never mind," I mumbled. "It's nothing. I just never knew lions …"

"What did you say?" he snapped.

"Really, never mind."

I knew how silly I would sound if I declared a lion had just spoken to me. Lance would have probably had me sit under a shade tree with a damp cloth on my forehead. I dug into the grub and devoured some sharp cheese and a hard roll.

"Are you okay?" Betty asked, trying to look me in the eye.

"I'm fine. Why?"

"You just seem a little quiet, that's all," she said. "You seem a little distant."

"I'll tell you later," I whispered.

"If we gonna catch *tembo*," Janga said, "we go now, Bwana."

"One more hour, and then we make camp," Lance said. "Are you okay, John? You just look out of sorts."

"I'm fine. Don't worry about me," I said, knowing that when a lion speaks to you, it sort of leaves you rattled.

We pushed hard over the next couple of days knowing we were closing in on the monarch. We had trailed his lone track to a sparse group of acacia trees on the edge of a rocky hill overlooking a basin.

"There he is," Lance said, pointing up the valley after spotting him about two miles away from our bluff.

He stood alone in the shade of a large tree, likely spent from the nearly fifty miles he had put down in the three days since our first encounter.

Temba tossed ashes to the wind and looked over the terrain. I could see the wheels churning in his head as he devised a plan to intercept our prize.

"We need to reduce our party," I said. "We'll all go, but we can leave the porters and gun bearers behind. Do you want to stay behind, Betty?"

"Nice try, mister."

"Let's draw straws to see who shoots him," I said. I picked some grass and made four strands, each one a different length, and then hid all but the even tops in my fist. "Long straw takes him with the double," I said.

I held them out so Lance could take the first pick, and he pulled out a shorty.

Jason started to laugh, and I held my finger to my lips. "We can talk, but let's not get rambunctious and spook that beast, unless you want to chase him another twenty miles."

Jason picked second, and his pulled up smaller than Lance's.

Betty reached out to take a straw, and it came out short again. Everybody knew I had the long straw remaining in my hand. Betty stood behind Jason and made a gesture to let him shoot the bull.

"Here, Jason," I said, "I'll trade you straws."

His eyes brightened. "No kidding, John? You would trade with me?"

"I'll trade, but you have to shoot him where I say."

He laughed quietly and whispered, "I'll shoot him in the middle of Timbuktu if you want me to."

"I want you to shoot him in the brain," I instructed sternly, "and it can be tricky, because it's about the size of a loaf of bread and shielded by heavy armor. If you don't hit him in the right spot, just behind the eye, we will both be in trouble."

Janga stealthily led us on through the bush and across the grassland, downwind from the resting beast. A gentle breeze blowing in the waist-high grass muffled our advance and hid us further from the elephant and his sensitive ears. Janga and Temba led the way, and we hunkered down so our heads fell just below the tops. We worked our way across the valley floor, edging to within five hundred yards, and still the big creature seemed unaware of our presence.

"*Shinda* (stay put)," Temba said, holding up his palm to the rest of us before motioning to Jason to follow him. "*Fuatilia*," he said.

Jason looked to me for help.

"He wants you to follow him carefully," I said, handing him my British double. "It's loaded up, and here, this is the safety. Now take these other rounds. You can put two rounds between your knuckles. You've seen me do this before."

Jason gave me an eager nod as he took the rifle.

"Hold it tight to your shoulder when you let the round go," I whispered. "And shoot for his brain." I loaded up his front pockets with five rounds each. "Now make sure these don't rattle around, or you may as well put bells on your shoes."

The wind remained in our face as we watched Temba, who was like a cat in the grass stalking a gazelle. Jason mimicked his every move. They settled in one hundred yards downrange, and Jason took careful aim at Temba's instruction. I grew anxious at every passing second.

The bark of the British rifle broke the calm, echoing through the hills.

The huge beast wheeled around in anger and let out a terrible roar that nearly shook the ground, flushing the birds out of the trees and scattering them in every direction. The elephant acted as if the shot had missed him clean, and he lunged forward in a charge. His trunk waved like a huge serpent, and he pounded the ground with his feet, sending faint vibrations to where we crouched. He stopped, though, after only a few steps.

Temba and Jason held their position, knowing well that the animal, like all elephants, had poor eyesight. Unless it heard you or smelled you, an elephant was not likely to see you if you remained still. Jason broke open the rifle and placed a fresh round in the chamber to prepare for a second shot, just as I had instructed him.

However, just as the beast was venting its anger, it lurched, wobbled, and then keeled over, falling dead in its tracks.

Jason jumped to his feet, but Temba grabbed him by the shirt, pulling him back down.

"What the boy lacks in wisdom he makes up for in enthusiasm," I said and chuckled quietly with Lance and Betty.

Once it was safe to move up, Janga led our party to the place where Temba and Jason waited. Betty took Jason in her arms and whispered something in his ear.

Temba gestured for us all to remain while he cautiously snuck up on the sleeping giant, all the time confident that, like a rodeo clown, he had the moves and the speed to elude a wounded elephant if he had to. At twenty yards, he picked up a stick and tossed it, hitting the beast with a thud to see if it might elicit a response. He gave us a thumbs-up and waved us to him.

I grabbed Jason's shirt as we moved up to his position. "Put another round in his brain," I said, "just for good measure."

Jason lifted the rifle, pointed it to the back of the elephant's head, and squeezed off another round, and the rifle's deafening blast knocked the kid back.

Janga took a pole and touched the eye of the elephant, and then we moved in closer to view his magnificence.

"I think I finally understand it," Betty said as she caressed his skin. "It's so incredible just to stand over a creature such as this and feel his power down in your soul. It's incredible to imagine being the first human to lay hands on him."

"The only thing I can compare it to," I replied, "is a mountain climber who is first to reach the summit of a well-known mountaintop. I know you've felt the tusks in my trophy room, Jason, but feel these and know that they belong to you now. There is nothing like the feeling of a tusk when it is still attached to the animal, knowing just seconds before his temper would have ground you into the dust."

"It's incredible to have silenced this monster after he almost killed me," Jason said, caressing the smooth ivory.

I could only imagine what was going on in his young brain. It seemed a terrible shame to me not to be able to salvage any of the meat, but with a long trek back to camp still ahead of us, we had no way to even try to attempt it. It would be several days before we were back, and by the time we returned, the carcass would be completely soured from the midday heat. Our natives worked quickly to separate the ivory from the elephant, and we all headed back to camp.

~~~~~~~~~~

One week later, the elephant march had been reduced to a thrilling memory. I hadn't heard any more voices coming from animals and hoped that I wouldn't anytime soon. We were enjoying a beautiful calm day, and I had dozed off in camp. When I awoke, I began to look for Betty and found her sitting along the river.

"I wondered where you were," I scolded. "You can't take off like this and not tell anyone, my dear."

"I have my rifle," she responded. "Besides, I did tell Janga, and he is right over there guarding me with his rifle."

"I stand corrected," I said, changing my tone. "This is a nice spot."

"Oh, this is a wonderful place, and just as soon as I'm done here with this letter to Mae, I'm going to dig out my fishing gear and wet a line."

"Looks like quite a letter there. How long have you been down here?"

"The better part of an hour, I guess," she said.

"What did you write about?"

"The elephant hunt. I thought she would be interested."

"You didn't tell her how many days we marched, did you?"

"I didn't tone down any of the hardship," she said, "but I might have played down some of the dangers. Here, I'm just about finished. Do you want me to read it to you?"

I looked around for a suitable place to sit and found a spot in the sand next to a stump. As I sat down and put my back against a branch, the cool air drifted off the flowing river. The birds spoke sharply as they danced in the treetops.

"Are you comfortable?" she asked.

"Okay, I'm ready."

"My dearest Mae," she began in her sweet voice. *"I am so delighted to report to you our progress, especially our wonderful fortune in taking a splendid bull elephant. John and Jason were like two boys gloating over an ice cream sundae, and for the first time I was able to understand why.*

"A week and a half ago we had a mild encounter with this magnificent bull while pursuing game in the bush country along the Mara. We retreated back to camp in the evening and then organized a tracking party to trail the monarch. What followed was a grueling five-day march, and had I known what we were up against, I might have gracefully declined to go along. Esther stayed back at camp and had a relaxing time reading her books. My wonderful man was as encouraging and helpful as he could have been. I tried to keep my grumbling to a minimum, just as you and I discussed in Chicago, complying with your wise council."

I chuckled to myself as Betty looked up from the page to catch my eye.

"Our guides are very much to be admired," she continued, *"since they have the senses of a winning field dog when it comes to tracking game. On this march we encountered a number of prized trophies, but passed them up for the silence of not spooking our elephant. But I must say, by the third morning I thought I would not get up from my bedroll. We had packed light enough not to become burdened by a load, and we had sufficient porters. But our provisions were such that we were limited to not more than six days out.*

"I will say that at no time were we in any danger, and since you have now received this word, it would make no sense for you to fret over me. Can one truly experience adventure without the threat of danger? And is not the threat of death the trap which keeps us all on the edge of life? How can anyone truly experience life if they have not had it hang in the balance?

"You know, Mammy, I would never write this to you so you might fuss over me. I write to you to tell you how much I am enjoying myself so you can take peace in the knowledge that I am exactly where I am supposed to be in my life right now. You know God is watching over me. I have had a lot of time to ponder on this adventure, and I have done a fair amount of questioning my lovely friend Esther, who has been helping me in my journey to find God. I can only say that I have learned a great deal, and that I feel like I am growing closer." Betty

paused, and a look of surprise appeared on her face as she studied my expression.

"What's the matter?" I asked.

"Just thought I might get a scowl from you for telling her about my search for God, that's all." Her eyes fell back to her letter, and she continued. "*I want to tell you about the elephant hunt. As I said, my body was about to give up on the third day when we finally came to encounter the beast. I had forgotten how massive his tusks were, and how foul his disposition. But Jason was picked to deliver the shot, and bring him down he did, and we are all safe and sound back at camp.*

"*I don't mean to bore you with unwanted details or to scare you with terrifying reality, but I did hope to give you a true sense of the awesome adventure we are experiencing here. I wanted to give you a firsthand account moment to moment, because of my commitment to you to keep you informed about our progress here in Africa.*" Betty paused again, dipping her quill pen in the inkbottle, and she carefully finished the letter, speaking each word slowly as she formed it on the page. "*My dearest Mae, now John has joined me on the east bank of the Ewuso Nyiro River as I pen the final words of this letter. We are sitting here together listening to the birds sing and the animals chat. We both express our love to you and write to tell you how much we miss your smile, your laughter, and your cooking. We really miss your cooking, but most of all your love. Give our best regards to Ralph and tell him he is in our thoughts as well. The last letter I received was several weeks ago on the second day of our trek. I can say what a joy it was to see the runner come into our camp carrying your lovely words from home. Promise me you will stay in touch, and I promise to continue to send my words to you. I love you. We love you, and we miss you. Betty, John, and Jason forever.*"

"That's a great letter," I said. "I think she will love it."
Betty smiled, and I leaned over and kissed her on the lips.

Chapter 17

A BROAD MIND

"I had a great time here in camp this past week and a half," Esther said as Betty and I settled into the camp chairs next to her. "I read my Bible and got to know Chuck. Quite a welcome break, don't you think, from the furious pace we took getting to our hunting grounds. I can't believe how the natives treat me like a queen. It's unlike anything I have ever experienced."

"Unlike the white people back in Nairobi," Betty said, shaking her head.

"Africa has been such a blessing for me," Esther continued, "to have the opportunity to serve God. I am so encouraged by the sheer volume of Christian work here, even though I feel helpless when I see the poverty and the condition in which these natives live. You know what?" she asked, putting her finger to her chin.

"What?" Betty asked.

"I actually count myself blessed to have been born from descendants who were captured and sold into slavery. I'm not discounting their suffering, nor am I forgetting the pain that my beloved family members endured. No, I believe it is terrible what happened to them. But I am quite aware of the fact that had not all this been allowed to take place, I would not be here today, speaking to these native people about God with such authority. Nor would I be married to Lance and have such special friends such as you."

"It does seem true that nothing of much good comes without suffering," Betty said. "What is old-fashioned hard work but simple suffering?"

"It's by God's design," Esther continued. "No child is born without the wrenching in a woman's womb to produce a new seed, and no teachable moment arrives in the life of a soul without the advent of some torment. Even the greatest event in the history of mankind, when God himself came to earth in the person of His Son to save humanity from the scourge of sin, was not accomplished without His own personal suffering and death on a cross."

Once again she just couldn't resist pushing her religion. But I had expected it this time and didn't feel like getting angry.

"I want so much to spread the Gospel here, but the barrier of language is so great and the influence of this culture is so intimidating. It's been very difficult for one lone black woman to have any real influence."

I knew she had to be looking for support from Betty, who remained silent. For darn sure she wasn't going to get any help from me.

"The sickness in these villages is devastating," she continued. "Had I realized this before, I might have been better prepared. It's my dream, of course, to have a medical clinic set up on our farm to care for the sick. Lance has tried to discourage me, claiming that we will attract multitudes of the sick and dying in what he said would be like 'flies on a carcass.'

"But if only we could reach them with more than the crude Gospel of Saint John, which is scratched out in Swahili, of which none of them are equipped to read anyway. And if that's not bad enough, the few converts that God has helped me to find have come under such incredible pressure from the witchcraft in their tribe. However, I might add, like the fire of a blast furnace, I can see how all this is serving to strengthen their faith and mine."

"Do you remember hearing about the trouble Dr. David Livingstone had evangelizing the natives?" Betty asked. "He scarcely won a single convert."

"His fame came from his explorations in Africa over fifty years ago," I explained, "and the discovery of Victoria Falls. Did you know that when he died they buried his heart under some Mvula tree near the east bank of Lake Tanganyika?"

"They did?" Betty asked.

"Sure did," I responded, "and then they manhandled his body out of the bush and sent it home to Britain, where they laid him to rest a whole year later."

"No kidding," Esther said. "I came to Africa thinking I would impact the Africans, but now I can see that I am here for all of you as well."

I knew I would have to chew on that for a while. *That is a little bit like the fisherman who tells the fish he is trying to catch them for their own good,* I thought, laughing to myself.

"When I married Lance, I knew he had a measure of faith," Esther said. "But I can see how that small seed has grown since we've been together."

I had to stop myself from bursting out laughing. When Esther was out of earshot, he talked like an old boatswain's mate, spewing out cuss words like billows of smoke off a cold fire.

"I'm thrilled to be on safari," Esther continued, "but my safari is much different than all of yours. If I might be so bold as to speak, I think you came to conquer Africa. Am I right, John?"

"You could put it like that," I said.

"I have come to serve God," she said gingerly, "and to serve Him for as long as He desires, to be His hands and His voice, and to let His light shine in the darkness. Do you understand what I mean?"

Her innocent demeanor drew me in as she talked. Her captivating smile and bright eyes had the effect of melting hard butter on a warm roll.

"Would you like some warm bread?" Bamira asked, holding out a platter of sliced bread.

"This looks wonderful," Betty said, taking a slice from the plate.

"Have a seat with us," Esther said.

Bamira took hold of the camp chair to sit down, and it creaked as he lowered his robust frame onto it. He had a very dark complexion and tight-wire curls cut short to his head. His face was wide and punctuated by thick lips and a wide nose. He had rough skin and heavy wrinkles from the hard years. He appeared to be in his late forties, but I had the impression he might have actually been much younger than that.

"What is this writing?" he asked.

"I'm writing in my journal, good sir," Esther answered, setting her booklet aside on a folding table.

"Can anyone here tell me a story about your Christianity so that I might decide what to follow?" he asked.

"Not me, Bamira," I said with a grin.

He squinted at me and then addressed us. "I think I will choose Christian, or maybe become a Mohammedan. I have been listening to Longerna, who is devoted to the prophet Mohammad, and what he tells seems very wise. But I am watching all of you also."

"How have I been doing?" Esther asked. "Have you found Christ in me to be worthy?"

"I don't know about this Christ. What story can you tell me to help me to gain some Christian knowing?"

"I've told you about the cross, have I not?" Esther asked.

"Yes, *Bibi* (madam)."

"And I have told you of His love and His power to forgive and to wash you clean?"

"Yes, *Bibi*."

I started to stand up, not wanting to be part of this conversation, but Betty grabbed my arm and I settled back.

"And who do you say that this Jesus of Nazareth is?" she asked.

"I don't know," he said, wrinkling his brow. "This man spoke for your god, I would say."

"Do you truly believe that He spoke for God?" Esther asked.

"I do suppose."

"If He spoke for God," she continued, "who is all that I have told you that He is, including my God who is angry because of sin, do you think this man could have lied and gotten away with it?"

"He died on a cross. Could that been his punishment?"

"What do you think?" she asked.

"I remember this man, and he was a good man, as you said, and you say he had no sin. If this is true, then he died for sins from all the world?"

"But even more than that, my dear Bamira. Who, pray tell, did He die for?"

"I don't know, *Memsahib*. Please, can you tell me?"

"I have told you before, and you did not hear. So now I can only say that you must search for the answer on your own."

"Why is that, *Mabibi*?"

"Because for me to hand you this gem is of no purpose," Esther said. "Unless you search to find it on your own, it will have no value for you. It is a gemstone of great value, but for you it has no worth."

How peculiar that she would not give him the answer. I knew it and wanted to pipe in and tell the poor man.

"How could I find such a treasure?" he asked. "And where would I look?"

"First, you must place a value on it to find it. Ask, and it will be given to you; seek, and you will find; knock, and the door will be opened to you. For everyone who asks receives; he who seeks finds; and to him who knocks, the door will be opened."

Bamira started to get up, thinking she had finished.

"Sit with me, Bamira, and I will tell you a story."

He looked at Betty and me, and then settled back in his seat as Esther flipped through her Bible.

"This is the story of Zacchaeus," she continued. "Jesus was passing through a town called Jericho, where a man named Zacchaeus lived. He was a chief tax collector and was a very wealthy man. A tax collector was much hated in these times, because he was collecting taxes for the Romans and at the same time he was lining his own pockets with the extra money he stole from the people."

"This man is a sinner, no?" Bamira asked.

"Yes, he was, and Zacchaeus wanted to see who Jesus was. But being a very short man, he could not, because of the crowd along the street. So he ran ahead and climbed a sycamore tree to see him, since Jesus was coming that way. When Jesus reached the spot, He looked up and said to him, 'Zacchaeus, come down immediately. I must stay at your house today.' So he came down at once and welcomed him gladly. Just imagine being called by name by a very famous man who you had never met before."

The whites of Bamira's eyes contrasted sharply against his dark skin as he listened wide-eyed, hanging on each word.

I, too, was intrigued, although I tried to remain skeptical. But the voice of the lion kept echoing in my head.

"All the people saw this and began to mutter, 'He has gone to be the guest of a sinner.' But Zacchaeus stood up and said to the Lord, 'Look, Lord! Here and now I give half of my possessions to the poor, and if I have cheated anybody out of anything, I will pay back four times this amount.' Jesus said to him, 'Today salvation has come to this house, because this man, too, is a son of Abraham. For the Son of man came to seek and to save what was lost.'"

"I should climb a tree to find this gemstone?" Bamira asked.

"Have you ever had a mind to climb the Mountain of Kilimanjaro?" she asked.

"No, mem. Bamira not like it cold, and the thought makes me tired."

"But if I told you a great treasure resides at the top," she continued, "and if you go that many riches and glory would come to you, would you then consider the journey?"

"If Bamira sure to find this worth, he will pack his sack."

"That is how you must search," she explained. "You see, at every point in your life that you have rejected Jesus, you have chopped a tree across this pathway. How many trees do you suppose are now across this path?"

As she spoke, I had a vision of the forest lying across my pathway, and a shiver went up my spine. But I shook it off.

"Many, I would presume," Bamira said. "From boyhood I have heard this teaching and had no want for it. If what you say is true, this path is much blocked."

"Then this pile of logs is now what you must climb to find the path leading to this pearl."

"But if I choose to follow Mohammed, will I not be acceptable in God's eye?"

"Do you think you can keep all of the laws that this religion teaches you must?" Esther asked. "Do you think you can work your way to heaven under your own power and will?"

"It could be very hard, mem."

"I know that you believe that Jesus was a great teacher and a prophet. Is that not true?"

"Indeed, memsahib! And if I decide to become Christian, then do I not also have to obey this law?"

"In the book of Matthew, chapter twenty-two," she continued, "Jesus taught that there is a foundation to the law. If you will love the Lord God with all of your heart, and all of your mind, and with all of your soul, and if you will love your neighbor as yourself, then you will not be tempted to break any of the law, because your love will protect you. It is true you will want to obey the teachings of Christ, which includes obeying the law, but when you fall, you are not condemned by your weakness. So we are all free from the judgment of the law because of Christ's death, and we are covered by His blood that saves us. Answer this one question for me," she said, pausing to look gently into Bamira's eyes.

Much like Bamira, I found myself captivated by her words, even though I wanted to run. Something was holding me in my seat. *Maybe it's Betty*, I thought.

"Yes, mem," he answered.

"Do you think you can save yourself by your own ability to please God?" Esther asked.

"This is a lot to consider," Bamira said, folding his arms tightly across his chest. "I must think on this."

"Your thinking will do you well," Esther said in her soft voice. "But if you can find it in your heart to pray and to ask God for this wisdom, you will find the truth. How would it be for you if we pray now?"

Again an opportunity had come for me to get up, and I was determined that if Betty grabbed me again, I would just pull away.

"No, please, mem," Bamira said, patting her arm, "I would need to think of this first before we summon your god."

I settled back in my seat, feeling relieved that Bamira had enough sense to stop her. But then I noticed that she had quit talking and had closed her eyes, and I remembered back to the incident with the men from the railroad on her front porch. I had seen something happen that day, and if something happened now ... well, nothing was going to happen now, anyway. I laughed to myself, wondering what Bamira thought about what he had just stepped into.

"Are you hungry, mem?" he asked, trying to get her attention.

"Yes, I am, but this one thing I must tell you."

"What is it, mem?"

"That this Jesus was God in heaven and came to earth as a man to make a way for you and me to be with God in eternity. You see, without a savior, we will all die in our sin. Jesus was punished and nailed to a cross because of our sins and the sins of the world. He died and was buried, and in three days He rose again from the dead. Then He appeared to His disciples and then to five hundred witnesses. That is the Gospel message: that He died on a cross for you and for me, Bamira, and if you receive it and believe it, you will live forever. If this message is not true, then nothing else in life really matters. But if it is true, it is the only thing that matters. If it is not true, then Apostle Paul said we as Christians are to be pitied above all people. Paul had put his life on the line for his faith. He was beaten and flogged and put in chains. He said if Christ has not risen from the dead, then we would not raise either, and if that is true, then we may as well eat and drink, for tomorrow we die." Esther paused in silence and turned her face up toward the sky, her eyes closed.

Bamira looked off in the distance, as if he were staring a thousand miles. "I am not ready to die, mem, but I am very hungry."

"What's for lunch?" she asked, opening her eyes after finishing her prayer.

"You stay here. Bamira make lunch ready now," he said and stood up.

He left for the cooking fires, and moments later I could smell the aroma from his soup drifting across the camp.

Esther thumbed the pages of her journal as we sat in silence, not knowing where to take the conversation from here.

"What is that you have written there?" Betty asked, trying to break the ice.

"This is my journal entry from this morning," she answered. "Would you like to hear it?"

Betty eagerly nodded her approval.

I had finally found my opportunity to exit. I moved to get up, but Betty grabbed my arm again. Anger simmered inside me. Why was Betty making me listen to Esther's syrupy dribble? Had they planned this?

Esther began reading from her journal entry, which was a poem of sorts:

"Oh, my dearest Lord,
I can feel you, although I cannot touch you with my hands.
I can see you, although I cannot visualize you with my eyes.
I can hear you, although I cannot listen with my ears.
I can know you, although I cannot look on your face.
I know you are sweet, although I cannot taste you or smell you.
But I hear your whisper in the wind.
Your song is in the birds,
your fragrance is in the wildflower,
your face is in all creation,
your voice is in your word,
and I can feel you in my heart.
Lord, you feed me, and I have no way to repay your kindness.
Lord, you are with me, even though I have a sense that I am alone.
Lord, you made me, and the world would have me believe it
was natural.
You speak, and they do not hear,
you nudge, and they do not respond,
you show them, but they do not see.
How awesome are your ways, how beautiful are your feet.
My heart flies on your wings and longs to be held in your hands.
I'll serve you for eternity. I am your friend and disciple.
I love you."

"That was beautiful," Betty said as Esther batted her long lashes. "I can't believe you wrote that just this morning!"

Finally, this conversation was over, and I could shake off the effects of everything I had been forced to listen to. The more I tried to deny everything, the more I became afraid that Esther's message was sinking in.

~~~~~~~~~

When we arrived at Bamira's lunch table, Chuck was just pulling a folding chair up to the table. As Betty and I approached, trailed by Esther, he scooted away from the table and jumped to his feat, and he and I nearly tripped over each other trying to push Betty's chair in

289

to seat her. Betty scooted in, and then Chuck and I found spots and bellied up to the table. Esther stood momentarily, then took hold of a chair and started to pull it away.

Out of nowhere, Betty reared back and hit me in the ribs with her elbow, and I straightened up, not knowing what I had done. She had my attention, and I looked into her squinting eyes as she mouthed the word, "Esther."

Esther had already begun to pull out a chair, and I jumped to my feet and helped her to get seated. We watched as the boy with white gloves poured red wine to the brim of my glass.

"Aren't you supposed to sample it first before they pour a full glass from a newly opened bottle?" Esther asked.

"Oh, sure, but that's only in the finest restaurants," I said. "Here you drink it even if it's rancid, I would imagine."

"Where is Lance?" Chuck asked.

"He is napping in the tent," Esther said.

"Should we wake him for lunch?" I asked.

"No, I think it best to let him rest," Esther said. "He felt warm this morning, so I gave him some quinine and insisted that he sleep."

"We don't need anyone getting sick from malaria," Betty said. "I do believe the march on the elephant took its toll on all of us. You were smart to stay behind."

"Have you seen young Jason today?" Chuck asked.

"He and Janga left this morning with his pooch in tow to find an African turkey they call a *bustard* for the evening stew pot," Betty said.

"The ones we heard squawking across the valley last week?" Chuck asked.

"That is the direction I sent them," I said.

"Would you like some wine?" Chuck asked, taking the empty glass from Esther's place and sliding it toward the young steward.

"Oh, no, tea is fine for me," she said.

"I suppose you think wine is evil," Chuck said with a sarcastic laugh.

"No, not at all," she said. "I just choose not to partake. I would sooner be filled with the spirit of God than drunk with alcohol. What have you been doing today, Chuck?"

Chuck brought his wine glass to his lips and took a small sip, then reached behind his chair and picked up a hardback book. "I have been reading this account from Lieutenant Colonel John Patterson called *In Grip of Nyika: Further Adventures in British East Africa.*"

"Ah, yes," Esther said. "*Nyika*—that means *wilderness* in Swahili. Tell me, how is this story?"

"It is a fascinating piece of literature. He has inspired my courage. I think I would like to write a book about our safari when we get back to Chicago."

"How will you portray me in your book?" Betty asked. "I guess I should be on my best behavior from here on out."

Chuck smiled warmly.

"If you tell me about this book you are reading," Esther said, "I will share mine with you."

I nearly had to laugh out loud at Chuck's eagerness to share the story. I knew he had forgotten the book that she was reading, and he was being led down a primrose path.

Chuck's gruff voice, not to mention the lines on his face, spoke volumes for the struggles he had endured in his life. I had compassion for my friend, knowing of the love he and his late wife had shared and how terrible her loss must have been for him. His eyes sparkled as he shared the simple storyline of John Patterson's adventure. Who hadn't heard about the accounts of his exploits with man-eating lions before? Surely everyone had. But I knew nothing of the other explorations of this man in more recent years, including his near death in the wilderness of East Africa.

Bamira escorted his server, who carried a steaming pot of soup on a platter, which he set before us.

"This looks wonderful, my brother," Esther said as Bamira beamed with pride.

The server began ladling the soup into the china bowls, and we clenched our spoons.

"May I give thanks?" Esther asked. She folded her hands and spewed forth another one of her many prayers.

"Oh my, that's up to his normal standard," Chuck said after digging into his lunch. "What is it?"

"Wildebeest is my special soup, just for you!" Bamira answered. "I think about what you say, mem, and I still think."

"That's good, Bamira," Esther responded. "When you decide, once and for all, that you want to discover this gift, I will agree to be your guide."

"Yes, mem ... yes," Bamira said as he backed away, nodding.

I looked at Chuck, who was focused intently on the bottom of his soup bowl as he continued to consume it.

"Did you know Bamira digs his own roots?" I asked. "He even gathers his own herbs to make this soup."

"He does?" Chuck asked.

"I would like to hear more about Patterson," Esther said.

"I'm afraid now," Chuck said with a laugh.

Esther smiled. "What do you mean, *afraid*?"

"Because I just remembered what book you intend to tell me about. It's the Bible, isn't it?"

"You caught me," she said and smiled again. "I'm guilty."

"I do respect you," Chuck said, "but I have no interest in your religion. You're not offended, are you?"

"No, not hardly, sir. You have every right to your opinion. And surely you must know that I have no intention of forcing the Gospel on anyone."

"Okay, my dear," he said, "just know that this old buzzard picks his carcasses very carefully, and Christianity is one carcass I choose to fly clear of."

Old Chuck had said a mouthful, and I could only hope that maybe he had put this subject to rest for a while. I knew Esther felt sincere about her faith, but it was making us all feel uneasy. I was glad that Chuck had the courage to put her in her place, and that maybe now I wouldn't have to take Lance aside and have a little talk with him about his wife.

"I understand totally," she said. "You know I wasn't always a Christian. Apostle Paul said in his second book to the church in Corinth that to one, Christ is the smell of death, and to the other, the fragrance of life. I know you don't understand me and you think I'm narrow-minded in my views, but I do remember full well what it was like to see Christ through the eyes of a nonbeliever. So not only do I understand the world from the perspective of Christ, but I truly know your point of view as well."

I knew I would have to ponder what she was saying, and I wondered if she really believed that she had the broader mind. While she had been studying the Bible, I had been studying the works of Darwin himself. How amusing that we were at full odds, both holding on to this coin in our pockets with two sides, and both unwilling to admit that the other person might have something. Well, at least my coin was shiny new. Hers had been tarnished by thousands of years of abuse. The ages had seen wars and suffering at the hands of greedy men who sought power from religion and money from the pulpit. Darwinism was like a breath of fresh air, and right now I really didn't care about the coin in her pocket. I wasn't going to take a look at her point of view, no matter what the lion had said.

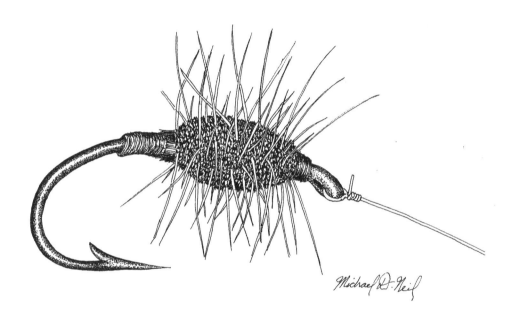

Michael D. Neil

Chapter 18

SHADY LADY

"Do you think the letter is acceptable?" Betty asked.
"It's a great letter," I said.

"No, really. I don't want you to say that to flatter me. I don't want to send the letter to Mae and have her die of worry."

"Dear, if I thought you shouldn't send the letter, I would tell you."

"Do you want to fish with me?" she asked.

"No. I'll cover you with my ought-six in case a croc or a hippo decides to come around."

Betty squinted as she threaded the braided silk line through the eyes of the fly-rod. The afternoon sun perched high over head, and the river's cool water flowed peacefully downstream. I thought about how Betty and I had grown in our marriage, about how our love had been renewed since I had agreed to share the one thing that had brought me such joy. It hadn't been that long—two years—since we'd hardly been speaking, but Africa had changed all that. I think it gave her real peace knowing that I was her protector.

There was literally no one else in the world that put this kind of importance on her, unless one considered Esther's case for God. But as to the validity of her view, who really knew? I could go only so far with the Gospel, maybe put it in my mouth for a taste. But as for swallowing, that was another matter altogether.

"What sort of wood is that rod made from?" I asked.

"Oh this?" she said. "It's a Hiram Leonard rod made out of bamboo. Daddy had a cheaper model made out of Greenheart, but he paid fifty dollars for this one. I almost hate to use it here, but it seems pretty safe in the wooden box he made for it." Betty began sorting through the little box, which contained her casting flies. "Now as they say, and as my daddy always told me, 'Match the hatch.' While I was writing that letter to Mae, I watched the dancing bugs on the river to see which ones the fish prefer. Of course, I'm no expert and couldn't name them one by one, but I do remember one with a bright red tail the fish seemed to enjoy.

"This is the one he would have thrown at 'em," she said, holding up a fly. "I remember he called it Red Bug. Funny what you remember in life, isn't it, John? I feel like a little girl again, having to be so careful with his delicate flies: Brown Buzz, Long-tail Drake, Hairy Spinner, Yellow Sally, Redhead Gnat, Wooly Bugger, and this one, the Shady Lady. Yeah, that's what he used to call me on the riverbank: his shady lady."

"He was right. You are a shady lady." I laughed, and she chuckled along with me.

"These little things always captivated me. I remember watching him hour after hour wrapping the yarn, the fur, and the feathers to make all these different patterns and shapes. The memories are thick, John, and they almost make me not want to use the little bugs at all. But at the same time, I know how thrilled he would have been to see me here on this riverbank using his homespun flies."

"I'm amazed you remember all the names."

"I'm telling ya, the memories are thick."

Betty looped the end of the finely tapered line through the eye of the hook and pulled it tightly into some fisherman's knot as if a day had not passed since her daddy had shown her the trick.

"Will you still remember how to fish?" I asked, looking on with anticipation.

"I think it's like riding a bicycle. I haven't ridden one in twenty years, but if we had a bike in camp, I wouldn't have to relearn it. My daddy taught me how to ride a bike, too. I remember him holding the back of it—I was just sure that he wouldn't let go—and when I looked back, he was running alongside, not holding on, and I was riding all by myself."

The clear water glistened under the morning sun as Betty stepped up to the edge of the water. "I wonder if these fish react to shadows like the ones back home. What do you think about me wading out?" she asked, looking over her shoulder with a little smile.

"Do I really have to remind you about the crocs?" I asked. "Even when the baboons drink, they dig a hole away from the water's edge and wait until it fills up so they don't have to stick their head in the river."

Betty turned her attention back to the river and then, like an old pro, brought the rod tip up and whipped the line behind her, letting out more line and making the line longer each time she whipped it back over her head. She then laid the red bug out on the top of the water. I had never seen this side of her before, and it gave me goose bumps to see her in this element. All these years of thinking I knew her, and now I wondered if I had known her at all. She let the fly drift down the river for a minute, and then she stripped out the line and made the loop bigger like a cattle roper. She picked up the bug, whipped it back over her head, and let it settle on another place on the river.

"You have to find the place where the fish are lying," she explained, "and you have to put this thing right where they can see it."

She continued without pause, whipping her line in and then tossing it back out. Time and again, she fought the river like a lion tamer with a bull whip, with nary a nibble.

"With all the talk about the great fishing here in Africa, either they aren't here, or they don't like my bug and they ain't fooled in the least." She let loose her cute little giggle.

I sat with her, trying to be patient as she whipped the river to a near froth. I knew they had to be here; not forty minutes earlier they had been feeding like a bunch of six-year-olds at a birthday party. Now, however, it seemed like an unwanted guest had arrived, and the fish were the only ones who knew it. I settled back on the bank, trying not to become impatient. I wished I'd brought my journal, which would have given me something to do. *Well, maybe a croc will swim by, and we'll get some real action.* I didn't want to question her ability, but I could truly feel boredom settling in on me.

"Why don't you just bait, hook, and put on a cork?" I suggested. "I think they'll go for bait better than a phony bug."

"Oh, sure, and you would have my daddy roll over in his grave, wouldn't you? If all you want to do is catch a fish, then that's how you would do it. But as far as I'm concerned, I would rather put them in a barrel and shoot them with your ought-six. Or maybe you would rather shoot a giraffe. Or how about taking an impala with your elephant gun?"

"Now that hurt!" I responded.

"I'm just explaining it in terms you will understand."

"I got your point."

Just then the water exploded in the vicinity of her little feathered decoy, and the line responded instantly, bending the flexible bamboo rod and making it bounce.

"I got 'em," she squealed.

I could feel her exhilaration as she hooked the fish. My heart raced as she put into play all the skills her daddy had taught her.

"This line isn't strong enough to hold a good fish like this one," she said, trying to subdue the excitement in her voice. "That's why you need a good, flexible rod to help reduce the stress on the line. The trick is to tire him, play him out, and take the fight out of him. Then when he's spent, you can drag him in. The problem is that I am very limited as to the amount of line I can give him before he has it all. If he has enough fight left when he reaches the end of the spool, then he'll be gone like a groom who got a better offer and left his bride at the altar."

I had to laugh at her illustrations. Deep in the fit of trying to fight a fish, she was giving me the blow-by-blow.

She let the stiff line slip through her fingers carefully as the rod nearly bent in half. Then the great fish splashed just under the surface, tossing white water as he shook his head and body and contorted himself to gain freedom from this snare. Then finally he broke the surface, dancing across the water on the tip of his tail, and we got our first glimpse of his silver form. The rod tip bowed and twitched, and again she gave him line to let him run. Then she tightened up on the line slowly and gripped the reel as she began to inch back some of her insurance.

"If I can just keep his head turned," she said with clenched teeth, "I might be able to stop him from making another run."

She began pulling in the line, holding it with her fingers and grasping the cork handle, then pulling another length of line and letting it fall on the beach at her feet. Now just forty feet of line remained from the tip of her rod, and the old boy broke the water with his dorsal fin. She pulled in several more feet of line, adding it to the pile, but too soon for glory. He must have sighted her standing above him, for he took off like a slug fired from a 50-caliber rifle.

I sprang to my feet to give her support. "That's some fish!"

"You're enjoying this, aren't you?"

"I never realized it involved so much skill. I just figured you let them eat the bait and then pulled them in, but this is exciting!"

"I tried to tell you. The art is knowing when to set the hook and then when to give him enough line to wear him down before he breaks it."

"Do you think you'll get him?"

"Yes, he's nearly spent now," she said with an air of confidence.

"He must be nearly twenty inches."

"Yeah, he's all of that."

She began pulling in the line again, and this time there was little fight left. As the final feet of line came in, we could see his beauty. He was still fighting to get his head around, but then he rolled over with a silver flash from the sun and let her pull him up into the shallows.

"This is quite a fish, Betty."

"He's a beauty, all right. He'll go twenty inches easy."

"What is it?" I asked as she pulled him up onto the riverbank.

"See these spots here? I guess I didn't really know what to expect from an African river. As far as I know, it could be a tilapia, or maybe a squeaker. I don't think it's a tiger fish. Anyway, who cares what it is. It's a beautiful fish. Besides, I'm sure Janga will know."

"Just as long as you can fry it in a pan," I said.

"You are such a grebe. Everything is food to you. When Daddy fished, most of the time he would put 'em back so he could catch 'em again on another day."

"He wouldn't eat them?"

"Sometimes, but most times, not."

"Well, I suppose catching them is pretty fun. I have to admit it, Betty, that was exciting."

"The challenge in this sport is in gaining the upper hand when you are on a level playing field," she said. "From my perspective, life is about fairness and choices. We are free to choose any path we want, and we have the freedom, absent the laws of men, to make any choice we want. I suppose it is just as Esther has said: that we are free to embrace or reject God. But if He made us love Him, it would be worth nothing at all to Him. God could, if He indeed is an all powerful God, and if He so desired, drop the water level in our pond and gaff us out one by one. But I guess He lets us make our own choice, because forced love is no love at all. At least that is how I see it."

I didn't have to respond because she knew how I felt, but she had just turned me into a fisherman. I was hooked. I would always prefer the bullet to the hook—the fur over the fin, so to speak—but over the course of the next several weeks I had her teach me how to fish. We caught tiger fish, yellowfish, three spot, Chesa, Nkupe, Bottlenose, Cornish Jack, bulldogs, barbel, tilapia, and a Vindu that I caught on a grub on a bare hook, letting it sink to the bottom. This was the bulk of the freshwater species in central Africa, and we never had a dull moment, which was how I had come to prefer everything in life. Dull moments were just not a part of my vocabulary.

~~~~~~~~~

That evening we had a mess of fish fried up in pork fat around the campfire as we listened to stories from Jason, who told us about his escapades during the great bustard pursuit. Jason … what a boy! I only wished I was his father, and I knew that Betty wished that she was more than merely a mother figure. I could have had a boy just like him, if only mine had not perished. And we should have had more children, if only Betty's womb had not failed her at such a young age. I knew her barrenness was a great disappointment to her, even though she would never speak those words out loud. I knew it had to be there, lurking in her thoughts. I knew there were many things that disappointed me about her that I could never say. We all had shortcomings that we were not able to admit, even to ourselves, and what good were they to be dug up like the contents of an outhouse for everyone to smell? No, they were better left buried so we were not reminded of the places where each of us fell short. I was certain that I had failed her, because I had failed myself in many cases. We should have been able to fill that big house in Chicago with the sound of children, and now my legacy was gone because of it. There would be no young Rivers to carry the torch into the next generation, no grandson or great-grandson to occupy the Riverses' mansion and carry on the family legacy. No grandchildren to bounce on my knee. But now I could see a glimmer of hope in Betty's eyes when she spoke of her relationship with Jason.

As Jason began his story, Betty sat on the edge of her seat. She was as anxious as a dancing spinner fly listening to the music of bullfrogs on a still morning at the pond. The campfire released its red sparks like fireflies, and the red and yellow flames leaped from the logs, making the faces of my friends flicker in the shimmering light. I took Betty's hand and held it on her knee, and while the fire warmed us from the outside, her hand, tightly clenched between mine, warmed me from the inside.

"I feel like a shady lady," she whispered.

I had to smile to myself thinking how much I loved her.

Chapter 19

SAVE THE PUP

"Yoo-hoo," I said, trying to get the boy's attention. "Jason, it's your turn."

"Is it my turn?" he asked, sitting on the edge of his chair.

My eyes strained to see past the open flames and the smoke drifting off the campfire.

"We've been waiting all evening to hear your story," Betty said.

"It's not as exciting as the story about your fishing," he answered. "I don't know where to start. The day seems like a lightning storm." Jason paused as he pondered the events of the day, and then he began to speak in his innocent way.

"Janga and I took a lunch with us and headed east, off in the direction where Betty had heard bustards calling a couple days ago. We took Buster, hoping he might help us sniff 'em up. You know how much he loves to chase little birds—I didn't know what he would do with a wild turkey. Janga took along an extra rifle, just in case we got into trouble with a lion or what all. We had walked for a couple hours, and then we scouted a dry riverbed, where we found fresh buffalo tracks in the sand."

"You found buff tracks?" I interrupted.

Betty grabbed my arm and threw me her look in the firelight.

"I wanted to go after 'em today, but Janga said we had to go for *bata mzinga* (turkey). I told him we could be heroes, packing back a buffalo head, but he just grinned, then turned and kept on moving up the sandy riverbed."

"You didn't tell me you found buffalo sign," I said. "How fresh were they?"

"Oh, they were real fresh," he said.

"Within the last day?" I snapped.

"Yep, definitely within the last day."

"Then it's settled," I said. "That's where we'll hunt tomorrow!"

"John, let him tell his story!" Betty insisted, protecting him like a mother hen.

"About a quarter hour later," he continued, "I spotted bustards sitting in the branches of a mimosa about two hundred and fifty yards up the valley. I pointed them out to Janga, but I figured he must have spotted 'em, too. Anyway, there were about ten. He asked me if I really wanted to shoot one, and I said, heck yeah, two or three or as many as we could get.

"Then he asked me how I might approach close enough to kill that many. I knew he was testing me to see if I was learning out here, and I had to think about how Janga would do it. I told him we should check the air to make sure we were downwind, and then try to close the distance to get a shot. He laughed at me for being too eager to settle for only one shot. I didn't know what to say, and he told me to take the lead.

"I tried to check the wind, but the air seemed so still. Then I started thinking—like a young feller would—and I decided those turkeys couldn't smell a thing." He paused to giggle. "Heck, a human has probably got better smell power than a bird. But I bet they can spot you coming a mile away. The fact is, they probably spotted us before we spotted them. Yeah, twenty sets of eyes all perched up there in the top of that tree. I looked for cover and tried to plan out my approach so I wouldn't become a laughingstock tonight as our black men sat around their campfire eating posho and telling stories. Then I gave him a nod that I was ready, and he gave me the lead.

"I put a tree between the flock and us and started reducing the distance for a shot at dinner. My mouth began to water just thinking about roast turkey, brown gravy, and potatoes. Then they were in range, and he whispered for me to settle in for a shot at the biggest one. Right about then, I noticed a bird soaring over their heads like a vulture. One of the birds on the limb launched to join him, and they flew away like paper kites on a string." He laughed. "That's when I realized I had been had."

"That's great," I said, laughing. "You deserve to be had."

"When I asked him why he did it," Jason said, "he said he wanted me to work on a problem without him. I opened my canteen and took a long, cool drink, hoping to recover my dignity, and when I stood up, the whole tree erupted with frantic vultures trying to escape. I made him promise that he wouldn't make me out as a laughingstock to the porters. All he said was that he would be kind, and he looked at me with a big grin. We've all heard their roaring laughter, and we all know that we are the source of their entertainment.

"We made headway, and as we approached the tree, my nose grabbed a whiff of something dead. I went to investigate, and we found the scattered bones and hair of a giraffe. The place looked like the morning after a rough-necker's beer brawl. The bones were picked clean, and they were whitewashed with vulture splatter.

"Then we found a lion track the size of a dinner plate," Jason said with wide eyes. "Hyena and vulture had trampled the whole area, but the lion track pressed into the soft ground right over the top of them, which meant he'd passed by just this morning. I asked Janga what he thought had killed the giraffe. He said mostly they die from fighting or being slow from old age. Nothing slow lasts much here. That's how the lion makes his day, by chasing the herd and seeing what's slow. That is what Janga said: everyone on the plain benefits from the lion kill. The hyena got a meal, and the jackal, the vulture, the raven, and right down to the sparrow and the mouse. Then the bug takes over, and the birds benefit again."

I glanced across the campfire as it flickered against the faces of Jason, Betty, Chuck, Lance, and Esther, who were waiting intently to hear the end of his story. Buster nudged Jason's hand with his nose and forced his head under it. Jason leaned back away from the heat of the flame and rubbed Buster's ear.

"I have read books and articles about hunting a field for fowl in Europe," Jason said, rubbing his chin, "and they use sporting dogs that point with their nose. Do you think we could teach Buster to point?"

"Nope, it's not in his blood," Chuck said. "I've had my share of dogs in my day. What I know is that it seems you can teach a pointer to flush, but you can't teach a flusher to point. Besides, I'm not sure you'd ever get a bustard to sit for a point."

"Anytime I ever saw one of those turkeys," I said, "you either had to get a shot off quick, or they'd fly off and you'd never see them again."

Betty nudged me in the ribs with her elbow. "Will you let him finish his story?"

"Anyway, I didn't kill one of those vultures," he continued. "I really didn't think you guys would appreciate me coming back with a smelly old buzzard for the stewpot."

Betty laughed. "I don't know about that. John is used to eating crow, and he probably wouldn't be able to tell the difference."

"That's my girl," I said, shaking my head with a smile.

"Anyways," Jason continued, "like you said, we did find one about five miles up the valley. I kept thinking about Mae's roasted turkey. Janga said, 'Aim small, miss small,' and told me to shoot its head off, which I did at his request, remembering your fine instruction, John."

"You did shoot the head off, didn't you?" Betty asked.

"Sure did," he said, beaming.

"What about Buster?" I asked. "What did he do?"

"Janga held his collar until after I shot, and then we let him go. I guess he has been around enough gunfire now that it doesn't bother him. He ran lickety-split down to the bustard and tried to bring it back, dragging it by a wing. He took possession immediately, showing off and acting like he wouldn't give it up. Janga threw the bird over his shoulder, dangling it by the feet, but I think Buster had designs on dragging it six miles back to camp, even if it killed him."

The group laughed, and silently I wondered what must have gone on in this little mind of Buster's. I had never seen such a devoted friend who loved a kid so much. *Imagine a friend who wouldn't compete with you for a position of power*, I thought, *who didn't care if you had money or if you were educated, who didn't care if you were eloquent or gainfully employed. He just loved you for who you were and not what you were. He could have picked anybody else, but he picked you. A friend who would never speak to others around the fire hydrant about your failures or the stupid things you do, but would accept you no matter what you did. A partner who was always glad to see you and patiently waited for your return, never angry that you left him behind and always happy just to have you close by.*

As Betty and Jason spoke, I began to think about what life really meant. I saw life as being totally relational. We wouldn't escape it. Even when we were alone, it consumed our thoughts. Even in our solitude we had a relationship with our self. It was this foothold on the ladder that signaled how we related to others: age, experience, education and birthright, religion, race, and gender. How tragic this was, although it was a fact of life that I doubted would ever change. I was amazed that only a few years ago here in Africa there had been slaves being kept against their will. Nothing could have been more absurd than to be allowed to own another person simply because they happened to be a different race or color on the outside when we were all the same on the inside.

I was glad that the black man had been freed in the U.S. after the Civil War. And I knew that even my father approved of the war, even though he had lost his father in the fight to free them. He had told me that he had always considered it his personal price to pay for their freedom. I couldn't imagine paying for their freedom with the death of my father. No amount of money could ever repay such a debt. What a shame that I had never known my grandfather.

"Is that the end of your story?" Betty asked.

"Janga, Buster, and I headed back for camp," Jason said. "Footloose and fancy-free, we figured we had accomplished our task, and we were feeling pretty smug that we had bagged what we'd set out for. We were moving right along when we came around a bush and ran smack into a herd of startled buffalo, not twenty yards away. We had no time to react. The bull of the band leveled his horns and came at us like a freight train."

Betty covered her mouth with her hand.

I sat up straight in my chair. "You didn't tell me about this."

"I know," Jason said, "and I wasn't sure if I should tell you."

"Let him finish his story," Betty whispered.

Jason cleared this throat. "I had no time to raise my rifle," he said, "and not thinking, I dropped everything and like a matador tried to avoid the glistening tips of his horns. I leaped one way, and Janga lunged the other. The old bull groaned and threw snot as he craned his neck to hook me, then he gave a kick as he passed that just missed my head. Buster growled and bared his teeth and nipped at his heels, and I yelled for Janga to shoot. But I could see that wasn't gonna happen, 'cause the bull ran between us. Then everything disappeared in a dust cloud, and we didn't fire one shot.

"I swore Janga to secrecy, 'cause I figured if you guys found out, I'd probably never be going out on this safari alone again. Heck, almost getting smashed by an elephant is bad enough. Remember how you said three strikes and you're out, Betty?"

"That's what I said," she answered.

"This wasn't strike two," he said, showing the palm of his hand, "because it wasn't that close a call, anyway."

I had to wonder why the kid was coming clean. Heck, he'd even put a gag order on Janga, just to cover his tracks, and now here he was spilling his guts to us, knowing how Betty would react.

"So why are you telling us all this?" I asked, catching a glimpse of Betty's face out of the corner of my eye. She had that familiar frown I could read like a book, and the frown said the kid was done hunting with Janga.

I glanced back at Jason, and he just looked at me with his puppy dog eyes and shrugged his shoulders. This book wasn't quite as easy to read. Surely if he hadn't been so clumsy while trying in haste to take a quick shot at the charging buffalo, he might not have dropped his rifle. The kid was going to have to be more careful and alert. He had a lot to learn. You couldn't just pluck a kid off the streets of Chicago, bring him to Africa, and expect him to survive here. If he didn't shape up, he was going to get himself killed, and I didn't know if Betty could take it. I wasn't sure how *I* would take it.

~~~~~~~~~~

The following morning revealed how tired we all were when the whole camp slept in well past daylight. I crawled out of the sack quietly so as not to awaken the sleeping princess. Lance was just throwing his tent flap back when I slipped out the opening of mine.

"Is Betty up?" he asked.

"Nope, sleeping like a baby," I said and chuckled quietly as I stepped away from the tent. "I think we should go after that buffalo up the valley."

Lance nodded enthusiastically. "I'll talk to Janga and see what he thinks. See if that buff was as big as Jason said it was."

I had to wonder if the bull was really that big.

Lance rolled his eyes and gave me a smile that said we were both on the same page. "You hungry?" he asked. "Let's find some coffee."

We spent the next half hour talking hunting and discussing how the safari was progressing. Not long afterward, the girls were up, bright-eyed and bushy-tailed, along with Jason and Chuck, and we sat down to a breakfast fit for a king.

"Pass me some more of that hog belly," Chuck said.

I looked up from my plate and saw movement through the bush behind him that immediately caught my attention.

Buster's ears perked up, and he let go a low growl.

"What is it?" Betty asked as she squinted over her shoulder.

"Trouble!" I answered just as a band of outlaw warriors came waltzing into our camp armed to the teeth with spears and shields.

Buster bolted headlong toward the men and held his ground, growling and barking, and everyone at the table took to their feet.

I couldn't have felt any more stupid or helpless, considering I had left my sidearm and my double back at my tent. I looked around, and not one of us had a rifle handy.

The lead native, who had a leopard skin draped over his shoulder, leveled his spear at Buster.

"Call him off, Jason," I cautioned. "He won't hesitate to spear him."

Willie began to jabber in an unfamiliar jargon with their leader, and the conversation quickly became heated.

"What is it, Willie?" Lance asked.

"Him say they own valley and demand payment to pass," Willie answered.

"What do they want?" Lance asked.

"They want the cow for our freedom."

"And if we don't agree?" I asked.

"They will fight," Willie said.

"You tell them that we'll report this to the British authorities," I said, "and they will send a detachment of soldiers to arrest them if they don't leave now!"

"We are a hundred miles from the authorities, and they know it," Lance said. "Let's not get tough with them just yet. Ask them if they will accept something else in exchange."

Willie's tongue fluttered in their native dialect while the outlaws stood sternly. He reacted with surprise and shook his head in disbelief when the leader pounded his long spear in the dirt and spit back a stern response.

"What do they want?" I asked.

"They want the bustard," Willie said.

"That's easy," Lance said. "Give them the dead bird, and let's be done with them."

"No, Sahib, the man want this dog: Bustard."

"Buster?" I asked. "They want Buster?"

"Yes, Bwana."

"I'll get my rifle," Jason said.

As he turned, Betty grabbed his arm in a death grip, and he stopped in his tracks.

"The dog is out of the question," I said.

"Tell them we will kill for them a buffalo," Lance said.

I nodded my approval, and Willie offered up the proposal, to which the leader spit back another angry reply.

"He said they will accept our cow and two buffalo," Willie said, "and they will stay at this place until we have returned."

"Tell them they are welcome in our camp," Lance said, "and that we agree to pay them two buffalo for coming into their territory."

"What about the cow?" Willie asked.

"Tell them we agree to kill them two buffalo, and that's it. No more."

"Are you sure this is a good idea?" I asked. "We are admitting to trespassing on land they don't own, and I'm afraid they will consider us weak and stupid. Talk about being buffaloed."

"I don't care what they think of us," Lance snapped, "just as long as they leave us alone and let us pass without a fight. They know what they're doing. Shoot, they have probably done this before, and it works every time."

Willie explained our position, and they walked over to a nearby tree and sat beneath it in the shade to discuss the proposal.

"I hope we can find those buffalo you and Janga saw yesterday," I said. "The only ones we have seen this whole trip were on the elephant march."

"Janga find buffalo, Bwana," Janga said.

I looked back over my shoulder, surprised that he had been here the whole time. "If you say so," I said. "I'm with you. Besides, as long as we take the cape and the horns, they can have all the meat they want."

"Me know swamp two days from here with many animals," Janga said, puffing up his chest. "You get rifles, supplies, and packers, and Janga take you there."

"I still think we can take 'em, John," Jason said.

"Are you crazy? And start a war? What's the matter with you, son? We might take 'em, but their whole tribe would be here tomorrow — and we will lose."

~~~~~~~~~

I felt uneasy about leaving Lance and Esther at camp like hostages. Esther would probably try to tell them about Jesus. But the more I thought about it, the more I became confident that Willie would take care of them. We discussed the possibilities of taking the Lizzy, or at least taking the horses, but Janga was the great discourager. My better judgment told me to stand firm, but he just wouldn't hear of it. So we left on foot.

Jason, Chuck, Betty, and I took off with Janga to kill a couple buffalo. We were hopeful we could connect quickly to save Buster from being taken. I didn't really care that much about the cow, although I appreciated the luxury of having cream in my coffee. We had the power, obviously, but we weren't going to start a war with anyone over a dog. Some of these tribes were always looking to identify an enemy. They loved a good war, and the best policy was to remain their friend. I resigned myself to the fact that, if we couldn't come up with the buffalo, we were probably going to have to give up our cow and the kid's dog as well.

We had packed lightly, just enough for two overnights, and rounded up enough porters to carry our supplies. If we got into buffalo, we would direct the tribesmen to the kill site and let them deal with the meat.

We beat feet along the same trail Jason and Janga had taken the day before. I was quite impressed with Janga as I watched him move catlike across the bush country. He was always on the alert for movement and continually reminded me that one must be on the lookout for a nose, an ear, a tail, or an eye. The buffalo would stand and wait for an approaching noise that he could not smell downwind to see what it might be. He was well armed, with his hefty blades firmly attached to the most powerful part of his body. He had respect for large predators, but he had no fear of them. Just like a bull in the ring, this buffalo was one tough hombre, and if you wounded him, he *would* get you. The old hunters liked to say that the buff could stomp even the most fleet-footed matador in the dirt, then hook him with his horn and literally make mincemeat out of him.

We had trekked several hours into the afternoon when Janga found a fresh sign from the small band they had seen the day before. He checked the wind to make sure our approach would be tenable.

I kept watching the ground to see if we were on Jason's track from yesterday. "Look here," I said. "Here's the buffalo tracks crossing the top of your boot prints. This is the spot you had your little encounter, isn't it, Jason?"

"Yep, this is it," he responded.

"You knew all I had to do was scrutinize the prints and I'd be able to put it together, didn't you?"

Jason gave me a wide grin and closed his eyes.

"I see here where you slipped and then jumped. It doesn't take much to put this all together."

"I knew you would," he said. "I knew you'd take one look at it and figure it out."

Janga continued toward the east as we stayed on the trail of the buff.

Jason took a step, cracking a dry stick, and Janga wheeled around, putting his finger to his lips while giving him a stern look.

We moved ahead cautiously, and Janga was like a leopard, always on the alert for the sound of the herd, ready to catch a whiff of their musk on the wind. The buffalo tracks were neatly printed in the soft clay as we continued to follow.

After several more hours of forging ahead in the afternoon heat, I could see that Chuck's face looked flushed, his feet heavy. He had begun to lag behind, and I tapped Janga on the shoulder to clue him in. I held up as we waited for Chuck to catch up to the group.

"Have you got enough water?" I asked.

"I'm fine," he answered in his gruff voice. "Don't worry about me."

"This track lead to swamp, maybe one hour from here," Janga said. "If we make camp, we can get good rest. Then we start fresh before light."

"In this heat, the buffalo will be holed up in the heavy reed grass," I said. "In the morning, they'll feed in the open."

We made camp and ate supper, but the whole time I could feel a thickness in the air. The armed natives back at our camp had left us tense and with heavy hearts. We roped up a canvas cover, and we all slept on the ground beneath it. Betty was restless, no doubt worrying about Esther and Lance back at camp, who were sitting on a powder keg ready to explode. The reason I knew Betty was tossing and turning was because I, too, couldn't sleep.

Janga seemed confident enough about this swamp, but really, how could he be so certain about the lay of the land? I had seen him cover up his small mistakes before, and I knew we were all hoping that we weren't being led on a wild goose chase.

I could have sworn I hadn't slept all night until someone tapped me on the shoulder, awakening me from a deep slumber.

"Time gets going," Janga said and then ducked outside.

I jumped out from under my blanket and started lacing up my boots.

"We'll leave camp right here, just as it is," I said. "And we'll leave the packers and porters here while we go on ahead to find the swamp."

"Are you sure Janga can find it?" Betty asked as she began to stir. "It's pitch black out."

"He seems to know what he is doing," I responded. "What other choice do we have but to trust him?"

The morning light gradually began to brighten in the eastern sky as we made our way into the swamp. We had trekked for an hour or so when Janga stopped. He motioned for us to follow through the bush to a rocky kopje, where he hunkered down. Then, crouching low, we quietly made our way to a lookout with a natural rock bench. The grass was heavy with dew, and the chilly morning fog laid out flat across the valley like a light blanket. Birds began to dance and sing across the treetops, greeting the advancing daybreak and announcing our presence.

"They come," Janga whispered and pointed down the valley toward the swamp, which was dotted with high reed grass along the edge and enclosed a pond.

I agreed, giving him a nod so as not to make any unnecessary sounds.

Betty drew the top of her jacket tightly around her neck. The locks of her dark hair tumbled from beneath her pith helmet and blew softly in the cool morning breeze. Her eyes lit up when we made eye contact, and she smiled sweetly before taking hold of her rifle with both hands, repositioning it across her lap.

Each minute seemed to drag on forever as we waited in anticipation. My throat felt tight and dry with excitement; I was confident now that Janga knew his business after having led us directly to the swamp. I hoped that Betty would make her first kill today. My eyes scanned every inch of the open glade for the slightest movement.

Janga cocked his head and tuned his ear, grimacing and holding up his index finger.

I held my breath, trying to listen through the deafening silence for the slightest noise. We froze, watching Janga for a sign.

Then he ducked his head low and pointed toward the edge of the clearing. Daylight was upon us, with the morning sky growing brighter by the moment.

I leaned over toward Betty and brought my lips to her ear, speaking softly, "Get ready. If this is the bull, he's yours."

Betty opened the bolt action of her .275 Rigby, sliding it back just far enough to check for the polished brass lying in the chamber. She carefully slid the bolt back into position and locked it over, resetting the safety. Then she looked up at me and nodded with determination.

"*Nyati* (buffalo)," Janga whispered, pointing along the edge of the dark mimosa grove to the left of the clearing.

The fog had begun to dissipate, and just then I saw the nose of Janga's buffalo poking out of the bush. "He's about one hundred and fifty yards straight away," I whispered.

"Take a place here on this rock," Janga instructed. He rubbed his hand on a natural rest, from where Betty could make a steady shot, as a cow came into the clearing first. "Let the cow go," he whispered.

"You can tell by a break in the horns on top of the head," I explained quietly. "The bulls have a solid cap."

Four cows came out of the heavy reed grass in full view, and then came a bull, his head emerging and exposing his massive horns.

"Hold your fire until the rest of the herd comes into the clearing," I said. "You guys find a rest and wait for a bull, but leave the lead bull for her."

Betty rested her rifle in the notch of the rock and stepped forward, taking a comfortable shooting position before bringing the rifle snugly against her shoulder. Chuck and Jason did the same as the old bull walked gracefully out into the open.

The bull stopped to look back over his shoulder, and then he turned and began to feed on the green grass. Three smaller cows followed him into the clearing, and one of the cows sidled alongside him, blocking Betty's shot.

She puckered her lip, but I whispered in her ear not to worry.

Then another bull poked his head out of the swamp and moved out into the open.

Jason tapped me on the shoulder and came close to my ear. "I never forget a face. That's the old boy who tried to kill me yesterday. He has to be because he has the same chunk out of the end of his horn on the right side."

"You claimed him," I said, "you take him."

They seemed as if they had begun to relax as several other bulls followed the pack out into the open.

"I'll take that second bull," Jason whispered so that both Chuck and Janga knew the plan.

"*Nyati mzuri* (good bull)," Janga whispered, probably knowing full well why Jason had chosen that one.

I pointed my British double downrange, ready to back Betty's shot. "Chuck, have you picked out your bull?" I whispered.

Chuck lay prone across a rock, his rifle trained at the herd. He lifted a finger to acknowledge his readiness.

More and more buffalo stepped out in the clearing, and then all three of the bulls moved so that we now had clear shots on all.

"On the count of three, let 'em have it," I whispered, thinking that maybe I should have picked out a bull to put my sights on. "Now, Betty, hold right behind the front leg and you will miss the shoulder bone and take out his heart."

Betty settled into the rifle, pulling it snugly against her shoulder. She inhaled, holding it just like I had taught her, and Jason did the same.

I began to count in a low voice, "One ... two ... three!"

Their rifles snorted in unison, belching black smoke and fire from the ends of the barrels and kicking the shooters back as the dead silence of the morning was broken. The bullets spoke as they smacked the massive bulls in the sides. Betty's bull stumbled and fell. Jason's lurched forward, glaring in our direction with a look that could have killed had he been able to locate us. And Chuck's turned with the cows and disappeared into the tall grass of the swamp.

Jason yanked on the bolt of his rifle and rammed home another follow-up round. Then the bull spun and faced us, pawing at the ground and throwing dirt clods behind him.

"Take another shot," I said. "Take him in the chest!"

Jason settled into the rifle again and squeezed off another round. The rifle bucked, and again I heard the smack of the bullet as it struck the bull in the side.

The bull stood for a second, then his knees began to wobble.

Betty ejected her empty cartridge and sent another fresh round to the open chamber, but her bull lay dead in its tracks. Jason reloaded and made ready to fire again when his bull's front legs gave out and the giant male crumpled in a huge black heap.

"Good job, Betty!" I yelled. "One shot! How about that?"

She dropped the rifle from her shoulder and peered out over the edge of the rocks at the two dead bulls sprawled out on the lush green grass at the edge of the swamp. "You got your bull, too, Jason," she said. "Nice shooting!" She set the butt of her rifle down, leaning it against a rock, and then turned and threw her arms around my neck.

"Wow," Chuck said. "One shot! Can you believe that? Mine is hit, but I don't think he's dead."

"I didn't think that old bugger I took was going down because of this light rifle," Jason said.

"It's not the size of the rifle so much as it is where to hit him," I said.

"Let's go take a look at 'em," Chuck said.

"Hold on," I cautioned. "Let's make sure they don't have any friends hanging around."

"Him hit hard," Janga said. "You whack bull hard, but give him time."

We waited for about ten minutes, then Janga motioned us to follow him, and we picked our way through the rocks single file. We moved slowly two hundred yards downrange to where the two bulls lay dead.

I could feel the hair on the back of my neck bristle.

"I don't like this," Jason said. "It's sort of eerie facing this brute after he tried to mash me under his hooves yesterday."

"You should be used to this after taking down that bull elephant," Chuck said.

I couldn't explain it either, but there was something in the air.

The grass rustled under our feet, the only sound any of us dared to make. At thirty yards, Janga slowed and held up his palm, signaling everyone to stop. Then the others held back while Janga and I approached Betty's bull while Jason's lay another twenty-five yards further to the west.

I knew we were in the most treacherous part of the hunt, but I tried to put it out of my mind, not wanting any fear to creep in on me.

The bulls looked dead as doornails. Janga poked the face of Betty's bull with a stick, and then I motioned the rest of them to move up. Jason hustled along, while Chuck and Betty followed close behind.

We waited for Jason to get in position behind Janga, and the kid brought his rifle up at the ready.

"Be ready," Janga said, pushing him forward. "You lead on."

I followed Janga and Jason at the ready, and I could see beads of sweat forming on the boy's forehead and another dripping down his cheek.

I hated cowardice. Not that I hated a coward, but I wouldn't choose a friend without a backbone. But mostly courage was what I strove for. I despised fear. I could read Jason as he inched forward, and I knew he had courage.

We placed each step cautiously and quietly so as not to wake or startle this sleeping giant. At twenty feet, I spotted his side rising and falling, so we maneuvered in to find the finishing shot to end his misery as quickly as possible. We gave him a wide berth as we angled for a head shot, and Janga and I stayed at Jason's heels, coaxing him on. I glanced away to make sure Betty and Chuck weren't in the line of fire.

The bull made eye contact, and he tried to lift his head. I figured he recognized Jason from the day before, and I wondered if now he regretted having tried to kill the boy.

Jason raised his rifle to his shoulder, taking a steady bead between the eyes.

The bull snorted and gave a low growl. The only thing that would be going through his mind in just a few seconds would be a hot piece of lead. He lay still.

Jason took a breath and then put his finger on the trigger, holding the rifle as steady as a rock.

I knew we were now safe, but still there seemed to be something very strange about how I felt. Uneasy, anxious, restless—I just couldn't put my finger on it. I had a sense his bullet might get away and hurt somebody, but somehow that didn't seem possible.

Finally, the rifle belched smoke, sending the round home. But before it could echo against the nearby hillside, the brush along the edge of the swamp erupted with an angry herd of black gristle and bone charging straight for us.

I turned and grabbed Betty's arm, and we began to run. Janga grabbed the back of Jason's shirt and jerked him away as we sprinted for the hillside.

I heard a shot ring out, and I turned to see Chuck holding his ground and sending another round into the thundering herd. I turned to continue my pursuit of the hill as a third shot echoed against the hillside. I looked back over my shoulder just in time to see the buffalo overtake him, and he disappeared under their hooves.

We scurried up the rocks to safety, and I saw Jason and Janga thirty yards to the east doing the same. The herd had veered off to the northeast and left a cloud of dust as they disappeared into the bush. It seemed as if there were dead buffalo strewn from one end of the marsh to the other. I counted five to be exact.

Then I spotted the lifeless body of our dear friend Chuck, who was sprawled out in the grass.

"Stay here," I said, leaving Betty on the rocks as I began sprinting off the hill for my pal.

Janga bolted after me, with Jason following his lead. I arrived just seconds before Janga and rolled Chuck onto his back, looking for signs of life.

"Are you okay, Chuck?" I asked, hoping for a response. I put my ear to his chest and then gently slapped his cheek. "Chuck ... Chuck!"

He twitched slightly as blood oozed from his nose. His forehead bore a large welt, and his shirt and pants were torn.

"He's alive!" I shouted just as Betty arrived.

She knelt at my side, struggling to catch her breath. "I think he's out cold," she said. "Look at this bump on his head! Chuck, you're going to be okay!"

His eyes moved under his lids, and he coughed, letting out a low groan.

"Chuck, are you okay?" I pleaded. "Chuck?"

He groaned, squinting up at the sun. "Did anybody see the guy driving that truck?"

"Thank God you're okay!" Betty said.

"I don't know about that. Help me sit up."

I took his hand while Betty supported his back, and he cried out in pain.

"What is it?" she asked.

"My knee," he said, grabbing it with both hands.

"Is it broken?" I asked.

"Just a minute. Let me get my breath." He looked toward the dead buffalo lying in the pathway of the charging herd. "Looks like

I did some damage before they got me. I was trying to turn them, but maybe I should have made a run for it, eh?"

"Maybe so," I said.

"I know," Chuck said, rubbing the goose egg on his forehead. "But heck, I never would have made it with this old knee of mine."

"What about your knee?" I asked.

"Yeah, this old knee has given me problems for twenty years."

Betty began poking and prodding him to check for injuries. She pulled at his torn clothing to see if there were any deep wounds that might need immediate attention.

"I think I might have broken my nose."

I pulled my canteen off my belt and gave him a drink of water.

He winced as he craned his neck, and he took a deep breath before exhaling with a sigh. "No broken ribs," he said. "That's a good sign. But I'm gonna be sore in the morning."

"At least you're lucky there's going to be another morning," Betty said.

"You know these buff," I said. "I can't believe they didn't stomp you or horn you. It really doesn't make any sense to me, unless you didn't wound any and the ones you hit you killed—and all the rest just ran off."

"I don't know, either," Chuck said. "All I know is I am alive. Here, John, give me a hand and help me to my feet."

I clasped Chuck's hand and pulled him up.

"Wow, a triple," Chuck said, looking at his dead buffalo.

"First time I saw," Janga said.

"At least we've got plenty of meat for our native friends," Betty said.

"What about that wounded bull?" Chuck asked. "Do we still need to go in the swamp after the wounded one?"

"Don't think so," I said. "I think the first one out of the reeds was the wounded bull, Chuck."

Out of the corner of my eye I caught movement on the rocky crest behind Jason, and I turned to see natives gathering on the hill. "Looks like we have company," I said.

Jason and Janga spun around to see them on the horizon.

"What do you make of it?" Chuck asked as he gazed toward the hill. "Could that be our porters?"

"Hard to say for sure," I said. "What do you think, Janga?"

He frowned as he squinted at the bunch on the hillside.

"Those are the scoundrels," Chuck said. "I thought they were going to wait for us back at camp."

"They followed us," Betty said.

"For the blood," I said. "They followed us for the blood."

"If they wanted our blood," Betty said, "why didn't they just kill us in camp?"

"Because they don't want *our* blood," I answered, "they want the buffalo blood."

"Why didn't they say?" she asked. "I would have given it all to them."

"Because it's so valuable to them," I said. "They probably never thought we wouldn't want it all for ourselves. Some of these tribes, believe it or not, haven't had that much contact with white men to know our customs."

"That's hard to imagine in this day and age," Chuck said.

Janga called out to them, and the natives, holding their swords and shields erect, came off the hill single file in a fast track, followed by their bare-chested women, who carried baskets and gourds—all total about fifty in number. I recognized their leader's fuzzy hair.

"I wonder how long you have to be in Africa to get used to bare-chested women," Jason said, his cheeks turning rosy. "I just can't imagine why they don't try to cover up."

We all had a chuckle, which helped us take our minds off what we had just faced.

The native women waded in and began taking the first buffalo apart without even a word. I guess in their eyes the agreement had already been struck, thus they saw no reason for any more talk.

Jason knelt down beside his bull to experience the old boy and his majesty. I didn't know if the kid felt shown up by Betty dropping her bull stone-dead with one shot. But I did know that even now I hadn't killed a trophy yet, and my trigger finger was getting a little itchy.

As I drew near to Jason's bull, all my anxieties vanished. Somehow I had sensed beforehand that something bad lay poised to strike. There was a lot to this life that we couldn't see or understand. Jason had killed a lion, an elephant, and a buffalo, gaining membership in a select group of African big game hunters. He only needed to add a leopard and a rhino to complete the "big five," something that only a limited number of sportsmen had achieved.

As I gazed at Jason's bull, my heart filled with emotion. I felt the thrill of victory for him, as well as a sense of sadness that the old bull had bitten the dust.

Jason reached out and put his hand on the horn. "This is incredible," he said with wide eyes, "to think you are the first person to have ever laid hands on him. But then how much remorse can you feel for someone who just yesterday tried to slit your throat. Look at the sheer power and bulk in the loins of this beast. I am humbled that little old me has claimed his life."

The natives made short work of his bull, leaving us with the nearly seventy pounds of head, cape, and horns. Our porters and skinners had come at the sound of our guns and worked to remove the skin from the skull and cut the horns away. We kept enough buffalo meat for our own camp needs and gladly parted with the rest.

"It's hard to believe," Jason said, "that their favorite parts were the lungs, entrails, brains, and blood."

"Did you see how they cut the meat into strips to dry in the sun?" I asked.

"I can't imagine not eating that juicy back strap cut an inch thick," he said and laughed. "I like it seared over hot coals and cooked to perfection with Bamira's herbs and some wild rice and boiled onions. Every person has his own taste, I guess."

We loaded up the trophy horns and capes and the portion of the meat we felt comfortable taking and departed the marshland. We had to make camp close by so Chuck could recover overnight before the long trek back to camp. I could feel an unspoken anxiety among us regarding the safety of the others. This band of outlaws seemed trustworthy to a point, but no one could say for sure what resentment lurked in their ranks or what evil motivations they might harbor. A chill ran down my spine as I envisioned returning to find only cold bodies littering the camp we had left two days before.

I tossed and turned all night, eventually breaking out in a cold sweat as I worried about Esther and Lance. The more I tried to reassure myself, the more I was consumed by terrifying images. I had received a premonition before Chuck's near death, the possibility that I was right again, that I might have some sort of sixth sense and could read the future, was frightening. I wanted to confide in Betty, but she lay fast asleep. I knew this would only upset her, and we were helpless to do anything, anyway. Finally the eastern horizon began to brighten, ushering in a new day. Never before had I welcomed a sight and dreaded it's coming all at the same time.

We arose with spirits high, even though Chuck's knee had swelled to twice its original size and his nose had turned black and blue. At Betty's suggestion, I had our men construct a litter out of sticks so that four of them could devote themselves to dragging Chuck back to camp. I was tempted to give the job to Janga for not letting us bring the Ford, or at least some of the horses.

"I can make it, really," Chuck said as Betty sat him down in the contraption they had tried to lash together.

"You're not going anywhere on that knee, mister," she scolded. "We have a long safari ahead of us, and we can't have anyone coming up lame. When we get you back to camp, we'll have to nurse you back on your feet."

"I just feel uncomfortable when people make a fuss over me," Chuck said, "that's all."

"Don't worry about it," I said. "We're not going to fuss over you. We just have to get you back to camp in one piece."

~~~~~~~~~~

Once more we were on the move across Africa on another unforgettable trek. The refreshing scent from the morning dew still clinging to the foliage filled my nostrils. The trudge over the rocky landscape slowed our going to a snail's pace since now we were burdened by the load of trophies and Chuck on the makeshift gurney. Every hundred yards or so, the lashing loosened, the sticks sagged, and the contraption began to fall apart under Chuck's robust frame. Each time I sent echoing curses to the surrounding hillsides. I wanted to blame our natives for my agony, but I realized it was making Chuck feel even guiltier for all the trouble.

We soon discarded the contraption after the huskiest of the men decided to lock theirs arms and lug Chuck's two-hundred-and-fifty-pound frame between them. But progress was slow. Four hours into the march, we'd scarcely covered five miles. What had taken only a couple of hours to travel just two days prior had become a grueling ordeal.

"We have to get back to camp tonight," I said. "I know if we don't, Lance will begin to worry."

"We'll never make it at this rate," Betty said. "We're going to have to make camp and start again in the morning."

"You'll make it tonight if you will just go on ahead," Chuck said. "I'll hobble on and follow the trail back. Just leave me with these black fellows, and we'll be just fine."

"We are not leaving you behind," Betty snapped. "I won't hear of it."

"Wait a minute, dear," I said. "Chuck might have something here. Jason, would you be willing to stay back with Chuck until I can get back to camp and fire up the Ford? I can probably cover the ground back here in less than an hour. Let's see," I said, pulling my pocket watch out of my coat, "it's one o'clock now, and we probably have a four-hour walk ahead of us if we pick 'em up and lay 'em down. If I grab the Ford and head right back, I should be back here shortly after dark."

"Works for me," Chuck said.

"We'll be fine," Jason said. "We'll wait here till you get back."

"I'm staying behind with them," Betty said.

"No, I want you with me," I said.

"It's fifteen miles back to camp," she said. "My legs are feeling like rubber."

"Buck up then," I insisted, "because I'm not letting you out of my sight. You just find your reserve."

"I will," she answered. "I think they call it *pluck,* don't they?"

"That's what they call it, and you've got it, sweetheart. I don't know what we will find back at camp. I'll go ahead and admit it: right now I need you with me."

"Okay," she answered. "It's good to know you need me."

"We'll leave you with a grub box, the matchsticks, and a tent," I said, "just in case. God forbid something should happen and I can't get back right away. I can't leave more behind than we can pack in the Ford when I return. And as soon as we get back to camp and make sure everything is okay, I'll be back."

Betty laid out lunch, and we made small talk, enjoying the afternoon sunshine together. Then she checked the feet of some of the black men and offered bandages. The boxes were closed up, and the gun bearers, porters, and packers gathered up their gear, after which we bade Jason and Chuck farewell.

Betty bent down and kissed Chuck on the top of his balding head. She then turned to Jason and embraced him like a son. "You be safe now until John gets back," she said, "and keep those rifles close to your fire."

I trotted ahead to catch up to Janga, who had already begun the march. As I looked back, I saw that Betty had paused to lean over and retie her bootstraps. "Let's go!" I shouted.

She jumped to her feet and began running to catch up. Then she stopped fifty yards down the trail, turned, and waved goodbye to the boys.

Chapter 20

FOUR OUT OF FIVE

W e hit the ground with intensity, putting one foot in front of
the other on a serious march back to camp. None of us knew
what awaited us, and the thought weighed heavily on me. Betty, too,
looked anxious.

As the late afternoon sun wore on, my feet began to feel like
two bricks.

"How are you doing?" I asked Betty.

Her grim face and wet shirt spoke volumes. "I'll be fine," she
answered with a stiff upper lip. "You told me not to come on this safari
and complain, and I'm not going to start now. I just hope everyone
is safe back at camp. Those natives were hard to read this morning.
I'm concerned because Janga is so concerned."

"I'm sure everything is fine," I answered, trying to reassure her,
even though the hard knot in my stomach wouldn't go away.

"How much further?" she asked.

"A couple of hours, that's all."

"How much daylight do we have left?" she asked.

"We're burning daylight. Probably about an hour and a half."

"Does that mean we'll be back at camp in an hour and a half?"

"Hope so," I answered, not wanting to tell her we would probably
not make it back before darkness fell. "Do you want to take a break?"

"Not if it means getting stuck out here in the dark. I didn't like
it much yesterday morning when we were prowling around before
daylight looking for that swamp."

"I figured you didn't," I said, panting as I spoke, "but you didn't complain."

"Am I complaining now?" she said. "You just keep marching and keep up with Janga, and we'll get back to camp before the sun sets."

I settled back into my stride, and I could almost feel Betty's breath on my back. Then I felt her hand on my shoulder, and I slowed in anticipation. "What is it?" I asked.

"You know you are my protector," she said. "No matter where we are, I always feel safe with you."

I reached down and patted my sidearm, then glanced over my shoulder and confirmed that I would watch out for her. I grabbed her hand and pulled her ahead of me so I could watch her backside as I walked behind. *What a girl*, I thought. *How could I have been married to her for all these years and really never know her at all? What a girl.*

As we put distance between us and Jason and Chuck, now I had new worries to contend with. I knew Chuck would watch out for the kid, but it worried me that maybe with his bum knee he might not be as capable.

What good was all this worry, anyway? Was it adding one day to my life? Was it changing anything, or making anything better? Not that I could see. It seemed to be burning a hole in my stomach, making me into an old man before my time, causing me to have doubts about myself and others. As far as I could tell, worry was nothing more than a sack of rocks in your pack. Now caution, there was a concept you could work with, and maybe worry could cause you to be more cautious. But worry in itself, as far as I could tell, was worthless.

~~~~~~~~~~

When we arrived at camp, we enjoyed a reunion that rivaled the joy experienced at the end of a war. We laughed and hugged and shared the story of the dead buffalo and Chuck's brush with death. All that worry over Lance and Esther had proved worthless, just as I had thought it would. No matter what happened in life, I thought, things would always work out for the best. Not that I was at a place that would allow me to say that my son's death had worked out for the best. But then, as I looked back at the events of the last year, I had to say that had Johnny not died nearly six years ago, I would have never given Jason a second look on that train that morning. And then there was the biggest question of them all: Would I have even discovered Africa?

I began loading up the Ford with provisions, just in case it broke down and I had to walk back or, even worse, had to spend the night in the bush alone. I knew Betty wasn't that excited about my trip, but she was more than willing to let me go to retrieve Jason and Chuck.

"Now don't worry about me," I told her. "I'll be just fine. I'll see how it goes, but don't expect me to drive back tonight. I'll probably go ahead and pitch a tent and spend the night with them and then head back fresh at first light."

"I'll be fine, too," she said.

"I know you will. You are in good hands. Here, give me a kiss," I said, reaching for her shoulder and pressing my lips to hers. As we embraced, I smelled her hair, and I just couldn't bring myself to wonder what it would be like to live my life without her.

I finally let go and then grabbed the wheel and sat down in the cushioned seat, and Lance gave the Lizzy a sharp crank.

"I'll be back in the morning," I said, letting out the clutch and heading off in the night with the headlamps piercing the darkness.

~~~~~~~~~~

Three hours later, and having fought the terrain every foot of the way, I finally retraced the nearly twenty miles through the darkness to find Chuck and Jason huddled around their fire. Jason jumped to his feet and began waving his hands. I brought the car up and turned off the spark, extinguishing the churning motor.

"Boy, it's good to see you!" Jason said. "Is everybody okay back at camp?"

"Everybody is fine," I answered. "Those natives were all talk."

"It's been a long day," Chuck said, "not that I didn't enjoy your company, Jason. I just hope we are done with that tribe. I'll be glad when we are on the move again."

"It's been a long day for me, as well," I said, "and I am dead tired. Besides, driving this thing in the dark is sort of sketchy. What do you say we just relax for a while? We'll sack out here and get a fresh start in the morning."

"Works for me," Jason said.

"What's that?" I asked, spotting a rolled-up hide lying next to Jason's gear."

"Oh yeah," Chuck said casually. "We killed a leopard."

"Who killed a leopard? Did you kill a leopard, Chuck?"

"Nope. Jason killed the leopard."

I wanted to be excited, but now the kid had taken one step closer to bagging the big five. I didn't know anyone who had done this in one safari, and I was afraid that the kid might get a big head, considering he was only fifteen years old and had achieved such a great accomplishment. I could only imagine what would happen back in Nairobi when they learned about a kid taking the big five.

"This is a great fire," I said, changing the subject. "That drive really did me in. I wouldn't mind just sitting around the fire and relaxing for a while."

"Did you bring any food?" Chuck asked.

"You don't have any food? We left you that chop box."

"Yeah, well, the natives were so eager they picked up that chop box and lugged it all the way back to camp. We were about to cut a piece of meat off that leopard until the hyenas got it."

"Yes, I brought food. I brought a pot of cold stew we can put on the fire."

"I'm starved," Jason said, holding his stomach.

"Let's eat," Chuck said. "Jason can tell you how he killed the leopard."

"Sure you don't want to save it?" I asked.

"No, you've got to hear the kid tell this one," Chuck insisted. "He'll tell it again when we get back tomorrow, but you'll want to hear it now."

"I'll get the stew," I said as I thought to myself, *I'm just dying to hear the kid rub my nose in his leopard kill.*

~~~~~~~~~

330

After dinner, with our bellies full of Bamira's stew and his fresh bread, we sat in the camp chairs I had tossed into the Lizzy.

"Tell him, kid," Chuck said. "Tell him about the leopard."

"Where do I start?" Jason asked.

"Don't ask me," Chuck said. "You're the storyteller."

"Okay, well, let's see … I had just finished packing an armload of limbs and sticks and was tossing them on that pile. The warm afternoon sun beat down on us, and the air seemed as still as death. Suddenly, the tranquility was broken by a snarl coming from a distant bush. I spotted something in the direction the noise had come from, and Chuck thought he saw a leopard. I was relieved that it wasn't a lion. That's when Chuck explained that a wounded leopard is much more dangerous than a lion, because they are vindictive and much more determined. He said a wounded lion is more likely to run and hide, but a leopard will come after you just to get revenge."

"That's right," I explained. "They say if you kill one, you better kill him all the way to the tip of his tail."

"Chuck said he'd heard tell of a man once who wounded a leopard in the foot," Jason continued with wide eyes. "It attacked him full force, taking his throat in its teeth and scratching his belly with his hind feet and spilling out his insides on the ground."

Chuck nodded his approval as the kid relayed the story.

"Anyway, he had my attention," Jason said. "Nothing much to mess with, that's for sure. Chuck said they are loners who feel most comfortable lurking in the darkness of the night. And they inhabit Africa in just about every corner. From what you read, next to the elephant, the leopard might be the most adaptable animal in all Africa. Right, Chuck?"

"You have been doing your homework," I said, "haven't you, Chuck?"

"Been doing lots of reading for many years," Chuck said. "Ever since you have been coming to Africa, that's for sure."

As I listened to the kid tell his story, it was as though I had been there with them all day. I was thoroughly immersed in the action.

~~~~~~~~~

"Don't you think we should whisper?" Jason asked, pulling back the bolt on his rifle to check the chamber for a live round. He crawled to a downed log and propped his rifle over it, taking a prone position and pointing downrange.

"If you get a crack at him," Chuck said, "take a heart shot. But if he charges, take him in the head. But take your time, and keep your cool."

Chuck moved to Jason's right. As he rolled over to get his legs under him, pain shot down his knee and brought tears to his eyes. He rolled back and tried to stretch out his knee.

"Are you okay?" Jason asked, hearing him groan.

"I shouldn't have sat down here. I guess my knee sort of tightened up on me."

Jason did a double-take downrange, and his eyes got bright. "There he is," he whispered.

Chuck studied the clump of brush and spotted the leopard standing a hundred and fifty yards straight away. "I'll back you up," he said.

Jason steadied himself for a shot, but like a cobra the leopard slithered away in the bush.

"He'll come out again," Chuck said. "Just hold your ground."

Jason held his breath for what seemed like minutes, and then he let it out with a short sigh. The two men sat in vigilance, waiting for the leopard to reappear.

~~~~~~~~~~

"We perched motionless," Jason continued. "Our eyes were fixed on the point where we had last seen the spotted cat. Minutes ticked away, and then nearly a half hour had passed without even a spot having shown itself. Neither of us spoke a peep, our eyes trained on every inch of foreground."

I could feel my heart begin to pound in my throat, and my chest felt tight as Jason's words drew me into the action all over again.

~~~~~~~~~~

"I think he's gone," Jason said, "don't you?"

"I think he's long gone," Chuck answered. "Are you getting hungry?"

"I am. I just hope that cat isn't," Jason said as they both chuckled under their breath.

"I suppose we ought to think about rousting up some dinner," Chuck said, "before the sun goes over the horizon."

"I'll fetch that grub box," Jason said as he got to his feet. He paused and looked around. "Hey, what did they do with that chop box?"

Chuck looked over to where they had piled up the gear they were going to leave behind, and everything was gone.

"Those idiots went off with the tent, too," Jason groaned.

"You'd think they would be happy to leave some of that stuff behind," Chuck said, shaking his head. "You'd think they would be relieved that they didn't have to carry it. But no, they have to go and pack it all away, even when they don't have to. I can't believe they took our dinner."

"It's gone. I just wasn't paying any attention to them when they headed off. I guess we were so distracted by saying goodbye to Betty that we weren't thinking of anything else."

"We'll be fine," Chuck said. "We had lunch a couple of hours ago. The boys put together a great fire for us, and they gathered up a good pile of wood that will last us all night. Even though the night might get a little chilly, we'll be just fine. That is, of course, as long as the lions don't find us."

Jason laughed. "And that leopard decides to find a new neighborhood to prowl."

~~~~~~~~~

"Our tensions were on edge the rest of the afternoon," Chuck said as the three of us sat staring into the fire. "Jason kept busy picking through the woodpile, keeping the fire going. This could have been a restful afternoon, sitting under this shade tree with the birds singing and the occasional squeak of a jackal coming to us from far off across the plain. In spite of the leopard, I had a tranquil time to reflect. And my thoughts drifted back to an earlier time in my life when everything was much happier. But then the kid spotted that cat again." Chuck paused, preparing to turn the narration over to Jason once again. "Now keep going with your story, Jason. You've got both of us on the edge of our seats here, and remember, I was there."

Jason obliged, picking up the story midstream.

~~~~~~~~~

"There he is, Chuck."

"Who?" Chuck asked, oblivious.

"The leopard," Jason whispered.

"Where?"

"Shush ..." Jason lifted his rifle, took careful aim, and began to squeeze the trigger.

"Don't miss!" Chuck whispered, picking up his rifle and getting ready for a backup shot.

Jason's rifle barked as fire flashed from his barrel. Then they caught a flash of spots in the brush just sixty yards away, which earned a second blast from his fire stick.

"I got him!" Jason shouted.

"You did?"

"I think so," Jason said, "but we'll wait before I investigate."

"You are learning," Chuck said. "Are you sure you hit him?"

"Pretty sure," he said as the two men sat there for as long as Jason could sit still. Finally, he spoke again. "Has it been long enough to go and check now?"

"Not hardly. Give him some time. We've got nothing but time, Jason. Let's just sit tight, and if we catch movement, we'll give him another piece of lead."

Ten minutes rolled by, and Jason was ready to move. "How about now?"

"Ten more minutes, and then we can begin to move up," Chuck said, looking at his watch.

Jason looked like a center waiting for the quarterback to call the signal, and Chuck set his watch out in front of them so the boy could see the time.

Finally, ten minutes passed, and Jason's fidgeting came to an end. "Now?" he asked.

"Carefully," Chuck warned, hobbling to his feet and wincing in pain. "I shouldn't have sat so long. This thing has really stiffened up on me."

"Wait here then," Jason said.

"Not hardly, Jason. I'll back you up." Chuck followed him as Jason moved silently and slowly, holding the rifle at the low, ready with his finger off the trigger.

~~~~~~~~~

As the kid explained every detail, it proved to me that he had been taught proper gun handling by the master himself: me. But by his own description, he was way too anxious to rush in on a wounded animal, and I just didn't know how to break him of it.

"I felt as if I were playing football hurt," Chuck said, breaking away from the action and bringing the moment back to the fireside. "If you want to win the game, sometimes it's necessary to play through the pain. Some people take this all too casually, and that's what gets them hurt. It's like climbing a mountain in a snowstorm. If you don't have respect for what you are doing, you just might be on your last climb. I knew my reflexes might have to be quick to beat a charging leopard.

"I used to shoot jackrabbits in the desert years ago, and you have to be up and on them quickly to get one with a small-bore rifle. Most people I know shoot them with a scatter gun and birdshot, but the guys I hunted with thought that wasn't sporting enough."

"Sorry, Jason," I said. "Finish your story."

Jason gave me a nod and rested his chin on his fist as he thought about how to get started again. "I expected the brush to explode at any minute."

~~~~~~~~~

Jason froze when he saw leopard spots in the bush. He put his rifle to his shoulder and held a steady bead. Chuck raised his rifle as well, and both men stood like statues trained on the cat.

In a flash, the leopard sprang, and Jason let go his shot, which caught the leopard just under the chin. The bullet took out the spine, and the cat collapsed in the dust, dead as a spotted mackerel and not twenty feet from where they stood. Jason worked the action, and the spent round landed at Chuck's feet. They clutched their rifles at the ready, the kid and the old man each holding his breath, and all went silent as they stood over the dead cat.

Finally, Jason eased his rifle down from his trembling arm and let the air out of his lungs.

"Man, oh, man," Chuck said. "You like to call 'em close, don't you?"

Jason stepped forward and nudged the leopard with the end of his rifle barrel, and not so much as a flinch came from the sleek spotted feline. "No, I don't like to call 'em close," he said as Chuck hobbled closer to get a better view. "But that one is as close as they get. Is that a particularly big leopard?"

"It's a female," Chuck said, bending down and running his hand over the plush spotted fur. "They don't get as big as the males. But she is probably, what do you figure, about a hundred and twenty pounds or so?"

"Would she have kittens?" Jason asked.

"They would be right here if she did, and if she had them denned up somewhere, she would still be nursing." Chuck reached down to check her belly. "You can see here that she isn't."

"Just look at those teeth!" Jason said, pulling up her lip to expose her canines. "They're like daggers!"

"You bet they are like daggers!" Chuck said as he took her front paw in his hands to look at her claws. "And if you don't think this little cat could take you apart, you're mistaken. You see this claw right here? This is the one they use most for catching and climbing. It acts like a fishhook. It's like a thumb on your hand. They are vulnerable to the big cats and the hyenas, so when they make a kill, they have to get it up a tree to consume it."

"No kidding?"

"Otherwise the rest of the competition just takes it away," Chuck said.

"Why do you think she was hanging around here?"

"Maybe she was returning to a kill," Chuck answered. "Your guess is as good as mine. Could be she has weaned kittens."

"Maybe I don't want to know that I just killed somebody's mother."

"I don't think you need to feel bad about killing that one. You did it in self-defense. If she were human, the prosecutor wouldn't even file charges."

"Sort of like a gunfight in the old West, right?"

"That's right. She could have left when she saw us, but she hung around, lurking and ready to pull a knife first."

Jason laughed. "Right, except she brought a knife to a gunfight."

"Did you bring yours?" Chuck asked. "You can start getting her undressed."

Jason laid his rifle in some soft grass and then reached for his belt and pulled his skinning knife from the sheath.

"I'll watch, Jason. Since I watched you do a lion before, this little gal ought to be a piece of cake."

~~~~~~~~~

Jason sat back in his chair as Chuck interrupted the action once again.

"He worked quickly, with the hands of a surgeon," Chuck said. "I watched as he pulled the hide off the legs and worked right on up to the head, ears, eyes, and nose. I saw only one place along the way where he cut a small hole by mistake, but other than that, he did a perfect job, just like an old pro. I had him drag the carcass out about a hundred and fifty yards from camp, just in case the hyenas came around. I found a comfortable spot to rest by the fire, and Jason rolled up his leopard and tied it up snug with a piece of cord."

"After that," Jason chimed in, "we sat around the fire and watched the sun go down. And by the way, that hole in the hide is nothing. As darkness came on us and the temperature dropped, I wished more and more we had that grub box. I asked Chuck what he thought about roasting a piece of that leopard back strap over the coals, and we agreed it might not be such a bad idea if we could find it in the dark."

"Neither of us has ever eaten cat before," Chuck said, "but I've heard tell it's pretty good."

"Yeah," Jason said, "but just then the sound of hyenas laughing far off in the distance grew out of nothing in a matter of seconds. They laughed like they knew exactly what they were doing. We could hear them fighting over that cat carcass. The noise subsided in less than twenty minutes, and then it faded away in the night."

"I imagine that little cat wasn't much of a morsel for them," I said.

"So then we just sat around the fire," Jason said, "resting until now, when you showed up, and now I'm awake and I don't know if I can sleep."

"You mentioned you had time to reflect on an earlier time in your life, Chuck," I said. "Want to share any of that with us?"

"I was just reflecting on my life with Helen," he said, shaking his head. "This old life has been filled with so much toil and stress. I can't believe all the stuff I put her through. But now I have come to this place in my retirement where I've found a measure of relaxation. If only Helen had lived long enough to enjoy this time. I can only imagine what a time her and those two girls would have had together."

I could see Chuck's face in the firelight. His eyes had welled up, and he appeared to be fighting back tears. I remembered Helen's last days, when she was terminally ill with cancer and Chuck was helpless to do anything about it.

"Too bad nobody knows the cause of cancer," he said. "Maybe someday they'll come up with a cure. What a shame she was struck down at such an early age. I've tried to find another wife, but no one could ever measure up to her.

"Helen Grace Newman was her name before she took my family name. I met her on the train to Chicago one spring afternoon. Twenty-three years old we were, and both of us full of life. I was a student at Cambridge University, and I had the world by the tail. The train car bounced and swayed as the Illinois scenery sped by the windows. This young flower of a woman sat quietly reading across the aisle from me. I remember trying not to stare at her little turned-up nose and long, dark ringlet curls. I had my nose in some boring book, and every few minutes I would look up to catch a glimpse of her beauty, at the same time laying out a strategy to get the courage to approach her.

"She looked up and then away, as if totally uninterested. I figured she was spoken for or maybe even married, but she didn't have a ring on her finger. Obviously she didn't know who I was: captain of the football team and all. Then I caught her eye, and we locked pupils. Her cheeks flushed pink instantly, and she batted her long lashes. Then, as if jumping off a cliff, she dove back into her book like a prairie dog fleeing from a red-tailed hawk back to his hole. But, like a patient hunter, I would have to wait until she was ready before I made my move.

"You know how you just know? From the very first moment I laid eyes on her, I knew she was the one. I wondered why, out of all those girls at school, I had never seen one as lovely as this. On her third glance, the corner of her lip came up just a little, and her eyes brightened. Then she wrinkled her brow and spoke in a voice that would have made a meadowlark jealous."

As Chuck told his story, his words captivated me. Maybe I was just tired, but my mind became entangled in his words as he spoke. It was as if I were sitting on the train, whisked up and mesmerized. No longer did I hear Chuck's voice, but imagined the moment as if I were actually there.

~~~~~~~~~

"Do I know you?" she asked.

"Not yet," I replied.

She rolled her eyes and went back to her book.

I had not been accustomed to being snubbed. Just to avoid any further damage to my pride, I decided to move to another car. But I caught her peeking at me out of the corner of her eye.

"Where are you bound for, madam?" I asked.

"Can't you see that I am busy?" she replied sharply.

And with that I grabbed my hat and coat and left without a word.

I thought about the possibility of never seeing her again when I departed the train. So I kept an eye out for her, expecting to encounter her at the station. I met my parents at their buggy and stayed at home for the next two months, and I worked with my father in his business until football practice began in late summer.

That same evening my parents held a dinner party for some friends and their families, and as you have probably already guessed, our parents were acquaintances. I nearly dropped my teeth when this lovely butterfly showed up for dinner with her family and we were introduced formally.

"Chucky,"—my mom always called me Chucky—"I want you to meet the Newmans. Phil and Victoria. And you will have to help me with your daughter's name."

"Helen," her mother said, pushing her forward as if she were ten years old.

I wanted to ask her if she intended to be as rude to me now as she had been on the train.

"Helen just returned from New York, where she studies music," her mother continued.

"Oh, a singer," I said as she batted her eyelashes, and her cheeks turned pink.

She had to be squirming inside, because neither of us admitted that we had met before. I could only imagine what she might be thinking. Funny, but now I knew for certain she would never be my type.

"What sort of music do you study?" I asked.

"The kind with notes," she replied with a devilish grin.

Our parents spotted some other friends and excused themselves, moving off and leaving us together.

"Do you hate all men, or is it just me?" I asked.

Her beautiful eyes brightened, just as I had seen them do on the train, and she smiled sheepishly. "I don't hate all men," she replied.

"Then it's just me?"

"No, I don't hate you," she said.

"Maybe, hate is a little strong then."

"I just don't know you, and maybe I'm a little leery of forward men."

"Confident men?" I asked.

"I have just not been around anyone who is so persistent."

"What are you looking for?"

"I don't know as I am looking," she said, batting her eyelashes. "I have a friend at school, and we get along quite fine, as a matter of fact."

"Is he a musician, too?"

"No, he is a dancer."

"Oh, I see," I said, rolling my eyes.

"What do you see?" she asked.

"I see a male dancer," I said and chuckled. "I've heard about these male dancers."

"He dances the ballet," she said smugly.

"That's surprising," I replied, not really caring for her attitude. Nor did I care if I offended her.

"What's so surprising?" she asked, lifting her chin and piercing me with her eyes. "I attend a school for the arts."

"It's just that most men who dance like that don't like girls."

She gritted her teeth and turned away to storm off, but I took her arm to stop her.

"I'm sorry," I said.

She glanced back with a scowl and then pulled her arm away, turning to face me. "You should be. That was a despicable thing to say."

"I'm sorry. You're right: that *was* a terrible thing to say. What I meant to say, or what I should have said was that this man, whoever he is, is one lucky chap to have your affection."

Her cheeks flushed pink, and she began to smile.

~~~~~~~~~

Chuck paused with his story, trying to hold back his emotions.

"She had spunk, didn't she?" I asked, trying to console him.

"Yeah, she was quite a woman," he said, wiping a tear from his cheek. "I got her a glass of punch, and we made small talk for the rest of the evening. And as we progressed, I began to realize that she was a very intelligent and lovely girl. She actually knew something about football, and we engaged in the topic — and we truly got engaged the following spring. Now, all these years later, her smile is still etched in my heart, and her laughter still rings in my ears. And just maybe if there is a hereafter, as Esther believes — and only the heavens know for sure — maybe I will see her again someday."

"Yeah, maybe, Chuck. I guess I'm the wrong person to ask about that. I have listened to Esther's point of view on religion, but I can't see myself taking on that perspective. I have always been a free spirit, taking life as it comes and under my own terms. I just don't see how I could ever give up my life to something like that."

"Obviously," Chuck said, "religion, as you have said many times, exists for the weak-minded, who need a crutch to get along in life. I don't need any crutches, and I am quite willing to get along under my own terms. It just seems a shame that life doesn't have more meaning than it does. You are here for a time, shining bright like a candle, and then when you are snuffed out, you are gone for all eternity."

"It's just nuts," I said. "That's all you can say … just nuts."

"Why don't you guys get some sleep?" Chuck said. "I'll keep watch for three hours. Then, Jason, you can watch the fire awhile, and I'll get a cat nap. John, you get some shuteye. You're the one who needs some rest."

Chuck didn't have to ask me twice. While Jason curled up in a ball just far enough from the fire to catch some of the warmth, I grabbed my bedding out of the car and made a place by the fire. I lay peacefully watching the flickering flames as Africa came alive with the sound of distant animals talking to the night under the diamond-studded sky.

With my rifle beside me, I could hear hyenas dominating the song of the African night. They were sopranos in the chorus, while the lion was the baritone, and the elephant the tenor and the bass.

I found myself dreaming of the hunt, of green grass and gentle breezes flowing from wide plains and rolling hills. I dreamed about the thrill of a clean kill. I knew I was dreaming at first, but then I felt as if I had been transported back to my life in Chicago.

The streets were busy, and I could feel the concrete jungle closing in around me. There were kids hocking papers, lame and indigent beggars looking for a handout, and delivery carts and horse teams hurrying by, and I took my life in my hands each time I tried to cross the street, picking up a little something extra on my shoes as I went.

I stepped off the boardwalk and onto the brick roadway, and suddenly a man in an auto began honking his horn at me. I had never heard such a horn before. I stopped to let him pass, but the idiot just kept on blasting his horn at me. I turned to see what his problem was, feeling anger well up inside me. I started up the street to have a little one on one with this fellow, when somebody grabbed my shoulder and started shaking it.

"John! John!" Chuck whispered.

My eyes popped open.

"Lion!" Jason screamed.

Then I heard a roar that sounded exactly like that guy's horn in Chicago. Jason put his rifle to his shoulder just as I picked mine up from the ground.

As I took hold of the stock, I glanced up to see this magnificent beast, his long black mane shimmering in the moonlight, as he came charging at us from the bush like a freight train at full speed.

Jason's rifle barked in the night, but the lion continued charging, now not fifty feet away.

I took aim and squeezed off a round, the flash from the muzzle convincing me that I had hit him dead on for a terminal head shot. He went down like a rag doll.

"You got him!" Jason yelled.

"You got your lion, John!" Chuck said.

"Let's wait till we know he's dead," Jason said, holding his rifle steady on the beast. "Can you smell this guy? This old boy stinks to high heaven!"

"I thought cats were supposed to be clean," Chuck replied. "I think you saved our life with your shot, John. One of us was about to get a handful of lion."

"I just took a last-ditch shot at him," I said, "but I think I got him in the head."

"Want me to shoot him again?" Jason asked.

"No, he's dead." I studied his lifeless body lying in the dirt not twenty feet away. "But look at him, Chuck. He's emaciated. He's a broken down old male looking for an easy meal."

"That's why he stinks," Chuck said. "He's been eating rotten meat, and he looks like he's been injured from a fight."

"Look at his front leg here," Jason said as he kicked it with his foot. "It's all infected."

I reached down to stroke the back of his mane and pulled out a handful of hair. "He's got mange, too," I said. I looked to the eastern horizon, which was glowing silver. "Is it morning already?"

"Yep," Chuck said. "You slept like a baby, while Jason and I traded off twice."

"It will be light pretty quick now," I said. "Let's break camp and pack up."

"What about this lion?" Jason asked.

"You must be kidding," I responded. "That thing is a waste."

"What about his claws or maybe his canine teeth?" Chuck asked.

"I've had enough of that stinking lion," I said. "Let's just get out of here."

"Give me a hand, John," Chuck said.

I reached for his arm and pulled him to his feet. Then Jason and I helped him hobble to the car, where we loaded him in the passenger seat. Jason quickly gathered up our gear and rifles, then came packing his rolled-up leopard hide over his shoulder.

The thought of the kid unveiling his leopard back at camp while all I'd downed was an emaciated lion didn't sit well with me.

"You'll have to show me that hide later," I insisted. "Is it a good one?"

"It's better than decent," he said, stashing it behind the seat and then walking around to the front of the car to give it a crank.

I revved up the Ford and turned the wheels toward camp. The lamps lit the trail, and we didn't have to worry about getting lost, thanks to the tire tracks I'd left last night in the sand. Every so often we passed a white flag tied to a branch in the brush.

"Now I see how you found us," Jason said.

"I'm good, but not that good," I said. "I would have gotten here earlier, but I popped a tire in some sharp rocks. I'll try to avoid them on the way back if I can."

The ride beat me up with all the bumps, the exhaust gave me a headache, the seat killed my back, and the motor hurt my ears. But amidst all this misery, I was glad we didn't have to walk—or watch Chuck being dragged back to camp. The horizon began to brighten, and slowly our headlamps faded as the morning sun began to approach. Then, before we knew it, the daylight was well upon us. I was glad I had slept like a baby, content to be safe and alive. And I swore to myself I would clear my mind and not dream any more about cars with funny sounding horns.

Chapter 21

INNOCENT

As we drove across the African bush, Chuck began to recount his brush with death, courtesy of the rampaging buffalo herd. I hung on every word. There were three parts that made a hunt exciting. First of all, there was getting close enough to the animal you were hunting to take him down. The second was hunting really big animals, and the third was hunting dangerous animals.

Every once in a while, Chuck would pause and then pick up the story again. But one time he paused a little too long. I glanced over at him, expecting him to start up again, but his head bobbed and bounced from the ride, his eyes shut tightly. I had a hard time believing that he could sleep through all the noise and jostling, but I guess he'd had a long day putting up with that energetic kid. I wondered for a second if Chuck had died on me or something, but then his eyes popped open as we hit a hole, and he picked up the story right where he'd left off. For a while, at least. Then he stopped mid-sentence and went right back to sawing logs.

I'd known this trip would be perilous all those many months ago when I planned it, and I had to think of all the things I had done in my life. I never considered myself a huge risk taker, but was I really gambling with my eternity? These of course were very personal thoughts that I could have never shared with anyone, but at that moment my mind began to wonder.

I thought about all the deep things in life that were so easy to ignore. I had to wonder if I really was more of a risk taker. I'd brought

Betty to a place where her life was under constant threat of harm, and I hadn't kept very good watch over my old friend and partner, Chuck. And how silly I was to have brought to Africa a young boy who was so naive about life! To let him go like a pup off-leash on the busy streets of a big city, where he could get stepped on or run over. What did it all mean, and what could be the purpose in this life, anyway? I knew it couldn't be to just pursue adventure. How long could that last, anyway? Were we really sojourners on a greater journey to somewhere else, or was this all there was? Where did the lion go when the bullet passed his brain and he fell silent in the dust? Why did he have to suffer? Was he gone forever? Because forever was a frightening concept that apparently would last a very long, long time indeed.

There just had to be something more here. Maybe we were reincarnated and couldn't remember our previous life, and the Hindus had it right. Or maybe we achieved perfection like the Buddhists believed and became nothing for all eternity. No pain, no suffering, no struggle, and no consciousness. What kind of a great deal was that? Or maybe the Muslims had it right, and we were surrounded in eternity with beautiful virgins who never grew old. *Now there's a thought!* I had to laugh to myself as the vision went through my mind. *Spending eternity with beautiful women who would remain virgins for all eternity—sounds like hell to me.*

There just had to be an easier answer than the one the Christians sold, which seemed too syrupy: a system of dos and don'ts, where everyone sat around feeling holy and proud because they were goody two-shoes, spouting that everything was to their god's glory, proud that he was like a personal genie who granted them any wish they desired. And then you had to do all this stuff to get to heaven, and it was all stuff I would have hated anyway.

At least where I was going, if that was hell, my friends would be there, too. They'd served me well in this life, and we would make the best of it in the next, if that was what we had to do. Besides, I was gonna be just fine, because I had already lived a pretty darn good life. Other than a few minor things, I had never done anything really bad. Anyway, I figured if this god graded on a curve, which he had to, he would likely grade me above the really bad guys who deserved to go to hell. Besides, I had never killed anyone, or stolen anything significant. I had tried to be a loving husband and remain faithful. I had always been a good person, but then, once again, I was certain he graded on a curve, if there really was such a thing as eternity. At least I could live my life the way I wanted to, and I didn't have to sell out. *I did it my way*, I thought. *That sounds like a great title for a song.*

I looked over my shoulder, and I could see that Jason was sleeping on his side in the backseat, with his hands tucked under his cheek. As I followed my tire tracks from the night before, I kept an eye out for a trophy. There were plenty of animals along the way, but nothing in the class I wanted.

Time slipped by, and before I knew it, we were pulling into camp.

"Thank goodness you're back safe," Betty said, rushing to the car.

I cut the motor and it sputtered. Chuck raised his head at the commotion, and Jason stretched, letting out a big yawn.

"Did I finish my story?" Chuck asked.

"Yeah," I answered, not really wanting to hear any more of it.

"Hey," Lance said, making his way across the camp, "I'm chomping at the bit to get going."

"Me, too," I answered. "I'm ready to find some big game."

I got some things out of the car and headed for our tent, with Betty at my heels.

"We didn't talk about this," she said, "but I was thinking that we should just stay put for a few days and recharge. Everyone is exhausted."

I could feel my blood beginning to boil as she spoke, and I tried to keep my composure. "We need to stay on schedule," I replied, trying to remain calm. "Besides, we've got to get out of this territory."

"Then it's time to revamp the schedule—before somebody gets killed."

"No," I replied sharply, "we need to move away from this native tribe before somebody gets killed."

"We're at peace with them now," she insisted.

"Betty, you heard Lance. He's chomping at the bit. Hey, where's my breakfast?" I asked, trying to change the subject.

"You missed it," Esther said as she approached our tent.

"We'll have to rustle up something," Betty said. "John is starved, and if I know that kid, he'll be starved, too."

"He's lucky to be alive," I said, and the ladies' eyes grew curious.

"I'm glad you guys made it back safe and sound," Lance said as he came walking across camp toward our tent. "Hey, I saw that leopard skin. Who got that?"

"What do you mean, he's lucky to be alive?" Betty asked, squinting at me.

"Oh, that leopard ... yeah, the boy scored another hit." I laughed, but inside my jealousy was eating away at me.

"Just a minute," Betty said. "What happened?"

"We had a lion come in on us last night in the dark, but I took care of him."

"Did you get attacked?" Esther asked.

"You're darn right we nearly got attacked," I answered.

"Where's the lion skin?" Lance asked.

"Not worth a hill of beans," I said. "The old boy was emaciated."

"Chuck said his knee is fine," Lance said, "but what do you think?"

"He's fine. That knee is going to give him some trouble for a while, but I think he'll be just fine."

"So what's the plan?" Lance asked. "As I said, I'm getting antsy to get on the move."

Betty's face turned red.

"I think we need a few days' rest," I said, stepping in before she exploded. "This is some pretty good hunting right here if you want to shoot gazelle and wildebeest."

"You've got to be kidding," Lance said. "I didn't come all the way out here to shoot gazelle and wildebeest. I could have stayed home and shot those. I want that hundred-pounder, and this isn't elephant country."

"We'll get there," Betty insisted.

"We've got at least five days ahead of us before we get there," Lance said. "It's what I have dreamed about since living here. We took that one side trip after that big bull, but we've just got to get to those herds."

"We need a break here, Lance," Betty snapped. "Everyone is getting tired. Are you that foolish not to see it?"

350

"I don't think you need to use that tone of voice with my husband," Esther said.

"Hold it, everyone, right now!" I yelled. "Maybe we have had just a little bit too much togetherness. But this trip is supposed to be fun and adventurous. Like Betty said, time is on our side. We set some goals for our itinerary, but if we don't reach them, it's not going to kill us."

"But pushing ahead when we are all exhausted will," Betty chimed in.

"Okay, I'll concede," Lance said. "I guess these last two days have been a bit eventful, to say the least, but what about those natives?"

"I could read that chief," Esther said. "He'll leave us alone. He was just running a bluff, and he got what he wanted."

"I'll shut my mouth then," Lance said, "until you guys are ready to move."

"Just be patient," Betty pleaded. "Chuck is in no condition to pack up. Let's relax a bit and enjoy our time together."

"She's right," Esther said, "and you know it, Lance. We haven't had any time together to visit and really get to know each other."

"Then it's settled!" Betty said. She sounded like she had just won a bet at a horserace, with her two-dollar ticket paying out odds of fifty to one.

"Don't gloat, my dear," I whispered to her as Esther and Lance began discussing lunch. "It's unbecoming."

Betty smiled and gave me a shove, acknowledging my teasing. But she knew I was half serious. She had gotten her way, which was all well and good, but she didn't need to rub anyone's nose in it.

"How about lunch?" I asked.

Bamira heard me and shouted from across the camp. "Soup and bread, Bwana!"

~~~~~~~~~~

I had wanted to take a jaunt after lunch to look at some of the country to the east, where the plains butted up to the green rolling hills. But there were villages between here and there, and Willie said we shouldn't go poking a stick in a beehive where it didn't belong.

They had already been stirred up once, and right now the less contact the better.

Chuck and Lance decided to take the kid for a ride in the Ford, and Betty and Esther were talking over coffee. I found a book and a quiet place under a shade tree, and I tried to read. But sleep came much too easily in the heat. This time, my dream came easily as well. I thought about this journey we were on and where we were going. I knew I couldn't turn back, even though I wanted to so desperately. I dreamed that I was in a boat on a raging river, being tossed and tipped at every turn, with the freeboard just inches away from swamping while all the time I had no paddle. I was on a one-way trip to eternity, but a voice in my head kept saying, *Go back. Turn around and go back.* Yet I couldn't. The river had me at her mercy. But the voice kept saying, *There is only one way ... one way ... and the only way to get there is to turn your life around.* But it was hopeless. I would need a miracle to turn the boat around.

I kept asking, "How can I go back? The riverbank is a sheer rock cliff, and the water is too swift." The whitewater roared, and all I could do was hold on for dear life. For dear life, or the lifeline would be broken. For dear life, or be plunged into the eternal darkness of death. What a terrifying thought: to end up dead for all eternity. Ashes to ashes, dust to dust. How many had gone before, and how many would follow? The graveyards were full of the decaying bones of those who, despite at one time being full of dreams and hopes for tomorrow, would spend the rest of forever in the cold darkness of a decomposing pine box. How cruel this life was to treat us with such dishonesty, to offer up false hope, when only the grave awaited us! All my hopes had been dashed on the rocks when Johnny had died, and the wind had been taken out of my sails.

My eyes opened to the red sky in the west, and I wiped the cold sweat that had collected on my forehead. I paused to reflect on my dream. Esther would know. I had to ask her what it all meant ... or would I?

I only knew one thing. I had come to this world as an infant, and nobody had really explained anything at all to me. They had just let me figure it out on my own. From what I could see, life had no real purpose at all. This was just a natural place that had come into existence all on its own. It had begun with a huge explosion. A bunch of matter had been tossed out into the universe, and this planet had evolved over a period of billions of years into what I now saw before me.

My only purpose was to enjoy what I had; to get as much as I could, including adventure; to live long, love much, and earn what I could when I could. Because my health, my wealth, and my happiness could all be snatched away in a finger snap. As the sages said, "Eat, drink, and be merry, for tomorrow we die." It was a tragic thought indeed, but no more tragic than spending your whole life searching for more than there was, or thinking you had found more where there wasn't. If there was any more to it than that, I would have to be shown firsthand, and probably soon, because I had been in so many scraps in my life that I had to be running out of luck. There was the time in my childhood when I had nearly drowned in a lake, but for my friend pulling me to shore. Or the time when I had slipped on a cliff and nearly plunged five hundred feet to a rocky death. Or the time ... now, as I thought back, there were far too many to recall. If this god did exist, then maybe he was watching over me. If not that, then lady luck was on my side.

I knew Esther would have quite a different view of all this, but her perspective about everything seemed so foreign to me—even silly, to be honest. She had an explanation for everything, but none of it made any sense or rested on any solid foundation. It all had to do with her faith in that silly book. Time and again she would spout quotes from some passage that she would hold onto as some shining truth, when in true fact, I could only take pity on her.

Somehow she had gotten sucked into the superstitious gibberish of uneducated men who couldn't have possibly understood the struggles we now faced in the modern world. How could one hope to take ancient writings and apply them to today? Christians called them enlightened. How absurd! If you wanted to be enlightened, talk to the lion. He had wisdom far beyond that of any ancient writer who had lived in a world that was long gone. *Let the world teach us about worldly things*, I thought, *and the heavens, well, let them speak to someone else, because I live in the here and now. And when I die,*

I'll be satisfied just to remain here in a cozy pine box with my best suit cut up the back.

I spotted Esther and Betty walking toward me and knew my quiet time had come to an end.

"Hello, ladies," I said.

"You were tired," Betty said. "You've been asleep here for about two hours."

"No kidding," I said. "Seems like two minutes. This is a really peaceful place. Good choice, Betty, to take some time to get our fires going again. Say, I was just thinking about you, Esther."

"Me?" She smiled, revealing her straight white teeth. "How so?"

I wanted to ask her about my dream, but I was truly afraid of the answer. I guess I actually knew the answer, and I didn't have to hear it out loud again.

"Nothing … it's nothing," I said, pausing to look up into her big brown eyes.

"What?" she said suspiciously.

"Oh, I don't know. It's nothing, that's all."

"Let me tell you a story, John," she said.

Oh great, I thought, *another one of her stories*.

"There was a certain man — we'll call him Chip," Esther said in her storytelling voice that always drew me in. "Chip was driving into town in his automobile. As he went along, he passed an acquaintance walking along. So he pulled over to see if his friend needed a ride. The man was extremely grateful and said that his car had broken down that morning. 'Where are you going?' Chip asked. 'To town,' answered the man as he jumped in the passenger seat.

"They made small talk, and then the man asked if he could make a stop at the bank before being dropped off at his destination. Chip agreed and made a turn and parked in front of the bank. He waited in the car until the man finished his business at the bank and got back into the car, asking if he could be taken to his final destination.

"While driving along, minding his own business, Chip looked into his rearview mirror and saw the police on his tail. They stopped him and drew their guns. Chip's passenger jumped from his seat and brandished a gun, but the police fired first, and the man fell dead, dropping loads of green cash from his pockets."

"He robbed the bank?" Betty asked.

Well, certainly the man robbed the bank, I thought. *The idiot got just what he deserved: shot dead by the coppers. But Chip didn't do anything wrong.*

"The police arrested Chip, even though he tried to explain he had nothing to do with it. The man had shot and killed the bank teller, the policemen informed him. Surely he'd heard the shot. 'My car was running,' Chip responded. 'I couldn't hear.' But the cops replied, 'You knew the man. He was a friend. You had a gun under your seat.' Chip started to panic. 'I always carry a gun under my seat,' he said.

"Chip was charged with bank robbery and murder. He hired the best attorneys, and they offered him a plea bargain. But he was innocent and refused to plea. The jury had no choice but to convict. He was innocent, and he appealed. But he lost his appeal, every one. He spent years in jail and in and out of courtrooms. He was a convicted murderer but insisted throughout that he was innocent."

"He *was* innocent," I said. "It's not fair."

"He was on death row," she continued. "He was convicted. Finally came the day of the hanging. He was hurt, he was angry, *he was innocent.* And at that final hour, the governor stepped in and issued a full pardon."

"Thank goodness someone had some sense," I said.

Betty nudged my ribs, and I frowned at her.

"The only condition to the pardon," Esther continued, "was that Chip had to admit his part in the murder. Just apologize to the family and admit he was wrong, and Chip could walk away a free man."

"That's easy," I said.

"Not for Chip. He was innocent, and he wasn't going to admit he was wrong. He would rather die than to humble himself."

"Didn't he take the pardon?" I asked.

"Nope, they hung him."

"That's the story?" I asked in disgust. "That's it? They hung him? That's ridiculous. Why didn't he take the pardon? All he had to do was say he was sorry."

"That's the whole point, John. We have all been pardoned from this death sentence. If we can just find it in our hearts to admit we are wrong and ask forgiveness, we can accept the pardon Christ has given us by his death on the cross."

"What do you want me to say?" I asked, feeling a little hood-winked by her story. "I don't know what to say."

Before Esther could respond, we heard the Ford approaching the camp.

"Here come the boys," I said, jumping up to greet them and feeling relieved to be done with Esther's story. "Come on, ladies, let's go see."

~~~~~~~~~

We ended up staying in that camp for five days while Chuck nursed himself back to life and got his strength up to travel. Esther's story continued to haunt me, and I continued to try to put it out of my mind. Chuck's knee injury, it turned out, wasn't as bad as we had expected. And finally, when none of us could bear to listen to the kid ask one more time when we were going to leave, we decided to head out for elephant country.

We were up early, and I was up even earlier. The sun was getting ready to peak his nose over the horizon. The camels were making such a racket I figured they were glad to be moving out of the camp as well. After having stayed in one place for nearly a week, it seemed like there was more preparation now than when we had packed up originally. Everyone on our crew scurried around, packing gear in boxes, stowing them on the mule cart, or assigning them out to porters for the day's jaunt. I spotted Chuck supervising his part of the camp and joined him to talk over the morning.

"How's that knee today?" I asked.

"It's getting better by the day," he said, flexing it about halfway a couple of times to prove his point.

"Will you be able to hike any stretches with it?"

"I find as I walk on it, it loosens up, but then she'll stiffen up on me at night. Just give me a few more days of rest—and keeping it limber. I just need to take it easy and work the kinks out, and I'll be just fine."

"When we get to elephant country," I said, "we'll be putting some miles on."

"I know, and I'll be ready."

"Ready for what?" Betty asked as she approached us.

"Ready for you," I said, trying to make light of her intrusion.

"Hey, I'm saddled up and ready to go," she said. "How about you?"

"The car is packed," I said. "My rifle is loaded, and my pistol is ready. Where is that kid and his dog?"

"He's chomping down a last bit of breakfast that Bamira was getting ready to feed to the birds," Betty said. "He's changing, you know."

"How's that?" Chuck asked.

"He's growing up fast here in Africa. I can tell. I can't quite put my finger on it, but if I compare him to the same kid I met last year, he is different."

"I see it, too," I said.

"I see a man emerging," Betty said. "It just seems strange to see a flower blossom right in front of your eyes."

"If you want to call the kid a flower," Chuck said. "But I would call him more of a cub—and well on his way to becoming a lion."

"That works for me, too," she said. "Do you need any help getting in the car, Chuck?"

"Do you need any help getting on your horse?" he replied with a devilish grin.

"Touché," she answered. "Well, anyway, I'll see you on the trail. I'll get Jason and have him bring his dog up to ride with you so he doesn't get stepped on."

"I love you," I said.

She rushed over and kissed my lips, wrapping her arms around my neck.

"I know, and me, too," she said, turning to run off.

I patted her behind as she departed and then glanced at Chuck, who was shaking his head and smiling with envy.

"I really admire what you have, John. You know that, don't you?"

"I certainly am a lucky man to have fallen in love with the same woman twice, aren't I?"

"No doubt you are a lucky man," he said as we stood for a minute watching her walk toward the horses.

We then shifted our gaze to the confusion unfolding around us. Our group might as well have been ants. Some ants carried sticks, others had eggs, and still others were carrying leaves. Together they were working toward a common goal: the good of the colony.

"Look like ants, don't they?" Chuck said.

I nearly laughed out loud as I nodded in agreement. *Men really don't have to talk to be on the same page.*

~~~~~~~~~

And then we were off, the Ford laboring uphill as I fought the wheel to steer around rocks and holes. Chuck, trying to stay in his seat and keep the dog in the car at the same time, had Buster in his lap.

"You know what?" I hollered over the motor. "Sometimes I think riding a horse would be way easier than riding in this thing."

Chuck nodded. He was still holding on to Buster, who now sat next to him on the bench seat. "It sure beats walking!" he answered.

"Not by much!" I said and laughed.

Up ahead, I could make out Lance, Esther, Betty, and Jason riding on horseback and leading our procession of porters and camels, followed with our guides and gun bearers, who were all on foot.

"How much petrol have you burned in this thing?" Chuck asked.

"The cans hold six gallons, and I put part of the sixth can in this morning."

"That's pretty good, isn't it?" he replied. "Do you think we'll get this thing back to the farm?"

"That's been the plan all along."

"Have we got enough for a side trip? I think we ought to go explore some of that low country."

Just then our conversation was interrupted by a rifle shot, and Chuck ducked instinctively. But when the steering wheel pulled hard to the left, I knew no one was shooting at us.

"Was that what I think it was?" Chuck asked.

I rolled my eyes, the steering wheel rocking, and nodded as I brought the Ford to a stop. "I could have gone all day without a flat tire," I said, wishing I knew why these little problems always gave me such grief.

"Maybe we're getting it out of the way early for the day," he said with a laugh.

I set the hand brake, and we both stepped from the Ford to look at the tire while I left the motor running.

"It doesn't look like the rubber is damaged," Chuck said. "It's probably just the tube."

"No, when you hear a blast like that, it has to be a hole in the tire. This thing is ruined."

Just then I heard what sounded like a horse at a full gallop. Yet the noise of the hooves pounding the dirt was distinctly different. Adrenalin was coursing through me before I even looked up. We turned to see a two-ton locomotive bearing down on us.

"Rhino!" Chuck yelled, instinctively jumping back in the car. "Let's go!"

"On a flat tire?" I yelled.

The rhino's big flat feet were sounding more like a rumble, and at that moment it seemed as if everything had slowed down to a crawl. I jumped behind the wheel and gave it all she had. Chuck grabbed his rifle off the floor and wheeled the barrel past my head. I looked down the barrel as it went by, and the hole looked as big as my thumb. At that point I didn't know which was more exciting: trying to outrun a charging rhino, or looking down the barrel of a four-fifty.

I popped the clutch as the motor churned, and dust and dirt kicked up from the back tire like a rooster's tail. As I fought to hold the steering steady, the car bounced and bucked. Trying to drive the Lizzy was difficult enough on the rough terrain without a flat. Chuck tried to hold a steady bead on the big gray monster, now not more than fifty feet behind us and closing fast, as I grabbed for second gear. I hurriedly glanced at Chuck, who was trying to steady his gun barrel for a shot on the rhino.

"Can't you find some flat ground?" he hollered in frustration.

"I'll drive!" I shouted back. "You shoot!"

I sped for flat ground and then glanced again at Chuck, who was still struggling to steady his rifle. Then I returned my attention to the terrain ahead of us just in time to see a big hole in our path. The car took a big jolt, and Chuck's finger accidentally bumped the trigger. His rifle belched smoke, missing the hulk by a mile, as he held on for dear life.

"You drive, and I'll shoot!" Chuck yelled as he jacked in another round. "But could you watch out for those holes?"

The Lizzy was slowly picking up speed, but still the massive beast gained precious feet on us. I aimed for level ground, and Chuck fired his rifle again, this time on purpose.

I looked back to see that the shot had missed its mark. Buster never flinched once from all the shooting, but watched the big rhino intently, never taking his eyes off of him.

"In a second you should be able to just hold the barrel up to his ear!" I shouted.

Buster began barking, no doubt in an attempt to show his toughness.

I swerved to try to miss a rock, and the rhino caught the back end of our car with the tip of his horn. It made a horrible sound on impact and raised our back wheels off the ground, and I fought to remain in control.

"He thinks we're a rhino, doesn't he?" Chuck yelled.

Just like Chuck, I thought. *He always wants to engage in conversation at the most inappropriate times.* "He's gonna kill us if you don't get down to business. I'm running out of ground!"

Up ahead not fifty yards away lay a thick line of brush that appeared quite impenetrable. This old boy was stout enough to roll our auto over in the dirt, and I knew the results of that would be disastrous.

Where is this so-called god right now? I wondered. *Too bad he's not in this. Maybe he could save us.* Some men might have started praying about now, but all I could do was drive. Besides, folding my hands and closing my eyes at this very moment wasn't going to save us.

"This is our last chance!" I shouted in frustration. "You've got to get him now!"

The brush line began to close in on us as the front tire separated from the rim and went rolling across the hot sand.

"Take him now!" I shouted in near panic.

Buster growled and barked again as the brute drew closer for another attack, and finally Chuck let go another round.

I looked back to see the rhino go down in a cloud of dust, making a divot in the dirt and rolling to a stop on his side. I hit the brakes and brought the car to a skidding stop just as we slipped into a ditch.

Buster leaped out of the Ford and ran toward the rhino, barking like a banshee. He nipped at the heels of the lifeless hulk. It seemed as if we had driven several miles, when in fact we had only been chased about a mile or so.

"Holy … holy," Chuck said, wiping his brow. "That was a close one."

I had to bite my tongue. I had lost some confidence in his ability to watch my back, and it took every ounce of effort to keep my composure. But this was not the time to talk about it. We were still in a fix, and I had to keep my head about me to get us out of it.

"Too close for me," I said, swinging my leg over the side of the car and stepping out. I braced myself for the worst and then took a gander at the front wheel. "It's worse than I thought," I said.

What had begun as a small problem had now blossomed into a gargantuan one. One of the spokes on the wheel had a crack in it, and the wheel was bent completely out of round. Worse, the car looked like it might be high centered in the ditch.

I unbuckled my belt and placed my sidearm between the seats on the floorboard, then checked the back where the rhino had horned us. "We took a pretty good hit here on the back end as well," I said. "Looks like I'll have to take a hammer to straighten it out." After coming around to the front, I climbed under the front axle to make sure there wasn't any worse damage.

"How bad is it?" Chuck asked as he walked back to look at his rhino.

"This rim is gone. I have two new tires in the trunk, but they aren't going to do us any good now. There are new rims in the mule cart," I said, sliding out from under the front end. "How's that rhino?"

"As dead as the rim, I suspect," Chuck said. "Can we catch up with them on foot?"

"Not likely. The safari is back that way. We probably drove two miles off course, and being chased by a rhino didn't help. By the time I get back to the trail, they will be just that much further ahead. I could try it, but I wouldn't catch them until they break for lunch."

"What do you think we should do?" Chuck asked.

"Maybe we should pray," I said.

"What?" Chuck asked, taken aback.

"Never mind."

He wrinkled his nose, refusing to let it go. "What did you say?"

"Ah, nothing."

"Did you say ... *pray?*"

"I was just wondering—"

"Did you fall down and bump your head? You're asking the wrong guy."

"Just forget it, then," I snapped.

"I think you've been hanging around Lance and Esther too much."

"Forget it," I insisted.

"What do you want to do?" Chuck asked.

"There's only one thing to do. We're going to have to drive on the rim and take it easy for as long as it holds out. Maybe we can catch the trailing porters and they can send a runner up the line."

"Maybe I should stay here with the rhino until you get back."

"No, forget the rhino. We'll deal with it later. When we catch them, we'll send some natives back to take care of it." I looked back to check him out. "Wow, that's a brute. I didn't really get a chance to see him that well when he was bearing down on us."

"I think he'll make a respectable trophy," Chuck said. "He's not the biggest I've seen, and he's not as big as my other rhino. But who says you always have to take the biggest and the best? He's got the best story going for him so far, that's for sure."

Chuck grabbed his rifle and laid it on the front seat, and Buster jumped in just ahead of Chuck. I took my spot in the control seat, revved the motor, and backed out of the ditch. Then we turned tail to catch the safari, not knowing of course how long our wheel would hold out.

The thought crossed my mind again that I should talk to this spirit in the sky. *Okay, if you're there, if you hear me, could you lend us a hand? There. I said it,* I thought. *If there is a god, and I'm not saying there is, then maybe ... well, anyway.*

The car bounced as I fought the rough terrain. But then finally, after about twenty minutes of bumping and thumping, we caught up with our trailing porters, who were carrying sixty-pound loads in bare feet on the hot sand. Immediately I quit complaining. We had a bent rim and were missing a tire, but at least we had a ride.

I jumped out and ran after the last man in the line, who turned and set down his load when he saw me. I asked him to come with me, and he followed me to the car. I attempted to explain in Swahili what our problem was, and how he could help, but he stood there with a blank expression on his face. But after showing him the demolished rim, it didn't take too much explaining. All he had to do was look; it was plain in any language. Then he rattled off what seemed like about five minutes worth of Swahili, of which I caught very little, and immediately trotted off through the trees and out of sight.

Funny about some things—how no one had to explain all the details of a situation before you got the clear picture. You could look at a thing, and you knew instinctively what needed to be done without hearing even a word. Life was like that a lot. You just knew you had been here before and you had dealt with a similar problem in the past. Maybe if there was a god, that was how he communicated with us. I didn't know. Yes, I did. There was no such god, and that was just the way it was. Too bad. Sometimes I thought it was a nice concept.

"What's wrong, John?" Chuck asked with a look of concern.

"Nothing."

"Are you all right?"

"I'm fine," I responded, trying to cover my tracks again. "I'm just fine."

"You just seem really troubled, that's all," he said. "More than I have seen you."

"I'm fine, really." No way could I confide in Chuck. He wouldn't understand what I was struggling with right now. "I guess we could jack up the front axle and take that wheel off so we'll be ready to go when and if they get back here with a new one." I opened the lid on the trunk and dug around for the jack, which was most likely on the bottom of all the gear we had packed tightly into this little compartment. "We're going to have to take all this stuff out of here to get to it."

"How far is the mule cart?" Chuck asked.

"I don't know. Right now, I'm looking for that jack. It must be here under this box of stuff. Let's stack this gear over there."

"Who put all this stuff in here?" Chuck asked.

"I did, and it looks like we're going to have to unload the whole thing." I started pulling out the pieces one by one and handing them to Chuck. "It took me half an hour to pack this in there this morning."

We worked and worked, me pulling out the boxes and handing them to Chuck, and him stacking them beside the car.

"Here it is, finally." I took it around the front and put it under the frame.

"Did you tell him about the rhino?" Chuck asked.

"Oh, shoot, I forgot all about the damn rhino. Wait here. I'll try to catch them on foot."

I took off running after the porter and ducked into the trees. It seemed like just a few minutes, but in all the distraction it must have been more like ten. I ran like a deer for at least two miles, trotting lightly in the sandy soil.

Something didn't seem right, but I just couldn't put my finger on it. Why did distractions always take you away from the most important things in life: the greatest tasks, the warmest friendships, your greatest love? Distractions always pulled you away from your aim and made you miss the target you were shooting for. And what happened if you missed your target? I could only imagine what might have happened this morning had Chuck missed his. Maybe we would both be dead right now.

I began to breathe heavily now, and I fell into a rhythm, pounding two strides on an in breath and two steps on an out breath. I felt so good running, light on my feet and such, and then it hit me like a ton of bricks: I had run off without my sidearm.

I stopped dead in my tracks. No wonder I felt so light on my feet. I had probably gone more than two miles, and I couldn't believe how quickly the line of porters had disappeared. I should have caught up to them by now. They had to be just in front of me, because their foot tracks were in the dirt just as plain as day.

As I studied them closer, I made sure they were the right ones. Here were the horse tracks, overlaid by camel prints, mule and cart tracks, and then by hundreds of bare feet weighing heavy in the sandy dirt. And all very fresh. So, unless I had missed a turn and there was another safari just like ours, I couldn't be lost. But good grief, they had disappeared, and I didn't think I had been sidetracked for that long not to have caught them by now. Either way, I would never catch them if I didn't start jogging again.

I should have gone back to get my sidearm, but the porters moved so quickly. I would never catch them if I did that. They could really hoof it, and probably even better now with a week's rest. They were probably longing to get back to their villages and their families — and now we were a week behind the itinerary. I didn't want to cut short our safari, but keeping such a large number of men employed for another week was going to add to my already hefty budget. Not that money was really an issue. But I had no employment now, and the pool drained a lot quicker when there was no head-works to keep it filled. They had to be just around the next bend.

I began to wonder if catching them was really the wisest move. I could have waited for the mule cart to return with the wheel if I had been more patient. Then we could have driven to catch the safari, and I could have told them about the rhino then. Sure, they wouldn't come prepared to deal with a dead rhino, but at least I would be alive. But it would have complicated things more by not having the proper men to take care of the rhino. The mule cart driver wasn't going to be any help. But we were going to have to drive to catch the safari, and by the time we got the wheel fixed on the Ford and drove to catch them, this whole thing was going to put us another full day behind schedule.

Problems. Why was life just a series of problems? Why couldn't things go trouble free and stay on course as planned? Why did it always have to take twists and turns that surprised us along the way, forcing us to adapt and change to bring things to a successful end? Maybe that was what made life so interesting. What good would it be if there were no surprises? No surprises meant no adventure. *Without adventure*, I reasoned, *you may as well be dead already.*

I thought I heard singing from the native packers, and I stopped dead in my tracks to listen. I cupped my ear to try to pinpoint their location. But as I turned my head, I couldn't believe what I was seeing. I couldn't believe how stupid this whole situation had become. I had even forgotten to fire off the signal shots!

"Ah, damn," I said and let out a breath in disgust. I wanted to kick myself.

Not twenty feet away stood the meanest-looking lion I had ever seen in my life. Maybe he just looked that way because of my proximity to him.

As he let out a low growl, I realized that this time I had really done it. His warm breath drifted to me like a cloud. It smelled like low tide at New York Harbor.

Without a gun, I could do nothing to defend myself. My life lay at his feet, and I laughed bitterly at how stupid I had been to leave my sidearm on the floorboard of the Ford. I had done plenty of stupid things in my life, but this had to take the cake. This was the Grand Poobah of stupidity. I wanted to shoot myself, which would mean a much quicker death than the one awaiting me now. I was facing a death sentence, although the only thing I was truly guilty of was stupidity. What a shame, really.

I didn't dare move a muscle, knowing that he was sizing me up for prey. Would he turn tail or say grace for the meal he was about to receive?

I did the only thing I could think of. Slowly, with both hands, I took my hat off and held it over my head to make myself a more imposing foe. I could feel my heart pounding in my chest from the two-mile run, but my pulse would have been doing the same thing even if I'd driven the Lizzy here.

They say your life passes before you just before death, and I waited with anticipation to once again experience my childhood before this beast tore me limb from limb. I had to wonder if it would hurt, or if the trauma of death would mask the pain. They also say that a lion will go for the soft tissue first after he breaks his prey's neck. This old boy looked like an experienced killer from the old West that had just gotten the drop on me at a poker table after catching me with an extra ace under my sleeve. Too bad I didn't have any aces left.

I tried not to make eye contact, because I knew it would only challenge him and make him want to kill me even more. But I'd heard it said that the eyes were the window to the soul, and if ever you wanted to peer into the future, all you had to do was look into the eyes of a lion. Of course, for me, unarmed and defenseless, that wasn't much of a future at all.

My future seemed crystal clear to me: my time was quickly coming to an end. My killer spirit was severely diminished by looking into this lion's piercing eyes, and as I stood there motionless, he took possession of me. And I suppose I took possession of him, predator facing predator. I thought about what a shame it was for him to end my life this way, and I swore to myself that if he were to let me go, I would return the favor.

The old boy blinked, and I had to wonder if he was really an old boy at all. He looked more like a young boy in his prime. I could almost read his thoughts as he stared at this gift handed to him on a silver platter. Yet I could feel an uncertainty about him. I remembered Esther telling me that every beast would require a reckoning for the life blood of man. So maybe, just maybe, he was thinking about it, too. If only I had a way to tell him.

Not wanting to move a muscle, I searched out of the corner of my eye for an escape route. But I could see only open ground, with no trees.

He lifted his nose to get a smell of me as he continued to size me up.

I hope he's not smelling his food. I wanted to laugh to myself, but nothing was really all that funny. *Food ... what a stupid time to be thinking about food.* I swore I could smell smoke rising from kudu tenderloins being seared over hot coals. I hoped that this wasn't the start of my life passing before me.

My lion stood his ground, and my arms began to shake from holding my hat aloft, and my knees became weak. He opened his mouth and let out another blood-chilling roar, one like I had heard so many times at night from a safe distance. Apparently, he didn't know quite what to do with me. He had probably never eaten a man before, and so he just stood there, wondering if I might taste good.

What do you do when you are backed into a corner? When the finality of death stares you in the face, when you have finally resigned yourself to the fact that your chips are all gone and you have no ante left to stay in the game?

This huge tyrant lifted his front paw and cunningly advanced a full step toward me, probably hoping I would bolt like a gazelle.

But I held my ground, because running at this point would be suicidal. I fought to keep my hat above my head. I was certain lions knew instinctively the difference between man and beast, and I hoped this one preferred the four-legged variety over the two. I didn't know where my courage was coming from, or how I had so far managed to keep my head while my heart was jumping out of my chest. It seemed as if I were looking directly into the face of God. This being had me on his terms, where now I stood at his mercy.

I thought about this god thing and prayer, but honestly it just didn't seem like part of the hand I had been dealt. I decided to play the cards, even though he had a royal flush and all I had was a pair of deuces. Still, I had something, and I hadn't folded yet. I just had to run this bluff like I had never done before at the poker table.

One step back lay a good-sized stick that I could see out of the corner of my right eye, and if I could reach it somehow, I might just have a chance to bop him on the nose when he decided this game had come to an end. I could tell he was getting anxious, that he'd grown bored of the face-off and was itching to act. Slowly, and as imperceptibly as possible, I stepped back and in one smooth motion slipped my right toe under the stick, hoping I might be able to flip it to my hand.

I scrutinized my lion one more time. He was *my lion* because by now we had become as one. The thought of becoming one with him, accompanied by the all too vivid image of him consuming me, gave me a chill.

I noticed a deep red in the corner of his lip and saw the glistening of wet blood. Then I looked just beyond him and noticed the hoof of a gazelle poking up from the grass. He had no doubt killed this thing just after the safari had passed, and then I had come blundering in on him. All I could think of was that he probably thought I wanted to steal his lunch.

There was a youthfulness in him, and finally I had an idea of just what kind of foe stood in front of me. This lion would have been far more treacherous as a fallen king tossed from his pride, eager for an easy meal after being fed by lionesses, who were the providers. A fallen king who had lost his pride and his feeling of self-worth was a dangerous foe indeed. But this young buck wasn't who he had presented himself to be in the beginning. Why, he wasn't the crusty killer I had taken him for. His gun was loaded, but I had to wonder if it was much more than a small caliber weapon. Not that a small caliber wouldn't kill you dead. They just weren't as imposing as looking down the barrel of a forty-four, that was all.

I began to feel like he wanted me to go away and leave him in peace while he finished his morning meal. I couldn't fault him for wanting to defend his food. I just didn't want to be the second course. If luck were on my side when I flipped this stick, I could grab it and the boy wouldn't be startled into launching himself at me in rage. Just maybe he might once again question his own wisdom, and think twice about his own mortality.

I felt as if I were a ringmaster in a circus taming a lion. It worked perfectly as planned. I let go of my hat with my right hand continuing to hold it above by head with my left. Lady luck flipped the stick in the air, and it made a wide arc and landed in my open hand like magic, as if someone handed it to me like a golden scepter. Now I had become a gladiator facing this lion, who had just been released from the den to eat a Christian for good Roman entertainment.

Well, maybe not a Christian.

His head cowered and his tail dropped, and that was when I knew I had him. He no longer looked at me as food, but now as his master.

I took the stick and swung it over my head, taking a step toward him. But again, I had to question my wisdom when he let out a terrible growl, obviously trying to regain the upper hand. But to no avail—he knew he had lost the contest. I had found the ace. My confidence grew as he stood just seconds away from what I thought would be his certain retreat.

Then like clockwork he turned and took a step back. He hesitated and glared at me, giving another growl just to let me know it wasn't over quite yet.

I foolishly stepped toward him and took another wide swing with the stick, all the time questioning my own courage and wisdom. I couldn't give him an inch, lest he think he had gained the upper hand. In all the maneuvering between us, the distance had now closed to less than fifteen feet. I couldn't have reached out and touched him with the stick, but he was uncomfortably close.

And then, just as quickly as it had begun, it ended. He turned his back to me and slowly inched away. My mammy had raised no fool, and I backed off, too, giving him his leeway and breaking the tension. He ran and pounced on his dinner, then turned again to watch me in a defensive crouch about thirty feet away. I backed off and continued to increase the distance until I felt comfortable to turn and walk away briskly.

I made a wide circle to get back on the path. I had to be going in the right direction to find it, so I just kept on going. But the further I went, the more I began to question myself. It suddenly felt good to be alive, and I had to catch myself from breaking down and sobbing. I had faced death more than once in my life, but this was one time when I had definitely cheated it soundly.

I had a lump in my throat as I walked, and I couldn't hold back a tear that rolled down my cheek. If I had not been so wrapped up in locating the trail, I might have sat under a tree and sobbed like a woman who had just lost her only child. I remembered back to when my son had died and how emotional it had been for both Betty and me. I had kept my composure throughout, never once losing control. But when it was your own life on the line, it was different. Now all of a sudden you knew just how close you had come to turning the light out forever. Facing your own mortality like that could make a Christian out of you. Well, maybe *you*, not me. *Live or die*, I thought, *nothing could ever make me do that*. I was lucky the cards had fallen my way and caused that lion to reconsider his options. I didn't want to think of what might have happened. The fact remained that I had my life and my wits. My courage had brought this to a successful closure, and by God I deserved to be commended.

Indeed, a lesser man would have never been able to hold his ground and face off a wild beast such as that. *And I did it with no help*, I thought. *This is a badge of courage I will always wear, even if there were no witnesses and even if no one will ever believe me. I will always know that I have done it.*

I came to a clearing and an overlook, from where I spotted the safari working through the trees about three miles ahead, as far as I could calculate. I picked up the pace and took a beeline toward their position, knowing that, if I could keep a heading with a rocky high point in the distance, I would intersect them. Instead of running, I walked briskly, keen as I was not to accidentally walk up on any more coiled rattlers.

As I worked across the bush, I became entangled at times trying to force my way through. The dead sticks were sharp, but I had to keep moving just to get out of this mess and get to the trail again. I couldn't believe that in all the confusion I had gotten turned around so badly and had gotten so far off track. And then I broke out onto the trail. But as I studied the dirt, I found myself behind the eight ball. I could tell by the layer of prints that someone, most likely Lance, had doubled back on horseback to find us.

There was nothing else to do but hoof it back to the Ford. All this effort had been for nothing. Here I had almost gotten myself eaten. If only I had waited for them to return, instead of heading off in a huff. I scurried on down the pathway behind the tracks of the mule cart, relieved to finally be back on track. I would soon be out of the woods.

A rifle shot broke the stillness of the morning and echoed across the valley, coming from the direction of where I had left Chuck, now seemingly hours ago. I waited for another report to try to pinpoint the location. A single shot like that was daunting to the mind. Without any clear confirmation from a follow-up report, all sorts of possibilities rattled around in your mind. Did someone have an accident? Did something charge? Was a wild shot taken that missed its mark, with the culprit hurting someone before escaping unscathed? Or had someone made such a marvelous single shot that no more were necessary?

The latter wasn't how my mind worked. I always tended to think of the worst possible scenario and then build that one up to the most horrible possible reality. I could only imagine that there had been an accidental discharge and that one of my friends now lay bleeding and dying on the trail. It was silly to work myself up into such a lather, but that was how my mind worked.

As I turned a corner, I spotted Luke, Betty's painted gelding, tied to a branch. I then caught movement through the trees and spotted Betty and Jason crouched near a jumble of rocks. My stomach turned as I realized I had seen the rock formation before.

I slowed down to catch my breath, and through the trees I could see Janga with them as they hunched over a carcass. I had been here just moments before, chatting with my lion.

God, I hope Jason hasn't popped that lion, I thought.

My heart sank as I realized this was exactly what had happened. Of all the scenarios I had conjured up, this one hadn't been among them. Okay, it was just a lion, but this one meant something special to me. I would be duty bound to praise him *again* for killing another lion, but my insides were burning up with anger. I hadn't shot a trophy lion on this trip—or a kudu, elephant, rhino, leopard, cape buffalo, or anything else. All I had killed was a desiccated old lion that smelled worse than it looked.

Whoopee! Who is the great white hunter on this trip, anyway? Who paid for the whole thing? My blood began to boil. *And now he has gone and shot my lion, too.*

The cat had appeared to be in the prime of his life, probably ready to take on a pride master and become the king of his own domain. But now all that had been stripped away from him. He would never know the respect of a woman, or be served and waited on. Jason had snuffed out his manhood and his courage with one small squeeze of a fingertip. His future—his life—had been torn from him. *What a terrible thought.*

"Oh, thank goodness," Betty said as I approached. "There you are. We heard you had a flat."

"Yeah, we got a flat," I said, trying to hold back my anger. "And it looks like Jason flattened another lion."

"Right," she said with a sheepish smile. "You probably would think that."

"Let me get a look at him," I said and then added bitterly, "He's probably not even dead yet." I turned green with envy and then red with anger as I stared down at my lion, now stone-cold dead, that Jason had stolen from me.

"Honey, you've scratched yourself," Betty said in a concerned voice, "and your shirt is ripped. Where have you been?"

"It's a long story," I said, checking the lion just to make sure it was mine. I pulled his head over to look at his left ear, and there I spotted the same white tip that I'd spotted during our encounter. "If I had been here, I would have told you not to shoot this lion."

"Why?" Betty asked.

"Because he could have killed me, but he let me go."

"When?" Janga asked.

"Not thirty minutes ago," I explained. "We shared this moment, a mutual understanding and respect for one another, and I vowed to spare him."

"Oh, come on, John," Betty said. "He's just another lion, and you know it. You would have taken a trophy lion like this. You're only jealous because now I have scored one and you don't have one yet. You don't even have the courage to congratulate me."

"What?" I said, smoldering. "This is yours?" I couldn't believe it. She had hit the nail on the head, but I knew I would have to deny every inch.

"That's right," she said. "I shot him dead with one shot right between the eyes."

"But Betty, look at him," I insisted. "He's just a young male, not much older than Jason in cat years."

"Stop it. He's a trophy, and you know it." She put her hands on her hips. "And he's mine now, and he's mature enough and beautiful enough to make a full mount. Look at him. He's not all scarred up like the one we have at home, or like most of the big males I've seen. Check out his mane. It's black as coal. And look at this little white tip in his ear."

"There's no doubt he's a fine specimen. It's just that ..." I paused as I spotted that look in her eye that said if I dwelled on this, there would be trouble.

"It's just that what?" she demanded.

"Oh, never mind."

This conversation had nowhere to go at the moment. If I were to speak my mind, she would bite my head off. But now I had to deal with this. I could only imagine the fuss everyone would make over her at camp. The thought of watching her prance around like a princess just because she'd shot a lion was nauseating. I would have to tolerate this whole thing being rubbed in my face. Damn, if I had only taken my sidearm with me when I'd left the car! I could have shot the lion dead, and this whole thing would be over.

"He's a beautiful lion," I said, "and that's why I'm glad I didn't shoot him."

"You would have shot him, and you know it, John," she said with her head cocked and her nose wrinkled. "I just know you too well."

"Maybe so, but I didn't. Besides, he and I gained mutual respect for one another at close range, not thirty minutes ago."

"Stop this right here," she said. "The only time you gain respect for one of these is when they bite the dust, and you know it. Why didn't you shoot him, really?"

I hesitated, not wanting to let the cat out of the bag.

"Hey, where's your rifle?" she asked.

I closed my eyes, not wanting to admit anything.

"Now you're scaring me, John. You left the car without a rifle?"

"Betty, I know," I said, holding my palms up with my fingers spread apart. "I thought I had my sidearm with me."

"No," she said, pointing her finger at my chest. "How many times have you harped on me to use my head out here? And Jason, too! And you think you can be careless with no one saying anything?"

"It was a mistake, okay?"

"A costly mistake," she spit back. "It could have cost you your life! And you would have ruined my life, too!"

"I was wrong, and I admit I was wrong. I won't do it again. There. Now can we get on with this? I've got a flat tire to worry about, a lion to take care of, a rhino, and a safari to catch. So do you think we could get going and discuss my shortcomings another time?"

"Rhino?" Janga asked.

"Yeah, we had a little bout with a rhino, and Chuck flattened him. That's why I came after the safari in the first place. I took my sidearm off while we were inspecting the Ford. When I went after the safari, I forgot about it."

"Willie sent a crew with the mule cart, just in case," Jason said. "We heard the shots and figured you had something down. Besides, he wanted to send enough help to fix the tire."

"I'll help you with the lion first," I said. "All the tools are in that cart, and Chuck knows how to change a wheel."

374

"I thought it was just a flat," Betty said.

"No, that wheel is ruined. When the rhino chased us, the only way to get away was to run that thing on the flat tire, and, well, let's just say we killed him. But by the time we caught up to the safari, we were done for. So when I left the car in a huff, I totally forgot I had taken off my sidearm and I ran headlong into this guy here."

"You're lucky he didn't kill you," Betty said.

"I got creative, that's all. I knew he probably hadn't had much contact with men in his short life. But they wise up pretty quickly after being speared at by natives or chased and shot at by white men. They get a really bad taste in their mouth where humans are concerned, and they run short on patience when it comes to face-to-face encounters. But this guy was special. I mean, it was sort of like he didn't know what to make of me."

"He was probably trying to decide if he wanted to use catsup on his steak," Jason said with a laugh, "but he didn't have any."

"Okay, okay, I suppose. But let's get to it. How sharp is your knife, Jason?"

"It's okay."

"Mine is just okay," I said, "and my stone is in the car."

"Mine like razor," Janga said, carefully handing his knife to Jason, who took the knife and felt the edge with his thumb.

"Easy there," Betty said. "That thing's sharp."

Jason rolled his eyes and refrained from saying anything.

Janga and I pulled on the brute to get him into position for Jason to go to work on him. Then he started cutting the lion up the front of his belly as he worked quickly, separating the hide with the hands of a surgeon.

"You're not going to make him ready for church, are you?" I asked.

Jason looked up with a wrinkled nose. "What do you mean?"

"Just wondering if you were going to make him holy."

Jason started to laugh, but Betty drowned out his genuine laughter with a sarcastic groan.

"Okay, sorry," I said. "Poor attempt at humor, I know."

Jason had just taken it down to the first paw and turned the skin so I could see the flesh side.

"Wow, where are all the holes?"

"Not a one, so far," he said proudly as he cut through the knuckles on the foot to release the big cat from that part of his clothes.

"I want the skull," Betty said.

"Oh, come on," I said. "What will you do with that?"

"I'm going to have it boiled and bleached."

Oh, great, I thought. *Now she'll have that thing on my mantle, and every time I look at it, I will be reminded of my stupidity at having left my sidearm in the car.*

"Are you sure?" I asked. "It's got a bullet hole right between the eyes."

"Yep," she answered, "that's why I want it. Don't you see?"

"Yeah, I see," I answered.

I saw all too well. I couldn't tell her what I was thinking, though. The vision I'd had looked like something I had stepped in, and now I would have to smell it on my foot for a very long time. Every time someone came into *my* trophy room, they would see her lion skull staring at them, and she would be there to tell the story of how she had killed him with one shot right between the eyes. And now she'd have the skull to prove it.

Jason continued to work, and finally he had skinned the entire lion.

"Don't forget my skull," Betty said.

"All right!" I snapped.

"What's wrong?"

"Nothing," I said, trying to hold my cards tightly to my chest.

She looked at me with a frown, as if to say, "We'll talk about this later, mister."

I didn't really know what to say. I felt confused, muddled. To discuss what had happened between me and the lion would only make matters worse. Betty wouldn't be sympathetic. She would just get mad. I didn't need it. I felt beat up enough right now as it was.

There seemed to be something quite symbolic in this act of removing the skinned head of my redeemer, who only hours before had let me live. Now I had to take his head. I felt like a puppy that had just been scolded for doing his business on the hardwood floors. Or maybe this God actually existed, and now He was trying to tell me something. Well, if it was true, He had a strange way of speaking.

Why couldn't He just talk to me? I remembered back to that day I thought I'd heard the lion speak. I must have been exhausted and at the edge of hallucination. I had to admit this safari had been different indeed. At every turn, another curveball had been tossed in my direction. *And who is this Esther? And why am I always faced with her silly perspective?* Or maybe it wasn't so silly.

I wasn't so sure what I believed anymore. I had been certain for so long, but lately things had been happening that had shaken my whole world. I knew I would just have to shake this one off, like an old dog returning to the beach after retrieving a stick from the lake. *Maybe I should turn this safari around and head back to Nairobi*, I thought, *and go back to my anthropological work.* At least when I dug, my life seemed to make far more sense. I wrapped the lion head in a cloth bag and handed it to Jason.

We saddled up, and I jumped on behind Betty. Jason took the tied-up skin and lashed it to his saddle horn. His horse took it well, considering. But still, the horse had wide eyes, smelling the lion perched that close to his backside. Then we rode on down the trail, following Janga to find Chuck, who was probably dealing with his rhino by now.

I didn't know why I treated Jason like a kid. I guess it was hard not to, considering his inexperience. But now I was in for it. I had let this safari get away from me by standing back and letting everyone else shoot game. I almost felt like it was not my safari anymore. It had been hijacked by the kid and now my own wife. *Maybe I should just be happy for her*, I thought. *Maybe I should just muster up some praise for her. I mean, for pity's sake, this is why I came on this safari in the first place: to let them experience Africa, to let them take a little piece of it back home with them.*

I had wanted Jason to become a man over here, and here he was, before my very eyes, doing exactly that. Still, it was hard. I felt like I'd been tossed out of my house and had found someone else sitting in my favorite chair.

As we made our way, I hoped something might cross our path. I could poke a hole in it with Betty's rifle—and just maybe regain a little bit of my self-esteem.

When we arrived at the Ford, Chuck had just finished up fixing the wheel and was brushing the dirt off his hands on his pant legs.

Bakshishi, the native cart driver, whose name meant *gift* in Swahili, gave a big grin. "*Memsahib alimpiga simba* (Mistress shot a lion)!" he said.

I nodded as politely as I could and smiled back. I couldn't see Betty's face, but I could feel her beaming in front of me as I held on with my arms wrapped around her waist. I jumped off the back of Luke, and Betty got down on her own and tied the horse to a branch.

"Bakshishi tried to tell me something about someone shooting something," Chuck said, "but I didn't know what he was trying to say."

"Yeah, they killed a lion."

"I heard a shot, but I couldn't tell exactly which way it came from. So the kid killed another lion, huh?"

"No, this time it was our mistress, *Memsahib*."

"Betty? Oh, that's great. *Memsahib*! I should have known. He kept saying that word, and I wasn't getting it. I've heard them use that before. I guess I just didn't know what it meant."

"You've been here in Africa long enough now, Chuck. You need to start picking up some of the lingo."

"*Memsahib alimpiga simba*," Bakshishi repeated as he climbed into his cart and got ready to go.

"Believe me," I said under my breath, "when we get to the camp tonight, the natives will be chanting that until they are blue in the face."

Tonight would be painful, and there would be much gloating, none of it by me. Sure, I had survived a face-off with a lion, but it was nothing to be proud of. It merely illustrated my own carelessness. Who would make such a big deal of me facing down a lion, anyway? I was lucky to be alive. The lion had let me live, and now he was dead as a doornail. And what that meant, I wasn't sure. But I vowed to make something of myself during the remainder of the safari, even if it killed me.

Chapter 22

EXALTATION

I jumped in the Ford, knowing the skinners would be able to take care of the rhino and then return in the mule cart with Boclay.

I turned to Betty. "Janga will lead you and Jason back to the safari. Chuck and I will probably take a little side trip since Luke is a little spooky around this car."

"How far ahead do you think they have gotten by now?" Chuck asked.

"Boy, I don't know," I answered. "With all the fiddling around we've done here this morning, who knows? We'll just have to see how long it takes to catch them. I know one thing: I'm going to take it easy so I don't blow another tire."

"We'll ride well ahead," Betty said, "because you're right: Luke hates that thing."

I sat back to wait for Betty, Janga, and Jason to gain a little distance on us.

Chuck, meanwhile, went around the front to give her a crank. "Are you ready?" he asked, pushing me just a little.

I tried to evaluate whether or not we had waited long enough. Against my better judgment, I said, "Go ahead."

Chuck gave a sharp pull, and the motor started abruptly as I revved it up.

Sure enough, Luke spooked, since they were only about fifty yards away. I felt helpless to do anything, and I knew I was in for it. He reared back, and Betty held on, clutching her horse around the neck. I cut the engine, and she grabbed the reins and fought to get him under control. Then she turned and gave me a glare. As soon as Luke had calmed, she came trotting back to the car. Chuck, still standing in front of the car, looked back at me and gritted his teeth.

"You and that damn car!" she yelled as she approached. "Can't you just ride a horse like everybody else?"

I didn't dare say a word in response, because I had seen her in this mood before. A wise man took the boiling pot off the fire instead of tossing gas on it with some sort of fool-headed remark. I jumped out of the car and ran up to her, stroking Luke's neck to calm him.

"What would you have me do?" I asked.

"What I asked you before: keep that car away from my horse." Then she leaned over and lowered her voice. "It would be nice to be on this safari with you. I spend every day when we are on the move with Lance, Esther, and Jason. Not that I don't like the kid's company, but it would be nice to spend some time with you."

"Okay, so what do I do with the car?"

"Chuck is perfectly capable of driving that thing. Besides, there are extra horses now that the safari has used up some of its provisions. If you wanted to ride with me, you could." Her big brown eyes always had a way of turning my heart to mush.

"We'll talk about it tonight when we get to camp," I said.

"Promise you won't just put me off."

I nodded and said, "Ride on ahead. We'll give you a little more space this time."

Betty put her foot into Luke's ribs, swinging him around by the reins, and then she settled in her saddle and trotted off to catch Jason and Janga.

What a girl, I thought. *There she is in all her glory.* Her rifle was slung over her shoulder, and she wore her bush jacket, khaki pants, and lace-up boots. Her dark curls were flowing in the gentle breeze. I admired her so, and I truly loved her. For the moment, there seemed to be this little problem of being shown up by her accomplishment. But I could never tell her that. I would have to deal with it on my own. Telling her wouldn't solve anything. It would just make her angry over what she would view as my stupidity. But I couldn't help how I felt. How could anyone control the outside forces that affected the way they felt?

"Come on, Jason," Betty said up ahead. "Let's get going before they fire that thing up again."

"If you find anything to shoot," I called after her, "call me and let me have first crack at it."

She laughed loudly so I could hear her. "I'll be sure and do that."

"You know, Chuck," I said, "I'm the only one here who doesn't have a trophy to my name."

"Yes, you do," he answered.

"No, I don't. Everybody else has been mowing stuff down, and my rifle ... well, I don't even know if it still shoots. I don't know why you would even say that. You know I don't have any trophies."

"That's what I'm talking about," Chuck said, pointing up ahead at the horses.

"What?"

"That's your trophy, right there," Chuck said. "Both you and Lance, you guys have your trophies. What more could you want?"

"I suppose."

"No, I'm serious," he said. "Listen to me."

"Yeah?"

"I had a wife who loved me," he continued, "and I took her for granted. And now she's gone, and I miss her so much."

I could hear sorrow and frustration in his voice. And as I began to look at things from his perspective, I suddenly realized how lucky I had been all these years to have Betty. I remembered back to my earlier times in Africa, when we had spent all those months apart. I remembered her depression and the sorrow she had packed around with her in Chicago like a box of rocks. I had never once missed her, even a little bit, back then. Even the train rides home had been filled with anxiety as I wondered what crisis I would face when I got home. I could always feel a flatness knowing that I would be leaving my freedom and adventure behind.

Of course, no way could I lay it all on her, because that college had put pressure on me, too, with deadlines and commitments and the little backstabbers and gossipers. The young people had been great: eager to learn and enthusiastic. I had loved working for Chuck, the one person I could count on. But even my colleagues had been jealous of my relationship with him as the president.

I know that burned most of them, I thought, *but I never really cared. Heck, I knew I was a brownnoser. Maybe all of my problems didn't stem from Betty, but I guess I never really realized it.* I laughed aloud.

"What's so funny?" Chuck asked.

"Oh, I was just thinking about Jason and remembering the first time he tried to get on that horse. He went right over the other side and nearly broke his neck."

Chuck laughed along and nodded.

Well, I'm not a liar, I thought, *but some things are better left unsaid. And by the way, that was a pretty darn good cover-up, if I do say so myself.*

I sat patiently until Jason and Betty had achieved a comfortable distance. Then I set my throttle and the spark advance, set my handbrake, and walked around the front to give the crank a hefty jerk. The motor started up like clockwork and resumed a comforting hum.

Then we were off, but at a crawl, so as not to crowd the horses. I turned off the path and came down the hill and out of the trees, and we stumbled upon the greenest plain I had ever seen. It must have been five miles across. Up ahead and across the expanse were hundreds of herd animals grazing and looking from a distance like ants.

"Is that what I think it is?" Chuck asked.

"Yeah, that's exactly what you think it is," I answered. "We'll get back to the trail, but we just gotta check this out." The grasslands were hard and flat, so I cranked it up and sped out across the level ground to get a closer look at the animals. "Are they buffalo?"

"Watch out for that ditch," Chuck warned, clenching his seat tightly.

I laughed. "You weren't this worried when we were running from the rhino."

"I guess I was looking backward the whole time and didn't realize how fast we were going. Besides, I think the whole time I was hoping you could go a little faster. But now I'm just hoping we don't hit a hole and flip this buggy."

I held on to the wheel as it vibrated under my palms, and my eyes watered from the warm wind blowing in my face.

"Maybe we ought to put the glass shield up so we can see," Chuck said.

"Yeah, maybe, but get your rifle ready. You can't shoot out the front with that in your way."

As we got closer, the dots began to take shape, and it became clear that they were all different species. All ears were up and locked on us as we made our way, and yard by yard we could begin to identify them. The cape buffalo were easy, those big lugs with their powerful horns; and the wildebeest, too; and there were zebra, along with all different kinds of gazelle and antelope.

I expected them to bolt at any second as we came into range: three hundred yards, two hundred, one hundred and fifty ... I drove up to within seventy yards, just to see how far I could take things, and then brought the Ford to a skidding stop. Apparently, they had never seen such a machine and didn't know to be afraid of it. We sat looking at them, and they stood staring back at us, dumbfounded.

"Should we shoot one?" Chuck asked.

"No," I said, "somehow that wouldn't be sporting. This is all about fair chase, and what's fair about that? This is like shooting fish in a barrel."

The big old buffaloes just stood there in a line with solemn faces, not willing to spend their precious energy running away, and for some reason not able to assess the threat. I had never been this close to a bunch of them before, and it felt incredible to watch them and look into their faces. Some stood chewing. Others twitched their ears, trying to keep the flies away. Others had drool coming from the corners of their lips. Those little birds called Ox-peckers, meanwhile, picked at their backs, eating little bugs and flitting back and forth between them. All of the buffalo had sad eyes—and a mean look on their faces.

"You know what they say," I quipped as Chuck looked on with curiosity. "Blaney always said a buffalo looks at you like you just ran off with his wife."

"Well, I guess he's right."

One of the old bulls began to paw the ground and snort at us.

"Uh, John," Chuck said, "maybe we ought to—"

"Yeah, maybe we ought to give them a little space."

"I have gained more than a little respect for these animals," Chuck said. "If they decide to charge all at once, we're in big trouble."

Just then a big bull pushed his way to the front and came out to challenge us.

"Like that guy right there," Chuck said. "Should I take him?"

"Look around us, Chuck. We are surrounded. You shoot him and we could start a stampede."

"Yeah," he said, laughing, "the only things they will find are bits of our clothes, some twisted metal, four rubber tires, and ten thousand hoofprints where they stomped us into the dirt. Hey, look! There's some giraffe. Come on, John. Let's go check 'em out."

"Okay," I said, revving the motor and moving the car out as the crowd of buffalo stepped back, lowered their heads, and made a path for us to drive through. "But we're just looking."

"I know," he responded as I passed through an opening in the herd.

"This is incredible," I said. "I've never seen this many animals in one place."

There were zebra, warthog, little tommies, heart beast, wildebeest, impala—all common animals I'd shot before.

The herds eventually thinned out, and then we saw why. About four hundred yards from them was a pride of lions sprawled out in the grass, their bellies bloated from gorging on their last meal. The vultures and jackals were working on the remains of a buffalo carcass nearby, and as we approached, the vultures took to wing and soared around us. The pride master raised his head as we hummed by, and I steered out and around to give them some space.

"There's your lion, John."

"Nah, not today. We've got a safari to catch."

The rest of the pride, about fifteen in all, raised their heads as we passed within a hundred yards. I had to wonder what they were thinking as our little jalopy bounced across the plain humming its monotone tune. Our heads were bobbing to and fro, bouncing from the springs, as the car went along.

"He was a good one," Chuck said. "You should have gotten him."

"I'm just not in the mood right now."

"Are you okay?"

"I'll be fine," I answered. "Getting a little wind in my face and seeing some great game will fix me."

But I knew that wasn't the case. And even if I had shot that lion, it wouldn't have eradicated what awaited me at camp. I didn't know how I would deal with it: the whole camp making a fuss over Betty's lion. What a blow to my male ego, being outshined by my wife. Shooting that lion back there wouldn't have changed anything, and I knew it.

I knew how the natives were going to look at this; they had been looking for a princess all along. Now they would have a reason to celebrate. When they found out, it would be nauseating, and somehow I would just have to endure it. Nothing I could do right now would change the outcome one iota. I wanted to confide in Chuck, but I knew his words wouldn't be consoling. I didn't need to confirm my stupidity right now, and I didn't need to hear repeated the thoughts that were already in my head.

Chuck kept looking over at me, as if trying to gauge my thoughts. Did my attitude really show through that much?

"There's a great eland right there," Chuck said. "That's a trophy, probably as good as you are ever going to find in all of Africa."

"Sure, he's two hundred and fifty yards away and standing still right now. But if we stop and line up on him, he'll take off running just sure as heck. Or maybe we could run him down with the car. But I'm telling you, I just don't have the stomach for shooting something from the car."

"You'd run him down on horseback," Chuck said, "wouldn't you?"

"Sure, I would," I answered, "but there's something different about doing it with a machine. They've never seen one of these before, and it just doesn't seem very sporting. I couldn't put him in my trophy room with the other heads. I think it would cheapen the whole den. Every one of those trophies has a story that I am proud to tell, but if you put one in there that I know isn't legitimate, then it's just a stuffed head."

"I can see your point," Chuck said.

"My trophy room is a testament to my character and my ability as a hunter, but if you cheat just a little to make it look better, you cheapen it."

"You're right," Chuck said. "So what do you think about the rhino we got this morning?"

"I think he's got a great story. After all, he was going to kill us, wasn't he? If we didn't get him first, he was going to get us—and that's a story."

Now the giraffe were right in front of us, munching on the green treetops not two hundred yards straight away.

"Aren't those majestic creatures?" Chuck said.

"Wow, they look like a patchwork quilt."

"Or like a jigsaw puzzle with legs," Chuck said and laughed. "They must be related to the camel or the llama."

"That must be why I can't bring myself to shoot one," I said.

"Ostrich!" Chuck shouted, pointing across the flats at the long-legged bird standing by an acacia tree about two hundred and fifty yards straight away. "Let's get us an ostrich."

I shut down the Ford and pulled out my Springfield from the back of the car, then snuck around the front and took a rest on the fender. The giraffes perked up and headed off across the plains in their graceful, awe-inspiring gallop, their legs opening and closing like long stepladders as they raced across the grasslands.

"Too bad they don't know me better," I said with a chuckle. "They could have saved their breath."

The ostrich stepped cautiously, probably feeling safe at this distance.

"Where are you going to aim for?" Chuck whispered.

"I'm just going to try to center punch him from this distance. Obviously, I'm not going to take a head shot from here."

I lined up on him and took a breath and held it, then squeezed off the shot. I could feel it break clean when the bullet left the barrel, and the rifle kicked me in the shoulder.

The ostrich reacted immediately and took off running, then wobbled and fell over in the grass.

"You got him!" Chuck yelled. "That was a magnificent shot."

I was more than a little skeptical of Chuck and his motives. I felt as if he was trying much too hard to get me pumped up. I pulled the empty brass out of the chamber and set the Springfield back behind the seat. Chuck ran around to the front, and I jumped behind the steering wheel while he cranked it up again.

"Let's go have a look at that thing," he said as he jumped in the seat. "What a shot!"

I revved up the Ford and drove it on a beeline to look at the enormous dead bird, pulling the car up to where it lay in the grass.

"That is a beautiful bird," Chuck said. "Can you eat 'em?"

"Oh, yeah, you bet you can. They have red meat like a beef cow."

"How much do you figure it weighs, John?"

"Two hundred, maybe two-fifty," I said. "It's a big male. Let's load it in the Ford, and we'll let our natives deal with the cleaning." I grabbed the legs, and Chuck grabbed the neck, and we horsed it up onto the back of the Ford.

"I'll get that piece of rope, and we'll lash it down," Chuck said. He looped the legs and tied the rope off to the undercarriage, and then did the same with the head on the other side of the car. "That ought to hold," he said, tugging on the rope to make sure it was taut. "Are you getting hungry yet, John?"

"Famished. It's been far too long a morning." I revved up the Ford. "Let's find our safari."

I tried to orient myself, my stomach growling and churning. I had some dried meat packed away in the rear compartment. But I knew if I held out, Bamira would put out one of his spreads. I cranked up the Ford and headed in what I thought was the right direction, weaving in and out of the sparse acacia trees, always picking out the best pathway, and staying in the most open places.

"There's only one road in Africa," Chuck said.

"Yeah, it's anywhere you want to go," I answered.

~~~~~~~~~~

A good thirty minutes had passed before we finally caught up with our trailing porters. We passed them on our way to the front, where Willie had already begun making preparations for lunch. I looked for

Betty and Jason's horses, and when I didn't see them tied up, I knew we had beaten them.

"Betty killed a lion!" Chuck shouted as Lance approached.

Lance's eyes grew as big as saucers. "You are joking, aren't you?"

I couldn't believe the first thing out of Chuck's mouth was the big bomb.

"No joke," he answered. "She and the kid rode right in on him. She calmly got off her horse and plugged him right between the eyes. One shot at one hundred yards, offhand, and he went down dead."

"The girl has ice water in her veins," Lance said.

Esther joined us, a book under her arm. "What did she do?"

"She killed a lion," Lance said. "*Single-handedly*."

"Let's get somebody over here to take care of this ostrich," I said to Willie.

"Who killed the ostrich?" Lance asked.

"I did," I said. "It was two hundred yards."

"Not like killing a lion, is it?"

Nope, I thought, *not like killing a lion.*

While we waited for Bamira and his crew to lay out the food, the porters collapsed to the ground for a much-needed break. But after a brief conversation with Chuck, Willie was barking orders at the porters, and they were once again scurrying about. They seemed restless and were abuzz about something. But as I sipped my wine under the stretched shade tarp, I tried not to pay much attention to it. Instead, Lance, Chuck, Esther, and I made small talk and discussed the events of the morning.

"Should we be getting concerned that Betty and the kid haven't shown up by now?" I asked, checking my watch.

"I'm not that worried," Lance said. "They are with Janga."

Just then, Buster took off like a shot, and I looked toward the end of the clearing to see Betty leading the way, riding high on Luke, with Jason right behind her, flanked by Janga on foot.

I couldn't believe my eyes when the sea of black men rose to their feet and began jumping and fighting to catch a glimpse of Betty.

"*Malkia aliuwa simba!*" they chanted in unison. "*Malkia aliuwa simba!*"

"Oh, brother," I said, shaking my head. "It's started."

"What are they saying?" Chuck asked.

"You don't know, Chuck? For heaven's sake! *Malkia* means queen, *aliuwa* means to kill, and you know what a *simba* is!"

"Queen killed a lion, eh?"

"That's right," I said. "They've promoted her from mistress to queen." I had known this would happen. None of them should have even heard the news yet. "I wonder how they heard about it."

I looked at Chuck, and he gave me a sheepish grin. Then I remembered him talking with Willie.

"Wow, that's impressive," Lance said.

Betty rode into camp, passing through the horde of worshippers, who, after parting to make room for her, pressed in at her, each man reaching up to touch her leg as if he might gain some power from it.

"Now that's nauseating," I replied.

Lance raised an eyebrow and gazed at me with a critical eye.

I wanted to say something to defend myself, but I knew I had an indefensible position. I wanted to blame her for killing my lion, but knew full well my own stupidity had created this whole affair.

"Hail to the queen!" I said as she pulled to a stop next to us.

She eyed me suspiciously and smirked. "Did you put them up to this?"

"Hardly," I said. "I suspected it, but I certainly didn't orchestrate it. And to be quite honest with you, I didn't even know they knew about it already."

"Hoo! Ha ! Hoo-hoo! Ha-hoo!" the natives chanted in a deep tone that echoed like the sound of drums. "*Malkia aliuwa simba*! *Malkia aliuwa simba*!"

"Can you help get me down off this horse?" Betty asked over the low roar of the chanting natives.

"You can't get down off a horse, silly," I said.

"What?" she asked.

"You can only get down off a goose or a duck," I answered.

Lance broke out in a belly laugh, but Betty just squinted at me and wrinkled her brow.

"Okay, so my timing isn't perfect. I'm still working on my vaudeville act. Here, let's get you off that horse so your subjects can worship you." I tried to wade in to take her hand, but the men were crowding me out. "Willie!" I shouted. "Can you get control of these men?"

Willie and Lance shouted at them, rattling off Swahili, and the crowd of men fell silent, backing away and then sitting down, their eyes still glued on Betty.

"Wow, I'm impressed," I said, struck by the eerie silence.

I grabbed hold of Luke's reins as Betty's feet touched the ground, and then I handed her horse off to the horse boy. Jason, who had already ridden around the crowd and given his horse off to the attendant, snatched his rifle from the scabbard.

"This is incredible," Chuck said. "There is no other word for it."

"I don't think they've ever heard of a woman killing a lion before," Lance said.

"Could be," Chuck said.

"It's a rite of passage for men," I said. "To kill a lion is a huge accomplishment, and plenty of them have never done it. It's an act set aside to establish greatness among the tribal men, but they have probably never seen or heard of it done by a woman."

"It's what catapults tribal leaders and kings," Lance said, "and as far as they are concerned, she has become the queen."

"She's always been a queen as far as I'm concerned," Jason said with a laugh as he joined us away from the crowds of sitting men.

"You better say that," Betty said, grinning widely and giving Jason a playful shove in his shoulder.

"Let's have lunch," Lance said and led us to the shade tarp the men had set up for us.

As we walked toward camp, suddenly I saw Betty in a different light. Maybe she *was* a queen. All I knew for sure was that I loved her, and even though she had shown me up something fierce, she still belonged to me, and I belonged to her. There were lots of things you had to get over in life; I decided right then and there to get over this one, too.

Chapter 23

THE VEIL

M y watch said three o'clock in the afternoon when we finally
settled in for lunch. It was pushing four when we finished.

"Shall we forge ahead?" Lance asked.

"I'd like to hold up until that oxcart arrives with my rhino,"
Chuck said.

"That oxcart will catch us for dinner or maybe later," Lance said.
"They'll be along, but we're burning daylight here. We've already
been held up several hours. I say we chug on. I can smell elephants."

"You can?" Jason said.

"Not now," Lance said. "But when we get there, you'll see
what I mean."

"I say we go," Esther said. "We're all fresh, our tummies are full,
and I for one am ready to go."

"I guess I'm just anxious to get a second look at my rhino," Chuck
said. "But I can wait."

I knew the only thing Chuck wanted to do was put his two rhino
horns together and see which one was bigger. He wanted to put them
on display so everyone could "ooh" and "ah" over them and tell
Chuck what a great white hunter he had become.

"Are you going to ride with me, John?" Betty asked.

"I think my saddle is in the oxcart."

"Nope, not that one," Lance said. "It's right over there on the
other cart."

"All the horses are already loaded up with gear," I said.

"Yes, Bwana," Willie said, "but Kumba, he been leading your horse by string since we begin."

"Well, if he's loaded down, then leave him loaded."

"No, Bwana, I have extra men to carry the load."

"I'll ride with Chuck," Jason said. "You can take Missy. She's gentle and alert, and you'll love her."

I hesitated to answer as I thought about the soft springy seat in the Ford and how much I had actually become attached to running that machine. Even though it was noisy, even though I had complained and actually at one point had wanted to get rid of her, now I had second thoughts rattling around in my head. After having seen how those animals responded to the car today, I had a new respect for her. But was it really sporting to shoot from the car?

Betty gave me a piercing look, and I remembered the deal we'd made.

"Chuck, you take the Ford," I said. "But remember, take it easy on second gear, or you'll grind it."

"I know," he answered. "I have watched you a hundred times."

"Sure, you did," I said, "but doing it is a lot different than watching it. I've babied that thing all the way from Nairobi, and I intend to get it back in one piece."

"I know how to drive, sonny. I was driving years before you were, and don't forget I had one of the first cars in Chicago."

"All right," I conceded, "you're right." I was still convinced that I was the better driver.

The African sun was poised to plunge over the edge of the world just hours from now as everyone got ready to depart. The winds were calm, but the tensions among us seemed high. I could feel the ropes binding us together beginning to chafe.

With my foot firmly planted in the stirrup, I swung my leg over the back of Jason's mare and settled into the saddle. It had been awhile since I had ridden, that was for sure, but I felt a sudden wholeness being back in the saddle. Betty beamed like a daffodil in full bloom on an early spring morning. I knew her vision for this safari had always included the two of us riding horseback together on a trail at sunset. Unlike me, of course, for whom the mere thought of a safari conjured up the sound of gunfire and the smell of cordite in my nostrils. It was the adventure of hunting animals that could kill you, of seeing them hit the ground after a well-placed first shot, of feeling the awesome power of victory over another.

Willie blew his whistle, and his men hoisted their sixty-pound loads onto their shoulders and formed a line that stretched several hundred yards. The remaining oxcart took the lead, followed by the camels and the pack string of horses. I tried to pick my horse out of the line, but I couldn't remember what it looked like.

"Let's ride ahead, John," Lance said.

He nudged his mare in the ribs and trotted past the crowd of men and beasts. Esther followed close behind him.

I tugged on my rifle butt to make sure it was snugly—but not too tightly—placed in Jason's scabbard. Then I reached back to feel my forty-four to make sure I had the snap on the holster firmly seated.

Betty smiled and then made a clicking sound with her mouth, and Luke responded without even a kick in the ribs. The girl had been born to ride a horse.

Jason and Buster were still milling around when Chuck called out, "Jason, give me a hand starting this Ford!"

"You better move my horse out before we try to start that thing," Jason said. "She won't like it much, either."

"I'm going," I said, turning her and then nudging her ribs for a little encouragement.

Now I remembered why I liked riding in the car. I had taken some nasty spills from this perch over the years. The problem with these darn things was that you had to sit up so high, and when you went down, you had so darn far to go before you hit the ground. And they were unpredictable as hell. It wasn't like walking, where all you had to do was watch where you were going. But you tended to put a measure of trust in the animal, hoping that they would watch where they were going. They didn't put the same value on your life that you did. Of course, they didn't want to fall, but I often wondered if they secretly thought about different ways of tossing you to make their life easier.

As Missy trotted up behind Luke to form a front line for the safari, with Lance and Esther leading the way, I felt a strange uneasiness come over me, sort of like a premonition that something terrible was about to happen. I tried to shake it off, and it gradually began to fade away. But I reached down and unsnapped my hog leg, anyway. I could hear the hum of the Ford in the background and turned to see it coming our way about two hundred yards back.

Then, without warning, it happened. I glimpsed a flash of a huge bronze form and then heard a roar as a massive lion struck me like a bolt of lightening. He grabbed me with an open mouth, and I turned away to protect my face. I had always imagined I would have time to react to a lion attack, but I froze in terror; nowhere to go, unable to make a sound.

My body jolted as I hit the ground, and he buried his teeth deep into the flesh of my left shoulder. I expected my life to flash before me, because I knew this beast would kill me first and then eat me. The account of Dr. Livingstone's journals raced through my mind, and I went limp as the lion began dragging my body along the ground. When attacked by a lion, Dr. Livingstone had simply gone limp, and apparently when the lion tasted human flesh, he lost interest.

The big cat began to shake me like a housecat would a mouse. Livingstone had said that this shaking created an almost hypnotic state as the body acids and chemicals mixed with the blood. The euphoric condition had to be God's way of allowing animals to be eaten alive with no fear of death or pain from the trauma. I knew I was done for, and I resigned myself to the few seconds remaining until darkness came over me.

It suddenly came to me in a fog: *What about God?* I had been lulled back to semiconsciousness by the screams from Betty pleading at Lance to shoot. Her voice seemed to be coming from the clouds, like the voice of an angel.

Then I said it, not through my mouth, but in my spirit. *Lord God, you know I'm a sinner. You know that I have lived my life denying you. God, if you are there, forgive me for everything I have ever done, and take my life to be with you in eternity. I admit it: you are my God. I give you my life, such as it is. To your glory, I give you my life. Lord, I am yours to do with as you wish.*

I dangled there, motionless in the mouth of the lion, and I could feel the ground moving again beneath me as my rump bumped along the grass and my arm dragged in the dirt. I had no pain, though I could feel the pressure on my shoulder from his bite. I could only wait now for the cat's next move. He would tear open my flesh to get at my heart and liver, the soft inner parts that were his delicacy. I had seen lions do it countless times to helpless antelope on the grasslands. Then a vision of my hog leg flashed in my mind. I tried to gather my wits to remember my right from my left. My right hand hung free, so with all the strength I could muster and with a renewed hope, I reached down to my belt. But my heart sank when I found the holster empty.

I could hear what sounded like a barking dog, and then a peace came over me as I heard the voice of God in a still, small whisper, almost as if the thought came from my own mind. *You are mine, and I have a plan for you. You must tell them about me. You will be a witness to my glory, and I will use you for the time I have decided to allow you to remain in this world.*

The growling became more intense, and the lion became agitated. He let out a roar from his open mouth, and I fell to the ground, hitting with a thud that snapped me back from my semiconscious state.

I opened my eyes to see Buster facing off the big male lion. He nipped at the lion's haunches, and the cat twisted to protect his flank. Then Buster let loose a deep guttural growl that would have impressed any German shepherd. The cat lunged forward and took a swipe at the pest, but Buster skillfully avoided his razor-sharp paw.

I tried to move, but my body was limp and my limbs seemed like they weighed a ton. I felt like someone trying to run in a dream. The cat stepped back to protect his fallen prey, which was me, and then Buster went on the attack again, leaping on the back of the lion. Buster grabbed its ear in his teeth and hung there on the side of his face, shaking his head and trying to rip it off.

Then, with me helpless to do anything, the whole incident came to a close in the snap of a finger. I watched as the lion swatted the little dog like a fly on a window and Buster went sprawling in the dirt. Then a single rifle shot rang out, and the big cat sprawled out, stone-cold dead.

I tried to keep my wits about me, but I must have passed out, because I could see a spirit from the heavens dressed in a long white robe. He drew toward me, and I looked into his piercing dark eyes. His pupils opened up, and I felt like I could be swallowed up by them.

He held out his hand, and there I saw a heavy gold ring that he took and placed on my finger.

"What's this for?" I asked.

The spirit angel just smiled, and then turned to leave.

I tried to hold on to his robe.

Do you really want to go where I am going? he asked. *I am allowing you to stay here where you are.*

I wanted to go with him. I desperately tried to hold on to him. But I finally let go, and he disappeared. And suddenly I felt as if I was drowning. I tried to swim, but my arms and my legs were like lead. I knew if I didn't kick, I would sink like a rock. I couldn't imagine how I had gotten stranded out in the middle of a lake.

I opened my eyes and saw everyone crowded around me as Lance emptied the last drops from his canteen over my face.

"Am I alive?" I asked, trying to focus my eyes on them.

I couldn't believe I had survived. Something seemed different, but I couldn't put my finger on it. Maybe I would feel like the same old person once I caught my breath and shook out the cobwebs a little bit. I looked at my hand, and there I saw this incredible gold ring on my finger sparkling in the sunlight.

"Your life was spared by that courageous dog," Chuck said.

"Where's Buster?" I asked as Betty helped me to sit. I gingerly touched my shoulder with my right hand. My shirt was soaked with blood. I reached under my shirt and put my finger into a huge, gaping hole left by a lion tooth.

"Can you move your arm?" she asked.

I squeezed my left hand and lifted my forearm just to be sure.

Jason stood behind Chuck, and I saw huge tears running down the boy's cheeks.

"I'll be okay, son," I said, thinking his tears were for me.

But then he stepped forward, and Chuck moved aside. Then I understood the source of his sorrow. Buster lay lifeless in his arms, his tongue dangling from his mouth, his open eyelids exposing the face of death.

"We saw the attack, and Chuck got here as quick as we could. But when we stopped, Buster bolted like a shot from a cannon. I tried to stop him, but it was no use. He had a mind to save you, and I knew he was no match for that cat."

"And neither was I. I tried to get to my forty-four, but I think it must be lying over there in the dirt."

"I'm sad, sir. But if I have to trade a life for a life, I'll take yours."

At that very moment, I finally got it. I realized what God had done in giving us His only Son to die in our place. Jesus Christ had traded His human life here on earth for our eternal life with Him. And now I had traded my own, but it wasn't so much a trade that I had made. It wasn't anything I had done, but a free gift God had given me. He had sent a lion so that all men might come to know Him.

"I'm sorry you had to trade, but I'm grateful for Buster's sacrifice."

"He was a courageous little dog," Chuck said.

"They say courage is not the absence of fear," Esther said, "but something you have to take that comes from outside of yourself."

"Esther, look at my ring," I said, gazing down at my empty finger. I looked in the dirt and felt around in the dust, thinking I had lost it like the forty-four falling from my unsnapped holster. "It must have slipped off."

"What?" Betty asked.

"He put a ring on my finger."

"Who?" Chuck asked.

"The angel!" I said in a panic.

"Come on, John," Lance said. "Let's get you out of this hot sun."

"He's delirious," Chuck said.

"I think he is going into shock," Betty whispered, perhaps thinking I might not hear her.

As I looked through a sort of fog, Lance and Willie hoisted me under their arms and carried me to a shade tree. Over my shoulder, I saw the big cat sprawled out, and I could see blood around his mouth that I knew belonged to me. They set me down with my back against a tree, and I could feel my shoulder separating under the pressure.

"That lion no angel, Bwana," Willie said. "My people know that is an evil spirit. When he crave human flesh, he take on the body of *simba* for just a while until it satisfied."

"Let me have a look at that shoulder," Esther said as she unbuttoned my shirt and peeled back the blood-soaked cotton fabric. She gritted her teeth, and Betty looked away.

"How bad is it?" I asked.

"Not bad," Esther said. "We just need to get you over the threat of infection. The puncture wounds from those fangs look like they missed the shoulder joint."

"And he didn't bury his claws into him anywhere that I can see," Lance said.

"That's good, because those scratch marks are the worst thing for infection," Esther said. "A big cat uses his claws for killing, and they are filled will germs."

"Bring me a bottle of vodka!" Lance shouted across to Willie, who was talking with some of his men.

"Are we going to celebrate my survival?" I asked.

"No, we're going to douse these wounds with a little alcohol to ward off infection."

"Esther, I have to tell you something," I said.

"Just rest. You can tell me later."

"No, I have to tell you now. I can tell the world later. Betty," I said, reaching out to take her hand, "I died out there."

"Not hardly," she said.

"No, that cat killed me just sure as anything, and I'm here to tell you. I'm different."

"What's he talking about?" Lance asked.

"I know what he's talking about," Esther said.

Lance poured the vodka onto my shoulder, and a burning pain shot through me. I must have passed out, because it felt like euphoria all over again, like being shaken by a lion. An inner peace came over me that I had never experienced before. It was like the most powerful drug I could imagine, replacing my pain with unmitigated tranquility.

~~~~~~~~~

I awoke in my tent lying on my cot. Betty sat in a camp chair beside me reading a book.

"Good morning," I said, bringing a bright smile to her face.

"Oh, darling, you had me worried. You were out like a candle all evening, and now the sun is setting."

"What are we doing here?" As I started to move, the pain shot through my shoulder. "Did I get run over by a team of horses or something?" I tried to move my neck, but it was as stiff as a board. "What happened to me?"

"You don't remember the lion?"

"Oh, the lion ... yeah," I said as it all came flooding back: the lion attack, the shaking, Buster, the rifle shot, and the spirit. Oh, and the prayer.

"The lion—I remember the lion—and Buster, too. Betty, something has happened to me."

"I know. You were nearly eaten by a lion."

"No, you don't understand. I was killed by that lion, but I was spared by God."

"Yes, you were spared by God," she said, patting my hand. "You didn't die."

"You don't get it. I died just as sure as you're sitting here. John Rivers is a dead man. The imposter who posed as John Rivers is gone, and now all you see is the real man."

Betty put her hand on my forehead.

"I know you think I'm talking nonsense, but hear me out."

Esther poked her head in the tent. "Is he awake? Did I hear you talking?"

"Esther, you have to baptize me right now!" I demanded.

"John, are you all right?" she asked.

"No, I'm not all right. I'm much better than that. I died yesterday afternoon, and now I'm still here and Christ is in me."

"Halleluiah!" Esther shouted. "We have witnessed a miracle of God in our presence. I've got to tell you that while you were being attacked, I prayed for you. I didn't understand what God was going to do, but I knew He would create a miracle. Lance!" she shouted outside the tent. "Come quick!" Then she turned and raised her hands, saying, "Praise God Almighty, for he has done it."

"What is it?" Lance asked as he cautiously pulled the tent flap back. "Don't tell me he's gone!"

"Oh, he's gone, all right," Esther said. "But for the first time in his life, I think he's alive!"

"Help me up," I said.

"Are you sure?" Betty asked.

"Yes, get me out of this bed. How far is that river we passed yesterday?"

"Probably two miles from here," Lance said.

"Perfect," I said, touching my feet to the canvas floor of the tent and sitting on the edge of my cot. I moved my neck to work the kinks out. "Man, I'm sore. That lion shook the soup out of me."

"How's your shoulder?" Esther asked.

I lifted my arm. At least it worked, even though the pain was tremendous.

"You're not thinking of going fishing, are you?" Lance asked with a laugh. "That cat really did get you, didn't he?"

"No. Esther is going to baptize me in the river."

"Now I know you bumped your head," Chuck said, peering inside the tent.

"Nope, I have awoken. It's like a veil has been lifted from my eyes. Now I can see. Like ear wax melting. Now I can hear."

"Oh, sure," Chuck said, raising his eyebrows.

"No, for the first time in my life, I know there is a God."

"How do you know that?" Chuck asked.

"Because I'm here. Because I asked Him to save me, and He did. And because He spoke to me."

"He didn't save you," Chuck countered. "That little dog saved you."

"I know what you are doing, Chuck. Remember, I was the master of that line of reasoning. I can't explain it. I don't know how it happened, or why. But don't you see that God used the dog?"

"No," Chuck said. "I see a man who is delirious, who was nearly killed by a lion, who has had a long day and is exhausted."

"Hear him out, Chuck," Esther said.

"We started out early this morning," Chuck growled. "We nearly got run over by a rhino, almost wrecked the car. Then he goes traipsing off in a huff to catch the safari. Heck, he almost got killed by a lion then, if lady luck hadn't been with him. But now he's just at the end of his rope. Why don't you get some rest? You'll be back to your old self tomorrow."

"I'm back to normal. This is where I was always supposed to be my whole life."

"Where's that?" Chuck asked. "Here in the view of Mount Kenya?"

"No, listen. My whole life I have been looking in a mirror, and the only thing I could see was me. Now that I can see, I know the glass was never a mirror at all, but a window to the universe. Life has never been about me. All along it was always about God and His purpose for my life. I just couldn't see."

"Preach it, brother," Chuck said and shook his head. "You need to get some rest, my friend." He patted me on the leg and then abruptly left the tent.

"He doesn't believe me."

"He's not the only one who isn't going to believe you," Esther said. "The world is full of nonbelievers just like you were a few hours ago. Now you'll spend the rest of your life telling them about Jesus. Some will respond, but most of them will remain unconvinced, just like you were for forty-six years."

"How can we convince them?"

"We can't," she said. "Not by clever arguments, not by the most convincing illustrations, and not by holding them down and force-feeding them the information. Nothing we can do will save them, because it's not for us to decide. God is in control, and that's the way he wants it."

"But I think they'll believe me if I tell them."

"Yeah, they will. But remember, it's not our work," Esther explained. "What would happen if the hammer started building by itself? The builder must first decide which boards are cut and which are nailed. There is a master plan to all this. Each board has a purpose, and one braces another until the structure is complete. You can't start building the roof before you finish the foundation."

"Then what is our place?" I asked.

"Our job is to remain ready when he needs us, and to be the best and sharpest tool in the box. If you needed a saw, wouldn't you want the best saw you had? Our part is to stay sharp by reading His word and knowing the Scriptures. Then God can use us. The more He is able to use us, the more He will use us. But we must first be willing to allow God to sharpen us, and sharpening is painful."

"Let's go down to the river," I demanded. "Right now!"

"It'll be dark shortly," Betty said. "Let's wait until morning."

"How's Jason?" I asked.

"He's pretty broken up," Betty said. "You know how he felt about that dog."

As I listened to her speak, the room began to spin and I felt lightheaded.

"Why don't you just lie back and get some rest," Esther said. "You'll feel much better with a good night's sleep."

I couldn't believe my shoulder pain, and I could only imagine how it would feel in the morning. Those big teeth had pierced my shoulder, and I was lucky they hadn't done more damage than they had. But I knew I wasn't out of the woods yet. Those nasty old boys were full of bugs that could attack you far more than their fangs or their claws. I had seen it all before, and I knew what fate awaited me. I had seen men swell up from infection, and I had seen limbs literally turn black and rot off. I had watched victims die even after enduring multiple amputations to stop the infection. I knew that only by the grace of God would I survive the week, and that only time would tell.

I kissed Betty, and the pain shot through my whole body as she laid me back on my bedroll.

"I'll leave you with a prayer if you like," Esther said.

"That would be good," I answered. "I can use all the help I can get right now."

Lance and Esther held hands, and Betty closed her eyes and bowed her head. I was amazed how Esther could talk to God. Her words flowed like a river as the Spirit filled her.

"Dear Lord," she began, "our gracious and heavenly God, we praise you for your grace and for your love. We thank you for rebuking us when we are wrong and instructing us along our pathway. Lord, we see clearly how you work in our lives and use every means to help us to proceed, including the things you have created and brought to this earth. Father, we know that you use every means possible to reach us, including even the lion, the king of beasts.

"Father, we thank you that this lion, even from his conception in his mother's womb, was created for a divine purpose and a divine appointment. We know that he was just a tool, as we are all tools in your hand. We thank you, Lord, for this great miracle of holy redemption, and for your great gift of faith and salvation, through your Son, Jesus Christ, the Lion of Judah. We thank you, Father, that there is no such thing as luck, and that the only true luck comes from following you.

"Lord God, now in our most humble terms, we ask another miracle that only you can perform. Lord, I know that you hear me. I know that you always hear me. But that those of us who are in this tent here today might come to know you more, and that they might truly see your hand at work here today, we stand as one in asking for your grace to work in John's life once more.

"Lord, we ask that through your mercy you would create a complete healing for John's shoulder, and that you would protect him from infection and deliver him from what might certainly be his earthly departure. Lord God, we trust in your infinite wisdom, and we are not asking that you go outside the realm of your deliberate will. Lord, do so only if it pleases you. And one more thing. We pray that you will bring peace to our dear Jason in the loss of his beloved pet. Father, we ask all this in the name of your precious and holy Son, Jesus Christ, our Lord ... Amen."

"Good night, sweetheart," Betty said. "I'll be right here next to you if you need me."

I didn't feel like I would die, even though over the next week or so I knew the infection could get me. But if it did, I thought, then so be it. Not that I wouldn't put up a fight and try to stay alive, but now my whole point of view had changed. For the first time in my life, I knew where I was going and why. As I thought about her prayer, I had to laugh to myself about the concept of luck. The girl had great wisdom, indeed.

My neck and shoulder were stiff as a board, and I wondered how I would be able to continue on with the safari. I figured that tomorrow we would begin making preparations for our long journey back to Nairobi, and that Lance's dream of seeing true elephant country would come to a close. Even riding in the Ford, with the bouncing and bumping, would be impossible for me. And riding a horse would be out of the question altogether. There were probably no less than a hundred billion *what ifs* in life, but if a person continually asked, *what if,* then life was worrisome and terrifying, a downward spiral that would eventually screw you into the ground.

All this didn't seem to matter anymore, because now I knew that God existed, He was watching over me, and He had always been watching over me. I didn't understand how that worked or why it worked, but now, for the first time in my life, I knew it to be true.

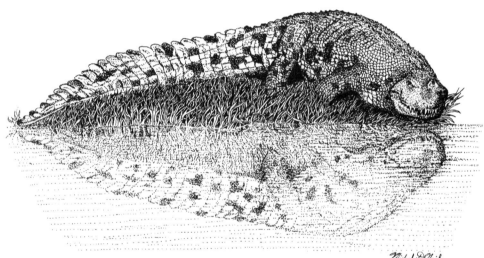

Chapter 24

THE FISHERMAN

The sun had already come up when I awoke, and the glow from the tent's white canvas made me squint. I rolled over and saw Betty's empty bed, which told me it was late morning. I stood up and grabbed my pants before I realized that I could move. I felt my shoulder and found the blood-stained dressings still covering my wound. Then I remembered Esther's prayer.

The thought crossed my mind that maybe God had authored another miracle. I stretched my neck, flexed my shoulder, and lifted my arm. It seemed incredible to me: not perfect by any means, but not what I had expected at all for the morning after. I got dressed and emerged from my tent, breathing in the fresh morning air.

Chuck and the ladies were sitting around the campfire sipping coffee when Betty caught sight of me. "John, what are you doing?" she yelled, leaping to her feet and rushing to my side.

"You need to stay down," Esther said, following close behind.

"It's a miracle, "I said. "I can't explain it, but I feel fine."

"You need to be in bed," Betty insisted.

"No, look," I said as I rotated my shoulder and flexed my neck. "I can lift my arm."

"Isn't it painful?" Esther asked.

"I can feel it, but it's not what I expected."

"I didn't think you would be able to get out of bed," Betty said.

"Oh, ye of little faith," I said with a smirk. "I think I'll be able to shoot in a few days."

"I don't know if I would go that far," Betty said. "Let's wait and see how you do."

"Are we going to take care of that deed this morning?" I asked.

"What is that?" Betty asked, her face turning pink.

"My baptism," I said, wondering what she might be thinking. "You haven't forgotten, have you?"

"I haven't forgotten," Esther said. "I just wasn't sure what shape you would be in this morning."

"Didn't you pray for me last night?"

"Yes," she answered. "But sometimes God doesn't always answer prayers the way you think He should. You have to be careful how you pray."

"Careful?" I asked.

"That's right. Ask for patience, and sometimes He will make you wait. Ask for humility, and He will give you humiliation. Ask for strength, and He will test you until He has strengthened you."

"That doesn't seem fair," I said. "Then what good is it to pray?"

Esther laughed. "Do I really need to respond to that?"

"Okay," I said, "but if God won't answer your prayers the way you want—"

"I see where you are going with this," she said, interrupting me. "But here is the deal. God isn't some genie in a bottle that responds to your every want every time you call on Him. He doesn't exist to serve you. He created us to serve *Him*. This life isn't about you; it's about God. Our prayers never change the unchangeable God, but they are designed to always change us. God doesn't care as much about our comfort here as he does about our commitment: our commitment to our faith, our commitment to love others, and our commitment to Him and the Gospel."

"I have a lot to learn," I said, "don't I?"

"Are you hungry?" Betty asked.

"Ravenous. I haven't eaten since lunch yesterday."

~~~~~~~~~

After a quick breakfast, Lance gassed up the Ford and the four of us took off for a drive to the river.

"Are you sure you know how to do this?" I asked.

"I've done them before," Esther said. "But no, in answer to your question, I am no expert. But believe me, God will be with us, and we will be blessed."

I couldn't help but stay alert for animals along the way as the Ford bounced and bumped along the grasslands. It was just what a hunter did all the time. As Lance steered around the sparse trees and patches of scrub brush, I looked down and saw Betty's rifle sitting comfortably between us. I thought about putting it to my shoulder and felt thankful that my right shoulder had not taken the brunt of the lion's attack. Thinking about killing again, I began to wonder about the hunt. *What about God, who created all these beautiful things here? Would He really approve of us killing them?*

Lance corrected his route as soon as the water appeared through the trees, and we sped on toward the riverbank. Then he picked a route to get us over the hill and skillfully brought the Ford to a flat sandy beach.

"It's beautiful," Betty said, "and the water is crystal clear."

"We'll send the water boys down later to fill the casks," Lance said.

"But for now, this is a prefect place for a soul washing," Esther said. She bounced out of the car and landed in the soft red sand.

"Wait just a minute," I said, considering what we had come to do. "Listen, I know I am changed, but I don't want to be a religious fanatic."

"You will only become what God decides to make you," Esther said. "In the words of John the Baptist, 'A man can receive only what is given to him from heaven, and if God should decide that you will become more, then so be it, and be it all to His glory.' Amen?"

"Amen," I replied, stepping out of the Ford.

"What about the crocs?" Betty asked.

"We'll be in and out before they know it," Esther said with a laugh.

"Is there a script to follow?" I asked.

"No, not really," she answered.

"What denomination am I, and how do I know this thing will take?"

"You are a Christian," she said.

"What denomination are you, Esther?"

"I am nondenominational. I'm not a member of one of the cults, nor am I a member of a religion that doesn't believe in the Holy Triune God."

"Triune God," I said. "What's that?"

"Maybe we should hold off on that conversation until another time."

"I just want to know what I am getting myself into."

She laughed. "Believe me, you are far past that. Okay, Triune God, or Holy Trinity, means one God in three persons."

"But that just complicates God to make Him one in three," Betty said.

"I didn't make Him one in three," Esther said. "He did. And He did it from eternity past. This is our God who is a God of fellowship. That is why He created mankind in the first place: to have fellowship. Imagine spending time in eternity alone. That is why God has always existed in three persons who are in agreement."

"That's still confusing," Betty said.

"Do you think we have a God who isn't complicated?" Esther asked. "It's meant to be confusing so that man can't get his brain around it. It's a concept of faith and an aspect of God that man is not able to understand on his own. You see this termite?" she said, reaching down and catching it in her fingers. "Now I want you to explain to him how your Ford runs. I want you to tell him the fine points of the internal combustion engine." She held the little bugger up toward her face, and I could see him struggling to get free.

"I'm not sure I understand it myself," I said. "I mean, I understand how it works with the fuel, the air, and the combustion and such, but I'm not really mechanically inclined. I've never taken one apart to see how it's all put together."

"But you know enough to know that if there is fuel in the tank and you turn the crank, it will purr like a kitten, right? And you believe that if you turn the crank, it should start?"

"That's about it," I said.

"Well then, even if we had the guy here who built it, do you think he could explain to this termite how it runs?"

"Now you're being silly," I said.

"Now you understand what Jesus was up against." Esther bent down and gently put the bug back in the sand, and it scurried off.

"So you're telling me that Christ was God," I said, "and that He knew everything."

"That's why He taught in parables, so that we could understand Him. He never gave the answer, but He always asked a question. And He let his listeners come up with the answer on their own."

"I'm a teacher, and I understand that," I said. "An answer given is just an answer, but an answer found is a treasure, and you never forget it."

"Jesus Christ *is* God, not *was* God," she continued. "He is a living God who came down in the flesh to free us from our sins. You see, prior to that, all man had was the Law of Moses, and the law only convicted us of our sin. The only way people had to ask for forgiveness was through the blood of animals. But God came down to make a sacrifice once and for all: to give us the gift of His cleansing blood, to wash us clean, and to allow us a way to heaven, that by our faith in Him we would receive through His grace this gift of eternal life."

"I still want to talk about these three Gods," Betty said.

"And that is the problem. There is one God the same way that water is just one thing. Heck, you're a scientist, John. You'll understand this one. Water is only water, but it exists in three forms, right?"

"Liquid, ice, and vapor."

"But it never changes; it's always water. And it's in every living thing. It's water that gives life. It's water that cleans us. It's Christ, the living water, that gives us eternal life. And it is the Holy Spirit that changes us and makes us clean from the inside out. Are you ready?"

"Don't you need to be a priest or something like that?" I asked.

"No, all Christians can baptize," she responded. "It's an authority given to them by God."

"Then I guess I already gave my life away. I might as well clean the part I have left."

I stepped toward the river, watching upstream and then down, and I spotted a crocodile sitting on the opposite shore, about a hundred yards away. "Get me the rifle!"

"Now what are you going to do with that?" Esther asked.

"I'm going to kill that croc down there before I get in the water."

Esther put her hand over her brow and squinted to see across the river. "Oh, come on. That thing isn't going to get us. Besides, now you're just killing to be killing."

"I suppose," I said, "but maybe I'm just a little overcautious right now."

"Yeah, but what would you do with it if you killed it outright, anyway?" she asked. "You couldn't get across the river to fetch it, and if you wounded it, it would just float downstream till it died. You have a lot to learn about the way the world works. Now it's going to be all new. You have always seen it through eyes of a man who rejected God and His principles. But now everything will change. You can no longer see things the way you did before, and you can no longer live the way you used to live. You always saw life as random circumstances that just happened by chance, but now you will see God's sovereignty and His hand in everything."

"It's a different perspective, that's for sure," I said as Esther reached out and took my hand.

"It's good and right that we are here now," Esther said. "God is with us and His blessings are on you, and with God's protection there is no way that croc will get us. Hey, take your shoes off," she said, bending over, untying the laces on her boots, and kicking them off.

I did the same.

"Everybody, take your shoes off," she said. "This is hallowed ground, because the Lord is here."

I followed Esther as she began wading out into the river. A chill came over me when my feet hit the water, but it felt good after all these weeks of sponge baths. I turned back and saw Betty standing at the water's edge while we continued to work our way out until we were waist deep.

"Lord God," Esther began, "we praise you, Father, for making a miracle here on the plains of Africa. We praise you, Lord, for the salvation of my friend John, who you have been watching over since the day of his birth. We praise you for making a way for all of us, for giving us power over Satan and freeing us all from eternal damnation. We thank you, Lord, for bringing us here together on this safari so that we are able to see clearly the true meaning of life and to understand our part in it. Now, Lord, help us to feel your presence. Help us to see the work of your hands, the power of your grace, and the wisdom of your spirit."

She opened her eyes and turned to me. "Are you ready?"

I realized she was talking to me and nodded eagerly.

"Father, since the dawn of time, your spirit has hovered over the water and your breath has made it a wellspring of holiness. Through the Flood you cleansed the world from sin, and through your spirit you made a new beginning of righteousness. Through the water of the Red Sea, you led Israel out of slavery, setting them free by an image of baptism. And in the waters of the Jordan River, your Son was baptized by his relative, John, because it was fitting that He do so."

As she spoke, I was amazed at her knowledge of the Bible—all this from a black woman who not fifty years ago would have been forbidden from even learning to read. Even today, in many parts of America, blacks were still repressed and treated like second-class citizens. And I had to admit that, even now, I couldn't believe how close we had grown since our introduction, when I had harbored all the same old prejudices so prevalent in our society.

It's all Darwin's hogwash! Even now I could see what evolution was doing to the world by claiming that man had evolved from monkeys, and by teaching us that we were no different than any of the other animals. There was no place for God in science, because there was only the natural world. Thus, man was nothing special, just another monkey—and not created in the image of God.

How cruel Satan was in trying to separate us from the truth of Jesus Christ! As I looked into Esther's big brown eyes, for the first time I could feel the love she had for me as a brother, and I could finally understand why my best friend had chosen to marry this magnificent woman. She was just as beautiful on the inside as she was on the outside.

"Father," she continued, "by the power of your Holy Spirit, unleash the wellspring and make this water holy by your name, the name of Jesus Christ that is above all others, and who will reign in the heavens forever."

Esther cupped her hands and filled them with water and then held them over my head. "In the name of the Father," she said and let the water cascade over my head and face. "In the name of the Son," she said, filling her hands full again and dumping the second load over my face. "And in the name of the Holy Spirit," she said and grabbed my shoulders, smiling at me with those big brown eyes.

She then pushed me under the water and held me down for just a few seconds longer than I thought she would. What a wonderful feeling it was to gasp for my first breath of life after being cleansed by God, to emerge with a new life as a new creation in Christ Jesus.

"Wow, I don't believe this is happening to me!" I said.

I felt free, liberated from my fear of death, whether it came tomorrow at the hands of another lion or in fifty years from old age. I was in Christ now and an eternal citizen of heaven. They could kill me now, but I wouldn't die.

My wet clothes hung heavily on me as we waded back toward shore, where Betty stood in the sand, gazing into my eyes. I stepped quickly to the shore and threw my arms around her.

"Me, too!" she said, just like she always did when I told her that I loved her.

"Yes, I love you," I said.

"No, me, too!" she said.

I looked at Esther, and she smiled, obviously understanding something about the situation that I didn't.

"It's my turn now," Betty said, taking Esther's hand.

"Alleluia, let's go, girl!" Esther exclaimed as she took her hand.

I followed them out into the water, having completely forgotten about my wounded shoulder and the dressings under my shirt that were now soaking wet. I held onto Betty until she was waist deep. I checked downstream to see if my friend was still sunning himself just in time to see him slip off into the water.

"Here he comes," I said.

"Who?" Betty asked.

"Mr. Croc!"

Esther looked over her shoulder and then cupped water in her hands. "I baptize you in the name of the Father," she said, pouring the water over Betty's head. "And in the name of the Son." She hastily splashed the second handful on her face. "And in the name of the Holy Spirit."

Then both of us dunked her under. The croc was now midstream and swimming straight for us. Betty came up with a gasp, rubbing the water from her eyes and grabbing her wet hair. Her face shone like a sunrise.

"I'm free ... I'm saved!" she shouted.

"Come on," I said. "He's making his move."

I grabbed both girls and gave them a jerk toward shore. We did the high-step, kicking water while Betty and Esther giggled like a couple teen-agers. I looked back to see the crocodile not twenty yards away and moving in quickly. As our feet hit the shore, I looked back again to see that he had closed the distance to just twenty feet. He came skidding up onto the beach on his belly, his jaws wide open. We sprinted up the sand toward the Ford, and Lance, who was standing with his rifle up at the ready, let him have it.

I felt the blast in my face. I had never actually been downrange of a rifle report, but now I knew what it felt like to see the muzzle flash before hearing the roar from the gun. I had heard veterans of war describe it as a terrifying experience. But in this instance the sound of the bullet whizzing by my ear came as a welcome relief. I stopped in my tracks and whirled around just in time to see the croc whip his tail to and fro in a wild display of his power. Then his jaw dropped, and he lay silent.

"Wow, you like to call 'em close, don't you?" Lance said, strutting down the beach.

"No," I responded. "You were the one who was calling it close. I would have killed him when he left the beach on the other shore. Besides, it was your wife who said he wouldn't attack."

"It's just God demonstrating His power and authority," Esther said. "Don't you see?"

Now, for the first time, I could see. Before now, I would have discounted her explanation as absurd and utterly devoid of logic, but now it was so obvious I couldn't believe I hadn't seen it before. God had protected us from that croc, and we had been able to do everything that He had intended us to do here. As a bonus, He had given us a trophy crocodile while providing for us a perfect illustration: Satan was always lurking in the shallows to harm us if we stepped away from God's protection.

"The most important thing is, John, that God has a lesson in all of this, and He wants you to learn what He is trying to teach you."

"Okay," I said and thought about what had just happened, hoping to make some sense of it.

"Can I try?" Betty asked.

"Absolutely," Esther said.

"God expects us from here on out to do His will," Betty said. "Even though He knows it will not be without trouble. The world is full of unbelievers who are content just to sit on the shore of life and sun themselves, preferring to be left alone. But if provoked, they will come after you. They are skilled killers of God's love and righteousness, and if you fail to take evasive action, they will eat you alive. But God's word is like that rifle. It will stop them dead in their tracks with a muzzle flash and a report so deafening there will be no mistaking its power. But like that croc, the master fisherman, God wants us to become fishers of men."

"That is why He chose that crocodile as the professor here in His classroom of life this morning," I said. "He is probably one of, if not *the best* fisherman in the entire world. Betty, you are a genius."

"No, John, it's not me. I never could have thought of this on my own. It has to be the Holy Spirit."

"But there's more," Esther said. "The croc is so successful at catching not just fish but young animals, too, who are unaware that he is approaching because he is hidden by the water. As Christians, the world sees us as crocodiles, lurking and ready to strike and take their life from them. So we do have to stay hidden to a certain extent so they won't avoid us altogether. Once the fish know you are a fisherman, they will simply swim away and hide under a log. Everything you say will be suspect. Your motives will be sincere to save them, but they will see it as you trying to take their life. The Scripture to us says that Christ's death on the cross means eternal life, but to those who are perishing it is the smell of death. And Jesus said, 'Whoever tries to save his life will lose it, but whoever loses his life for my sake will find it.'"

I took Betty's hand, and I could feel her shaking, chilled from the wet clothes.

"Let's get you back to camp and get you into some dry clothes," Lance said.

"Aren't you going to be baptized?" Betty asked.

"Me?" Lance asked. "Oh, I was baptized as a young boy, and you really only need to be baptized once."

"It's hard to imagine how this works," Betty said. "I mean, I stepped into that river as my old self, but something happened out there. I think the river was changed. Heck, I've been a fisher girl since I was a little kid, and I know rivers. But this one is different. It really and truly is like I drowned out there a few minutes ago. It's like my doubts about God were washed away. I just don't get it."

"That is the point," Lance said. "You did get it. You got the Holy Ghost. Here, take my coat before you catch your death."

"That was it, wasn't it?" Betty said.

"Yes," Esther said.

"That was my death," Betty said. "I never knew it would be so easy, dying that way." Betty took Lance's coat. "Turn around, Lance," she said and removed her wet shirt before slipping into the jacket. "That's better."

"I'll start the Ford," Lance said.

"I'll give you a hand," I said.

"What about your shoulder?" Betty asked.

"What about those dressings?" Esther asked. "I never even thought about them when I dunked you."

"It's a little late now," I said with a wide grin.

"Let's get your shirt off and change those bandages," Betty said as she began to undo the buttons on my shirt.

"I'll get the kit," Esther said, stepping toward the car.

Betty opened my shirt and began to remove the bandage, which was soaked with water and still stained with blood. Her eyes popped open, and her jaw dropped. "Esther!"

Esther stopped dead in her tracks. "What is it?"

"Take a look at this!"

"How bad is it?" I asked.

"It's a miracle!" Esther said, coming in for a closer look. "We have witnessed a true miracle."

I reached over and felt my shoulder, where just hours before I had put my hand on a terrible wound. The gaping holes, swelling, and soreness were gone. I flexed my arm with virtually no pain. "I can't believe it!" I exclaimed.

"Why is it that we always say we believe in God and His power," Esther said, "but then when we see a miracle, we say we can't believe?"

"Because it is unbelievable," Lance said. "But miracles always are, and that is what makes them so special. If they were believable, they wouldn't be miraculous."

"Get on your knees, everyone," Esther said, putting her palms in the sand and kneeling down.

She put her head in her hands, and we all followed suit and knelt in a circle.

"This is hallowed ground, for the Lord has been here," she said. "Let us pray to the Lord.

"Dear Heavenly Father, we praise you for your loving kindness. We praise you for your grace and your gift of faith to those who seek your face in their heart of hearts. We thank you, Father, for hiding your face from the world and then showing your power at the times of your choosing. Father, thank you for this miracle that you have given us here today. Lord, we feel as if we have seen the burning bush with our own eyes. Father, we cannot comprehend the total will you have for us. But Lord, we see with our eyes, we know with our hearts, and we are witnesses to your power. We believe because there is no other explanation. And so, Father, we are left with nothing more but to honor you and to love you with all of our hearts.

"Dear Heavenly Father, be with John and Betty in these days to come as you test their faith to make it strong, as we know you will. Help them, Lord, to stand firm and to prove to you and themselves that they are worthy of the calling that you have given them. We pray all of this in the name of your precious and Holy Son, Jesus Christ, our Lord."

Lance bounced up and prepared to start the Ford. I got to my feet and wiped the tears from my face. Betty put her arm around me and kissed my bare shoulder.

"Who is this God, and just what is He capable of?" I asked. "It almost makes you want to be frightened of His power."

"When you realize who He is, then you should be," Esther said. "In the book of Psalms, it is said that the fear of the Lord is the beginning of wisdom. Think back to when you were a kid. Didn't you fear your father?"

"Most definitely."

"Didn't you have a different relationship with your parents?" she said. "Your mother nurtured you and coddled you, but your father held you accountable. Although he loved you, he would never put up with your nonsense, and if you tried to deceive him, he could always see right through it."

"You remember him well, don't you, Esther?"

"I do. He was just like my father."

"And like mine!" Betty said.

I took my seat behind the wheel while Lance turned the crank, and the engine kicked over and began singing its tune.

"You better let me take her," Lance said, approaching the driver's side.

"Yeah, that'll be fine," I said. "Hey, what about your croc?"

"I'll send a skinner back for the leather. We're not going to move him. He probably weighs three, maybe four hundred pounds."

"I've never eaten croc before," I said.

Lance laughed. "Because it probably tastes a little like an old merganser."

I stepped out and took the backseat, and as we started out, I realized that another miracle had just happened. I had always been the kind of man who would fight to be in control. It had always been in my nature. I was the kind of man who called the shots. If I didn't have control in putting the shots on target from my own rifle, then I had to give direction on where to shoot. Maybe I could see a glimpse of my old nature being replaced with that of humility.

~~~~~~~~~~

When we arrived at camp, the three of us changed into dry clothes, and when we came out of our tents, Lance started barking orders to Willie to get packing.

"Wait a minute, Lance," Esther said. "We're not leaving until we make sure John is okay."

"Are you ready to go, John?" Lance asked.

"I'm game. You know me." I felt like a horse at the gate. The hunt lived in my heart: the competition, the danger, the conquest, the excitement, and the thirst for victory. There was joy in the winner's circle, which was full of pomp and circumstance. Was it all about ego and personal glory? *Oh God, I hope not! Let it not be so.*

"I, for one, say we get going, as long as John feels up to it," Lance insisted.

"What about the hunt, Esther?" I asked as I fastened my pistol belt and holster around my waist. "Do you think God approves of all this killing?"

"If it's done with a pure heart and pure motives," she said. "All God's creation was made for man, and it's part of the blessings He bestows upon us."

"How would our motives be pure?" I asked.

"Well, since you asked—now don't be offended."

"No, I guess I need the straight scoop."

"Then you have to examine your own heart to decide what the trophy means to you," she said.

"I love to look at them," I answered. "They are beautiful, and I would someday like to complete my collection before I get too old."

"Find your motive," Esther said. "You have to search deep in your heart. Ask God to reveal it to you, even if it's hidden away in darkness."

"I don't know if my motives are pure," I answered. "But I suspect not."

"Then ask God to lead you to purity."

"But in all this killing, does God give us His approval?"

"If you were destroying them," she continued, "and not giving them back to God just as He gave them to you, that would make Him angry."

"What do you mean? You are not saying that they live eternally, are you?"

"Why wouldn't they? There are a lot of things in life that God chooses to keep secret. I don't believe you can go beyond Scripture to explain things that He has decided not to share, but surely the Bible tells us about the mind of God regarding His creatures."

"Tell me more," I said.

"In regards to taking the life of an animal, it was God who made the first kill. When Adam and Eve sinned in the Garden of Eden, God clothed them with animal skins, making atonement for their sin. God gave Adam dominion over the animals, and after the Flood, He gave Noah the right to eat them for food. When Noah made a sacrifice to God after the waters subsided, the Bible describes the burnt offering as an aroma pleasing to the Lord. God blessed Abraham when He took a knife to the throat of a ram in place of his son Isaac.

"When Moses faced down the Pharaoh of Egypt, God told Moses to have the Israelites take the blood of little lambs and sprinkle it over the doorposts of their houses to save them from the destroyers' Passover. God blessed men like David for killing bears and lions that threatened his flocks. And Jesus helped the disciples trap and execute thousands of unsuspecting fish, who were caught up in his disciples' nets. He also sent evil spirits into a herd of pigs, who ran off a cliff. If just one of those two thousand pigs had died an eternal death, wouldn't that be cruelty?

"So the question is do animals live eternally? I think only God knows the answer to that for sure, but I believe it would go against God's very nature to discard something so precious as the innocent creation He had made for His own pleasure."

Just when I thought we were really getting somewhere with this conversation, Jason interrupted us.

"Hey, boss, I liked riding in your car. Do you think I might take a backseat with you and Chuck today?"

"You can have the front seat," I said.

"Oh, no, sir. You should have the front."

"I'm not riding in the Ford."

"What?" he asked, pursing his lips.

"You heard me," I said. "I'm riding my gelding today."

"What about your shoulder, sir?"

"Listen, I thought we got over this 'sir' stuff a long time ago. Why aren't you calling me John?"

"I'm sorry," he answered, "but what about your shoulder?"

"Take a look for yourself," I said, unbuttoning my shirt and pulling back the fabric.

"Wrong shoulder," he said and chuckled.

"No, it's my left shoulder, remember? You said it was good that the lion didn't get my shooting side."

"Well, I'll be a monkey. Look at that cotton-picking thing!"

Esther turned her face away and wrinkled her nose.

"Can you believe it?" I said. "It's all healed up. It's a miracle. Glory be to God!"

Jason squinted at me in confusion again. "What?"

"It was God, Jason. It has always been God, and I just couldn't see Him."

"What happened?" he asked.

"I prayed He would save me, and He did. It's been a long time coming."

"All right then. You'll have to tell me sometime. Look, I'll go tell Chuck that it's him and me in the Ford."

"I'll go find Lance to see how close he is to loading up," Esther said.

"Jason, hold up a minute, son."

Jason stopped in his tracks and faced me as I walked over to him.

I put my arm around his shoulder and then whispered in his ear, "You need to choose your words more carefully."

"What did I say?"

"You have to be more sensitive. You can't go around calling something a cotton picker in front of Esther and not hurt her feelings."

"Oh, you're right. I never even thought about it."

"Esther is a very sensitive lady, and we need to treat her with dignity. Do you understand me? She's no different than Betty."

"I guess I never thought of it before."

"Well, think about it," I said in a stern voice. "From now on, there are a whole lot of things that are going to change on this safari: how we treat one another, how we act toward the animals, the way we interact with the natives, and the way we view God."

"That's everything, isn't it?"

"That's everything we need. You see, Jason, life is all about relationships: how we see ourselves, the role we believe we have earned, and the shelf on which we decide to place the book that tells our story."

"What do you mean?" he asked.

"Life is all about top shelf and bottom shelf." I paused, thinking. "Let's just call them top and bottom *self*. You put your book on the top self, and you are filled with pride. Everything else is a servant to you. You don't have to work at relationships; everyone else has to work at them with you. It's a great place to be, on that top self. Life seems easier there because everybody has to kiss your behind, and you don't have to apologize to anyone because you are always right."

"So tell me," he said, "what's so good about the bottom self?"

"Nothing. There's nothing good about the bottom self."

"I don't get it, then."

"Bottom self is no better or any worse than the other," I explained, amazed at my perspective. "Bottom self creates the same kind of evil in our lives that top self does. It fills you with envy. You become bitter at your life and covet everyone and everything. Bottom self is a world of wants, and as long as all you long for is top self, God will hold you back. Most of the time, those who are on the bottom self have more pride than the toppers, because they are trying to make up for their shortcomings."

"Those are the sins of pride and envy, aren't they?"

"The worst of the worst," I responded.

"So how do you get around them?" he asked. "I only see two choices."

"By putting God in the place of honor in our life," I answered. "Until that happens, nothing makes sense at all. It's all confusion, covered by mist and veiled from our view. Only God can part the waters that surround us and allow the waves and wind to be still. But there is a natural longing in our spirit to know God. I have known it for forty-six years. I have always denied it, because I never wanted to give up the top self and move over for God."

Jason's eyes were like magnets pulling the words from my soul. I had never spoken like this before, nor could I comprehend why or how this conversion had begun or by what power it continued. At that very moment, I believed God to be speaking through my mouth, and the instruction had taken place as much for me as it had for the kid.

"This is what God is, Jason. Our Father is a humble God. He will never take your soul away from you without your permission. This life was His gift to you, and to take it back by force would be a betrayal. He is a loving and gracious spirit who waits patiently for us to come to Him on our own. Now there is an evil enemy in this world who God uses to help us to seek out His protection, but I don't think He will ever allow Satan to tempt us more than we can handle. I don't know; that might even be in the Bible somewhere. I heard someone say that to me once.

"We are given free will. If God controlled everything, if we were mere puppets on a string, our love would be meaningless to Him. He gave us this temporary, unhealthy, and vulnerable condition, such as it is, to test our spirit to see if we would trade it in for a perfect life with Him in eternity. But we have to give it. He won't take it on His own. That's not how He works. But if we don't give it to Him, we will spend the rest of eternity wishing we had. It's sort of like being at the roulette wheel with a pile of chips and betting it all on just one more spin until it's gone. But we can cash in anytime we like for the big jackpot."

"Sounds like you must have hit the jackpot, John."

"More than you know right now," I said.

"Are you two ready to go, or are you just gonna stand around all day chewing the fat?" Chuck asked, packing his rifle toward the automobile.

"Hey, Chuck, I'm riding with you," Jason said.

"Get your things. I'm ready to go," he insisted.

Jason headed off and then stopped, spinning around in his tracks. "I don't know how to think about this right now," he said to me.

"The only difference between a believer and a nonbeliever is someone who hasn't met Christ yet."

"Maybe someday I'll believe."

"Yeah, someday you will—that's for sure. You just need to make sure you're still alive the day you do. If you look for God, you will find Him, Jason."

"I'm gonna try and think about it. Believe me ... I'm gonna try."

I made my way over to the horses and found my horse boy just finishing saddling up my gelding.

"How is this horse?" I asked, not sure if he understood English. "Has he been ridden?"

"Good horse, Bwana," he said in his heavy Swahili accent.

"What's his name?"

"Name, Bwana?"

"Jina (*name*)," I said, and his lights came on.

"Maua, him Maua."

"Maua?" I asked.

The boy crouched down and plucked a flower growing under a bush. "Maua," he said, holding the bloom with a wide grin.

"I can't ride a horse named Flower!"

"What's wrong, John?" Betty asked, leading her horse from the makeshift corral.

"They named my horse after some daisy," I said.

Betty broke out in laughter, grabbing her stomach and trying to control herself.

"Hey, just yuck it up," I said.

"Climb up there. I want to see you riding high on your majestic steed named Daisy."

Willie came over to see what all the laughter was about. "What is funny, Bwana?" he asked.

"They named my horse Maua," I said, "that's what."

Willie began to laugh along with Betty. "This is a liana flower," he said, trying to control his laughter. "We can change, Bwana."

"That's a good idea," I said and laughed. Betty's laughter was contagious.

"Let's call him Trigger," I said. "What's that in Swahili?"

"Trigger?" the native horseman asked.

"Yeah, Trigger: the part on a rifle you pull to make it shoot."

Willie looked at me with a blank face.

I pulled my hog leg, and the native horseman cowered.

"No, it's okay," I said, pointing to the trigger and holding it by the barrel. "This is trigger," I said.

"I know what it is, but there is no word, Bwana," Willie said. He rattled off Swahili to the native, who began to grin.

"Besides, Trigger is a stupid name," Betty said. "Nobody would ever name a horse Trigger. But if you like Trigger, it doesn't have to be a Swahili name."

"Not if you think it's stupid," I said. "Hmm ... how about ... Gun Smoke? Is there a Swahili name for Gun Smoke?"

"*Bunduki-fukia*," Willie answered. "That mean, gun gives smoke."

"Well, you call him Bunduki-fukia, and I'll call him Gun Smoke."

"Are you sure you're up to this?" Betty asked.

"They say lightning never strikes twice, right?"

"Maybe so," she answered, "but a lion ain't no lightning bolt."

"That's right, but now I'm immortal. And whatever happens now happens for a reason. If God decides to take me out now, then I know He is finished with me here and has a greater purpose for me in the next life."

"It is strange, isn't it?" Betty said. "I'm not afraid anymore. Since I know that my life is in God's hands, there is a peace over me."

"I guess I'm not ready to go quite yet," I said. "But the difference is that I'm willing, and I'm ready if He calls."

"I suppose," she replied, "I just don't want to get left behind."

"But the strangest thing is," I said, "the one thing I have truly loved in this world—my burning desire for the kill, just for the sake of the kill—isn't there. It's not that I'm against it, or that I don't still crave the adventure and the challenge, but to kill something so I can put it on my ego leaves me cold right now."

"I don't think that's what a hunt is all about, is it?"

"I hope not. But just yesterday I was feeling pretty down because I hadn't taken one trophy this whole trip, but now none of that matters. We didn't come on this safari to find the perfect trophy."

"Right," she said. "I guess all along we didn't know it, but we came here to find God perfectly."

"Who would have thought He was right in front of us the whole time, like a brass ring on a merry-go-round, and I just wouldn't reach out and take it?"

"Yeah," she said, "I guess we never realized the ring was pure gold and not brass."

"You know, there's something funny about the English language. When you start looking at the words and how they are formed together, you see how God created it, and how the prince of this world tries to get in the way of God."

"How do you mean?" she asked.

"Okay, well, take *word*, for example. God's word is truth, but the world confuses it and tries to change it. And Lucifer with his lies confounds the *L*, which God had preserved for His love, and makes the word into His *world*, with all of its temptations. And look at the word *God*. If you insert the letter *L*, you end up with gold. And that's the one thing that Satan always uses to put between the people and God."

"Wow," she said with bright eyes. "And you take a three-letter word that is triune and insert Satan and you get the one thing that all mankind worships in this world, which by the way is a four-letter word. Are there more?"

"Probably. I'll bet if you did a study on it, there are all kinds of hidden truths in the words. Well, let's see ... here's one. Take *word* again and put an *S* on the front of it, with *S* standing for *spirit*, and you get the word *sword*. That is what the Bible is: *Spirit Word*. I remember Esther telling me that her Bible was the sword of the Spirit. She said it was sharper than any double-edged sword and divides the soul and the spirit."

"And with the hilt on the sword," Betty said, "it is made into the form of a cross, the most powerful image in the entire world."

"I know one thing for sure," I replied. "I have been like a hound dog, barking up the wrong tree all these years."

"Yeah," Betty said with a laugh, "you never find the critter you're looking for when your dog is barking up the wrong tree."

"I think the enemy changes and confounds things to make people think it is wisdom, but in the end it's a road leading to nowhere. I can't believe I spent my whole life's work trying to prove something right that was wrong all along." I slipped my foot into the stirrup and swung my leg over Gun Smoke's back.

"I have an idea," she said, following my lead and settling into her saddle to come up to my eye level.

"What is it?" I asked.

Betty looked over her shoulder to where Chuck and Jason were making last-minute preparations with the Ford. Then she looked back with her soft eyes. "You remember how we always said we loved Jason, and if we ever had another son, we would want him to be just like him?"

"I do," I answered, "and I remember suggesting adoption, but you were the one cold on the idea."

"I was never closed to the idea," she said. "I just wanted to be cautious. I think the time has come, and when we get back to civilization, I'd like to make it official. What do you think, John?"

"I think it's a great idea, but I don't know for sure how he'll see it. He's already been talking about staying in Africa with Lance and Esther."

"That's just a kid talking," she said. "He'll go home with us if we adopt him."

"Don't be so sure he won't decide to just stay here in Africa, Betty."

~~~~~~~~~~

Willie led the safari another twenty miles that day toward elephant country. Betty and I enjoyed being together on the trail, making small talk and enjoying the sights. I had forgotten how relaxing riding horseback could be, not having to fight the wheel from the bumpy terrain while instead letting the horse choose the way some of the time. Of course, I never dropped my guard, having learned my lesson. But at the same time, I had no regrets about getting attacked. I just hoped for no repeat.

Betty had been able to spend a lot of time with her horse and to develop a relationship with it. There was an advantage in building trust with a horse. The horse wouldn't throw the rider, and the horse would feel as comfortable with the rider as the rider felt with the horse. You could almost become one with a horse. I wondered if that was the way we developed a relationship with God. I wanted so much to begin this friendship with Jesus Christ, to be able to trust Him with the little things, to let Him work out the details, instead of always trying to do it on my own. This would be my first day as a Christian, and I knew there was much to learn. With much anticipation in my heart, I began my new life.

Chapter 25

GOD'S GIFT

That evening when we arrived at camp, Betty couldn't wait to pop the question to Jason. She reminded me of a little kid at Christmas, having sat on the news all day. If it didn't come out quickly, I was afraid she might explode with excitement.

"How far behind do you think they are?" she asked. "I just can't wait to tell him."

"You can tell him right now," I said as the faint noise of the Ford began to emerge from the bush. "Can you hear it?"

"Now I can," she said. "But you know, it's funny: we never heard one shot all day."

"We saw plenty of game," I answered, "but nothing worth shooting. They were probably in the same boat."

The Ford showed its face, appearing along the edge of the trees about a mile off. The zebras that were grazing on the plain bolted, and a cloud of dust arose while their song mixed with the tune of the Ford in a very special moment.

"It's funny, isn't it, about fleeting moments?" I asked Betty as we stood waiting for the pair to arrive in the Ford.

"Why?" she asked with her cute little nose wrinkled up.

"Life passes much too quickly," I answered, "and you want to catch it all, but our hands are just too small. Heck, our whole life is too small."

"I know," she said, "but you just let it go and enjoy all that you can. We haven't heard from Mae for such a very long time. I hope my letters are getting through, but we have no way of knowing."

"I can't believe how faithful you have been in keeping her updated," I said. "Are you going to tell her about the lion?"

"I'm going to tell her about our newfound faith, but I'll leave the lion story until we get home."

"Amazing, isn't it?" I said. "That God sent a lion so that all men might come to know Him."

"What do you mean?"

"There are lions all around us," I explained, "even in Chicago."

"Yeah, I suppose so," she said.

"I think God uses lions to draw people to Him."

"I never thought of it that way."

"He uses the devil," I continued, "who prowls around like a roaring lion looking for someone to devour, and he uses His Son Jesus, who is the lion of Judah. One lion saves us, and the other one tries to destroy us. But both lions have the power to make us want to seek God. Satan is the storm, while Christ is the wings of the mother hen. Satan is the wolf, while Christ is the good shepherd."

I pondered the power of the statement I had just uttered. Was it God who did bad stuff, or was it Satan? That was probably the question of the ages. If one could answer that question, then the rest would be easy. If God was sovereign, then He could stop all of the bad things from happening. But if all the bad stuff quit happening, then no one would need God. And if all the bad stuff just happened by chance, then God wasn't really sovereign at all.

According to Esther, Jesus said in the New Testament that "not one small sparrow falls to the ground outside of the Father's will." If that wasn't His sovereignty, then I didn't know what it was.

In the world I had just left, suffering was random. It was no wonder that I was so terrified all the time. God was not capable of evil, but then man defined evil for himself. Only God knew the difference between good and evil. That had to be the whole point in the Garden of Eden, where Eve ate from the forbidden fruit. Satan had told her that she would be like God, knowing the difference between good and evil. Man had a certain sense of good and evil, but an inability to understanding the mind of God.

I could see for the first time a difference between the good lessons that God taught us and the evil that caused us to sin. Obviously, sin could cause our suffering, but there were lots of things in life that caused suffering that God used to help us grow. Not everything that caused us to grow came from evil. Case in point: the lion that had nearly killed me. I thanked God for the lions in life, because without them we might never find Him at all.

Jason waved to us as Chuck brought the buggy across the grassland and closed the final hundred yards.

"Now give him a breath before you pounce on him," I cautioned Betty.

"Oh, John, give me a little credit."

The Ford pulled up, and Chuck shut her down, and suddenly we could hear the birds in the trees and the porters chanting as they helped set up camp.

"How was your day?" Betty asked while the two prepared to exit the car.

"We saw a herd of elephants," Jason said, standing with his hands on his hips, his hair a little windblown, and looking like the true African hunter that he had become. "The minute they spotted us, they disappeared in the heavy bush, and we never saw them again."

"Willie said they can hear that thing coming for twenty miles."

"Really?" Jason asked.

"Betty and I could hear it from probably two miles away just now," I said, "and just imagine what an elephant can hear. I mean, look at the size of their ears."

"Wow," Jason said, his eyes wide as he stepped out of the car.

"I can't help it, John," Betty whispered. "I just have to ask him." She turned to squarely address him. "Jason, John and I were talking, and well, we don't know how you would feel about this, but we wanted to ask you something very important."

His eyes narrowed as he focused on Betty's voice. Then his face brightened in anticipation of what she was about to say. "What is it? Are you going to let me drive the car?"

"We'll have to talk about that one," I answered with a laugh.

"We were wondering how you would feel about becoming our son," she asked.

"Oh, my goodness," he said, lifting his eyebrows. "It's what I have always dreamed about. Ever since I first met you on the train,

John, I have secretly wished that I could have a father just like you. If you had asked me only two days ago, I would have leaped at the chance. Actually, I can't even believe right now that I am saying this."

"Don't give us an answer right now if you're not sure," I said.

"We want you to think about it first," Betty said, "and consider all your options."

"It's just that me and Chuck had a good chance to talk about a lot of things today. And well, a bunch of stuff has happened in this camp over the last couple of days, and things have changed."

"What's changed?" Betty asked.

"Ah, shoot ... you know, don't make me say. Besides, I might not be going with you back to Chicago."

"But Jason," she said, stopping to show restraint.

"School has never been my cup of tea, and if I go back, I know my life will just turn into a pile of bookwork."

"Life is work," I said, "but unless you are going to build a life, find a girl, and make a go of it, that's what you've got to do."

"Maybe so, but I think I can make a go of it here, and to me this ain't work."

"Believe me, someday it will turn into work," I said. "When you're my age and you get tired of adventure and maybe even the killing, then you are going to want to fall back on an education."

"What do you think, Chuck?" Betty asked.

"Everybody needs a mom and a dad. In spite of what I said today, Jason, you need to think about this."

I could only imagine what Chuck had told the kid today, but I was grateful now that he was supporting us in this way, even though I knew how he felt about our newfound faith. Betty's eyes began to well up, and a tear appeared, dripping down the side of her cheek.

"I don't want you to think I'm not beholden to you, ma'am. I mean, you guys have been so great. You took me in when I had nothing in my life, you brought me along on this trip, and you have treated me like a son. It's just ... it's just that you gave me Africa, and now I don't know if I want to give her back."

"She's not ours to keep, Jason," Betty said. "But you are your own man, and you have to make up your own mind."

"She's right, Jason," I explained. "It's the same thing with God."

"I'm going to go see how they are doing with my tent," Chuck said, rolling his eyes and then briskly exiting.

Betty squinted and shook her head just once.

"Anyway," I continued, "the offer has been made, and you know what that means. You would be our only heir, Jason. Everything we have would someday be yours."

"Oh," he said as if a streetlight had just been lit, "I hadn't considered that."

"It sweetens it for sure," I continued, "but the real deal is not our money. It's the plan of Jesus Christ to take our place in death, His forgiveness and His promise of eternal paradise. I never knew, Jason. For forty-six years, I denied it, and I can only wonder about all the people who never got it because of my stupidity. I can't change that, but I can do something about it now. And that's what I intend to do. Tell everyone that God is real."

"Let me think about it," he answered. "Can you give me a day?"

"We'll give you as long as it takes to decide," Betty said.

"Our offer stands as stated," I said with an assuring voice.

Jason spontaneously threw himself at Betty and hugged her neck like a ten-year-old.

"You are quite a boy," she said. "Quite a *man* ... your own man. I love you, Jason." Betty's eyes welled up, and a tear leaked out and came streaming down her cheek.

I had been witness to so many tears over the years from this woman, and seeing them again put a pit in my stomach. I couldn't believe Jason's reaction, and I was terrified to think how this might affect Betty's peace of mind, especially if ultimately he said no. She had been so different over this last year, and I didn't want this to push her over the edge, back into her state of depression.

"I better go see if Willie needs any help prepping the camp," he said, letting go and turning to leave. Then he stopped and turned to face us. "Thanks. However I decide, thank you." He turned again and ran across the clearing to where Willie and his men were setting up the kitchen.

"The kid has a good work ethic," I said. "Are you okay?"

"I'm fine. I guess I just thought we should let him decide one thing at a time. If he comes to us as our son, we will have a lifetime to tell him about Jesus. You need to be a fisher of men. I guess I'll have to tell you about fishing sometime. But a fisherman is just a little cagey about how he fishes. He will throw out bait and wait for the fish to come to him. Don't jump in the river and try to catch them with your hands. The way I see it, if God wants me to have a son in this life, then he'll give me one. I'm not going to worry about it. I'm going to let God work out the details. Maybe God only wants me to have one son for eternity.

"I remember my friend Rose once told me that if you claim to have faith, then you have to live your faith. I didn't know what she meant at the time, but I guess it's time for me to start living my faith. Even though it has only been one day, I feel privileged to be in Christ, and I want to please Him. Esther said the Lord will give you back the years the locusts have eaten; it's in the Bible somewhere. She said the Lord will give you the desire of your heart, and having a family has always been the desire of my heart."

"And mine, too," I replied.

"You know the other thing that Esther pointed out to me during all of my discussions with her here in Africa?"

"What's that?" I asked.

"She showed how much Job misunderstood God. You know, when I read the book before, I thought it was just about Job's crummy life and all the things God had let Satan do to him. It really didn't seem fair to me that such a good man had gotten such a raw deal. But I was so focused on my own troubles and loss that I never realized that Job did figure the whole thing out in the end. Here, let me show you." She reached into her saddlebag and pulled out a black leather-bound Bible.

"Where did you get that?" I asked. "Are you holding out on me?"

"Esther gave it to me, and I have been carrying it with me since that day I attended church with her." Betty opened the book and began to flip through the pages.

"Will you let me borrow it?" I asked.

"Anytime you like," she said, clearing her throat and settling in to read. *"I have heard of thee by the hearing of the ear, but now mine eye seeth thee. Wherefore, I abhor myself, and repent in dust and ashes."*

"Wow, he repented," I said, "and he figured it out in the last chapter?"

"Yes, and listen to this," she continued. *"Also the Lord gave Job twice as much as he had before. Then came there unto him all his brethren, and all his sisters, and all they that had been of his acquaintance before, and did eat bread with him in his house. And they bemoaned him, and comforted him over all the evil that the Lord had brought upon him. Every man also gave him a piece of money, and every one an earring of gold. So the Lord blessed the latter end of Job more than his beginning,: for he had fourteen thousand sheep, and six thousand camels, and a thousand yoke of oxen, and a thousand she asses. He had also seven sons and three daughters.*

"Now when I read this book, all I see is a man who was self-righteous. He was proud, because he thought he was better than everyone else and he didn't deserve what he thought God had done to him."

"But he got it right in the end," I said, "and God gave him twice as much as he had before."

"And that's why I'm not worried anymore about having what I want," she said. "I know that God will give me what I need and my life will turn out exactly how He intends if I just learn to seek Him more. I can't focus on what I think will make me happy, because if I just let go, then God can work in my life to give me all that He intends for me to have."

"I'm getting hungry," I said, although I felt torn between soothing my hunger pains and finishing this fascinating discussion with my beautiful wife. "How about you?"

~~~~~~~~~

About an hour of light still remained after dinner, so I took my writing things and Betty's Bible and found a quiet place at the edge of camp to be alone with my thoughts. All the excitement about elephants had everyone in a stir, and Lance just couldn't stand the thought of waiting another day to find his bull. I thought he was going to wet his pants.

Lance and Esther had taken a short side trip in the afternoon, and he, too, had seen fresh signs from a large herd. He swore that one of the tracks he had seen measured twenty-three inches in diameter. Willie said we were ahead of schedule and that tomorrow we would be in the heart of elephant country, in a place where the herds returned every year at the conclusion of the rainy season.

There was very little known about elephants, and I was convinced they would make a fascinating study for the right scientist. They seemed to be very social and congregated in small bands of mothers, sisters, and aunts. The men folk lived separately from the ladies, except when mating season came along. Mothers even sent their sons off to be with the old men at the age of five or so. It was a great system: the men raised the boys, and the ladies raised the girls.

They had an incredible sense of smell and maybe even better hearing. Scientifically, it was likely impossible to calculate how much more they could smell or hear than a human. Most of what was known about the beast came from men whose only desire was to kill them. We seemed to know everything there was about their feeding habits and their migration, where to place a bullet for a brain shot or a heart shot, and how far to push a bull before he stomped you in the dirt. They were extremely wary and shy, and when you hunted them in the jungle, you never actually got a look at them in full view—only pieces of their trunk, an ear, or their tail wagging at you as they fled.

This time of year with the dry foliage and the noise it created, it was near impossible to sneak up on them unless you found a spot where you were upwind and you could set up an ambush. But in the rainy season the foliage was so thick it was hard to see them at all. They must have been able to communicate over long distances, because their shrill voice could travel across the plains for miles. If I could hear it miles away, I could only imagine what an elephant might hear. Perhaps it was the low tones that traveled miles and miles, the ones that a human ear could not hear because the range was so low. This had to be how the elephant communicated over long distances.

It was funny, really. We all lived in the same world, but our perception of things varied from one to the other. It was impossible to imagine what an elephant understood about the world. Many of them had never seen a white man before, let alone understood where he came from or who he was. So for a human to understand an elephant's world was an equal impossibility. Other than the lion, which occasionally separated baby elephants from the herd, man was the elephant's only serious threat. What sort of emotions did they feel? Did they experience love and hate as well as fear? If their devotion to family and their distain for man were any indication, the answer was yes.

Stories about elephants were passed from hunter to hunter. I heard tell once, after a big bull went down with a bullet wound, his companions got him to his feet and pushed him along and out of sight into the thick bush, where the hunters were unable to track him. But did they think or reason, or was their life shallower than that? I had a hunch that man's understanding of them was so shallow that we only saw them as stupid animals in pursuit of food, water, family, and safety.

The real difference, however, between man and animals was our ability to use tools, make a place to live, and to prepare food. But all that came from man's ability to reason. Thus, although an animal had free will, his destiny depended largely upon instinct. But even there, I wasn't so sure. I had to consider the pride lion or the big bull elephant. There was obviously a drive to be the top dog among them, to take charge of the women, and to reap all the benefits that went along with that position. Was this instinct, social conditioning, or both?

Was man any different? Man placed himself so high above the animals in his own mind that he couldn't see what God was trying to tell him. Maybe this was the secret of God and His creation: that man believed in his superiority because of his ability to converse with one another in both spoken and written language. It had to be the word that set man apart from the rest of creation. Esther had told me to look in the book of John. Was that in the Old Testament or New? I hurriedly searched the index and found it in the New Testament. Here it was: *In the beginning was the Word, and the Word was with God, and the Word was God. The same was in the beginning with God.*

That was a difficult concept, but if Christ was the *word*, then He was God in the flesh. That was what set man apart from the animals. We were made in the image of God. To the animals, when they saw man, they were seeing God. That was where their wisdom came from: the fear of man. Man got his wisdom from the fear of God.

There was a mystery here that no one could answer. Did God speak to the animals and use them for His purpose? Why had He put them here to experience the pain and suffering associated with this temporary moment in the vast expanse of the universe?

These were all questions that God refused to answer in His infinite wisdom. The answers were better left with the master. I would trust in Him that He knew best.

"What are you doing, darling?" Betty asked.

I looked up to see her and Esther approaching, the western sky blazing orange behind them.

"I'm writing in my journal, just pondering life. Look at that sunset. Isn't that beautiful?"

"What have you concluded?" Esther asked.

"That our God is amazing. It is incredible that He chooses to keep so many answers about this place a mystery."

"But that is what makes Him God," she said. "And for those of us who acknowledge Him, it keeps us humble."

"What amazes me is the way man is wired," I said. "Here you have a God who gives man this incredible gift of life, and then man takes it and uses it for his own glory. Man is so self-serving. He craves everything that goes along with power."

"God knew that would happen," Esther said, "and that is why He is constantly testing our hearts to see if we are real."

"That's what this place is," I said, "a testing ground. It's a place where He can send us to find out if we are worthy to be with Him in eternity. It's not a place where we come to earn our salvation, but a place where He can determine by looking at our hearts if we are worthy of His gift of faith by His grace."

"I have a question for you, Esther," Betty said. Her eyes began to turn red, and she blinked to hold back the tears. "I've never asked anyone this, and maybe I don't want to know the answer."

"What is it?" Esther said.

"What about my son? Is he with Christ in heaven? You know he had no faith. Heck, *we* had no faith. And he was just a little boy."

"This is how I see it," Esther said. "The Scripture says we are saved by God's grace and not by what we do, so that no one can boast of their works. But how big is our God? I mean, really, look at the universe and ask yourself, how big is my God? How big is His grace? I believe He sits on His throne as a prefect judge in every way. With wisdom and understanding, compassion, mercy, humility, patience, and His love and His grace, He will pass judgment. But remember this: He is a jealous god. He hates sin. And though He is slow to anger, He is not immune. He is not just a happy old grandpa who will fail to hold us accountable. But for the innocent, there will be no penalty. No one will ever say, *that's not fair, God*.

"We look at life from an earthly perspective, and it's easy to fall short of understanding. But when we get there, I think we will hit ourselves in the forehead with the heel of our hand and ask why we were so stupid not to see."

Betty started to speak but then held her tongue.

"King David lost a son," Esther continued, "and he said that one day he would be with him again. I am certain your child was not old enough to understand God. But I believe that everyone will be judged by God, and those of us who are covered by the blood of Christ will be saved automatically. At the same time, we who are in the light will be disciplined more swiftly for our sins than those who live in darkness. We will be held to a higher accountability. We don't spank our neighbor's children, but our father will be quick to take us to the woodshed.

"You see, Jesus paid the debt of our sins on the cross, and now we are forgiven and washed clean. There has to be a rejection of God in the heart, and that only comes at an age where a child is able to reject Him. I believe the loss of that little boy may have been your pathway to God, and that it was in God's will for you to suffer in such a way that you would turn to Him for comfort. I believe that little boy by the grace of the one who made him will be waiting to show you all that he has seen when you arrive.

"But remember this: a day of the Lord is as a thousand years here on earth. When you arrive in heaven, say twenty or forty or even sixty years from now, you will be reunited with him. But it will be as if he has only been there for a few minutes. And this life and all of its pain and sorrow won't matter to you anymore. You will look back at the price you paid and will say, 'For all this I would have endured one thousand times the pain to get here.' You will be what God intended you to become from the beginning of time: the beauty, the splendor, and God's majesty will overtake you, and you will be in awe of what

He has done. The Scripture says … let's see, it's in Isaiah sixty-four, yes, here it is. *For since the beginning of the world, men have not heard, nor perceived by the ear, neither hath the eye seen, O God, beside thee, what he hath prepared for him that waiteth for him."*

"That does make me feel better," Betty said. "Does it give you peace, John?"

"Plenty," I said. "So what do you think about the animals? When they die, is it just like blowing out a candle? Are they no more forever?"

"Do you remember I said I would research that question?" Esther asked.

"Yes, and I am persistent. Did you find anything?"

"This is what I found," she said, pausing to give me her wide smile and making me want to wag my tail, if I had one. "The animals are like the angels, except they have earthly bodies. An angel cannot receive salvation the same way that mankind can, but they are eternal creatures. Man was created in the image of God, and the Scripture says we will reign with Him in heaven. To reign, there must be something to reign over. It wouldn't be to rule over nonbelievers, because they will be eternally separated from God.

"In the book of Genesis, chapter one," she said, opening her Bible, "verse twenty-six, God made creation and gave it to man to rule over, the same way I believe it will be in heaven. You see, mother earth acts as a womb for God. He sends spirits here to become what He has chosen them to be, and after they have gone through a period of instruction, suffering, and testing, He moves them along to the next phase of their life. Apostle Paul said we are predestined, but that doesn't mean some were predestined to go to hell and others predestined to be with Christ. Everyone is predestined to be with God in heaven, but many chose to reject Christ. There is only one unforgivable sin, which is blasphemy of the Holy Spirit. God cannot forgive you if you have chosen to reject Him in your heart all your days, and if you chose to fly off into eternity holding that line.

"But because an animal has no choice about God, they aren't held responsible for their sins. God will not punish them or hold them accountable. Animals were not created to one day rule with God in heaven, nor were the angels, and therefore they are not held to this higher level of accountability as is man. It's the same with Satan, who wanted to be like God. Satan was created as an angel. When he wanted to be God, God tossed him out of heaven and he landed here as the prince of this world.

"God is a perfect judge, and animals are not responsible for the law that He set down for man. He didn't tell the animals, 'Thou shalt not kill,' or give them any of the other nine commandments. The animal will not be held accountable for his greed, or his prejudice, or for coveting another female. But they will have to give an account. Look here, in the book of Genesis, chapter nine. God says He will require an account from man as well as every beast. So when you get there, be ready, because if you have been cruel or mistreated an animal, they will be waiting there to testify against you.

"I think God will use all His creation as members of His jury on judgment day. They will be with Him in paradise, because He created them. In the book of Hebrews, it says Christ is the heir of all things. Look around at the things God created, and then you tell me what Christ is heir to. If your father was a great painter and left you as the sole heir to all of his paintings, but on the last day before he passed on he had them all burned, would that not be a betrayal to you as his son?"

"My father left me everything he had," I said.

"And that is what God the Father has done for His Son. All God's creation will be given to Him. Everything, that is, except the ones who have chosen in their heart to reject Him. Everything God created will be taken up, and everything that does not seem so beautiful here will become beautiful to our eyes, and we will understand its beauty and its eternal purpose. We will be thankful for all the evil that drove us to God's sanctuary, like the lion that was waiting to devour you. And every hardship, every heartache, every trial, and every storm that you endured will have been worth every nickel you shelled out."

"So what about the person who has never heard about Jesus?" Betty asked. "Are they doomed to hell?"

"No, it's just like your infant son who is in heaven. A person has to actually reject Christ in their heart. If they never heard about Christ, how can they reject Him?"

"Thank you, Esther," I said. "Thank you for being our guide and helping us to see God."

"Don't thank me. It was God who did it."

"Maybe so," I said, "but it was your willingness and your boldness to speak the truth."

"But it was God who gave me the words and put me here in this place."

"I just hope when we get home," I said, "that I can be as good as you are at leading others to the truth."

"Yeah," Betty said with a laugh, "if we ever get home."

"Hey, don't be talking like that," I said.

"I know," Betty said. "But lately I'm feeling like I need to go home. And here we are out here in the middle of nowhere, just east or maybe west of Timbuktu—heck, I don't know. There are dangers all around us, and we have traipsed what seems like halfway across Africa to get to who-knows-where and for God-knows-what. Sometimes I wonder. I mean, I just want to get in a warm bath and crawl into a clean, fluffy bed."

"We have all that back in Nairobi," Esther said.

"Okay," she continued, "but we are still a long ways from Nairobi. I'm feeling like I just climbed to the summit of a mountain, and now I have to start the long trek down. I guess I used up nearly every bit of what I had, and I'm feeling a little like I don't have what it takes to get back."

Esther and I just sat quietly, not knowing exactly what to say.

"And if Jason says no, my heart will be broken. I already lost a son, and now I might be losing another. Except this one will be stillborn." Betty's eyes turned red and welled up.

As Esther embraced her, I began to burn with anger over the selfishness of that kid.

"I'm going to have a little chat with the lad right now," I said.

"No, John, let him be. I don't want his forced love. If you back him into a corner and I toss the net over him, I'll always wonder how it might have been if he decided on his own."

"But he needs to know what's at stake here," I said.

"I think he knows it's a lot more than money. He knows what he means to me. He knows what he means to *us*. I'm not sure he knows how much it is tormenting me or how much I desire to have him for a son. But I know he loves me. I just hope I win out over Africa."

"That's it, isn't it?" Esther said.

"In a nutshell," Betty said. "The boy is torn."

"No," Esther said. "God is showing you what He has gone through since He created you and placed you here in this world. It has always been a choice between our love for Him and our love for the World. Now you can step back and see a clear illustration of the personal struggle that you went through, and the one you put God through—the same struggle Jason is having right now."

Betty and I looked at each other, and I could see in her eyes a frightened little girl who was afraid that she might be hurt again.

The western sky had faded, brilliant red replaced by a small red hue on the horizon, and darkness had begun to consume the African bush.

"Let's get back to camp," Betty said. "I don't want to get caught out here without a moon or a lamp."

We trudged the ten minutes back to find Jason, Chuck, and Lance sitting around the campfire. We couldn't hear what they were saying, but Chuck saw us and nudged Jason, and they both looked up as if they had been talking behind our back.

"Hope we're not interrupting anything," Betty said.

Chuck shrugged his shoulders, and Jason looked like a cat that had just eaten the family's pet canary.

Lance started in with an off-the-wall question, just as it looked like there might be an opportunity to focus on the central issue of the day. "What sort of trophy do you treasure the most in all of Africa?" he asked.

"I want to know what you guys were talking about when we got here," Betty insisted.

"I'll answer the first question first," Chuck said. "Without a doubt, the rhino, especially since that old boy nearly flattened me a couple of days ago in the Ford. That's going to be quite a story when I show off his handsome head mount. You know what they call a herd of rhino, don't you?"

Everybody sat silent, knowing this conversation had bounced far off track.

"Okay," he continued, "lions are a pride, geese are a flock, buffalo are a herd, wolves are a pack, and whales are a pod, right?" he said, waiting for an answer.

"And vultures are a committee," I said, laughing.

"Yeah, and dolphins are a social," Esther chimed in.

"Hey, a group of crows are a murder," Lance said.

Jason laughed, clearly confused. "A murder? Why a murder?"

"Ever known a crow that wasn't out to murder something?" Lance asked. "They are rotten to the core when it comes to stealing babies from a nest."

"Okay, but how about rhinos?" Chuck asked.

We sat with blank faces. I knew the answer, but I wanted Chuck to have his moment in the sun.

"Here's a hint. A rhino can run thirty miles an hour, but he can only see about fifty feet in front of him."

"Okay," Esther said, "so what's the hint?"

"A group of rhino are called a crash," he said, and we all broke out with a good laugh.

"That's why God put a horn on their nose," Jason said between laughs, holding his stomach. "Too bad he can't blow on that darn thing to warn everybody he's coming."

"He's so big he doesn't have to," Esther said.

"Yeah, it's up to whatever's in his way to get out of his way or get flattened," Chuck said.

"How about you, John?" Lance said. "What's the most treasured trophy for you in all Africa?"

I paused to think. The most treasured thing I had gotten from Africa was my newfound faith in God, but I knew right now wasn't a good time to lay that one on the table again with Chuck and Jason. It hadn't been that long since hearing about Jesus had made me sick to my stomach from having it forced down my throat.

"What's the matter with you, John?" Lance asked. "I would have thought that your most treasured trophy in all Africa would be right on the tip of your tongue."

"My most treasured African trophy has always been the bongo. You know that. But before I just blurted it out, I had to really think about how I feel now."

"Is that your final answer?" he asked with a suspicious grin on his face.

"I don't know. Overall, I guess. I like the bongo, but I would have to say that I have gained a new respect for the lion. To me, he has always been the most majestic in all Africa. He is a symbol of power and authority. He demands respect, and he puts up with very little monkey business. If I have to choose my all-time favorite trophy now, I guess it would definitely have to be the lion."

"How about you, Betty?" Chuck asked.

I could see the gears churning in her mind, and I knew right now that Jason was her greatest trophy. Bringing home a son from Africa would complete her life.

"From a woman's perspective, the lion is not my favorite anymore. Not after seeing him almost rip your head off, John. The lion is a nightmare to me. I guess I love the giraffe. But I would never want to kill one, so that's really not a trophy. But as far as being the most graceful and gentle animal, they win in my estimation. But for a trophy, I guess I would have to say the buffalo."

"Why's that?" Jason asked.

"Because he's like an old bulldog, and he's solid and strong. He holds his ground in a fight. He's loyal and defends his friends and his family." Betty paused as she thought about what to say. "He's a symbol of the kind of man I married." She looked up at me with those big brown eyes, and I could feel my heart melting under the spell of her smile.

"Okay, you two," Chuck said, laughing, "let's not get mushy."

"Tell him, Chuck," Lance said.

"Ah, not now," Chuck groaned.

"Tell me what?" I asked.

"Well, maybe this isn't the best time," Chuck said.

"It's okay," Lance said.

"Well, I've been talking to Lance, that's all, and I'm thinking about staying in Nairobi."

"And doing what?" I asked.

"We haven't worked out all the details yet."

"I could use a partner," Lance said. "Looks like Chuck is ready to throw in with me."

"And I suppose you are staying on, too," Betty said, looking directly at Jason.

The boy dropped his head and stared at the ground.

I nudged Betty and rolled my eyes. I couldn't believe she was pressing him again. She just couldn't let it go and give him the time he needed.

"Well, actually," he said, the firelight flickering against his face as he looked up from the ground, "I know you're gonna be disappointed with me, ma'am, but I have some bad news."

I knew it! I thought. *Chuck has been talking with Jason, and all along they have been making plans to stay in Africa together.* I began to burn inside. I couldn't believe my good friend had betrayed me like this. I saw the corners of his lips curl up, forming a little smirk on his face. I couldn't believe that somehow he thought this might be funny.

"Chuck and Lance have made me an offer to stay with them and start a guide service out of Nairobi."

"So that's it, is it?" Betty said, dropping her face in her palms with her elbows resting on her knees.

"But I won't be staying there in Nairobi very long," Jason said.

Betty looked up and watched his face intently.

"Just a few days or so when we get back."

Betty wrinkled her nose, shrugged her shoulders, and held her hands palms up, waiting for an answer.

"What are you thinking?" I asked.

"Well, Nairobi is fine and all, and you know how I love the bush country. And all along I've been thinking that maybe I could have a future in being a big game hunter."

"Yes?" Betty said in a suspicious tone.

"Well, Chuck has offered to let me stay with him here in Nairobi, but I have bad news."

Betty slid back from the edge of her chair, preparing herself for the worst.

"I won't be staying with Chuck."

"Where will you go?" Betty asked.

"You see, ma'am, there's this nice couple who have asked me to come and be their son in Chicago," Jason said with a wide grin. "Do you know them?"

Betty sucked in a breath of air and held it, putting her hands over her mouth.

"So I guess I must have a new mom and dad, if they'll take me."

Betty began sobbing as she leaped out of her chair and held her arms out.

Jason got to his feet, and they embraced. "I didn't mean to make you cry," he said. "I thought you would be happy."

"It's okay, Jason," Esther said with big wet tears running down her cheeks. She approached them and joined in their embrace. "That's just a girl thing."

I had a lump in my throat, as well, as I stood up, but I wasn't going to cry. I could only think about the day I had met Jason on the train. I had known then that he was a quality kid—with so much potential. The minute I had met him, I had known that he and Betty would hit it off. And now, to see this, and to see what this whole thing had become—it was incredible. Jason looked up and saw me standing there, and he broke away from the women and extended his hand.

I took his hand with a firm grip. That was what men did: they shook hands. There was an invisible boundary between them, and they didn't show affection, lest someone talk behind their back. But Jason surprised me and threw his arms around my neck and embraced me. My immediate reaction was to feel uncomfortable, but the warmth and the love I felt from this kid melted my heart.

"I dreamed about this day when we got to Chicago on that first night," Jason said, pulling away and leaving his hands on my shoulders.

"Why didn't you tell me?" I asked.

"What was I going to say? Oh, by the way, it looks like I'm going to be your new son."

"Yeah, I suppose that wouldn't have worked out so well. But it doesn't matter now, does it, son?" I pulled him to me and embraced him, and the lump in my throat began to hurt as Betty and Esther both looked on with silly grins and wet cheeks.

"Where do we go from here?" Jason asked.

"We're going to get a trophy elephant," Lance said.

"I know that," Jason said, "but what about doing the formalities on this sonhood thing I just agreed to?"

"All in good time," I said. "We can check with the government in Nairobi, but my guess is we will have to wait until we get back to American soil before we do anything formal."

"Until then, Jason," Betty said, "we can agree we all have a new relationship."

"I declare right now," I said, "that you are our son, formal or not. In our hearts, we belong to each other. But I can't wait to get home and make it official."

"I'm so excited," Betty said. "I just want to head back right now."

"We are right on the edge of elephant country," Lance said. "One more day and we'll be where we set out for. You won't believe the size of the bulls! And now you're talking about heading for home."

"No, not now," I responded. "We're here for the hunt, and our heart is still in it."

"We're just excited about this new chapter in our life," Betty said, "that's all."

"That's fine, and I'm happy for you, too," Chuck said, hoisting himself up off his chair and turning to leave for his tent.

"Where are you going?" I asked.

"I'm turning in. It's been a long day."

"We'll be up early," Lance said.

"I'll be up with the vultures," he said, continuing toward his tent without turning around.

We looked at each other with blank faces. Nobody spoke as Chuck slipped into his tent, which sat across the clearing some twenty yards away.

"What's the matter with him?" Betty whispered.

"I think he thought Jason would be staying here in Africa with us," Esther said.

"I think he's taken quite a shine to you, Jason, as we all have."

"I didn't want to hurt him, but now I feel bad."

"Don't feel bad," I said. "You made a choice, and life is all about choices. This isn't the first time you have probably made a choice that disappointed someone, and it won't be your last."

"But part of growing up and becoming a man is standing on your promises," Lance said, "and considering your options carefully. You weighed the pros and the cons and then made your final decision."

"And once you have decided, then stand firm and stay the course," Esther said.

"If I've hurt my friend, then I'm sorry. But I will never regret my decision to become Jason Rivers."

"Nor will we, Jason," Betty said.

"Nor will we," I echoed. I felt relieved that the kid had made the right choice.

Michael D. Neil

Chapter 26

A BITE OF FAITH

The following day, we were once again treated to a brilliant blue sky and another warm winter afternoon. It was not the sort of winter I had grown to expect in Chicago, where a person could literally freeze to death on the street. The thing I loved most about the African winter was the lack of rain—and the fact that the animals had to congregate around water holes.

We saw plenty of plains game, including a small band of giraffe. Betty's spirit soared as she poked fun and flirted with her new son. Jason seemed to have a new lease on life and appeared to sit taller in the saddle. He spoke clearer, joked better, and listened harder.

As the day wore on and my canteen wore down, we still had not seen hide nor hair of the elephants. We knew they were all around us. We had seen dung piles and tracks, but the really fresh tracks were all too small to waste time following. The whine from the Ford echoed across the plains as Chuck explored the outer edges of the safari alone to find us an elephant herd. But every time I heard him wind that motor, I could feel my blood begin to boil. He had to know that we would be leaving the Ford behind in short order. No self-respecting elephant would sit still for two seconds listening to that thing approach. Some of the animals, having never experienced such a racket before, came out to investigate the commotion. But I had more respect for the elephant, their cunning, and their seeming intelligence. They were smart enough to recognize a manmade sound and move on before it could get too close.

"It's beautiful today, isn't it?" Betty said.

"Oh boy, you can say that again," Jason said.

"Okay, it's beautiful today," she said and giggled.

"How's your water holding out, Betty?" I asked.

"Down below a quarter."

"We'll be at the river crossing any time," I said.

"Isn't that the same river we were at yesterday?" Jason asked.

"Yep, but it makes a huge bend," Lance said, "and we took a straight line. We'll be upstream a long ways from there."

"We couldn't have crossed it back there," I said. "You saw how deep it was."

"Yeah," responded Lance, "another river joins it about five miles downstream. That's why it was so wide and deep."

"I don't know how to break it to Chuck," I said, "but it's the end of the line for the Ford."

"Why is that?" Betty asked.

"Because we have used almost half of the petrol we brought. Even if we had more, we wouldn't get that thing across the river."

"What will he do?" she asked.

"He'll have to ride a horse like the rest of us," I said. "That car has always been a luxury item from the beginning. I was never sure just how far it would really make it, anyway. I really thought it would break down before this."

"I'd say nearly three hundred and fifty miles ain't too bad," Lance said.

"Wow, is that how far we've come?" Jason asked with wide eyes.

"That's about the size of it," I said. "There's a mile counter on the speed dial if you want to check it."

"Hey, there's the river!" Jason shouted, kicking his horse in the ribs and trotting off ahead.

We could see that the porters had already begun to cross in a line, holding their loads above their heads and wading in chest-high, with the short ones going in neck-deep. As we rode to the riverbank, Jason stood talking with Willie. Jason walked over to where he had tied his horse and pulled his rifle out of the scabbard. He then went back with Willie, who had his rifle at the ready, guarding the porters from any crocodile attacks.

We could hear the irritating hum as Chuck came motoring in behind us in the mechanical beast, and he ran it on ahead, skidding on the sandy beach. He set the brake, shut her down, and stood up behind the steering wheel, peering over the windshield.

"How are we going to get this thing across?" he asked.

"We're not," I said. "This is the end of the line for Old Betsy."

"Who?" Betty snapped.

"Betsy," I said.

"Who's Betsy?"

"Nobody. It's just a name for the car. Remember, Davy Crockett use to refer to his rifle as Old Betsy."

"Oh, all right then," she said, rolling her eyes.

"Are you sure we can't get her across?" Chuck asked. "I could look for a better place."

"This is the best place, and there is no way. See that big tree right there? That's where we're leaving her."

"That's fine with me," Chuck said. "But you know the natives will wreck it when they find it."

"We'll have to chance it," I said.

"For how long?"

"Three weeks," I said. "Maybe a month."

"Hey, it's your machine. But I'm warning you right now: they'll pull the mirrors off and any chrome they can dislodge. They'll flatten the tires and try to steal the seats."

"I got an idea," Jason said.

"What's that?" I asked.

"You know how superstitious they are about evil spirits? Well, I was thinking. Do you hear those crows upstream?"

"Yeah, what's your idea?" Lance asked with a furrowed brow.

"How about I take a shotgun up the river and collect some birds, and we'll hang 'em on strings in the branches all about where we park the car?"

"Nah ... won't work," Lance said, folding his arms across his chest.

"Ever tried it?" Betty asked.

"Don't have to," he answered. "Besides, those crows will see you coming a mile off, and they'll scatter to hell and gone. You'll never even get a shot at *one*."

"I'll get the shotgun," I said, kicking my horse in the ribs and trotting toward the mule cart, eager to have Jason prove him wrong. I heard Betty praising the kid for his brilliant idea.

The native teamster didn't have to dig very far to find the scatter gun, and Jason came alongside and took it from him, filling his pockets with shot shells.

"It won't work," Lance said as he tied his horse and threw in another of his two bits. "I'm telling you, even if you do get a crow, the natives are superstitious, but they'll see right through this."

"Don't be so sure," Chuck said. "I mean, I want to keep going on in the car. But if we have to leave it, we should do something to protect it."

"Wish me luck," Jason said.

Willie shouted to one of his men to accompany the kid.

"It's not like we can cover it up with a bunch of sticks and hide the darn thing," I said.

"Exactly," Chuck said. "Those natives are expert trackers. They'll follow the tire marks to a pile of sticks, and then they'll dismantle it piece by piece: the windshield, the headlamps. Whatever they can't get off they'll smash."

"I like Jason's idea," Betty said.

"Heck, you've seen 'em around dead stuff, Lance," I said. "I've seen them avoid it like the plague."

"Seems to me if there were dead things hanging all around it," Esther said, "there might be like an omen or something here. They have a strong belief in the spirits. That's why they live in round huts. Do you know why?"

"No," Betty said.

"Because they believe evil spirits like to hide in the corners," Esther said, "so they make their houses without them."

"That's funny," Betty said.

"They think we are just as strange," Esther said, "believe me. When I present the Gospel to them, they are shocked."

"What are the roots of their religion?" Betty asked.

"They believe that their god, *Ngai,* lives on Mount Kenya, and that he gave all the land to the first two people, and that all the other Kikuyu clans came from their children."

"Why do so many of the natives seem to follow Mohammad?" Betty asked.

"I think they can identify better with the Arab influence than with the Jewish tradition. There has been little or no Jewish influence here because the Arabs came here to capture and sell slaves. And it's possible Mohammad seems more contemporary than Jesus, and therefore more correct. They like the idea of a prophet, but this whole concept of God coming to earth in the form of a man is a difficult one for them. In the African world, spirits are everywhere: in people, trees, rivers, animals, rocks, mountains, and even personal effects and objects. They would see that car as being alive and running by the power of a spirit. They even believe that people can be possessed by evil spirits."

"If they are so convinced that a person can be possessed by an evil spirit," Betty said, "then why can't they grasp that a person could allow the Holy Spirit to come into their life?"

"I don't know," Esther said. "It seems like a natural jump to me. But there has been many an evangelist who has come up empty-handed in Africa, that's for sure."

We heard a series of shotgun blasts from upriver and stopped talking. Jason's horse flinched and pulled hard on its rope, which was tied off to a tree. I counted the shots as their reports came, five in total. Betty handed me her reins and dismounted quickly to calm his mare, when five more shots broke through the silence.

"Are you sure we can't get this tin can across the river?" Chuck asked.

"I'm afraid she would drown," I answered. "You saw those porters. They were up to their necks. As it is, we're going to get a little wet, but that car would get totally waterlogged."

"What about me?" Chuck asked. "I don't even have a horse."

"We've got you a horse," Betty said.

"Oh, great. The first time I get on my horse I have to take him across a river. How's that going to work? What a way to begin a relationship."

"You have to start somewhere," Betty said.

"I just don't need to get off on the wrong foot with him. How do you build trust with an animal when the first thing they know you for is a bad experience?"

"Okay, we'll go first so he doesn't think this whole thing was your idea," Lance said, and we all broke into laughter.

Chuck laughed along on the outside, but I knew how he felt on the inside. He had become much too attached to that machine, and even though we might have found a place to bring it across far upstream, I was content to leave it behind, if for no other reason than the noise factor. Besides, we were running low on fuel.

"Who said this would be a bad experience for a horse?" Betty said. "They don't mind getting wet."

Just then, Jason and the native came running with their hands full of dead crows.

"How many did you get?" I yelled.

"I got 'em!" he yelled back from about a hundred and fifty yards upstream.

"Looks like he showed me up," Lance said. "He's got five or six of them."

"Hey, the kid is quite a dead eye with that shotgun," I said. "What can we say? He's showed us all up."

"How many did you get?" Betty shouted, knowing that he hadn't heard me the first time.

"Eight! I got eight!" he yelled in an excited voice, gasping for breath and holding up his prizes in both hands, with his shotgun dangling off his shoulder by the leather sling. "I hit one more, but we lost him in the brush," he said with a grin as they plopped the crows at Lance's feet.

"Okay, kid, you proved me wrong," Lance said, folding his arms across his chest.

"Sure are dressed up pretty from the kind of crows I'm used to," Chuck said.

"They're called *pied crows*," I said. "They're related to the ones back home, except they have that white on their belly and their backs."

"So how'd you do it?" Chuck asked.

"When I snuck in on 'em, I picked out the lead bird."

"Oh, come on," Lance said. "How'd you know which one was the lead bird?"

"Just let him tell his story, Lance," Betty said, wrinkling her brow.

"Like I said, Lance, I've been watching flocks like this since I was a kid. These African crows are just like the ones back home. So I took a careful aim on the first shot, just to knock the lead crow down."

Lance rolled his eyes and smirked, and Betty glared at him.

"You see, I figured I didn't want to kill the lead bird, just wound him so he would make a lot of racket and all his buddies would come to his rescue. Well, anyway, it worked. On my first shot, he fell out of the tree, and instead of the flock flying off, he started screaming. They circled and came down to help him, and when they did, I let 'em have it. Even when I reloaded, they still kept hanging around."

"Okay," I said, ribbing him just to get a reaction, "but you shot ten rounds and only got eight birds."

"Okay, I missed one clean," he said in a quick defense. "And I knocked another one down that I couldn't find."

"Ah, I'm only kidding," I said. "That's incredible shooting. I don't know if I've ever even heard of anyone doing such a thing."

"Obviously not me," Lance said. "Heck, I was the guy who said you wouldn't even get one."

"We remember," Betty said with a smirk.

"Praise God," Esther said. "It was the Lord who allowed you to take them."

"I want to believe in your god," Jason said, "but it's going to take a miracle for me to believe."

"Ask, and it shall be given you; seek, and ye shall find; knock, and it shall be opened unto you," Esther said, quoting the book of Matthew.

Jason sobered up and paused long enough to consider the words Esther had spoken, apparently taking them to heart.

"Okay, Jason, what do you think?" I asked. "Where should we park this tin can, and how should we display your trophies?"

"That wide tree right there," he answered. "Pull it right under those high branches. We'll take the string, tie a rock on one end, and toss them over the branches."

"You better hang those high enough so the hyenas don't pick them off like cherries," Lance snapped. "And you better not hang any directly over the car, or else you'll have jackal traipsing from one end to the other trying to get a free meal. You'll wish the natives had taken a few trinkets off of it when you get back and find the hyenas and vultures have used it for an outhouse."

"Oh, Lance, for heaven's sake," Betty said.

"Don't you see?" he said. "Those dead birds are going to act like fish bait. I think it's a stupid idea."

"I never claimed to have all the answers," Jason said, throwing up his hands. "I was just trying to help."

"Okay, John, you're in charge," Lance said.

"Lance, don't turn this into a big deal," Betty insisted.

"I'm not. It's your car. Whatever you want to do is fine with me. Let's go, Esther. Are you ready?" Lance swung his leg up over his horse and grabbed the reins. "Let's get across the river while it's clear of crocs."

Esther followed suit and looked back at Betty, shrugging her shoulders and raising her eyebrows. Lance nudged his horse in the ribs, and Esther followed as the horses entered the river, kicking up water with their hooves.

"What's going on with him?" Jason asked.

"I don't know for sure," Betty said. "I think we're all tired, and I think we've had far too much togetherness. People just get edgy and irritable, that's all."

"Well," I said, "I still think the crows are a good idea. Here's some string, so let's start hanging them."

"Do you think we ought to hang 'em by the feet or by the neck?" Jason asked.

"What do you think?" Betty asked. "Hang them by the feet, and they might look like you killed 'em and put 'em there. But hang 'em by the neck, and they'll think they were caught alive and hung by the neck until they died."

"That makes sense," Chuck said. "It will obviously add more of a mystery to it."

"Also, it's like hanging a glass upside down," I said. "I think they would tend to believe the spirit is still present when it's tipped right-side up. It just might work. Not that I have ever heard of it being done before."

"If it works," Betty said, "you'll have an original idea to your credit."

"Not that you will ever be famous or make any money off of it," Chuck said with a laugh.

"No, but that's how people get rich," Betty said, "just like that. Some crazy idea that nobody has ever heard of before. It's called innovation."

"I predict that someday every home in America will have one of those things they call a radio," Jason said, "and families will huddle around them and listen to music and tell stories. And someday, they will even be able to send moving pictures to that radio through the air."

"Now that's a little farfetched, don't you think?" Chuck said, laughing in unison with Betty.

I had to chuckle along with them at the kid's crazy ideas, knowing that nothing could ever take the place of a good book.

"Hey, you laugh," Jason said, "but if I had any money, I would be putting it on radio."

"Maybe so," I said, "but I'm content to keep my money diversified in the sure bet of the American stock market. I'm not going to invest in somebody else's goofy dreams."

Jason got busy decorating the tree like Christmas had come to Africa, and Chuck positioned the car with precision so as not to make a platform for wild dogs.

"Besides," I said, "I don't think animals will be the problem. It's the natives we should be worried about.

"There," Jason said, stringing up the last of the dead crows. "How's that?"

"Looks morbid to me," Betty said.

"That's the whole idea," he said.

"It beats trying to push that waterlogged hulk across the river," I said, "and then having to fight to get it to light up again."

"No thanks," Chuck said. "There has been enough frustration on this trip without that headache."

"I'll take my chances that the natives don't get to it," I said. "The thought of whipping it like a drowned horse leaves me cold."

"Are you guys ready to cross?" Chuck asked, taking the reins of the horse that Willie had saddled up for him.

"Wow, how's that knee doing?" Betty asked.

"Pretty good."

"You look like an old pro up there," I said.

"I may look good now, but I can only imagine how my butt is going to feel after a couple of days of this."

"Just keep your humor about you," I said. "We don't need two cranky people in our midst."

"I'll give it my best shot."

"I think I'm going to take my boots off," Jason said. "I hate the thought of wet feet all day."

"Let's just go," Betty insisted. "We'll all have wet feet. At least you'll be in good company."

As she led the way into the river, our horses waded in up to their bellies, which put us knee-deep in the water. Jason lifted his feet above the water and balanced on his saddle, trying to avoid the water.

"Think you're pretty smart there," Betty said.

Jason began to laugh. Then his butt slipped, and he grabbed the saddle horn, catching himself just before going into the river head first. He sat up straight and dipped his feet in the water, catching the stirrups and clinging to his horse.

"Hey, Jason," I warned, "you need to take that rifle out of your scabbard before it gets wet."

I looked upstream and saw that our porters were unloading the wagons onto a log raft that had been built and attached to a long rope, with a group of men waiting to pull it across.

"That's quite a project they've got going up there," Chuck said.

"Yep," I responded, "Willie sent men ahead two days ago."

The water soaked through to my toes, and the temperature felt soothing to my legs and feet. Gun Smoke seemed to like the water, too, and I saw him drinking as we crossed. The sound of the horses moving through the gentle water, the afternoon sun hanging high overhead, a quiet breeze moving the fresh air downstream—*serenity* seemed to be the only word that could properly describe the moment.

Suddenly, without warning, the mood changed. Like the devil himself, this prehistoric menace shaped in the form of a twelve-foot crocodile came out of nowhere.

"Jason, look out!" I yelled as the croc's head emerged with open jaws, aiming straight for Jason's leg.

In one fluid motion, I unsnapped my forty-four Colt, drew, and cocked the hammer back. It reminded me of the old days, when a man had been caught cheating at cards and went for his gun. I raised the pistol up to eye level and focused on the front sight.

Jason jerked his leg, but too little too late. The croc snapped, attaching himself to Jason's boot. Jason winced, grabbing the horn on his saddle with his free hand, and tried to reach the bolt on his rifle, which was cradled in his armpit. His eyes were as wide as his horse's.

I had but one chance for a head shot on the croc, which meant hitting a brain the size of a chestnut. *If only this horse can remain steady and calm.* I knew if I missed, that thing would begin spinning like a top to twist his prey, and Jason would be ripped off his horse by the force and chomped and killed.

After giving a little pull back on the reins with my left hand to hold Gun Smoke steady, I dropped them and took a steady aim, gripping the pistol with both hands.

Jason started to squirm to pull his foot free.

Jason, hold steady, I thought as I held the front sight midway between his eye and the ear hole. I needed to punch the brain. Knowing every second counted, I squeezed the trigger.

The report from the Magnum round spoke with authority and bucked under my grip. Then—*smack!*—went the big round-nose lead as it punched the croc's skull.

Gun Smoke flinched, and the croc reared back with his mouth wide open, releasing Jason's foot from the vice.

Smoke rose from the barrel of my gun as I held steady, pulling the hammer back, waiting for a follow-up shot. Betty screamed, Jason jumped, pulling his foot away, and Chuck's horse reared back. Chuck lost his grip and went splashing into the river on his back, disappearing under the surface.

And the croc ... well, the croc rolled over belly-up, stone-cold dead, with blood oozing from his nostrils and turning the river red. Then he sank out of sight.

Chuck came up spitting water, soaking wet, his hair matted against his face.

No one spoke. We were too stunned at what had just happened.

"Let's get to shore before we get hit again!" Betty shouted. "Let's go! *Let's go!*" she yelled, kicking her horse in the ribs with her feet under the water and making a swift get away.

"You need help?" I asked as Chuck hobbled in the water shoulder-deep, trying to get back on his horse.

"No, I got it," he said, dragging himself back on.

Betty led the way, and we all followed suit. In the forefront of everyone's mind, I was sure, loomed the possibility that Jason's foot had been crushed or badly damaged by the teeth of the crocodile. They were also probably thinking about what an incredible shot I was with that forty-four, and how I had just saved the kid's life.

Then I realized that whatever happened, our God was in charge. I remembered Esther saying that not one small sparrow fell to the ground outside of the Father's will. So I prayed silently:

Dear Lord, I know I am not worthy of asking, but I know now that you are my father, and so I feel that as a son I can ask and you will hear me. And so, Father, that your glory might be revealed to my son, Jason, I pray that his foot would not be injured and that he would see your hand at work in his life. You said, Lord, that whatever we ask in your name will be given. So by faith, Lord, I claim it, and I ask you now so that my son might come to know you. In the name of your precious and Holy Son, Jesus Christ, I pray for this miracle. Amen.

"Hey, are you okay?" Betty asked with a look of concern as we approached the shore.

"I'm okay," I answered.

"What are you trying to do—get some sleep on your horse?"

"No, I was praying for Jason's foot."

Jason looked back over his shoulder, wrinkling his brow. "Too late for that," he said. "He got me good."

His horse rose up out of the water as we reached the bank, and Jason slipped his rifle back into the scabbard. I focused on his boot and the gaping holes in the leather. Betty bounded from Luke, and her feet hit the beach as she dropped her reins, running to help Jason off his saddle.

"Let's get you down and have a look at that foot," she said.

"I don't want to look. I know it's gonna be bad," he said as he hobbled off his horse and sat down in the sand, while Betty went to work on his bootlaces.

She pulled them free and gently tugged on the boot. Jason gritted his teeth as she took hold of the heel and peeled the wet boot off the woolen sock. He rolled his ankle and wiggled his toes, and I reached in to roll the wet sock off his foot, revealing clean skin without even a scratch.

"Wow!" he exclaimed. "How did that happen? He never even touched me."

"Aren't you glad I told you to keep your boots on now?" Betty asked.

"Yeah, but look at my boot. It's ruined."

"We've got plenty of boots," Betty said with a sigh of relief.

"But those were my favorite boots. I just hate the thought of breaking in a new pair."

"Jason, look at your foot, not your boot!" Betty said.

"You're right. Hey, John, you saw that croc. He had me dead to rights with a full mouth grip. I was a second away from being ripped off my horse and being devoured by that monster. I saw the bite, and I knew that even though you might kill him, my foot was in trouble. But you prayed, didn't you? I could have sworn that croc got me." Jason paused and then looked up. "You don't think ..."

"It's not important what I think," I answered, "because I already know. But what do you think, Jason?"

"I think you are a darn good shot with that forty-four," he said, "but other than that, I don't know what to think. I wanted to believe, and I don't know why, but something stopped me. I mean, I guess I believed there was a god, but I always thought he was so big and powerful that he wouldn't have time for me until just now."

"I wish Esther had been here to see this," Betty said, clutching Jason's bare foot in her hands.

"I saw God do a miracle with you, John," Jason said. "I saw it with my own eyes, but now I see with my heart. You know, after Esther quoted that Scripture, I prayed that somehow God would reveal Himself to me. It's just different when it happens to you, isn't it?"

"Oh, please," Chuck said, sitting high on his horse. "The croc just missed the kid's foot, that's all." He tossed a coin into the air, and it landed in the dirt next to us. "Just because you called tails doesn't make it a miracle."

"That's right," Betty said. "It only makes it a miracle if you believe that God made it land tails."

I reached down and picked up the coin, which was showing tails.

"You'll never convince me, John," Chuck said. "You'll never convince me there is some invisible force lurking behind what we can see, controlling every outcome."

"I'm not going to try to convince you," I said. "This is your life, and you can do with it whatever you want to. If you can't see the work of God all around you, you are fooling yourself. How do you think all this creation got here?"

"Ah, John, it's all foolishness. Look here. It's me, John."

"That's the point, Chuck. Remember, it's me, too—your old buddy John. The same old guy who laughed at God my whole life."

"I remember," he said with a groan, "and that's why I know that you'll snap out of this. I think you just got scared to death when that lion took you. One of these mornings you're going to wake up, and everything will be back to normal again."

"Maybe so, Chuck, but I don't think so. There is no going back once you have seen the light. I never once heard of anybody turning their life around after finding atheism."

Betty and Jason began speaking to each other softly as Chuck and I continued our vigorous discourse.

"Something just wasn't adding up for me, Chuck. The more I wanted to prove Darwinism, the more obstacles I found. It's like he came up with a theory that seems to make sense if there is no God, and now everyone is scurrying around trying to prove it. Heck, you know all the evidence that disproves anything Darwin said has been brushed under the carpet, and then we bring forth everything that supports it. What kind of science is that? But now, for the first time in my life, everything makes sense."

"Oh yeah? How?" he asked, folding his arms.

"Just take a look around us," I said. "Everything you see has been created by God and left behind as a footprint of His existence. In fact, when you think about it, it's really all overkill so that man would be without an excuse. Here, I just read this passage yesterday," I said, pulling my Bible from my saddlebag and fumbling to find the book of Romans. "Yeah, here it is. Chapter one, verse twenty. Listen to this: *For the invisible things of him from the creation of the world are clearly seen, being understood by the things that are made, even his eternal power and Godhead; so that they are without excuse.*"

"I just don't understand how you could have abandoned everything you believed in," Chuck said. "What happened to you out there, John? I don't see how you could have changed so much in just a couple of days."

"You want to look at my arm again?" I asked. "It's easy when you die and come back alive spiritually. I can't explain it. It's nothing I thought of or decided to do on my own, but it was something that happened to me. Esther calls it the grace of God and the power of the Holy Ghost."

"Oh great, so now you believe in ghosts, do you? John, you didn't die. That lion didn't kill you. Wake up. I want my friend back."

"What you see is what you get," I said. "I can't make any excuses for God or for what He decides to do. That's as absurd as the hyena complaining that he wasn't born a lion."

"This whole conversation is absurd. All I can say is that I've lived a good life. I've never killed anyone. I've tried to be a good person. And I don't think that, if there is a god, he would send me to hell just because I don't happen to believe a certain way. Heck, what about all these natives? They don't believe in Christ. Does that mean they're all going to hell, too?"

"Look, Chuck, that's between them and God. If that works for you and you're okay with what you believe, then that's your business. No one is forcing anything down your throat, are they?"

"Well, no, I guess not," he admitted.

"You're just betting your life that your point of view is all right," I said. "I myself am betting my life on Christ, who died on a cross, rose from the dead, and said that if a man believes in Him, he will never die. He never once said, live a good life and you will live forever. He said, take up your cross and follow me."

"But what about those people who never heard about Christ? What about them?"

"It's not as much about them and God as it is about you and God. If you feel so strongly about them that someone needs to tell them, then maybe that someone is you."

Chuck laughed. "Right."

"God won't force Himself on anyone," I continued. "We live in this world with free will, free to make our life anything we want to. If we reject God, that is our business. But if a man rejects God his whole life, then God will respect his wishes."

"Hey, let's get that croc out of the river," Chuck said, conveniently changing the subject.

"What would you do with him?" I asked.

"How about a pair of cowboy boots?" Jason asked.

"Or maybe a handbag," Betty said.

I looked out the corner of my eye and saw Willie wading across the river. He was holding his rifle over his head and making his way to our side of the river.

"He's big enough," I said with a laugh, "you could make a coffin out of him."

"Yeah, he was almost *my* coffin," Jason said.

"You'll never get him. He sank like a rock."

Just then, the water began to boil, and several crocs began thrashing in the water as they pulled his carcass apart. In a matter of seconds, the crocs were feeding on him like a pack of hyenas.

"Nature sure has a way of taking care of its own," Betty said.

Jason got to his feet with one bare foot in the sand.

"You are one lucky dude there," Chuck said.

I wanted so desperately to correct him and explain again that there was no such thing as luck, but I knew that would just lead back to our argument. Anyway, our conversations about God were taking us nowhere at the moment. I knew from all my years of experience that trying to convince a religious person that the theory of evolution made sense was impossible. I could see now that the same could be said in reverse. Salvation had to be the work of God. Only He could awaken a man's soul. God did it this way so that no one could ever take the credit for someone else's salvation. Not that I wouldn't continue to speak my mind, but arguments were worthless. I doubted anyone had ever been argued into heaven. Esther was right: one had to wait for teachable moments, and otherwise just seek God and live by faith. It amazed me to think this way, because for so many years I had kept God at bay. Now to embrace Him seemed so foreign to me.

As Betty rode off toward the men loading the wagons, Willie came ashore, dripping wet. "Did he get you?" he asked.

"Not a scratch," I said.

"One more miracle," Chuck said, rolling his eyes and mocking me.

"Isn't that Temba and his scouts?" Jason asked, pointing toward the tree line.

"They'll have news," Willie said. He picked up the torn boot from the sand and frowned while he inspected the damage. "Not even scratch?"

"It's just like Chuck said," I explained, rubbing his nose in his own comment.

Then Temba and some of his scouts arrived and began to give Willie a report in Swahili.

The foothills of Mount Kenya rose in the distance, and we could see dense forests looming ahead. I had been in forest country like this before. Thick groves of tall papyrus stood in a dense jungle, laced together with creepers, clumps of thorn brush, endless patches of thick bamboo, and tangled masses of climbing morning glories. Screaming monkeys flying overhead would sound the alarm of an approaching man, as would flocks of birds of every color, size, and shape, some with elaborate songs and others with simple whistles.

Betty galloped back to us while holding a new pair of boots by the laces. She tossed them at Jason's feet, and he sat in the sand and went to work putting them on. "I got you some dry socks, too," she said, tossing them in his lap.

"Don't you think this boot is patchable?" Jason asked as he pulled on the dry socks and began to lace up the new boots.

"You must be kidding," I said, getting a chuckle out of the gaping hole ripped in the toe. A big patch of leather was missing from the side.

"I'm kidding," he said, getting to his feet. He snatched up the torn boot and began swinging it over his head by the laces.

"Hey, are you sure you don't want to keep it as a souvenir?" Chuck said.

"Nah," Jason said, "I don't need to be reminded about almost being eaten." Then he gave it a fling, watching it as it flew out over the water and splashed into the river. "At least I have one left. Those were my favorite boots."

One of the men standing with Willie bolted toward the river, and we all jerked our heads in his direction.

"*Basi* (stop)! *Basi!*" Willie shouted as the scout waded out and grabbed the boot.

The man paddled with his hands, holding the boot laces in his teeth, and made haste toward the shore, watching over his shoulder as he swam.

"Oops," Jason said with a sheepish grin. "I guess I never thought someone else might want that boot."

"Willie," I said, "what does Temba have to report?"

"Good report," he answered. "You tell them, Temba."

"*Tembo* (elephants) smash *kikuyu shambas* (crops) at *usiku* (night). *Tembo* hide in *magugu* (jungle) all day. *Kibwana* (prince) in *chengo* (village) make *utashi*."

"*Utashi*," I repeated. "That means urgent request."

"Yes, Bwana," Temba said. "Him make utashi to kill tembo."

"How far away is it?" I asked.

Temba wrinkled his nose and looked toward Willie, who hesitated. I knew Willie, instead of jumping in yet again to help us communicate, wanted to let us figure it out between us.

"Uh, let's see," I said, struggling to think of the words. "*Masafa* (measure of distance) *chengo* (village)?"

"Chengo two hours, Bwana," Temba said.

"Let's ride," I said, fetching my horse and climbing into the saddle.

Jason handed his other boot to the native, who stood on the sandy shore soaking wet with the torn one. The native grinned ear to ear with his white straight teeth as he took it from Jason, putting his hands together and bowing low, showing his gratitude.

"You made his day," Chuck said with a laugh as Jason sprinted for his horse.

Willie motioned to his men, and they trotted off to catch up to his porters.

"I bet he'll beat us to that village, won't he?" Jason said, climbing into his saddle.

"Yeah, he is one tough hombre," I answered.

"When I get to camp every night," Chuck said, "I am bushed just from riding in that Ford all day. But that man has been jogging and walking all day, and he's still barking orders well into the evening."

"Yep, and he'll be up before us in the morning," I said, "and he'll do it all again the next day. That's why Lance was so happy to get him."

Jason nudged his horse in the ribs, and we all followed suit.

Michael D. Neil

Chapter 27

A BAD TASTE

W e rode on for the next two hours along the edge of the foot-hills, where Samburu huts dotted the landscape. We saw dozens of small farm plots called *shambas*, where the major crop was millet and corn. Lance and Esther had ridden ahead of us, and I fully expected to find them waiting along the way. Our line of porters stretched out several hundred yards, and in the sparse timber and sometimes thick bush, we couldn't see the front. I assumed that Willie had caught up to them by now and he would be leading the pack.

We encountered several native men, who were naked save for a blanket slung over the shoulder. They greeted us and gave us encouragement to continue on to their main village. As we approached it, we could hear drumming. Then, as we crested a knoll, we saw that they were having a festival, with literally hundreds of native men dancing to the drums.

We felt like a liberating army as we entered the encampment. The men carried bright shields made from what looked like rhino hide, but with all those shields, there wouldn't have been a rhino left alive in all of Africa. Some or most of them had to be made from buffalo. The men's bodies and faces were painted brilliant red and yellow in bold patterns. A long spear glistened in each man's right hand, and I could sense a great chain of command among their ranks: sergeants, lieutenants, captains, and generals. They wore beads, brass armbands, and anklets, and a small number of the very privileged wore headdresses of lion mane and white plumes from the Colobus monkey. The drums thundered as columns of men jumped like spring bucks, chanting in unison in their war tones.

Their prince, who looked like he had only been on the earth for about fourteen years, greeted us with his entourage. He no doubt intended to spur us on to victory over the nighttime invaders who threatened the stability of his community by taking food from the mouth of his citizens. We dismounted to honor him, and when he raised his hands, the drums fell silent, the dancing stopped, and a hush fell over the army of warriors. Then a thousand eyes stared at us. Women, children, and men young and old waited in silence.

As we had predicted, Willie had beaten us to the celebration. Now he was ready to translate the prince's greeting and proposal.

Jason looked around with a wrinkled brow. "Where are Esther and Lance?"

Betty looked around as well and shrugged her shoulders.

The prince began his speech, which seemed eloquent, but totally incomprehensible.

Willie listened intently, then turned to translate. "The prince say every night the raids begin, and he hope that our guns will kill tembo. He hope that we can kill all, but he hope, too, we frighten so will go away."

"Where is their king?" Betty asked. "Why have they sent this boy?"

"Oh, no, memsahib, is not good to ask," Willie said, shaking his head. "This boy has much power, but if king sick, the village never tell to outsider and make them look like weakness. But maybe them size you and not give you the pleasing of a king greeting. So king send warriors to dance to show power and send prince to keep you small."

"Well, I can see that," Betty said, "but if their king is ill, we could give them some medicine."

"You make them hurt feeling," Willie said.

"How?" she asked.

"Them no want you medicine," he said. "Them will think you need witchdoctor, because you medicine not drive out evil spirits that is caused for sickness. Great pride in witchdoctor, and you to offer medicine hurt this pride." Willie returned his attention to the prince, who resumed his speech.

As I studied the crowd of natives, I could see them listening intently to his every word.

"Prince Eakarro say them prepare a great feast in honor for you, and to stir in you courage to kill all tembo."

"Well, I would like to oblige him," I said. "But you know we only have permits for five elephants, and I prefer to kill only bulls. My guess is that there are no bulls here at all, and just a bunch of cows and yearlings. It doesn't take very many elephants to make a mess out of a farm plot."

Willie told the prince about our government permits, and the prince responded intensely, as if he were arguing. Willie laughed, and then the prince joined him in laughter.

"What's so funny?" I asked.

"Prince Eakarro say, 'Permit? We don't need no stinking permit.' Him say government approve slaughter if tembo threaten village."

"Is he right?" I asked.

"He is," Willie said.

"I'm just not so sure we can deliver what he thinks we can," I said.

"We'd probably have to kill thirty elephants to make a dent," Chuck said.

"Well, that ain't going to happen," I said.

The prince turned to his subjects and lifted his staff, and the natives all dropped to a knee. We and the prince were the only ones left standing. He began rattling off more words I couldn't understand, and Willie nodded and then dropped to a knee. He looked back and waved his hand, and we all dropped as well, except for Chuck, who sat to keep his bad knee straight.

"What's going on?" I whispered.

Willie put his finger to his lips and squinted at me. He whispered, forming the word prominently with his lips, "Blessing."

The prince stood with his staff held high and delivered the blessing. *What confidence for such a young boy!* I thought. He finished, then lowered his staff, and the natives all rose, cheering and chanting. The drums resumed, and the warriors started dancing again.

"He give you blessing," Willie said over the sound of the drums, "so that when you kill many tembo it be by his power."

"Quite impressive," Chuck said. "What just happened?"

"If we kill any elephants," I explained, "it will be because of his power, and not our hunting skills or our rifles. All of his people will be singing his praises for our success."

"Are you okay with that?" Jason asked.

"I'm fine with it," I said, "unless you want to tell the Samburu masses that it's you and not their prince. Even if you could, they wouldn't believe you, anyway. Personally, I'm content to take the humble posture."

Jason climbed onto his horse and shaded his eyes with his hand, looking left and right. "Here they come, Mom. Let's go see Esther and tell her about the croc. I just gotta tell her."

Betty turned to me and mouthed the words, "He called me Mom." She put her hand over her heart and climbed onto Luke, grinning widely.

"Meet us in the main village!" I called after them as they trotted off together.

Chuck and I followed the prince and his generals to the village, where we could smell goats being roasted over a fire. Women came out of their huts as we went by and stared at the strange sight. They looked like me the first time I'd witnessed a flying machine.

"Good thing we left our Ford across the river," I said. "They might have all run off."

"Guess they don't have many visitors here," Chuck said.

"They have seen plenty of whites here before," I said. "We can't be that odd."

I looked back to Jason and Betty being followed by Lance and Esther as they rode to catch up to us. Native women and children continued to appear and stare at us as if they'd never seen anything like us before. As the prince led our entourage, groups of women began to congregate, speaking jubilantly and gazing in awe. Then some men joined them and pointed, and I looked back and saw that Esther appeared to be the main attraction.

"They have never seen a woman with their color of skin riding on a horse," I said.

"Do you think that's it?" Esther asked.

"I know that's it," I said. "You're the talk of the town."

~~~~~~~~~~

That evening, we feasted on Samburu cuisine, such as it was. The women brought in the pots of food, while the male leaders of the tribe washed their hands in a common bowl of warm water.

"It is rude not to wash first," Willie said as the bowl was passed to him.

I had asked Willie to join us to help translate our dinner conversations.

"Apparently, it is considered very rude not to wash before eating because we will be eating with our fingers," Esther said.

They served a delight called *ugali na sukuma wiki,* which was a stiff dough made out of maize, or white corn flower, followed by *sukuma wiki,* which was similar to collard greens and boiled with tomatoes, onions, and roasted goat.

"This goat is a rare treat," I said, taking a bite. "Not served rare, but well done. But served rare ... uh, seldom—I mean, not rare."

Jason started to laugh, and the others joined in.

"What I mean to say is that Samburu very seldom eat meat because their goats are much more valuable to them for milk than for meat. It's what they use for currency here. It would be like us eating money."

"This must be quite a special occasion for them," Betty said, rolling her eyes to the others and obviously hoping I wouldn't notice.

Jason dug a coin out of his pocket and put it between his teeth.

"Yeah, careful, smarty," Betty warned. "Don't choke on that thing."

I knew some of their language and could pick up bits and pieces of the native conversation, but speaking quickly as they did made it impossible to follow. I felt at ease, as if we had won their confidence to a certain extent. But I was still curious about their king.

"Can you ask them about their king, Willie?" I asked.

"Is not important right now," he answered.

"But I want to know."

"They don't tell," he said.

"Why not?" I asked.

"Okay, Bwana, just for you I ask."

481

Willie said something in their language, and the faces of the men turned cold. Prince Eakarro answered him with wild hand gestures, making what looked like lame excuses. I had always been able to pick out a truth or lie in any language, because men's faces all spoke the same.

"He say king leave on journey and them wait him return."

"Does that mean that he died?" I asked.

"If he died, or even if he is sick," Lance said, "that could still mean he is on a journey."

"Now Bwana, you see?" Willie said. "Them not tell. Not want other tribes find them with no king or if he much sick. It same that I explain."

"They must have great respect for their king," Chuck said, "to allow this kid to command their armies. That's all I have to say."

~~~~~~~~~~

Our men had set up camp just outside of the village, and after dinner we geared up for a night hunt. The elephants apparently had been coming out of the jungle every night to raid the farmlands. The natives had driven them off with torches and drums, but plenty of their men had been killed trying to challenge angry elephants in the dark. We had decided not to wait another night, so we set up for their arrival, hoping to put the spotlight on them with our artificial torch. But would the elephants realize something was awry and fail to show?

As we sat patiently in the darkness, my eyes were heavy, and I had to fight to stay awake. The elephants talked back and forth, breaking the silence of the night, and it felt like they were right on top of us.

"My goodness," Betty said, "don't these critters need some sleep? I know I do."

"I know," I said. "I'm beat. I can hardly hold my eyes open."

"What time is it?" Jason asked.

"Why?" I responded.

"I just want to know if it's past midnight," he said.

I reached into my pocket and pulled out a matchbook, which I struck to illuminate my watch. "It's just after midnight ... ten after."

"Wow," Jason said.

"Yeah, wow," Betty said. "It's really late."

"No, I'm really old," Jason said.

"It's your birthday!" Betty said in a loud whisper.

"Today?" I said. "Jason, I totally forgot. You're sixteen today."

"I didn't forget," Betty whispered. "I wanted to surprise you. I have something for you back at camp."

"What is it?" he asked.

"You'll see," she insisted. "You'll just have to wait."

Just then, we heard the brush begin to crack along the edge of the jungle, about two hundred yards from the farm plot.

"Pardon me if I don't sing," I whispered. "Listen."

In the darkness I could just make out an elephant stepping out and making a run for the farmer's goodies. One of the Samburu men started jabbering and pointing.

"Shush!" I ordered. "Shut him up."

Willie turned and grabbed the man, and he fell silent.

"I told you we shouldn't have brought any natives out here," I said.

"But him own shamba, Bwana."

I didn't have to respond. I just shook my head in the darkness. Night vision was something you could acquire over time as you trained your eyes to collect light. I had always felt I could see better under low light conditions than most people. Tonight, a cloud cover had moved in and blanketed the night sky, making it extremely dark. The trick was that you never wanted to look directly at the object you were trying to see. Instead, you moved your eyes just to the left or to the right of it. I didn't know why it worked. But it did.

"Can you see it?" Betty whispered.

"Yeah, it's a cow," I answered, "and here come two more."

"Where?"

"Two hundred yards, straight out." I pointed so Betty could see them.

"How do you know it's a cow?" she asked.

"Because she's got a calf with her," I explained, "and the other two are young: probably her older children."

"I can't see a thing," Jason said. "Where are you looking?"

"Shh! You just hold the light," I ordered. "Here comes another one. Maybe this is the bull. Get that torch ready."

"Is it a bull?" Betty whispered.

"Yeah, here he comes," I whispered.

The elephants all stopped, ears up. More elephants arrived, and then the growing band continued in our direction. A breeze blew in our faces ever so gently, muting their powerful sense of smell. They continued on unexpectedly as we hunkered down with our rifles at the ready. When they were no more than fifty yards out, I tapped Jason on the shoulder to hit them with the light. I had actually never aimed an artificial light at elephants at night, and I didn't know what to expect. Plains game would freeze solid, blinded by it, but I didn't think elephants would be as apt to. They really weren't afraid of running into anything; they could just run over it.

Jason hit the light, and the whole area lit up. The elephants stopped in front of us, looking surprised, as if someone had just turned on the day.

The bull raised his trunk in defiance and held his ground, looking quite intimidating, confident he had the power to frighten men. Shooting him seemed more like murder than hunting at this point. To many people, turkey shooting was very exciting. But to me, I needed some element of fair chase. I knew I would have to shoot him, but I wasn't too excited about it. This wasn't one of the old bulls we were looking for. He was mature, but not a trophy by any means. This would have to be a mercy killing to protect the villagers—not the sort of hunting I had come to Africa for, that was for sure.

We had already planned that Chuck would take the shot on the bull. It was safe to say this was a younger bull, because the bigger mature bulls didn't hang out with women. We had decided to kill the lead cow, not the one with the calf but the herd matriarch, to disrupt them and make them want to leave. We had to do something to change their feeding habits, and a murder in their ranks, taking out the two leaders of the clan, would certainly take care of the situation.

Elephants seemed very sensitive when it came to the death of friends or family. I had witnessed it personally. When they came to a kill site of a fallen comrade, they often caressed the bones of the loved one. It was as if they were remembering the dead and grieving over the remains. I had heard it said that elephants would avoid places where their family members had gone down.

My train of thought was broken when Chuck lifted his rifle to his shoulder. I wanted to instruct him about where to shoot, but then I hesitated, fearful that I might insult his intelligence. Yet we were in a very tenuous position here. If he were to wound this animal and just make him mad, one or more of us could die.

I leaned over and whispered in his ear, "Remember the brain shot."

We had agreed earlier for Lance to take the lead cow, and I was confident in his ability to pick her out and put her down. But in these tense seconds, all kinds of scenarios raced through my head. The worst case was always good to expect and plan for, but this plan I felt hadn't been laid out sufficiently to any degree.

"If this young bruiser decides to charge us, he could just run for the light," I cautioned.

I brought my five hundred double up to my shoulder. It did seem that very few of these African animals took kindly to the thought of being killed, and if you gave them half a chance, they would try to take you with them.

I had schooled my companions on the preference of a brain shot; however, the skull of the elephant was tricky, and angles were everything. Penetration was not always a sure bet, and hitting this ten-pound loaf of bread deeply encased in heavy armor was risky. If you scored the hit, you had done both the beast and yourself a tremendous service. But if you missed the mark, you left yourself open to a dreadful attack. Even with the heavy five hundred nitro, a brain shot was uncertain. On the cow, I had suggested a heart shot. But on the bull, who I knew would charge if given half a chance, I had recommended the skull shot at this range. I would be at the ready with my British double to back up Chuck, just in case he were to miss the mark.

"What are you waiting for?" I whispered.

The bull stood just fifty yards downrange. I trained the barrel of my heavy rifle just in front of the beast's ear canal, halfway between the bull's eye and his ear.

Both shots rang out in rapid succession, piercing the night with a belching of fire that lit up the field like a flash from a photographer. The bull flinched, and the cows turned and ran across the field into the darkness. He lifted his trunk and trumpeted, sending a shiver up my spine. His ears opened and he stepped toward us, and I let him have it with my own thunder stick, putting my bullet in the frontal brain region.

The rifle barked, and the bullet smacked against the bull. The light caught the cloud of smoke, obstructing my view, but as I recovered from the recoil, I saw the bruiser's knees buckle. And then down he came, like a ton of bricks that shook the ground when he hit. The cows crashed through the heavy jungle at the edge of the shamba, sounding like a runaway freight train before the noise finally subsided.

The native farmers erupted in cheers and dancing, like a dog whose master had just unclipped its lead.

"Willie, tell them to hush," I insisted. "We don't know if this is over yet!"

Willie barked at them, and they went silent as we trained our ears toward any sounds of danger. Jason continued to hold the light, which was turning amber as the juice in the battery drained.

"Is he dead?" Chuck asked.

"No," I said, "he is still taking breath. Listen."

We could hear wheezing, but not from the bull. Jason shined the light on him, and we could see that he laid stone-cold dead just forty yards away. Obviously, a dead-on hit to the vital spot in his head had done him in.

"Cut the light," I said as I realized it might be easier to see without it.

Everything went black, and it took half a minute or so for my eyes to adjust once again to the low light generated by the overcast sky. I could see a bump lying in the middle of the field, a hundred yards or so straight away.

"She is down, but not out," I said.

"Now it's time to end her misery," Lance said.

"Wait here," I said to the others.

I opened my breech and replaced the empty casing with a loaded round. Lance and I advanced past the dead bull and toward the mound lying helplessly in the dark.

"Can you see her?" I asked.

"I can just barely make her out," he answered.

We could hear her fighting for her breath, and then she let loose a moan like I had never heard before. I felt a lump in my throat, knowing we had just mortally wounded somebody's mother. We approached cautiously, even though she appeared to be down hard. Obviously, an elephant wasn't going to jump to its feet and tromp you, but that didn't mean another elephant wouldn't come out of the darkness to defend her.

"I really don't like this," I said.

"What?" answered Lance. "Do you think she is still a threat?"

"No, I just hate killing cow elephants."

"Yeah, me, too."

"No, you don't understand," I said. "I *really* hate this. Will you finish her off quickly, please? That wheezing is getting to me."

I could see Jason's light throwing shadows across the field as they looked over the dead bull. Lance raised his rifle.

"Make it clean," I said just before he let go the round from fifteen yards away.

The flash and the report were blinding and deafening.

"Wow!" I said as the roar of his gun echoed through the foothills. I could feel my ears ringing. "That can't be good for your ears."

"I think that did it," he said.

The old girl lay silent, stone-cold dead in the blackness of the night. Light dew had begun to form in the grass, and I could feel the dampness in my feet.

"That does it," I said. "We aren't doing that again. We'll leave these animals to the villagers, and they can do with them what they want. I would sooner just forget this whole incident, and tomorrow we'll go after bachelor bulls and leave the women and children alone."

"We'll be heroes tomorrow in the village," Lance said.

"I suppose, but that still won't make me feel good about it. Let's go find our tents. I'm spent."

We returned to the others and found Jason sporting a grin from ear to ear.

"Wow," he said. "What a hunt, eh?"

"No, Jason," I scolded, "not hardly. That was a terrible hunt, and nothing to be proud of. I feel like we just shot an unarmed woman on a street corner."

"Oh, John, it can't be that bad," Betty said. "These elephants aren't exactly that innocent, you know."

"I know, I'm just not proud of what we had to do, that's all. Blaney Percival is a personal friend of mine, and I'm not sure he would approve."

"We saved a village," Esther said.

"I suppose that's the way to look at it," I said. "I'm just not a fan of spotlighting."

"Look, it's going to be light in a few hours," Lance said. "I think we should get some sleep while we can."

"What about the elephants?" Jason asked.

"As always, we'll let the natives handle them," I said. "The sun will be up in a few hours, and they will reduce both of these elephants to dried meat strips hanging off everything they can find."

When my head hit the pillow, my body said *sleep*, but my heart was sick and my eyelids felt like they were spring-loaded. Discouragement and exhaustion mixed to bring me to a new low. I had failed myself and God. I had gone against everything I believed and everything I stood for. For the first time on this safari, I wanted to turn around and go home to Chicago. I tossed and turned all night, or what there was of it, before light from the rising sun began to invade our tent. I knew that no one in our party would be awake for hours, but trying to sleep for me had become a waste of time. I could only imagine what sort of reception we would get from the villagers this time.

I patted Betty on her rear end and leaned over and kissed her ear. Her hair smelled intoxicating, and memories of all the years together flashed in my mind. A joy filled me from the inside out, and I took peace knowing I had been faithful to her even when I had stood on the edge of infidelity years ago. Not that this made me clean in the eyes of God or better than anyone else who had failed the test. It was just something for me and me alone to enjoy, like a gift from God. I could take no pride in thinking that I had done it, because it was God all along who had given me the strength to resist. I just hadn't known Him then. He had been raising me up all along for some great purpose, although even now I had no clue what He had in mind. All I could do was learn and grow in my faith.

I stepped out of the tent to see the eastern sky lit up crimson red. The mountains rose majestically above the jungle floor. It never seemed to matter how early I emerged from my tent; Willie always beat me. I was beginning to wonder if the man slept at all. Still, this morning I felt thankful because he had coffee brewing over the campfire. As I joined him, he poured a cup of his steaming brew.

If our plan was to shoot a trophy bull elephant, we had probably just successfully driven every elephant within ten miles of this place deep into the jungle.

"What's our best bet for a trophy bull now?" I asked.

"Temba and Janga be back today to tell if they find tembo."

"But if they don't come in today, I want to get started on a hunt. This is elephant country, and we'll find them. I don't need to wait for them."

"No, Bwana, we need wait. They come. You see. Temba put herd to bed, and they come quick now to tell."

"I guess I'm in no hurry, really. The rest of the clan won't even stir for a couple of hours."

"Them sleepy bunch," Willie said and laughed.

"Everybody needs their rest, including you. Somebody will just end up getting hurt or sick if we don't rest."

"I hear sound from elephant far up valley in night. They will hear, too, and we find. Is not easy to hunt. Bulls run in jungle and hide in thickets. Very hard to find."

"I know. We've hunted there before," I said. "But then, that's a hunt as far as I'm concerned, unlike last night's fiasco."

"Fiasco?" Willie asked, stumbling on the word. "What is that?"

"It's like a mistake. Something that shouldn't have happened, that's all."

"But we made happen, Bwana. Was no mistake."

"I know we did, but it doesn't take away my regrets about shooting sitting ducks."

"Sitting duck?"

"A sitting duck has no chance, because the shooter has given him no chance. The duck is on the pond, and the hunter pops over the dike and blasts him on the water with no chance. To be fair, the duck needs to be on the wing, the same way the elephant needs to be chased in the jungle and given every advantage. Otherwise, it's not sporting. It's just murder."

"I see it, Bwana. You are man of principle, honor, and discipline. I have much respect for this. Yours is not man of pride. You are man of humility, and that makes man of *courage*."

"How is that?" I asked, intrigued by his comment.

"Because most man live from his pride and believe courage come from his absent from fear. But I know that no fear is to be stupid. And see, this man of pride is a much fool. For this man of humble, his courage real, because real courage not come from no fear at all. But this courage come from the man with no self. Only then can this man have true honor, when his focus to serve is not on him. And you, Bwana, you are the man."

I wanted to be puffed up by his perception of me, but then his words cut to the quick. *Humility*. If that was my asset, I had to take it to heart. How could a humble man boast, or take pride in the praise given him by others? I sat silently pondering what I had just heard, and I realized I had never really talked to Willie before, just the two of us. He had much more depth than I had ever given him credit for. True, he had perception in the field and could look at a target and determine range. He could figure bullet drop to calculate a hit. And he had more accurate depth perception than anyone I had ever met. But he was more than a hunter, more than a tracker. He had wisdom. At that moment, I realized that God could speak to you through others, and Willie's message of humility and service had come straight from God Almighty.

I thought of all that needed to be done before we could go after big bulls down in the valley. But why should I have to worry about all the chores? We had hired men to take care of them so we could concentrate on the hunt. Willie had carved this safari into a well-oiled machine, and there were no worries left for me. All I had to do was get Betty ready for the jungle and get my gear together for a tough day ahead. I could leave the safari details to Willie, Temba, and Janga. Those men I had hired had true servant hearts. It made me wonder if I could ever become a servant in the truest sense.

Many of my colleagues referred to their native porters as boys, but now I preferred to call them men, which gave them the dignity and respect they deserved. After all, they were loyal and had sacrificed so much to come along, leaving their families behind to serve us. Yes, we had paid them quite well for their services, but not one had deserted us. For each knew the importance of his role. Willie had instilled that sense of teamwork in them from the very beginning. He had their respect and was able to encourage them when needed. I hadn't realized the depth of his character and the height of his wisdom until this morning.

We'd had nothing to do with the elephants from the night before. The villagers had made short work of them in the early morning hours while we had slept. Drying meat now hung in long strips outside every hut. I had breakfast from Bamira's day-old bread, a block of sharp cheese, and hot coffee. I felt raring to go.

Finally, Jason stumbled out of his tent. I knew the kid would be the first one up, ready to find a trophy elephant.

"I figured you couldn't sleep in," I said as he approached the campfire, where I had been sitting in the canvas chair.

"I heard those elephants last night," he said, "and I knew you wouldn't sleep in, either."

"Okay, so we are two peas in a pod, just like Betty said." We both laughed.

"Yeah, I guess Mom has us pegged," he said.

The word *Mom* felt like a gold nugget pulled from the stream.

"How do you think we ought to go after them?"

"They will be in the heavy jungle in that rolling hill country to the south."

Jason's eyes perked up, and he pointed behind me. "Look!" he said excitedly.

I turned to see Janga and Temba with two of their scouts returning.

"Willie, your men are here," I said.

Willie looked up from his conversation with Ducar, one of his camel men, and he headed off to greet them.

"Let's go," I said, encouraging Jason.

We made quick steps, following Willie. The men began to speak in Swahili as we all came together. I felt somewhat comfortable in following the conversation, but Jason looked at the ground and began kicking a rock.

"What are they saying?" he asked.

"They located six bachelor bulls, all eighty-pounders or better."

"Where are they?" he asked.

I held up my palm to silence him while I listened. The faster the scouts spoke, the harder it was to understand them. After a moment, I thought I'd got the gist of it.

"They are in a swale about eight miles south, not spooked, and they have no reason to leave. They are old bulls past their prime, but loaded down with heavy armament, as the men put it. They have probably encountered white hunters before in their lifetime, but not for many years. We should be able to get on them quickly today and bring down one or two nice trophies."

"Is that it?" Jason asked. "Don't they have a game plan?"

"Hold on," I said, waiting for the men to finish. "Okay, here it is. They suggest that we form two parties. One will leave before the other and make a wide circle. In case the bulls spook, the others will hold back, then set up on the leeward side. They said we should leave sooner rather than later because these are rare trophy bulls. Go get Lance. This is what we came for. I'll get that sleepyhead girlfriend of mine up and moving."

Jason sprinted for the tents in world-class time, quickly leaving me in the dust.

"Are you awake?" I said, pulling the tent flap back and peering inside at the sleeping beauty.

"It can't be morning already," she said.

"It's time, unless you want to stay behind. Temba's scouts have located trophy bulls down the valley. Maybe the ones we heard last night. Apparently they are well worth the effort. Are you game?"

"I'm always game. Is there breakfast?"

"There's always breakfast."

"I'll get ready to roll, and you find me some food," she said.

"It's a deal."

~~~~~~~~~

We were all up and ready to go in an hour. I could feel the excitement in the air, knowing we had finally reached the place we had set out for so many months ago.

"Come gather around," Betty said, motioning to the others. "You know what today is, don't you?"

"Yes, Mom, it's my birthday."

"You know I didn't forget. Wait here," she said, walking briskly toward our tent.

"What's she doing?" Jason asked.

"You'll see," I said, folding my arms in anticipation.

She emerged cradling something hidden under her coat.

"You got me a gift?"

"No, I got you a companion," she said, opening up her jacket and pulling out a puppy.

"It's a Samburu puppy! Oh, Mom! Oh my goodness!" he said excitedly, taking the little brown dog in his hands and cuddling it to his face. "How old is he?"

"Willie said he's about three months old," she answered.

"How did you find him?" Jason asked.

"John asked the prince at dinner last night. The natives came through for us and found him in a village hut."

"What sort of dog is he?" Jason asked, cradling him in his hands and scrutinizing his features. He laughed at the dog's little face.

"I don't know what they call them. I guess he's just a Samburu mutt."

"He's no mutt to me. I'll have to come up with a great African name for him. How about Kiku?"

"What about a Christian name?" Esther said.

"Do you have one in mind?"

"I like Isaac," she said.

"What does it mean?" he asked in an excited voice. "Is it in the Bible?"

"It's not an *it*. The word Isaac is a *he*. Without taking an hour to tell you, let me give you the short version. Want to hear it?"

Betty eagerly nodded with a grin, and Jason agreed.

"In the book of Genesis," Esther began, "Abraham was married to his wife Sarah. They never had any children of their own, even though God had promised him that his descendants would be as numerous as the stars in the heaven. Abraham lived two thousand years before Christ. He and Sarah had grown far past the age of childbearing, so to help God, Abraham slept with his maidservant, and she conceived a son that he named Ishmael. But then one day God visited Abraham, and He told him that he and Sarah would have a child. Sarah laughed at the idea, which was ludicrous. Abraham was one hundred, and Sarah was ninety years old. So when Sarah gave birth to their son, they called him Isaac."

"What's it mean?" Jason asked.

"It means *laughter*," Esther said.

"This little guy sure makes me laugh," Jason said, "so Isaac must be an appropriate name." He paused as he admired his new dog. "What about Ishmael and Isaac? Did they become great friends and live happily ever after?"

"That would be a great story, wouldn't it? But that isn't how it went. Sarah didn't like her maidservant's son around, so Abraham sent the mother and the boy away. God told Hagar, the maidservant, that He would make Ishmael into a great nation."

"Did He?"

"Ishmael became the father to the Arab nations, while Isaac became the father of Israel."

"They still get along, right?" Jason asked.

"Like oil and water," she said with a grin. "There was a prophet who came along about three hundred years after Christ and decided to write down the things he heard from a spirit that he thought to be God. He claimed to be speaking for God when he changed the story written in the Bible and said that it was Ishmael who was the favorite son of their father, Abraham. In the Bible, it is told that to test Abraham's love for Him, He told Abraham to take His son Isaac to a mountain to sacrifice him."

"God did that?"

"Yes, and Abraham was obedient to God and took Isaac on a three-day journey, made an altar, and put wood on it for a burnt offering. He was ready to kill Isaac, when God told him not to and instead provided a ram for the sacrifice. God knew that because Abraham was willing to give up his son, he loved God more than life itself."

"So what about Ishmael?" Jason asked.

"This prophet named Mohammed, who I told you about, wrote in his book they call the Koran that it was Ishmael who Abraham had taken to the mountaintop that day. He said that Ishmael, being the eldest son, was the favorite son, and that the Mohammedans were God's chosen people. Apparently, Moses had gotten parts of the story wrong, even though he'd written his account about seventeen hundred years before Mohammed was born. At the time Abraham wrote his story, the events had only passed about six hundred years before. But now Mohammed said that his account was the true story. In this Koran, Christ is considered only as a prophet, and not God. He was just another teacher who taught people to love their neighbor and told them that if they were good and obeyed God's commandments, they would live forever.

"Isn't that true?" Jason asked.

"No," she answered, "you can't believe that Christ was a great teacher and then not believe what He taught. He was either a vicious liar who wanted glory for himself, a crazy man who didn't know what He was saying, or the Son of God. If you choose to believe He was telling the truth, then He was born of a virgin, He did come down from heaven after being with God from the beginning, He lived as a man tempted by the devil, He lived a perfect life without sin, and He made himself a sacrifice, once and for all paying the debt for sin and freeing all those who believe from eternal damnation. And the most important thing of all is that He rose from the dead and sits at the right had of God the Father. You see, just like Abraham, we all have false gods that we worship, and we don't even know it. Things slip between us and God. They get in the way of our fellowship. For most people, the God they worship is their own life. Day after day, they seek glory to feed their inner flesh, and they try to pump up this lagging tire, which bounces on the rim along the road of life.

"That is what Christ demonstrated through the washing of His disciples' feet: how they should treat others. But remember, it was the night before He was arrested and put on trial and then crucified. He said he had given them an example and that they should do as He had done. The following day, he went to the cross and died. This is the ultimate expression of our love for God: to give Him back everything He has given us. The most precious gift is the very life we live.

"When Christ told the rich young ruler what he must do to have eternal life, He said, go and sell everything you have, give all the money to the poor, and follow me. The rich young ruler couldn't do it, because he would have to give up his power and his glory. But that is what God wants from all of us. He wants our humility, and He wants us to give Him our love and our honor. He loves you so much that He sent His only Son to suffer and to die for you. It's the least we can give in return for His great sacrifice. What earthly price could we possibly put on eternal life with Christ?"

We all sat stunned by Esther's sermon. It was the most beautiful presentation of the Gospel message I had ever heard, and all this from the naming of a puppy.

"I have never actually heard that story put in those terms before," Chuck said.

"You've given me a lot to think about," Jason said. "What will we do with Isaac while we are gone?"

"Willie has taken care of everything," Betty said. "Give him to that native girl right there, and she'll take care of him while you're gone."

"They were her pups," I said, "and she has the mother."

"Enough of all this talk," Lance said. "Let's get down to business."

"One more thing," Betty said, holding out a sealed envelope. "Don't open this now. It's sort of like a birthday card, just to let you know ... well, you can read it later." Betty handed the envelope to Jason, and he stuffed it in his shirt.

"We need to decide how to split up the hunt," I said. "Who is going with me?"

"You have to ask?" Betty said. "I'm going with you."

"And I'm going with you, too," Jason said.

"Guess that leaves us," Lance said. "Who's gonna make the circle, John?"

"We'll make the wide circle," I said, "since Chuck is still nursing that knee. Sounds like we'll have about twelve miles, and you guys will have about five or six. We're ready to go, so you guys can hold back awhile if you like, since we have quite a ways. You guys take your pick of guides."

"We'll take Janga if you don't mind," Lance said.

Jason handed off his pup to the native girl, and he followed her toward his tent.

"I knew you would take Janga," I said and laughed.

"What about the signal?" Lance asked. "The same one?"

"Yep," I responded. "Two quick shots, followed by a third. Wait five minutes to the second hand, and repeat it. Just like always."

"What about Jason? Does he know?" Esther asked.

"Oh, I'm sure he knows," I said. "Besides, we're staying together."

Betty eagerly agreed with me, nodding enthusiastically.

"Let's put everything together and get on the trail," I said, grabbing my British double and handing it to my gun bearer.

I took my knapsack and slipped one of the straps over my shoulder. "We may decide to spend the night in the jungle, but we won't stay two. If we're not back on the second evening, you can send scouts out after us. But trust me: we won't get lost as long as we are alive. Temba has a sense for the jungle, even though I don't know if he knows this particular place. I wouldn't expect that you would have to stay out overnight, Lance, since you won't be that far from camp. But you ought to go prepared. Just in case we score, you'll want to hook up with us."

"Don't worry, John," Chuck said, "we'll be back at camp frying elephant tenderloins over the fire by the time the sun goes down."

"Do elephants have tenderloins?" Betty asked.

"Oh yeah, back strap, too," I said. "Ever eaten mule before?"

Everybody traded confused glances, not knowing if I was serious or not.

"Well," I said, "a sixty-year-old elephant probably tastes a little bit like a twenty-five-year-old mule. But I ain't never had any of that before, neither."

We all broke out laughing.

"I would try some," Betty said.

"What? Mule?" I asked.

"No," she said. "Elephant."

"Willie," I said, "send Bamira to get some meat out of the top of the elephant trunk, or else fetch the feet off one of those we bagged last night. When we get back to camp, you can roast some up for us."

"You are boss, Bwana, but Willie eat gazelle tonight if that okay."

We all had a good laugh as we got ready to leave camp.

Chapter 28

THE SNAPSHOT

As we set out, I felt a certain satisfaction that we were finally on the hunt we had planned for, all those many months ago. Now I finally had a great sense of elephant country. As we walked along, there were tracks, old and new; dung piles, fresh and stale; and signs of destruction, where the elephants had knocked the mopane trees over to get at the limb tops. They were creatures of habit. Once they had established familiar surroundings, they liked to stay unless something (like last night's kill) disrupted their patterns. Not that they didn't travel. But when they found a place where there was plenty of food, they would stay put as long as they could hold out. For some reason, this native tribe hadn't mastered poison arrows like the Wakamba had. I didn't ask, because I didn't approve of the practice. I didn't know why. Poison just seemed so extreme.

Following Temba again made me realize how quickly his feet moved along the trail. He hurried up the elephant path lickety-split, and Betty looked over at me and shook her head, not saying a thing. Neither of us had to wonder what she'd meant. I knew that, to keep her happy, I would have to find a way to slow him down.

"*Una haraka gani* (What's your hurry)?" I asked.

"*Hakuna harake, Bwana* (No hurry, Bwana)," he answered.

"*Memsahib hawezi kuendelea na huu muendo* (Memsahib cannot keep up at this pace)," I explained.

"Temba do," he said, resuming his march at nearly the same rate.

Betty rolled her eyes, and I laughed and shook my head. But Jason stayed with him stride for stride. We stayed close, watching ahead to keep them in sight, and now and again I would see Temba look back to make sure we were still following. I could tell the porters were pleased that we were along on the journey, which meant they didn't have to keep up with him, either. He had the same reputation among the natives.

It was just his nature, and I knew you couldn't change somebody's nature. Funny, but that was God's work, not man's. We all liked to think we could win over others to our point of view, but winning an argument just pushed someone further away from the truth. On top of that, it made the loser's heart just a little dimmer and the winner's just a little more prideful. There was room for strong debate, however, because a good debate was like iron sharpening iron. But debate was only worthwhile if it offered food for thought in a supportive atmosphere. If it turned into a wrestling match, where one opponent was pinned down and force-fed the other's opinion, then the outcome was null and void. Sort of like shooting big game at night with a light; even if he hunter scored nothing seemed fair about the game — and everybody knew it.

Unless truths were offered at teachable moments, they were wasted and fell on deaf ears. Unsolicited truth given as good advice was as useful as a blanket on a hot day. *But wait for the weather to change*, I thought, *and the chilled will come seeking warmth*. Christ had always taught by asking questions, which helped his followers come to answers on their own. An answer you had to work for had much greater meaning than wisdom handed to you on a silver platter.

We rounded a corner and found Jason and Temba waiting for us. We all rested on the trail to catch our breath.

"Hey, John," Jason asked, "how did you know the elephants you heard last night were mature bulls?"

"We didn't," I said. "They just heard them and scouted them. They all sound like they're blowing the same horn. Whether it's a squeak, a purr, a growl, or a roar, I don't think you can tell one from the other."

"They must be talking to each other," Betty said. "I wonder what they are saying. I don't think they're as dumb as we humans think.

For as many sounds as they make, I'll bet it's a learned language. Certain trumpets mean alert while others mean food."

"No doubt," I answered, "but maybe the trained ear can tell the difference between a mature bull and a cow. But you have to spend a lot of time with them to know that."

"I suppose it's like anything else," Jason said.

Temba motioned with his head, and he started up the trail again, with the three of us following.

"The more time you spend learning about something," Betty said, "the more familiar you become."

"That's why Esther has such a powerful faith," I said, "because she spends so much time reading her Bible and praying. I think the more time you spend with God listening to Him, the better you become at hearing His voice and understanding what He is telling you."

"That makes a lot of sense," Jason said. "I suppose if you were with elephants twenty-four hours a day, maybe if you had the same likes and dislikes, or if you understood their emotions and fears, then you could understand what they were saying."

"That's right," I said, trying to stay on pace to keep up with Temba. "That's what makes our God understandable to us. We can identify with Him, because He is not just this invisible force in the universe that created the heavens and the earth. He came here in the flesh, and just like us, He was tempted by sin. But He lived a perfect life. Imagine if you were falsely accused and falsely beaten for it, but yet you still forgave them just before you were crucified. You see, our God knows what it's like to suffer in this life. We don't have a God who is so far above us that we can't understand Him. When He speaks, He talks in our native language, and He speaks directly to our heart and soul by passing up our ears and our minds, which tend to act as filters for most of the things we experience in the world."

"What about Chuck?" Jason asked. "How do you get through to him?"

"It's not up to me, thankfully. That takes all the pressure off and relieves me from all the guilt of not being able to save him myself. I just need to remember to pray for him so that his heart will hear from God. I can be ready at those teachable moments for God to use me, but as far as his salvation goes, that's up to God. There is nothing we can do to be saved. Our faith doesn't come from us; it comes from God and His infinite grace. It's a gift from God. When I was attacked by that lion, God used that moment to show me His hand at work.

"The Israelites were sure they would die when Moses led them out of Egypt and straight to the banks of the Red Sea. They could see Pharaoh's army coming, and they knew they would all be annihilated by the sword. But then God used Moses in a mighty way and opened the waters, and all **two** million people crossed over to dry ground. Then when the last Israelite made it, God closed the sea back and all of Egypt's army drowned. That was a gift of faith, the same way you knew God saved you from the jaws of that croc. It was nothing you did; you just knew it was by God's mercy that He saved you."

I looked up and saw Temba waiting on the trail ahead. He was squinting at us and had his hands on his hips. He didn't have to say a word, because I knew his body language.

"We're talking too much," I whispered.

As we approached Temba, I could see he was ready to explain a few things to me in Swahili. This is how it translated into English. "These bulls will hear you, Bwana. You don't understand them, but I do. They will know we are coming unless we have complete silence. If you want to talk, then we can go back to camp. Or if you want to take a walk, then we can go a different direction just to enjoy the view. But where we are going, I thought you wanted to shoot an elephant. To shoot elephant we have to get close to them, and if you don't be quiet, you are wasting my time. Understand?"

I nodded in agreement. I had known as much, and I felt silly that I had to be scolded.

Temba pointed to Jason and Betty, and I quickly brought them up to speed.

"We are being too noisy," I said, "and I stand corrected."

"Sort of what I thought," Betty said. "I could tell by the tone of his voice."

"*Tupo tayari* (Are we ready)?" Temba asked.

I tapped my index finger to my lips, and Betty and Jason nodded. Temba smiled and then resumed his march. Although I had been humbled, I felt good about my relationship with Temba. I liked it that he felt comfortable enough with me to be stern with me when needed.

For the next hour, we strolled through forest paths worn down by a thousand years of elephant migration. Funny how these big bruisers just rambled along where countless herds had gone before. I knew they were creatures of habit, even though it appeared they really didn't live in any one certain place. Throughout Africa, with its many diverse habitats, where you could find a variety of wildlife preferring one place over the other, there was always one constant: the elephant. Even though they preferred certain habitats, they could be found wandering everywhere. Not that I had been to every place in Africa to see this firsthand, but I had talked to enough travelers over the years to know it was so. It was always the elephant that travelers spotted, whatever corner of this great continent they were exploring. My guess was that someday a researcher would come along to explain such things to us, assuming the elephants didn't disappear as more white men came to take over the land.

Man, by contrast, seemed to resist following the old pathways. He was constantly searching for a new road to take him in a direction. He was not content to keep his feet on the ground, as God had intended for him to do. No, he had to invent a flying machine to take him above the clouds, and he had to create mechanical ways to make his life easier, with railroads, skyscrapers, motorcars, airplanes, ships, and bicycles. Man had this inborn desire to make life easier and better, and he resisted following the paths set for him thousands of years before by wise men who had followed God and recorded what had happened for those who would come after.

The Bible had always been there, staring me in the face and challenging me. The story of the Savior had been with me since my boyhood, and I had wrestled with it time and again, rejecting it as merely a myth, like the story of *Gilgamesh* or *The Odyssey*. Of all the books ever written, it was the one that had to be taken as fact. We could not continually evaluate it for truth, because it had been written by God and not men.

We spotted a small band of cape buffalo standing among the trees and watching our approach, and we stopped dead in our tracks. I spotted a decent bull that I could have brought down, but buffalo were not on the menu today. They spooked, crashing off through the heavy brush and rumbling like a freight train leaving the station.

Betty widened her eyes, patted her chest, and stuck out her tongue. Jason mouthed the word *wow*.

Temba motioned for us to continue, and I could see him stepping carefully now so as not to crack any twigs. He stopped and checked the wind with a handful of dust, and it gently came back, landing on his feet.

"That is the reason we walked up on this herd of buffalo," I whispered softly in Betty's ear. "The wind is in our face, and they couldn't smell us."

Temba looked back and frowned at me for speaking, and Betty pointed at me. She smirked playfully, knowing I had just been scolded again by Temba.

I knew he meant business. His reputation as an elephant guide depended on his ability to get us within range of an old bull, and I could tell he had no intention of coming back empty-handed. If we didn't get a bull, it didn't matter that much to me. I had killed them before. A trophy was always nice, but my reputation didn't depend on it. It was sort of like a painter who worked in his studio. If he produced a work that he was not satisfied with, he would paint over it, rather than release it to the world and cheapen his reputation. To me, it was just an adventure. But to Temba, it was his life's work. Likewise, if I was giving a lecture on the origin of species, I wanted to speak with authority, clarity, and conviction, because I knew that every word would be judged by my critics.

A chill went up my spine suddenly as I realized my life's work had changed. I had made a complete turnaround. The things I had bet my life on before were no longer valid. Darwin's theory was just a theory to me now, since I truly believed that God had created the earth in seven days. How amazing that I hadn't thought of this until just now! God had put me in a dilemma. Everything I had worked for, everything I had stood for and come to rely on had gone up in a puff of smoke. Not that I was distraught, mind you, because God was everything to me now, and none of that Darwinism amounted to a hill of beans. But I suddenly realized that if I tried to go back to my old life of teaching science in the same way, it would be impossible. I could still teach science, but I would have to rethink everything.

I remembered a story in Greek history where Alexander the Great landed his army on the shores of Persia. To cut off their retreat, he ordered all their ships burned. I didn't want to retreat to my old life, where I lived in a world where God didn't exist. I wondered how I could have lived all those years in a random dimension between luck and chance. I almost laughed out loud when I realized the word *luck* was just an acronym for Living Under Christ's Kingdom. But without God, nothing made sense here, and everything hinged on probability. If you were successful, you owed it all to yourself and your own hard work and good fortune. Life had no purpose beyond just being here and making the biggest pile and leaving the biggest name. No one wanted to face the reality of death, of slipping into the abyss at the end and becoming nothing for all eternity, a fate so terrifying that we avoided the thought at all cost and focused on the now, our toys, and ourselves.

I had always wondered what it might be like to believe in God, but I realized I could never have given up my life, because I had nothing else. And that was the key. If you were not sure about God and the promise of eternal life, then how could you give up the only thing you had? Jesus said, "Whoever finds his life will lose it, and whoever loses his life for my sake will find it." How amazingly true this one simple statement had become to me! This truth, spoken nineteen hundred years ago, was as relevant now as it had been the day Jesus said it.

Temba stopped dead in his tracks and crouched on the trail, and we did the same. We heard a trumpet blast from an elephant that sounded like it had come from about a half mile away. We hadn't heard any elephants until now, and we knew they were close. Temba signaled us to stay put. Then he crept forward to a tree and slowly rose to his feet. Another trumpet blast echoed through the hills.

Throughout the ages, God had announced His presence with the sound of a trumpet, and it was written that Christ would do the same when he returned. I wondered what the elephants really knew about God, and if there might be more behind this great elephant call. In Matthew, Christ had said that on the last day "all the tribes of the earth will mourn when they see the Son of man coming in the clouds of heaven with power and great glory, and he shall send his angels with a sound of a trumpet, and they shall gather together his elect from the four winds, from one end of the heavens to the other." And in Exodus, when the people were shown the glory of God on Mount Sinai and it erupted with fire and smoke like a huge volcano, they heard the sound of a trumpet blast, and it grew louder and louder. I had heard these elephants a thousand times before, but now, after spending my mornings reading the Bible, everything in life had so much more meaning for me.

I knew that God was speaking to me personally through every means possible. I knew that He spoke to me through His word, that it wasn't just a book, that it was living and active. I knew that He spoke to me through His Spirit in a still, small voice, that if I listened, I could hear it in my soul. And I knew that He spoke to me through other people, our circumstances ... and perhaps other creatures in His kingdom.

Temba motioned for us to move up, and then he put his index finger to his lips and pointed to the ground for us to watch our step. He moved like a cat stalking a gazelle, and we followed, moving silently in the direction of the trumpets. The trees were thick in spots, but then as we moved, there were grassy openings that allowed us to see fifty to a hundred yards out. Temba avoided the temptation to advance in the open grass, and we stayed in the trees, using the ancient elephant trails. The afternoon winds began to blow gently straight into our faces.

I heard a crack behind me, and we all turned around to see one of our porters named Zamba cringe as a twig broke under his foot. Temba took the man's load, setting it down, and whispered to him sternly in Swahili. Then he continued forward, and we left our porters behind safely near a tree. Only our gun bearers followed us.

"Make sure you are loaded up now, and keep your safety on," I whispered.

I opened the breach on my double barrel to check it one more time. The greatest thing about hunting was not knowing what was going to happen next. This was not only true in hunting, but it was true in all adventure, as well as life itself. But this was *pure* adventure, stalking these elephants and knowing full well that they were the big ones and were capable of killing us.

I knew Temba had a plan, but I wasn't sure about the details. I hated not being in charge, but for the moment I had to trust Temba and his knowledge of elephants. That was another reason why unbelievers had such a hard time with God, because they liked being in control and not having to answer to anyone. *This is my life*, I had once thought. *I will live it my way.* I had heard it said once that if you wanted to hear God laugh, tell Him your plans.

The bush got thicker, and I could see we were right on the edge of the jungle wall. I recalled the plan Willie had described—encircling the herd to get them between us and the other team—and I realized that Temba didn't seem to be following through with the agreement. It probably had a lot to do with the winds and the lay of the land. Most likely, Temba couldn't follow the plan to the letter because he just wanted to do the best to help us lay a trophy down. We were startled by a huge crack as a fair-sized tree broke and then crashed to the ground.

"They are feeding," I whispered to Betty and Jason.

Temba moved stealthily, one foot at a time, toward our unsuspecting prey. They were busy stripping limbs, bark, and foliage from the freshly downed tree, and they purred amongst each other.

Then I spotted movement through the trees about two hundred yards ahead, and Temba froze in his tracks. Elephants had terrible eyesight and relied almost entirely on their sense of smell and hearing. It made me wonder what sort of world they lived in. I wondered if they had a sense of eternity, or if they knew that God had a plan for their life. There were a lot of mysteries to this life, and there were many questions that remained unanswerable.

I could barely hear my own footsteps over the crashing limbs and feeding of the elephants. The wind had slowed, but we had no doubt about the direction; we could strongly smell elephant urine and fresh dung. Temba looked back with a wide grin. Now three bulls stood about one hundred and fifty yards out, but we still had no clear shot through the heavy brush.

Our eyes were trained on the big ivory, and just the thought gave me butterflies. I didn't want to get greedy, but if we could get a couple, or even all three, that would be a great day, indeed. I still had great respect for the situation, knowing those old boys were dangerous. You couldn't live for fifty to seventy years without seeing a lot of stuff. White hunters had been in this land for all their lives, and the bulls had probably watched their own fathers die at the sound of gunfire. If they could get a chance to snuff you out, they would take it.

Temba crouched low and stepped lightly, carefully planning each move so as not to make a sound. These old bulls were so sensitive to noise. They were always on the alert because of what they carried. Their massive ivory marked them and put a price on their heads, and they seemed to sense it.

It was sad that they had to die, but I had a much healthier perspective on hunting than I'd ever had before. It had once been all about me and putting the trophy on my ego, but now I knew they were a gift from God. We praised Him for His creation. Without God, we had nothing and were nothing. To be successful in a hunt was a humbling moment. God smiled on our life and blessed us with the great gift of His creation.

One of the bulls let out a trumpet blast that nearly shook the ground. We were just over one hundred yards away now. I knew we were in a great position to take them, and we only had to work our way in to find a clear shot before they moved on or got tired of feeding on this downed tree. The other thing that could happen right now without warning was that the wind might shift, in which case they would run for cover in the heavy jungle.

Temba knew we needed to find a hole in the trees to get shots on the various bulls. He knew the layout needed. We needed to put as many of them down as we could without wounding any or putting any of us at risk. Weeks ago, we had seen just how cranky these old boys could be when Jason had almost been killed. Even though danger was a big factor in adventure, it was one aspect I hoped to avoid.

We looked for an open spot in the trees to get a crack at them. Any little sound would be enough now to spook them, but we had time on our side as long as they continued to feed. We could see one of them moving away, headed from our left to our right. The big bruiser moved up and went to work knocking down another tree about eighty yards straight away. We had a fairly open corridor to the right of the tree he was pushing on. As he shoved the tree, a loud crack echoed through the bush, and the tree went over, taking with it other foliage and giving us a clear view of his wide head.

His tusks were massive. He wasn't the biggest elephant I had ever seen, but was definitely in the top five. Temba froze, and the rest of us followed his lead, not moving a muscle. Then a smaller bull came out and began munching on leaves. Now we had two shooters well within range.

I was worried Jason's rifle might be too small to bring down one of these bulls, but I knew a well-placed shot in the heart would lay either of them out. I knew we would have to speak to each other before we lined up, just to make sure we were each on the same page.

"You take the big bull on the right, Jason," I whispered. "I'll take the one on the left."

Just then, the bull of the woods came over to get in on the downed tree, and we had three decent bulls right in front of us.

"Do you feel confident, dear?" I whispered in Betty's ear.

"Which one do I shoot?" she asked, whispering directly in my ear.

"The middle one," I whispered back. "Wait till he's broadside, and then shoot him right behind the front shoulder. He's a little smaller, but still a very nice bull."

Just then, the bull on the right let out a scream. His ears flapped like huge sails, and he lifted his trunk, facing us. He then advanced in our direction, closing the distance to within about fifty yards. Then he stopped and shook his head.

Without warning, Jason touched off a round. My heart sank. My first reaction was to be angry, but with no time to scold him, I raised my rifle, and the charging bull turned and headed off in a southerly direction. The other two bulls flinched, and Temba motioned us to move so we could get a clear shot. He ran up about ten steps to an open spot, and we followed. Betty's bull stood broadside, and I had a good head shot on the biggest one as they stood together, quartering away from us. They must have thought the shot had come from the other direction, because the echo had bounced off a nearby hill.

"Squeeze it off," I whispered. "Right behind the front shoulder. On three. One, two, three."

Her rifle belched, and I followed a split second later with my own report, still holding a steady bead for a brain shot. My 50-caliber jumped, socking me in the shoulder like a baseball smoking the catcher's mitt. Between the kick and the smoke, I lost sight of the elephants. I peered through the fog, and they were gone.

"What happened?" Betty asked.

"I don't know," I said. "They disappeared."

"*Tembo chini* (elephant down)," Temba said, giving a toothy grin and pointing through the trees.

"*Wapi* (where)?" I asked.

He didn't speak but only motioned for us to advance, and my eyes were fixed on the place where Temba said my bull had fallen. He moved quietly and deliberately up to get a closer look, and I opened my rifle and dropped in another round. Betty's gun bearer handed her the second rifle that was fully loaded and took her rifle from her. Then he worked the bolt action.

We spotted the big hulk rolled over in the tall grass. All eyes were alert as we made our way in on the motionless mound.

"Where did the other one go?" Betty asked.

"I don't know." I said. "Did you hit him?"

"I don't see how I could have missed. The thing was as big as a barn, and I know I can hit the broad side of a barn. I had a clean break on the trigger, and I know my sights are hitting dead on at this range."

When we came on the bull elephant, he lay dead in his tracks. His tusks were massive: no less than a hundred pounds a side. Not the largest bull, by any means. The largest elephant tusks I'd heard tell of weighed around two hundred and thirty pounds a side killed by an Arab hunter in 1899. But I was pleased with this bull, which was just the trophy I had set out for all those months ago when we left Chicago. I turned around to congratulate Jason, and he was gone.

Betty looked back, and she furrowed her brow. "Where's Jason?" she squealed. "Jason! Jason!" The sound of her voice absorbed in the bush, falling dead silent.

I shrugged my shoulders, confident that he had probably followed after his wounded bull and that he wouldn't go too far. "He'll be back. He just went to see if the other bull is down or hit."

Temba walked past the downed bull and began searching the grass for a blood trail on Betty's elephant. "*Memsahib piga tembo* (Madam shoot elephant)," he said.

"Shall we sound the signal?" Betty asked.

"Not just yet. They will have heard our shots, and they'll know. Let's find out where your elephant is. Besides, Jason is tracking his bull, and if it's wounded, we won't want to push it any."

"Okay," she conceded, "let's go find my bull."

"No, not just yet," I said. "Let's give him some time. If he's hit good, he'll be down in twenty minutes. But if we push him now, he could run off a mile in the heavy jungle."

"Does Jason know that?" she asked.

"Don't worry," I said, "he'll keep his head."

We sat silently waiting at the kill site, and I continued to admire the tusks on the old bull. Secretly, I was terrified that Jason was missing, but I wasn't going to alarm Betty.

"How old do you think he is?" she asked after a few minutes of silence.

"Hard to say for sure. We can look at his teeth and get an idea. But just by the size of his ivory, he could be well over sixty years old."

"His ivory is beautiful," she said.

"I've seen them before where they've been broken off from digging or fighting, but this one has perfect polished ivory."

"I'm getting worried, John. Maybe Jason thinks you're mad at him for shooting early."

"I am, and when he gets back here, I'm going to give him a piece of my mind. There was no call for that."

"Hey, he just got excited, that's all."

"Right, and there is no call for that in hunting. It's totally unacceptable. That's how people get hurt. Excitement comes from the threat of harm in this sport. When you're dealing with high-powered rifles, there is no room for error. Bull fever is just plain stupidity."

"Okay," she said, "get it out of your system right now, and take it out on me."

"Oh, I'll be good with him. We've come a long way since Nairobi. You'll see."

"But I really am getting worried, John. Don't you think we should go after him? We can trail my bull later."

"Let's give him some space," I said. "If he wanted help, he would have waited. He wants to do something on his own. He's sixteen years old, for heaven's sake. Heck, when I was sixteen, I was taking my father's sailboat out on Lake Michigan by myself."

"Okay, but that still isn't the darkest jungles of Africa."

"Well," I said, "let's give him some rope and stop babying him. He'll appreciate that more than if we continue to hover over him."

"I thought you were going to say, 'like a bee on honey.'"

"I was," I said. "How'd you know?"

"Because you always make a metaphor when you talk."

"I hadn't really thought of it, Betty, but I suppose I do."

Temba rose from his crouched position and walked out into the tall grass, looking for more blood.

"He went this way," Temba said in Swahili. "He's hit hard. He'll be down by now."

"What did he say?" Betty asked.

"He thinks the elephant is down," I answered.

I knew Betty really didn't want to track the bull. Her desire was to find Jason and find him fast. But she followed reluctantly as we made our separation with Jason wider by the minute. Two hundred yards turned into four hundred yards, and four hundred yards turned into a half mile. Still, the blood trail had left a significant mark on the land. The bull had made it to the edge of the grass and then plunged headlong into the heavy jungle.

"This will be rough going, but he has lost a lot of blood," I said. "It should be like an old salmon struggling at the end of a fishing line. He has enough energy for one more run, but now we are reeling him in."

"See what I mean?" she said with a laugh. "Another metaphor."

"I know, but you're used to it," I replied, laughing along. I realized once again how wonderful it was to have a woman who loved you.

The thick jungle undergrowth made our headway extremely difficult. It became increasingly difficult for Temba to identify the track, but he followed the freshly broken low-hanging limbs and the blood-splattered foliage. We had gone another two hundred and fifty yards in, when Temba ducked under a leaning tree and there lay our prize. This one was a bit smaller than mine, but in any circle of sportsmen this was a great trophy elephant, indeed.

"This bull is bigger than yours," Betty said, tongue in cheek.

"Yeah, right," I said and laughed.

"Okay," Betty said, "now that we found my elephant, let's go find Jason."

I looked at my watch. It had been well over an hour since we had put shots on these bulls. I figured Jason hadn't found his bull yet, otherwise we would have heard the signal or at least the kill shot. Maybe he had missed it clean and had already returned to the other bull, where our porters were probably already getting to work.

"Let's give the signal shots now," Betty said.

"All right, give me your rifle," I said, handing my double off to my gun bearer.

Betty eagerly handed her rifle over to me.

"We'll see," I said, "but I think this canopy will smother the noise." I turned to Temba and spoke in Swahili. "We will summon help."

Betty covered her ears as I pointed the muzzle up into the tree branches. I fired off the signal shots, but they seemed to just get eaten by the jungle canopy.

"Now we can go back to our first kill," I said, handing her the rifle.

"They'll hear us," Betty said.

Temba made his move, and we struggled to stay up with him as he worked his way out of the jungle. I stopped every twenty or thirty yards and tied off a red piece of flagging to the low-hanging branches. By the time we'd escaped the entanglement, another fifteen minutes had passed. With Temba leading, we followed our trail a half mile back and found that our porters had already gone to work on the big bull. I could feel the air escape from Betty's soul. Jason was still gone.

"Let's signal again," Betty insisted. "Just in case you're right and he didn't hear the first ones."

I reluctantly agreed and fired off another series of shots with her rifle. This time, I felt confident that Jason would hear them and find his way back any minute.

We waited and watched the men as they worked diligently on my elephant, but as the clock continued to tick, we had more cause for concern. I didn't dare say a word, because I knew she stood on the edge of panic. I couldn't face her emotions. Right now, I wasn't even sure I could deal with mine.

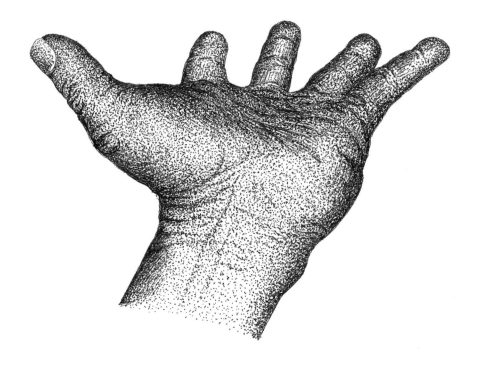

Chapter 29

AN OPEN HAND

W e heard rustling in the bush, and Betty's eyes lit up.
"It's Jason!" she said excitedly. "*Jason!*"

Then Janga emerged from the tree line on foot, followed by Lance, Esther, and Chuck, all on horseback.

"Oh," I said, "you guys."

"Did you see Jason?" Betty asked.

"No," Lance said, dismounting and tying his mare to a tree. "Isn't he with you?"

"He went after a wounded bull," I said, "and we're getting worried."

"Why did you let him go after a wounded bull?" Chuck asked. He got off his horse and hobbled on his stiff knee.

"We didn't let him," I said. "He just disappeared."

"I'm really worried," Betty said. "Let's go after him now. It's going to be dark in a few hours."

"Wow, what a bull!" Lance exclaimed.

"Yeah, he's quite a trophy all right," I answered.

"Is this one yours, Betty?" Chuck asked

"No, mine is about a mile away, tucked on the edge of the jungle."

"You got two?" Esther asked.

"We might have three when Jason gets back," I said.

"Let's go after him, John," Betty pleaded. "Right now."

"Okay, okay. Let's go find the mutt."

Betty tightened her lip and glared at me.

515

"Janga," I said, "let's see if we can find any blood from the other bull. Do you guys want to head back to camp?"

"Chuck," Lance said, "you take the ladies back, and I'll stay here and help find Jason."

"Not on your life," Betty said. "I'm staying until we find him."

"We could be spending the night in the bush," I said.

"I came prepared to stay when we left," she said, "but I didn't come prepared to lose my son."

"My men make camp here," Janga said. "We find him. Temba track."

Betty began to cry, and Esther put her arms around her.

I took Lance aside so I could confide in him man to man.

"What happened?" he asked.

"I don't know. I didn't think he would go far, but now I'm damn worried. If he was in trouble, he would have signaled. It's going on two hours, and he should have been back here by now. I don't want to alarm Betty, but it's not a good situation."

Lance gritted his teeth and nodded. "I thought you had this cured way back at the farm," he said, "when the kid went after the lion by himself."

"I know. Betty stopped me then from being too hard on him," I whispered. "I just don't know."

"Let's pray to the Lord," Esther said as she and Betty joined us. "He is testing us. But for some reason, I don't have any bad feelings about it. Maybe it's a woman's intuition, but my gut says that he's safe."

"I hope you're right," Betty said. "If anything happens to him, I'm afraid I will die."

"No, listen to me," Esther said. "If God has allowed this to happen, then you must accept the hand He has dealt. But believe God is testing you. Do you remember when you lost your son, how you blamed God and refused to let him go? Day after day, you struggled with the answer to the never-ending question *why*, and you suffered over the loss. Nothing in this world compares to the loss of a child. God does not intend for you to become broken from that loss, but to grow and produce eternal fruit from your suffering."

"If the Scripture says that God will not give us more than we can bear," Betty asked, "then why are there suicides?"

"Because that's not what the Scripture says," Esther said. "Specifically, in first Corinthians it says that God 'is faithful and will not suffer you to be tempted above that ye are able; but will with the temptation also make a way to escape, that ye may be able to bear it.' So it is not suffering that He will not overburden you with, but it is temptation. Temptation is about sin, and it is the devil that tempts us, while God uses Satan to test us. Some just choose not to take the path of escape and so fall into sin. The world looks at suffering and sees it as evil, but God sees suffering as good. And while He hates sin, He does not hate our suffering, because it always makes us grow."

"Yeah, if it don't kill us first," Lance said to the wrinkled brow of his wife.

"If anything were to happen to him," Betty said, "I'm just afraid of the depression all over again, and this time I don't know what I might do to myself. I'm terrified."

"Well, you have to know that suicide is never an option," Esther said. "While I do not believe it is an unforgivable sin, I do believe if you show up early, you will miss out on all the great blessings God has planned for your life. The blessings He has set aside for you will be missed in the same way that if you hold on to anything in this life too tight and try to keep it for yourself. Besides, suicide is the most selfish act. It's usually done to get back at someone else for the hurt they have caused, or else it's done because the person has no hope and just wants to end the agony."

"So what would you have me do?" Betty asked.

"You remember the story of Isaac?"

"How could I forget?"

"Then take this boy and give him to God," she insisted. "He belongs to God and not to you. Guard your heart so that you have not lifted him to a place where you are worshipping him above God. Remember that idols come in many different forms, and they can slip in before we know what we have done. Are you ready to pray for Jason?"

Betty eagerly nodded for Esther to begin her prayer.

"Come, gather around," Esther said. "We're going to pray."

"*Hakuna damu* (No blood)!" Temba shouted, searching through the grass.

"Tembo not hit," Janga said. "We must go now and track Jason. No time for praying."

"Oh, yes there is," I said. "We will all pray before we head out, and you will see what God will do."

Janga rolled his eyes and summoned Temba, who protested at Janga's insistence.

As we gathered, I watched Chuck out of the corner of my eye, knowing he was still on the outside of this whole dilemma he had created in his mind—an outlook I still felt somewhat responsible for, after all the years of preaching darkness to him and having him take to heart everything that I said all those years.

"Let us pray to the Lord," Esther said, bowing her head. "To the God of Abraham, Isaac, and Jacob; to the great *I Am*, who was, who is, and who will always be. To the same God who came to earth as a man to wash us clean from our sins. Lord, we praise you for watching over us and protecting us from harm. We praise you for your love and your grace. We praise you, Lord, as the God of provision and our great provider. We praise you, Lord, for your holiness, for being the rock we can always count on, for being unchanging from yesterday, today, and tomorrow. Lord, we thank you, knowing that you will always love, always wait, and always hope that we will turn our face to you and ask for your forgiveness.

"Lord, we know that we have sinned, that we have gone astray and lived a life that was only pleasing to us. Father, forgive us, for we know that we are not worthy to ask for anything. Quickly," she said. "Take your shoes off."

"What?" Chuck asked.

"Take your shoes off now," she insisted. "The Lord is here, and we are standing on holy ground."

Esther reached down and began unlacing her boots, and Betty and I eagerly followed suit, with the others doing so reluctantly.

"*Vua viatu vyako sasa*," Janga said to Temba, who looked bewildered but finally kicked off his sandals.

"Now let's get on our knees and bow to the Lord," Esther insisted.

"I can't get on my knees," Chuck said.

"Here," she said, "sit on this limb right here next to me. Let's form a circle.

"Father, we feel you, we know you are near, and Lord, we come to humbly beseech thee, and we ask that you grant this request by your will. Father, as your servant, Abraham offered you his son Isaac. Lord, now we offer up this precious boy, and we hold him in our open hands to you. Everybody, hold your hands open to God."

We looked up, and Esther was holding open hands to the Lord, and everyone followed her lead, including Chuck.

"Father, for everything we have held, including our very lives, we give it all to you. We take this precious son, Jason, and we give him to you, Lord. You made him, you gave him to us for a time, and now, Lord, we take peace in knowing that if it be in your plan to allow us to once more witness his smile, to look into his bright eyes, and to hear his voice, we know it is by your grace and your mercy.

"Father, keep him safe and watch over and protect him, bring him back to us safely, and grant us peace. And Lord, should it be in your will to once more prune us, help us to understand. Help us to let go, and help us to grow by the power of your Holy Spirit. Give us true wisdom that transcends all understanding. Lord, be with the trackers now, and be especially with Temba and Janga as they use every ounce of skill that you have given them to find our treasured companion, friend, and son. All this we pray in the name of your beloved Son and our Eternal Savior, Jesus Christ our Lord, Amen."

I looked up and saw that Temba's eyes were still shut tightly. Janga nudged him to let him know that we were finished. No one spoke as we dug through the pile of shoes to find our own, and we brushed our socks and pulled on our boots in silence.

I could feel a tear on my cheek as I remembered two days earlier, when I had watched Jason lace on the new pair of boots at the river's edge and had listened to the excitement in his voice at having witnessed the miracle of salvation. Now here we were just two days later, and I had a terrible feeling that either we wouldn't find him at all, or if we did, he would be dead, having been flattened by a bull elephant. It was going on two and a half hours now since we had killed the elephants. With late afternoon wearing on, sunlight was in short supply. I saw Janga talking to the other men, and two of them left abruptly. I caught Janga's eye.

"I send them back to camp to get help for these dead bulls," he said.

Temba began scouring the ground like an old hound dog sniffing for a fox. We all jumped in and started searching the tall grass for a blood trail or for Jason's footprint. Finding the elephant track and identifying the correct one would be difficult, since the area was littered with tracks like a barnyard covered in chicken feet.

"Bwana!" Temba shouted and motioned for us to come. "*Unyayo wake* (boy track)."

"I'll go with Temba," I said, "and I'll take the electric torch."

"I'm going with you!" Betty insisted.

I could see it in her face. To argue with her now would be futile.

"Chuck," Lance said, "can you stay here with Esther and take care of her? I'm going with the rest of them."

"I'll stay here," he said with a laugh, "but she will probably be the one taking care of us both."

"We've got about an hour of daylight left," I said privately to Chuck, "and when I find him, I won't know whether to hug him or punch him."

"Oh, John, stop it," Betty said, having overheard my comment. "He's got a perfect explanation."

"I suppose, and I'm anxious to hear it. *Tangulia* (lead on)," I said to Temba.

He began bird-dogging the trail, followed by Janga.

I struggled to see the trail in the sparse grass as Temba made his way along. Now and again, I would pick up just a piece of boot print. There were elephant tracks everywhere, and I couldn't believe Temba could identify the right ones and stay on them. We had gone about a mile when the track turned straight for the heaviest part of the jungle. Tracking wasn't at all like marching behind Temba, and the mile had burned up almost thirty minutes of our precious daylight. The sun positioned itself to wave goodbye for the day, hanging low in the sky just over the western horizon.

"*Unyayo nzun* (good track)," Temba said.

"But I am concerned that the boy has gone to be with the spirits," Janga whispered so that Betty couldn't hear.

"*Tutaendelea mpaka tumpate au mpaka tutakapofikia muda ambao hatutaweza kumfuato tema* (We'll go until we find him, or until we can't follow anymore)," Temba said.

"What did he say?" Betty asked.

"He said we are still on the track. Don't worry. We'll find him." I cupped my hands over my mouth and yelled at the top of my lungs, "Jason! Jason!" The noise sank in the trees like a rock tossed into thick mud.

Betty followed suit with a shrill shout of her own. "Jason!" she called out. She turned to me. "I'm really worried, John."

"We'll find him. We just have to trust God. Remember what Esther said: worry is the opposite of faith, and we have to consider it pure joy when we face all kinds of troubles such as this, because we know that God is testing our hearts. He is teaching us perseverance and patience and ultimately making us stronger. It's like the runner who trains each day. His body becomes stronger as he gains endurance. It is just that way with our faith. God puts us in situations to test us so that we are better able to finish the race. As the book of James says, hope is born of suffering."

"For some reason, we get the whole flesh thing," she said, "but we forget about the work our God has for our spirit."

Temba continued on, and the four of us followed him. We could see where the elephant had broken trail through the heavy underbrush, and I couldn't believe Jason had followed the bruiser, knowing he had not put a bullet in it. We had not seen even a speck of blood. Was it possible Jason had? I couldn't understand why he had chosen to follow this bull. Besides, one would have thought the boy had a healthy fear of these animals, having nearly been killed by one only weeks ago. The further we went, the more angry I became wondering just what in the hell had possessed him to go it alone.

The canopy shaded out the remaining sun, and darkness began to close in on us. I could tell Temba had begun to struggle in locating Jason's track, but still he pushed on. I pulled the electric torch out of my knapsack and lit up the ground. It startled Temba. But when I looked in his eyes, I could see the signs of his despair.

"*Je tumelipoteza* (Have we lost it)?" I asked.

"*Ndiyo, Bwana, inaonekana tumefuatilia unyayo mbaya* (Yes, Bwana, I must have taken a wrong turn. We must go back)."

"*Kuipata au kuifuatilia tena* (To pick it up again)?" Janga asked.

"*Hapana, turudi kampuni tusubirie mchana* (No, back to camp and wait for daybreak)," he insisted. "*Hili jangwa linaridhisha na ni rahisi kupoteza mwenendo gizani. Na isitoshe chui huwinda muda kama hua na ni hatari sana* (This jungle is very deceiving in the dark, and it is easy to get turned around. Besides, the leopard hunts here, and it is very dangerous in the dark)."

"*Memsahib, hatapenda, tupoteze matumaini* (Memsahib will not like that we are giving up)," I said.

"*Ni vizuri tupoteze mmoja tu, Bwana* (Better to only lose one, Bwana)," Temba said.

"What did he say, John?" Betty asked, her voice on the edge of panic.

"He said we have a good track, but it will be easier to follow in the morning when we are all rested and we have good light."

"You must be joking," she said, clenching her jaw.

"No, he's not," I explained.

"How do you expect me to get any sleep when Jason is out here in the jungle somewhere? Besides, I know about the leopards. I heard him say *chui huwinda*. I'm not stupid. I know that means *leopard hunts*. I say we keep going until we find him. He could be injured, and he might not last the night."

"We'll find him," Lance said, "but this pursuit is madness."

"You might think that," Betty snapped, "but I lost one son, and I don't intend to lose another."

"You know what I think?" I said. "We need to let go, and let God."

"Somehow I knew you were going to say that," she said. "I have to tell you that it bugs me that it was my idea to begin going to church, and now you're claiming you found God and have left me in the dust. What am I supposed to think?"

"I don't know, because I didn't do it," I said. "If I'd had a choice, I would have continued down the same road of unbelief. Come on. Let's go have dinner. I promise you we'll be up at daybreak and we'll find him. Besides, for all we know, he'll be waiting for us around the campfire when we get back."

"Not likely," Lance said. "Chuck would have fired off a shot if he came in."

"I can't believe he hasn't signaled us if he's okay," Betty said. "John, I'm just not ready to let him go."

I put my arm around her to comfort her.

"Jason!" Betty yelled. "Jason!"

We listened as the stone-cold silence of the dark jungle consumed the sound of her voice.

"Fire off a signal round, John!"

"There has been enough shooting," Janga said. "Let's head back."

I had to use the torch to find the trail, and we made our way out of the jungle, trudging back to camp. As we came back out of the heavy jungle and trudged across the grasslands, I could see the flickering of the firelight through the trees. I couldn't remember a more welcome sight. The only thing better would have been seeing Jason joking with Chuck and Esther around the fire.

Esther spotted our light and ran to greet us. "Did you find him?"

"No," I said, "we're going to get some rest and start again in the morning."

Betty ran to Esther. They embraced, and Betty began to sob uncontrollably.

"I know, dear, I'm sorry," Esther said, "but we'll find him."

"Not if we don't look," she said, sobbing. "I think we should have kept on. I'm terrified. I don't know what possessed him. I just can't bear to think of him laying out there injured or worse." The tears rolled off her cheeks, glistening in the firelight.

"Let me get you something to eat," Esther said.

"I don't think I can eat," she said. "I'm hungry, but my stomach is in a knot."

"Come and sit by the fire and have some tea, and let's talk," Esther said, helping Betty to a log that had been pushed up to the fire.

"No luck, eh?" Chuck said.

I motioned him aside as Esther and Lance sat down with Betty.

"I don't like it," I said, putting my hand on Chuck's shoulder and speaking in a low voice. "I wanted to keep going, but that jungle is forbidding. Temba just lost the track, that's all. He'll pick it up in the morning, and we'll find him."

"Hope he knows enough just to sit tight if he's turned around," Chuck said.

"Yeah," I answered, "the only trouble with being lost is sometimes you don't know it, or you won't admit it." I had to stop myself from saying something about Chuck's salvation. I paused, and I could almost hear the wheels churning in his head.

"I know what you are saying," he said with a wink. "I'm listening to a point."

I didn't say anything more, because I knew I had said it all.

Chuck put his hand on my shoulder like a father figure. "You'll find him. I just have the feeling he's okay."

"I hope you're right," I said. "Have you eaten anything?"

"We have," Chuck said, "but there is plenty of food. Let me get you some."

When I turned around, Esther was deep in conversation with Betty at the fire.

"Our life is like a song," she said. "It is beautiful as the notes are played one on the other, moving up and down the scale and creating beautiful melodies. The high notes cause our soul to fly like butterflies, and the low notes are dark and mysterious. But all work together to create beautiful music. It is life. All the notes work together, and we have to embrace them."

Betty sat silently, the firelight flickering on her face as she listened intently to Esther's wisdom. It felt like Esther's words came straight from God.

"Let me tell you a story," she continued. "Do you remember a man named Horatio Spafford?

Betty wrinkled her brow, then nodded. "Yes, Spafford. A prominent Chicago attorney some forty years ago. Disappeared after the Chicago fire, I believe. I remember my father spoke of him."

"Did you know he wrote a song?" Esther asked.

"No, not hardly," Betty answered. "What sort of song?"

"Seems he had rather a tough go of it," Esther said, "but despite all his troubles, he penned a Christian hymn entitled 'It Is Well with My Soul.'"

"What sort of trouble?" Betty asked.

"What I know of the story," Esther said, "is that Spafford and his wife Anna lost a son to the fever when he was only four years old. Something you would know about quite well. Just a year later, they lost everything in the great Chicago fire in 1871. Devastated by the blow, he took stock of his life and decided to move to Jerusalem to start over. When he and Anna and their three young daughters arrived in New York, he got word that a last-minute business deal had fallen through and he needed to return to Chicago.

"Since tickets had already been purchased aboard the French steamer *Ville de Havre*, he urged Anna to take their girls and go on ahead. Around the first of November in 1873, the steamer collided with an English vessel in the Atlantic and sank in twelve minutes, claiming the lives of over two hundred people. Anna was saved by clinging to a floating plank, but never laid eyes on her children again. It is said that she heard a voice that told her, 'You were saved for a purpose.'

"Just nine days after leaving his wife in New York, Horatio received a telegram from Anna that stated simply, *Saved alone*. Now obviously distraught, Spafford boarded the next steamer bound for England. The story goes that the ship's captain called Horatio to the bridge when they reached the spot where the *de Havre* had gone down. Spafford returned to his cabin and penned the now famous lyrics to the hymn, which he wrote from a Bible story."

"What was the Bible story?" Betty asked.

"The story is about a well-to-do Shunammite woman found in the book of Second Kings, chapter four, who had no children and an aging husband. The great prophet Elijah had a servant named Elisha, who, after Elijah was taken up to heaven in a chariot of fire, became a man of God in his own right.

"This Shunammite woman had convinced her husband to build him a room to stay when he visited them. Elisha was so touched by her generosity that he offered to speak to the king or the commander of the army on their behalf. But she had no desire for such privilege. Elisha asked his servant for a suggestion, and he said the woman had a great desire for a child. Then Elisha summoned her and told her that she would have a child this time next year.

"She became terrified that she would get her hopes up, only to have them dashed. It came to pass that everything Elisha told her came true, and she gave birth to a son. One day, the young boy complained of a headache and then died in his mother's arms. Immediately, she saddled a donkey and traveled some distance to find Elisha. When he saw her approach, he sent his servant to ask if it was 'well with thee,' and she answered, 'It is well.'"

"How is it that it was well with these people?" Betty asked. "Horatio Spafford had just lost his daughters, and this woman in the Bible had just lost her precious son."

"Because their joy was not in their circumstances," Esther answered, "but in the Lord. And even in great sorrow, they knew that happiness wasn't dependant on a set of conditions. They knew that this life is temporary, that the part that makes it *well with our soul* is found in God and the eternal heavens, not in the briefness of our earthly condition. Even Jesus's half brother James, in the beginning of his letter, said to count it all joy when you have trouble, because hope and patience emerge from suffering. Let me ask you this question: what is your purpose here?"

"Purpose?" Betty repeated, shrugging her shoulders and widening her eyes. "I'm not sure. I guess it would be to build a life and to enjoy it, raise healthy and happy children, and leave a legacy. Looks like I'm not doing so hot at number two."

"Think about this for a purpose: to serve God and to be obedient to His will." Esther paused while Betty quietly let the words sink deep into her soul. "Let me ask you another question."

"Okay, I'm ready," Betty said.

"What is the most important thing in your life right now?" Esther asked as she sat up straight and let go of Betty's shoulder.

Betty sat quietly thinking, and then answered, "Jason. Jason is the most important thing to me right now." She looked at me out of the corner of her eye and gave me a sweet smile. "Oh, John, you know what I mean. You're the most important thing in my life, okay? But Jason is a close second. I love this boy like my own son. Heck, he is my own. It just isn't official yet. I love my husband and my home back in Chicago. I love Mammy Mae. I love you, Esther, and all of my dear friends. I love all you guys. Everything I have right here and back in Chicago are the most important things in my life."

"Anything else?" Esther asked, giving a squint.

"I can't think of anything I left out."

"Are you sure?" Esther asked.

Betty gave a concerned look as she internalized the inquiry.

"What about God?" Esther asked.

"Oh," Betty said, "of course. But it goes without saying that I love God."

"But that wasn't the first thing that came to your mind," Esther said. "Where is He on your list?"

"Well, right now, I don't know," Betty said. "I haven't exactly come to that place where it will be well with my soul if we don't find Jason tomorrow." Betty's eyes began to well up again, and a tear rolled down her cheek.

"God is testing you, my dear," Esther said, "just like he tested Abraham. You need to hold this boy in an open hand to the Lord. You need to make a choice and prove to God who is most important. What is the first commandment?"

"I don't know," Betty said.

"Oh, yes, you do. Think about it."

Betty sat quietly and put her finger to her lips. "I guess I do. You shall have no other gods before me, right?"

"That's right, and are you violating that commandment?"

"Absolutely not," she snapped. "There is no other God but the Lord."

"But have you elevated Jason to the place of God in your life? Are you worshipping him? And the big question: Can you give him over to God and let go? And now I'm going to ask a really difficult question. Are you ready for this one?"

"I don't know," Betty answered. "I'm feeling a bit beat up right now, but maybe one more punch isn't going to matter, as long as it isn't the knockout punch."

"Have you ever been able to let go of Johnny? Not the memory, and not the joy he brought you. But have you ever been able to let go of his soul and give him to God? Can you let him go and let go of the grudge you are holding against God for cutting him out of your life? Can you move on?"

Betty took a deep breath and let it out slowly. "What's the matter with me?" she said. "Why can't I?"

Esther put her hand on Betty's shoulder. "It's the same struggle man has had from the beginning. Just imagine how Eve felt when her sons quarreled and Cain killed Abel. She lost them both, because Cain was banished by God. There are only two ways to escape the pain of life. One way is to have never been born at all, and the other is to be *born again* and to love God with all your heart, mind, body, and soul."

"But how do you love God like that when you can't see Him?" Betty asked.

"That's the question for the ages. Don't you see that is the point? That's why God created this place in the beginning. We can't love something we don't know, or something we can't experience, but thankfully that isn't the case with our God. He is living and active, and He left us a book by which we can know Him: a firsthand account, written by people who did know Him. Even one account was written by his best friend, the Apostle John, who called himself the disciple who Jesus loved. When Jesus hung there on the cross, He gave John His mother and told her that now John was her son.

"But just imagine how this made John's mother feel. Her name was Salome, and she was Mary's sister, which made Jesus and John first cousins. Salome had been a very proud mother, and in fact, she had brought her sons to him and asked that they be allowed to sit on his right and his left in his kingdom. Being related, she probably figured they had an in with Jesus. Imagine what a humbling thing this would have been for Salome, who felt she had played a part in His movement, only to have Jesus give the apple of her eye away to her sister.

"Mary had already received such a great blessing by being the mother of Jesus, and for Salome to be told that John was now her sister's son—this would have been a tremendous test for her and would have taken a great act of humility to get past it. Just imagine being at the cross at the very moment when Christ was to speak his last words, and to be given a test of humility in that way. Isn't that just how God works in our life to bring us to this place of humility even today?"

"That's it, isn't it?" Betty said.

"In a nutshell," Esther said. "Only through our humility are we able to truly find Christ."

"What about the song?" Betty asked. "'It Is Well with My Soul.'"

"I have sung it before many times," Esther said. "It is very inspirational, and when you get back to Chicago, it will be in the hymnal in the church pew."

"What about the rest of it?" Betty asked.

"That's all I know," Esther answered.

"No, I mean, do you think I have been putting Johnny between me and God?"

"I don't know. That's not for me to say exactly, but that's for you to decide, Betty. From an outsider's perspective, maybe. But I am an evangelist who looks at a set of circumstances the way a doctor examines symptoms to diagnose an illness. I have to sit at the bedside and tell the patient what's wrong and try to help them to participate in the treatment."

"Well, I'm taking the cure right now, Esther. It's time for this to be well with my soul. Do you know the words?"

"I know some of them, Betty. I know how it starts. Let's see ... 'When peace like a river attendeth my way. When sorrows like sea billows roll. Whatever my lot, thou has taught me to say, it is well, it is well with my soul.' I don't remember the other verses. Like I said, you'll have to find them when you get back to Chicago. Oh, let's see ... I think I remember the last verse. 'And Lord haste the day when my faith shall be sight, the clouds be rolled back as a scroll. The trump shall resound and the Lord shall descend, even so, it is well with my soul.'"

"Can I pray?" Betty asked.

"This would be as good a time as any," Esther said.

"How should I start?"

"Start by praising Him for who He is, thank Him for what He has done, and ask forgiveness for all that you have done. Then you can ask what you will in His will."

"Dear Lord God," Betty began as we bowed our heads, "the God of the heavens. The God of Abraham, Isaac, and Jacob. The One who brought the Israelites out of Egypt, and the God who came down to earth as a man and gave His life for the forgiveness of our sins. We praise you for your patience, because you wait for us to come to you. We praise you for your perfect timing, because you know when to speak at the very moment our hearts are ready to listen.

"We thank you, Lord, for Africa, and for what it has meant to all of us, and all that it has meant to me. I thank you for Jason, Lord, and for giving me the hope that one day I would have a son again. And now, Lord, I know it was you that gave me that hope again.

"Please forgive me for not loving you, Lord, with all my heart, mind, body, and soul. Forgive me, Lord, for having other gods before you, and for not making you the most important thing in my life. And now, Lord, I take this precious son, and I bring him to the altar of God, and I hold him in an open hand to you. I say without reservation that you are my God. And should you decide to take him out of this open hand, then he is yours, and has always been. And Lord, in the other hand I hold up: Johnny. Lord, forgive me for holding on to him all these years, and for questioning your will and trying to make my own plans supersede your own."

I opened my eyes slightly and saw that Betty had both palms open to the heavens.

"And Lord," she continued, "you know I have never done this. I have held on to this boy since the day he was born, and then even tighter on the day he died ... until now. All of his memories have belonged to me alone. Lord, forgive me for thinking that it was you who took him from me. I realize now that life isn't all about me, but it is all about you, since you created the world and everything in it. That you are the one who knit me in my mother's womb and gave me the breath of life. That I took no part in it, and that it has always been you guiding me, loving me, and waiting for me. Lord, you are my God from this day forward, and never again will I let something come between us to cloud our communication and darken our relationship.

"And Lord, last of all, I pray for Jason. Not for his return so that I may worship him, but for his safe return so that you can use him. Lord, he belongs to you, and I believe now that I can truly say, no matter how this all turns out, that it is well with my soul. Because you are my God and I am your humble servant, it is well. It is well with my soul." Betty paused and put her hand on Esther's knee. "Will you finish the prayer?"

"Lord God, we thank you," Esther said. "We thank you for the courage and for the faith of our dear sister. Lord, grant us wisdom to understand *why*, give us courage to face the *what* and the *what-if*, and gift us with your grace, your peace, and your mercy so that we might answer the *who, when, where,* and *how*. Because, Lord, those are all the questions there ever were and there ever will be in all the universe, and your grace is sufficient to answer them all. And so they are all summed up with this one prayer, given by you, Lord, all those many years ago.

"Our Father, which art in heaven, hallowed be thy name. Thy kingdom come. Thy will be done in earth, as it is in heaven. Give us this day our daily bread. And forgive us our debts, as we forgive our debtors. And lead us not into temptation, but deliver us from evil: For thine is the kingdom, and the power, and the glory, forever.

"And Lord, watch over and protect Jason on this dark night, and lead him by your Spirit back to us. Lord, we have so much hope that he will return to us safely, or that we will find him tomorrow safe and sound. And we ask you, Lord, to grant us this and to smile on our lives with your great mercy. We pray all of this by the power of your name in the Father, and in the Son, and in the Holy Spirit. Amen."

I looked up first and saw that Chuck appeared to be asleep, cradling his face in his palms. But he looked up directly after Esther's prayer, and I realized that he might have been participating.

"I'm hungry now," Betty said. "Finally, I have peace. Not that I can bear to think of Jason's fate, but I know, whatever our lot in life, God is watching over us. And should the unthinkable happen, I know that God will have a greater purpose in it, and he will bless me for letting go."

"That's the spirit," Esther said. "Let's get you some dinner."

We sat around the fire and listened to the sounds of the African night for the next couple of hours. Then we stoked the fire once more before crawling into our bags for a welcome rest. Janga posted guards to keep the fire ablaze and watch for the night marauders.

I wanted to sleep, but I kept imagining Jason might walk in and surprise us at any minute. But the more likely scenario kept creeping in on me: we would probably have to bury him here in the mountains when we found him tomorrow.

Finally, I fell asleep. When I awoke, the eastern sky radiated a faint pink as the sun began to arrive for the day.

"You ready to go?" I asked, rubbing Betty's shoulder.

She stirred and rolled over. "Yeah, let's get going," she said, crawling out of her sleeping sack and grabbing for her boots.

One of Janga's men heard us stir and jumped up to stoke the fire.

"Go ahead and get ready," I said. "I'm just going to sit here for a little while and ponder things. If that's okay."

"For a minute," Betty said. "Then we're going to have to get going."

The cool morning air had a bite to it. I slipped out of my bedroll and found my jacket. The eastern sky was ablaze now as Betty commenced to stir the camp to life.

Oh, Jason, I thought as I sat on a log with my Bible in my lap, *why have you done this to us? If you're alive, I'm going to wring your little neck. How inconsiderate to put yourself in harm's way when Betty is in such a fragile state!* But then I started thinking about what God was doing, and as Betty got herself ready to go, I sat quietly on a rock and pondered everything. *Can I really blame Jason for what he has done, or do I give thanks to God for what he is doing?* Last night, Betty had come to the realization that she was valuing her family over God. That would have never occurred if Jason had been here sitting around the fire with us.

For what was this life but a flash in a pan? God had no greater gift than to call us home to be with him for all eternity. It was so obvious that suffering was the pathway to God. He could not use us the way He intended if we didn't have the right relationship. We could never truly know Him when there were things in our life that cut us off from hearing His voice and seeing His hand at work. And sometimes, the only way he could get our attention was to take the very thing away that had stood between us. Pruning was a gift from God that made us ready for the next growing season in our life. It helped us to produce the kind of fruit that only an arborist knew about. We thought we were the ones who found God, but without His pruning, we had no reason to seek Him at all.

So it was not us who saved ourselves. I thumbed through my Bible and found the book of Ephesians, chapter two, verse eight, and I began to read silently. *For by grace are ye saved through faith; and that not of yourselves. It is the gift of God. Not of works, lest any man should boast.* I had always thought that you could work your way to heaven by being a good person and living a good life. I had figured that God graded on a curve, and the really bad people were condemned to hell. If you had never killed anyone, you would probably make it in by default. I had hated Christians all those years precisely because they were raising the bar. By living a life of faith, they were discounting the impact my good life would have in the end.

I assumed all religions led to heaven, no matter what they taught. But now I wasn't so sure. Did Satan worshippers go to heaven? The answer was no, of course. But what about the other great religions? What god were they worshipping? There was only one true God. We were called to worship Him in spirit and in truth, and truth was nothing more than purity. We were called to worship the one who said, *You shall have no other gods before me.*

I thought of the Gospel of John and searched for a certain passage. I found it and read to myself Jesus's words. *I am the way, the truth, and the life. No man cometh to the Father, but by me.* This was the one true God and His Son Jesus Christ.

Jesus defined his three-in-one nature when he said, *I will pray to the Father, and He shall give you another Comforter, that He may abide with you forever.* Then Jesus went on to explain that this comforter was the Holy Spirit, *whom the world cannot receive, because no one can see Him nor do they know Him.* But Jesus said that we would know Him because He would live in us. This one true God was three in one: one what, and three who. This was a concept that man could not understand through human reason. We would only believe it by faith.

In the book of Genesis, chapter eighteen, this three-in-one God visited Abraham near the great oaks of Mamre, where three men spoke with one voice. Moses, traditionally considered the author of Genesis, just wrote down what the Holy Spirit told him to and didn't question what he was told—all this from a man who was himself a murderer, taking the life of an Egyptian man because he had beaten a Hebrew slave. Now how could it be that Moses became a friend of God after living a life that would have landed him in hell, according to what the world thought was the test for salvation?

Yet God used him in a mighty way, despite the fact that he was damaged goods. And he used King David, who sent the husband of his lover to the front lines of a war, where he was killed, leaving blood on David's hands. But by his faith David was saved, as was Moses. The same was true for us. We were saved by our faith in Jesus Christ. There was no sin too great that it could not be forgiven, except for the final sin of rejecting God, which was known as blasphemy of the Holy Spirit. Reject God, and He could not save you. The shepherd would stay with those in the flock who stayed with Him, and He would come to rescue his wayward sheep. But if you refused to come, He would not force you. Embracing God could not happen unless this faith was given as a gift from God by His grace, and then we would live with Him for all eternity. Our unwilling heart could be as cold as ice, and we could refuse to see and refuse to believe, no matter how hard God tried.

"Are we going?" Betty asked, piercing my solitary thoughts. "It's light enough right now."

"Are Janga and Temba ready to go?" I asked.

"Everyone is ready except you," she said, tapping her toe in the dirt.

"He might just come wandering into camp," Chuck said as he approached us, "and if he does, I'll signal you."

"What's that chopping sound?" Betty asked.

"Must be the natives working on my elephant," I said.

"They've been doing that for the last hour," she said. "Not only that, but they must have had to walk half the night to get here from the main camp."

"You must have slept like a log," I said, "because I kept hearing noises all night that kept me awake."

"I'm telling you, John, I have a peace right now," Betty said. "I can't explain it, but somehow I just feel like everything is going to be all right. I know that's completely out of character for me."

"That's my girl," I said. "Through Christ, we will have strength and peace."

Somehow I felt peace, too, but I also knew the prospects were grim for finding Jason alive. We had heard nary a peep from him all night. If he were lost, surely he would have given us a rifle signal by now. No, I had to prepare myself to deal with the reality of finding him still and cold. And I knew Betty would need every ounce of faith she could muster to deal with this.

I had looked up the passage about the Shunammite woman last night to learn more about the story. It turned out Elisha had lain on her dead son, and the boy had miraculously come back to life. I just wondered if God could do such a thing for us, or if he would continue to test our faith. *No matter, Lord,* I thought. *You are in charge, and however you decide to orchestrate and conduct this symphony of life, I will find joy and peace with you for all eternity.*

"Who is going, and who is staying?" Lance asked. "I know that I for one would like to accompany you. Janga said he would stay and supervise the elephant butchering. He said Temba is a better tracker."

"Now that it's daylight," I said, "we'll have a better chance at picking up the trail."

"Did you ever camp before coming on this safari?" Esther asked, putting her arm around Betty.

I motioned Lance aside as the ladies continued their small talk.

"I know I'll never convince Betty to stay behind," I said to Lance. "I'm afraid of what we are going to find out there. The scene could be rather gruesome. Heck, Lance, you've seen what an angry elephant will do to a man."

"Yes," he answered, "I remember that guy we saw on the Maru six years ago."

"I'll never forget it," I said. "That vision has always been etched in my head, seeing him flat as a pancake. When we find him, Lance, I'm going to have to deal with her, and I'm just not sure how."

"You better prepare her for the worst," he warned.

"What are you men talking about over there?" Betty asked.

"We are just trying to lay out a plan," I said.

"Well," she said in a stern voice, "I'm going to go with you, just in case you were making any other plans."

"I know," I said, "but I am just trying to protect you and prepare you."

Betty glanced past me, and her face turned white and her eyes widened. "Jason!" she screamed. "Jason!"

She jumped up and started to run, but I grabbed her shirt and jerked her back.

"It's him!" she screamed. "Let me go!" She broke free of my grip. "Jason!"

"Where?" I said, as we all looked in the direction she was running but saw nothing.

"She's delirious, John," Lance said in a loud voice.

I ran to catch her. Then I spotted him, bedraggled and bewildered, wandering toward us, his shirt tattered and his hair tussled.

Betty hurried to him and embraced him.

I trotted up behind her and threw my arms around them both. As we shared this silent moment and sweet reunion, a dozen questions raced through my head.

"Oh, Jason," she sobbed, "I thought I had lost you!"

"I don't know what got into me," he said. "Can you ever forgive me for putting you through this?"

"I've already forgotten it," she answered.

Then the rest of them showed up: Janga, Temba, Lance, Esther, and Chuck. We all came together to greet him like a warrior home from the front lines.

"God has granted us a miracle!" Esther squealed. "Praise be to God Almighty."

"Where's your rifle?" I asked sternly. "We kept waiting for a signal."

"Smashed by the elephant. It's in pieces. I was just lucky to get out of there alive and in one piece."

"There are more rifles," I said.

"But there is only one you," Betty said. "You are my son, Jason, from this day forward. I am your mom, and you are my son. Born this day, he was dead, but now he is alive. Praise God."

"Like the prodigal son in the book of Luke," Esther said. "He was dead but is alive again. He was lost and now is found. Praise be to God in the highest."

"You must be starved," I said.

"I'm just glad to be alive."

"What happened?" Betty asked.

"I don't know. I thought I wounded him. So I took off, thinking I could get him. I guess in the heat of the hunt, I just forgot everything and tried to get him. I should have had more respect for him, but I kept thinking I could get a clear shot. But the minutes turned into hours. I don't know why I didn't consider the approaching darkness. I guess that's the way life is for so many people. They don't consider the approaching darkness and the power of the beast that is trying to kill them. They are just living day by day, pursuing glory in the world for themselves, and they forget."

"Yeah, yeah," Chuck said, rolling his eyes. "Get to the point."

"That is the point, Chuck," I said.

"I finally did get a shot, but only when he broke out of the bush on a full charge. I took a bead and squeezed off on a dead chamber, and the rifle went *click*."

"Dead chamber?" I asked.

"I know," he answered. "I really hesitated to tell you at all."

"How did you end up with a dead chamber?" Betty asked.

"I've gone over that in my head a thousand times. Maybe I had a dead primer, or I had an empty chamber altogether. But when I turned to run, I stepped in a hole and dropped the rifle. I scrambled to my feet and got out of his way, just before he could get me. I actually think dropping the gun was a good thing, because he turned his attention on it and stomped it to smithereens. At that point, I ran and ran to get away, aware of how narrowly I had just escaped death. When I realized I was safe, I stopped, but my sense of direction was completely gone. I knew I couldn't go any direction, and that just maybe I would hear your signal. Then the darkness came caving in on me, and before the total blackness arrived, I found a soft spot to curl up for the night. I kept thinking you would fire off another shot, because I heard the signal well before dark. But then you guys just went silent."

"See, John, I told you," Betty said.

"Okay," I said, "what can I say?"

There was nothing to say. Last night, I had been convinced Jason was dead.

"So how'd you find your way out?" Lance asked.

"I prayed. At first light, I prayed that God would lead me out, and like Esther said, it was a miracle."

"Come," Esther said, "I have a Scripture. Let's pray and give thanks to the Lord."

Esther skipped off toward the campfire encouraging us to follow her. Betty would not let go of the boy and held him around his neck as we walked back to camp.

Esther was hurriedly fingering through her Bible to find her passage when we came walking in as a group. "Here it is," she said. "Let me start with this one first. By the power of the living God, who has granted us all authority as His saints to heal the sick and comfort the dying, I now declare this day as holy and sacred. John, step toward Betty and stand right here, and Jason, you stand between them. Now on this day you are born again. You were dead, but now you have come home and are alive once more. I declare this by the power vested in me as a believer in Jesus Christ, as a child of God, and as a disciple of the one who died on the cross and rose from the dead. I read these words that Jesus told his best friend John as He hung there dying on the cross.

"So, John and Betty, I tell you just as Christ said all those hundreds and hundreds of years ago in the book of John, chapter nineteen: 'Dear woman, behold thy son.' Then he said to John His disciple, 'Behold, thy mother.'" Esther looked up at us like a preacher presiding over a wedding. "Is there anyone here among these witnesses who disagrees or takes exception?" She paused, waiting for a response. "Then by the power of God Almighty ..." Esther leaned forward and made the sign of the cross on my forehead. She did the same for Betty, and then finally Jason. "Let me read to you these words of the young woman Mary as she carried the Lord in her womb," Esther continued. "She said this in the presence of her relative Elisabeth, who was pregnant as well with John the Baptist. Mary was told by the Holy Spirit that Elisabeth was pregnant in her old age, but when Mary entered her house, Elisabeth knew that Mary would be giving birth to the Lord without Mary saying a word.

"All these things Luke said he understood perfectly, because he likely conducted a thorough investigation that included personal interviews with Mary herself. These words she gave to Luke to write in his letter to Theophilus, probably a friend and high Roman official."

Esther closed her eyes and recited the passage from her memory. We were all touched by the moment and by her ability to recite Scripture from memory.

"And Mary said, 'My soul has magnified the Lord, and my spirit has rejoiced in God my Savior. For he has regarded the low estate of his handmaiden. For, behold, from henceforth all generations shall call me blessed. For he that is mighty has done to me great things; and holy is his name. And his mercy is on them that fear him from generation to generation. He has demonstrated strength with his arm; he has scattered the proud in the imagination of their hearts. He has put down the mighty from their seats, and exalted them of low degree. He has filled the hungry with good things; and the rich he has sent away empty. He has helped his servant Israel, in remembrance of his mercy; as he spoke to our fathers, to Abraham, and to his seed forever.'" Esther looked up at us. "I now declare you parents and son in the eyes of God, which is more official than any government license, in the name of the Father, and of the Son, and of the Holy Spirit."

"Thank you, Esther," Betty said. "That was wonderful. You know what, everybody?"

"What are you thinking?" I asked.

"Would you be terribly offended," she said, wrinkling her brow, "if I made a suggestion here that might not be too terribly popular right now?"

I hesitated to ask, wondering what goofy thing she was going to think of now that would be so unpopular. "What is it?" I asked.

"Can we go home?" she asked. "I have loved this trip, every inch of it. You know that. But I'm ready to go home."

I looked around at the faces of our companions, and everyone seemed amenable. I actually had no qualms about it myself. I had just experienced one of the most jubilant moments of my life: seeing my son return to me in one piece, saved from the depths of the jungle and now safe in the arms of my lifelong love. I had to admit from the depths of my soul that I was ready to return. I was ready to go home.

"I'm ready if you are," I said. "How about you, Jason? Are you ready?"

"I've had enough," he answered. "I could even be ready to go back to school."

"Sounds good to me," Chuck said.

"Then we're all in agreement?" I asked.

I looked at Esther and Lance, who nodded in the affirmative.

I couldn't believe we had come to the end. Well, not the end, but at least the halfway mark. We had to work our way back to Nairobi, back across miles and miles of African bush, and we had all those many weeks of travel still ahead of us.

EPILOGUE

A nd so we made the long journey back to the ranch in the Ford, which was still in perfect working order, thanks to the hanging crows. We shot various antelope, buffalo, and gazelle, and by the time we got to Nairobi, we'd had our fill of safari and our fill of African adventure.

Oh, Africa ... She was alive, from the grasses that exploded underfoot with insects, to the teeming waters filled with fishes, frogs, bugs, floating flowers, hippos, and crocs. From the forestland, thick with birds of all colors, shapes, sizes, and song, to the trees that housed the monkeys, baboons, and leopards. From the tiniest antelope, incapable of harming a flea, to the largest bull elephant, a beast as social as it was unpredictable, as gentle and majestic as it was brutal and terrifying. From the thorny scrub brush to the multitude of wildflowers, whose fragrance was the aroma of God Himself.

Africa was a hard place of survival, where the circle of life played out day after day. A place upon which God's hand rested. But I had the feeling that He wasn't finished putting the final touches on His masterpiece. And I knew that she was a place of miracles, where even the smallest movement belonged to a larger symphony. The musicians knew their parts well, but only the conductor knew the next movement to be played.

This great swath of land, so often referred to as the Dark Continent, was anything but. It was a vibrant place, where sunrise and sunset were indistinguishable in their glory, where the night sky shone more beautifully than anywhere on earth. But only the naïve were unaware of the dangers that lurked beneath her beauty. This was a dwelling place of God, where, if you listened carefully, you could hear His heartbeat and feel His breath on your cheek.

After bidding a final goodbye to Lance, Esther, and their new partner Chuck, we never returned to Africa. We never saw Lance or Esther again, in fact, although the stories they told in their subsequent letters—about setting up a medical clinic and evangelizing the natives—could fill a book.

I have always looked back fondly on those times, now a distant memory, and I hold dear all that happened to us in the bush. God bless the memory of Betty. May she rest in the arms of Christ, having gone to meet the Lord two years ago. I loved her, and she loved me. She was mine, and I was hers. I relish her memory and take great peace in all the wonderful times we shared in our later life as we spread the Gospel with a great revival in Chicago. We were so thankful that Jason survived the great World War, and I am reminded of that now, as we face this enemy a second time and war looms once again on the horizon.

Jason finished school, going on to become a prominent Chicago lawyer. He met and married a beautiful woman named Susanne, who gave us four wonderful grandchildren to take care of me in my old age.

Chuck, for his part, returned home after some years. He continued his work in the academic world and, to the amazement of us all, found Christ in his old age. Before he passed on, we often reminisced about Africa, never forgetting the many adventures that helped shape us. Now, at age seventy-five, I find myself looking back as much as I look forward. While I am eager for a reunion with Betty in heaven, should God will it, I will always look back with fondness at our time in the bush, where we received the gift of faith. I will never forget the miracle of Africa.